Karen Turner Ward
Hampton University

Kendall Hunt
publishing company

Cover images taken by Jack Manning, Jacqueline Bontemps, and Lina Cordoba

Kendall Hunt
publishing company

www.kendallhunt.com
Send all inquiries to:
4050 Westmark Drive
Dubuque, IA 52004-1840

ISBN 978-0-7575-7766-6

Printed in the United States of America
10 9 8 7 6 5 4 3 2 1

Contents

Preface

When I was first exposed to the study of communication, there were no laptops. There were no computers. No one knew what it meant to have a HD television, nor dreamed that anyone would one day watch television on a cell phone. In fact, cell phones were only a concept at that time. Needless to say, communication, specifically mass communication, has drastically changed to the point of redefining itself during the last twenty five years. At the expense of exposing my age, it is well worth the cost if it provides us with a moment of reflection and extends an opportunity for us to really discuss the complexity of communication study and how technology has affected the manner in which we communicate on a daily basis.

While it has been years since I sat as a student in a communication theory class, I can attest to the fact that the diverse nature of communication has contributed to its value in the academic preparation of today's college student. Its rapid growth and diversity innately support the position that communication is valuable and necessary to the success of students who wish to be competitive in today's job market. We live in an age where we share the experience of a moment with millions of other people, a world where it's not just important, but imperative that students are prepared to tackle the challenges presented in every type of communication scenario. This fresh textbook offers valuable help towards that task.

Communication for Today's Student strategically addresses communication issues that have become critical to success in contemporary society by examining the principals of communication, interpersonal communication , public communication and leadership and group dynamics. **Communication for Today's Student** is a new interactive text that includes multiple scenarios highlighting the value of communication skills in an evolving global community –in personal, professional, and multicultural contexts. First-time public communicators and other students will find the accessible guidance they need to identify and implement creative solutions, and to evaluate when communication works well and when it can be enhanced for greater effectiveness.

Now, let's get started.

There is a popular saying that has been used in many of the speeches I have heard during my career in academe, "*To whom much is given, much is expected.*" Since I am a firm believer in this quote, I believe it is only right that I acknowledge all those who have given so much to bring this project to fruition and give thanks to them for their contributions.

I would like to thank all of my students for their inspiration. They have helped me challenge myself and grow as an educator during the past thirty years. To the numerous students I have had the privilege of instructing like Matthew Mosley, who have texted me, not telephoned nor written but texted me to say, " I want to be a public speaker just like you ." I say thank you.

To the faculty in the Department of Fine and Performing Arts, Mrs. Jamantha Watson, Dr. Robin Boisseau, and Dr. Curtis Perry Otto, thank you for your input and never ending support.

Ms. Chelonda Walker, I appreciate your long days and attention to detail. You have the patience of a "saint." The synergy of Bresean Jenkins, creative prowess of Dr. Jacqueline F. Bontemps, and the aesthetic ingenuity of Mr. Joseph Martin made this textbook visually arresting. You are one terrific creative team! Much appreciation is extended to Mr. Scott Brewer, Mr. Jack Manning, Ms. Laura Flagg and Ms. Lena Cordoba for their wonderful photographs.

Words cannot express my gratitude to Dr. Charrita D. Danley and Ms. Virgelia Jade Banks for their contributions. Without you, this would not have been possible.

I would be remiss if I did extend my appreciation to entire team at Kendall Hunt, especially Mr. Curtis Ross and Ms. Stefani DeMoss. Thank you for your professionalism and patience. To Ms. Joanna Finch and the staff at Great River Technologies, thank you for all your hard work on the online site.

Thank you Dr. Robert Schihl, Professor and Associate Dean for Academics, School of Communication and the Arts at Regent University for encouraging me to pursue the doctorate in communication. I extend my sincerest gratitude to Dr. Mamie E. Locke, my dean and my friend; you have been a lighthouse in the middle of a very large ocean.

But most of all I would like to acknowledge Dr. William R. Harvey, the President of Hampton University who took a chance on hiring a young academician twenty years ago and instilled in her through his wisdom, leadership and vision that "there's no such word as no."

About the Author

Dr. Karen Turner Ward is a Professor and the Chair of the Department of Fine and Performing Arts at Hampton University. She holds a Bachelor of Arts Degree in Drama and African American Studies from the University of Virginia, a Master in Fine Arts Degree in Acting from Virginia Commonwealth University, and a doctorate in Communications from Regent University. Dr. Ward's professional activity includes writing, producing, directing and acting. She has presented papers at professional conferences on the state, regional and national levels,

1

Communication for Today's Student: An Introduction

After reading this chapter, you should be able to:

- ❐ Define communication.
- ❐ Explain the communication process as it relates to a situations in your life.
- ❐ Discuss the different models of communication.
- ❐ Describe the function of each element in the communication process.
- ❐ Explain the importance of ethical communication.

Key Terms

Channel
Communication
Computer-Mediated Communication (CMC)
Context
Culture
Decoding
Encoding
Ethical
External noise
Interactive Communication
Intercultural Communication
Intrapersonal Communication
Internal Noise
Linear Communication
Message
Noise
Nonverbal feedback
Public Communication
Psychological noise
Sender-receivers
Small-group Communication
Symbol
Transactional Communication
Topophobia
Verbal feedback

1 Scenario

Nathalie held her breath as she looked over the Nancy Williams Cafeteria, affectionately known as the "Big Café" by students. She exhaled as she scanned the room for a place to sit. She had been cooped up in her room the past two days, studying for her first round of midterms as a college student. Mathematical equations, genetic makeup, and sonnets of Shakespeare consumed her like a tidal wave and she had finally emerged to the surface to eat.

"Nathalie," Nathalie's eyes darted as she tried to find the source of the masculine voice that spoke her name. "Nat Nat!"

Finally her eyes rested on the source. She smiled sweetly as Christopher waved her over to his table. She walked over slowly and sat down across from him. She was surprised Chris was even in the cafeteria. He usually skipped it, opting for the Raider Grille rather than the jerk chicken in the cafeteria. When he did decide to take a gamble with the café he was usually surrounded by his entourage, but today he was alone.

"How are you Miss Lady?" he asked, as he wiped his mouth.

To say that her stomach was doing somersaults was an understatement. Nathalie had always had a thing for Chris ever since she met him in the summer at pre- college. They both were taking Introduction to University Life, a class introducing the freshmen class to the history and culture of the university. Their friendship started simply with a question, "Do you have a pencil?" Sounds very cliché but Nathalie liked it. It resembled the love stories she would see in books and movies.

"I'm fine, just overwhelmed with studying for midterms," Nathalie confessed as she took a bite of her roast beef. "I've been in my room for the past two days!"

Chris nodded, "Me too. Been in there so long my boys left me and went to dinner without me."

"Same here," said Nathalie.

"You know what? We should take a break," Chris said.

Nathalie chuckled, "I am. Right now."

"Nah, I mean a real break. We should go to a party. My boy is having a party in the Docks at 13C." Chris told her.

"Boy, I got a GPA and a scholarship to maintain." Nathalie said, as she began to open her dessert.

"Me too, Nat. But look, we're not gonna do well if we don't relax." Chris reasoned, "Look, we'll go over there, take a few Jell-O shots and chill."

"Jell-O shots?"

"Yea. We'll take some shots, drink some of my man's good tea and chill."

Nathalie shifted in her seat. She prided herself for not indulging in underage drinking her first semester in college. She was usually the one who looked out for her girls when they went out. She saw what happened when people didn't drink responsibly.

Chris sighed, "I see you're not down. Forget it. I'll check you later."

Chris gathered his tray. Nathalie bit her lip. Her mind began to race.

"*Come on Nathalie. He's never asked you to chill with him before. This could be your way in there with him. And besides you are a little drained from studying and little drink may relax you...*"

"Chris! Wait!" Nathalie called out across the café. Chris paused at the door.

Let's Communicate

Communication is a part of every human being's daily life. From an infant's cries for milk, to a teenager's request to drive, to a college student's questions in class, to Chris and Nathalie's discussion of the party, to an employer's instructions to employees, communication is taking place. Many people take communication for granted because it happens so often in our daily interactions with one another. However, communication should never be taken for granted; it is the foundation of our human interaction.

Children communicate with their parents and caregivers to ensure that their basic needs are being met. Students communicate with teachers and professors to ensure that they are acquiring the knowledge being taught and meeting the expectations that have been set. As individuals, we communicate with our peers to form relationships and friendships. As family members, we communicate with those who are related to us as we build familial bonds based on shared relationships. As employers and employees, we communicate to meet the goals and objectives set before us and to fulfill the mission of our organizations.

Communication with our parents and caregivers ensure our basic needs are met.

These are but a few examples of the ways in which we communicate. If you were to take a few moments and reflect upon your daily activities as a college student, you would notice that they involve a significant amount of communication with various individuals for unique purposes in different settings and contexts. Take a moment to think about the communication that you have had over the past 3 hours. How many individuals were involved? What was the purpose of the exchange? Was it successful?

Why Study Communication?

Having thought of how often you communicate and knowing that you have been actively engaged in some form of communication since birth, you may wonder why it is important for you to be enrolled in a communication course. Well, it is important for you to be enrolled in this course because it teaches you how to communicate EFFECTIVELY. The fact that you engage in communication daily, does not mean that your communication is effective.

How many times have you felt that the person you were talking to did not understand what you were saying? How often have you wished that people would "get the point"? Have you ever felt that no matter how many times you explained yourself, the listener did not respond appropriately? Have you ever tried to think of other ways to say what you wanted to say? Has a person's facial expressions ever signaled to you that you said the wrong thing? Have your facial expressions ever hurt someone's feelings? Have you ever said something you wished you could take back? Has your tone of voice ever been inappropriate for the situation? Have you ever been in a situation similar to Nathalie and Chris?

More than likely, everyone reading this text answered "yes" to several of the questions. That is why it is important for you to take a communication course. This course will prepare you to communicate effectively in both your personal and professional lives.

Personal Communication

Personal communication is the foundation of building relationships. As a college student, a great deal of your personal communication resolves around your interaction with family members and friends. These are the people who you consider a part of your circle, the people that you trust with your thoughts and feelings. These are the people who influence you.

Communication is a direct reflection of identity. Who you are is largely determined by your personal communication. Consider the children whose parents tell them, "You can be anything you want in life!" These children usually have a positive self-image and believe that the sky is the limit for them. Unfortunately, there are other children who are sometimes told, "You will never amount to anything!" Not having the encouragement and the reinforcement necessary for a positive self- image, these children sometimes fall prey to the negative communication spoken into their lives and do not reach their potential.

Children whose parents tell them, you can be anything you want in life usually have a positive self-esteem.

As you can see, your personal communication with family members and friends can affect who you are as a person. In college, you meet many new people from different places with different backgrounds, cultures, and ways of thinking. Many of these individuals become your life-long friends. It is important to communicate positively with your peers in order to not only learn from them, but to also provide them with the support and encouragement that they need to be successful students. What you say and hear makes a difference in your life and the lives of others. Therefore, it is important to say the right thing, at the right time, in the right manner. It is important to communicate effectively in your personal communication with family and friends.

Professional Communication

As a college student, you are preparing yourself for the professional world of work. Consequently, you must be prepared to communicate on a professional level. The communication styles and techniques you engage in with your family, friends, and peers are often more informal than the communication expected in the professional world.

The way in which you communicate professionally is a major factor in your success as a professional. You must communicate with your employer, other employees, business partners, clients, and various constituencies related to your profession of choice. No matter what career path you choose, at some point, you must engage in professional communication with other people.

One of the first instances when an employer gets an opportunity to evaluate your communication skills is during the face-to-face interview. At this time, both your verbal and non-verbal communication skills are on display. You should want potential employers to be impressed by your ability to communicate, but they will not be impressed if your communication in the interview is the same as your communication with family and friends.

It is important to know the difference between various modes of communication and when it is appropriate to use each. You will learn this information from your communications class. Becoming an effective communicator in your professional life is just as important as becoming an effective communicator in your personal life. This text will teach you both.

Now that you understand why it is important for you to study communication, you will be introduced to the foundations of effective communication, the different types and methods of communication will be explained to you, and you will be prepared to become an effective communicator in various settings and situations.

In order to become an effective communicator, you must know what communication is and be equipped with the tools necessary to communicate effectively.

Communication: Defined

Communication is a process described as the exchange of ideas by using symbols which represent abstract and concrete ideas. Like all processes, the communication process is comprised of elements or components. The critical components work together to fulfill the objectives of the process.

To understand fully how the communication process works, let's use the model to explicate the role each element or component plays in the process.

The critical components work together to fulfill the objectives of the process.

The Communication Model

In our opening scenario between Nathalie and Chris, we can see the communication model in action.

When Nathalie decides to go to the cafeteria after being cooped up in her room for days, she was engaging in **intrapersonal** communication. When she arrived in the cafeteria and heard her named bellowed across the room, she took a seat next to Chris and began engaging in conversation. At this point, Nathalie and Chris become sender and receiver within the communication process.

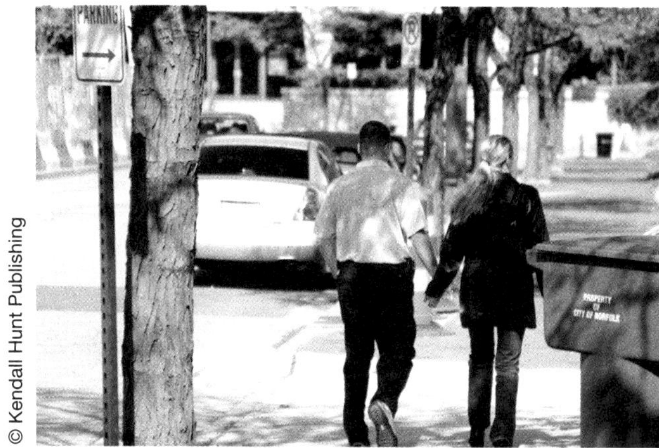

Communication is a process in action.

What does this mean? Once a communicator gets an impulse or has a mental image in mind, it must take the form of a **symbol**, or words in this case. The process of transforming mental images into words and placing these words into logical messages with meaning is called **encoding**. The process continues as the sender sends the message to the intended recipient or receiver, who in turns, **decodes** the message and attaches meaning to it. The message can be verbal or nonverbal, conscious or unconscious.

The message can travel on various types of channels to include telephone, letter, text, computer mediated and, of course, the most common channel, face-to-face.

Once the message is perceived and understood by the receiver, the decoding process occurs and that process is reversed. The receiver's feelings and thoughts are sent back to the sender for decoding. In the case of Nathalie and Chris, when Nathalie sat down and began sharing the reasons for not attending the Café for the past couple of days, they were operating as sender and receiver. Basically, the couple was sending messages back and forth using a face-to-face channel. Each communicator was engaged in the process and was giving feedback to the messages they received. At some points in their communication, they gave **nonverbal feedback** and at other points their messages took the format of **verbal feedback**.

Messages can travel on various channels.

Most communication in interpersonal situations is two way. Each time the opportunity is given for the receiver to react to the message, the communication is open to feedback and is characterized as two-way. Where the communication process takes place is as critical as these elements are to the process of communication. The place that communication occurs is called the **context or setting**. The context refers not only to the physical environment, but also the personal perceptions, attitudes, beliefs and background each speaker brings to the communication context or setting. This, of course, affects how the sender and receiver will respond to the message being sent and, therefore, affects the feedback of each. Nathalie and Chris have their communication in the cafeteria which of course is the physical environment, but an even greater factor in their communication with each other is the fact that they are attracted to each other and have been previously involved.

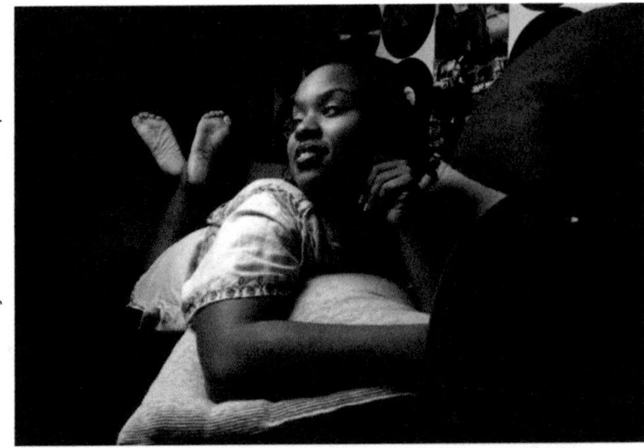

Communication open to feedback is characterized as two-way.

As Nathalie and Chris sat in the cafeteria discussing what they had been doing and deliberating about going to the party that night, they communicated openly and freely because they had shared knowledge and experiences. They were successful in communicating their mental images because they were able to understand one another. There was no breakdown in the communication context or setting, even though there may have been the presence of what social scientists like to call "noise." When speakers approach communication from different contexts, this can lead to ineffective communication. When noise occurs in the communication context, it also interferes to the success of the process. **Noise**, or interference as some like to call it, is anything within the communication context that prevents the message from being transmitted successfully.

© 2009. Courtesy of JaxonPhotoGroup.

Noise is interference in the process. Sometimes noise is external, other times it may be internal or psychological.

There are three types of noise: **external**, **internal** and **psychological**. **External noise** or interference includes any factors outside of the communicators that make it difficult or prevent the message from being understood. For example, a loud motor of an air conditioner in a small classroom or a large dog barking in a reception area would interfere with a message being transferred between two speakers. **Internal noise** refers to interference which occurs within the speaker. A speaker that has a speech impediment, such as a severe stutter or hoarseness from laryngitis, would have difficulty being understood. Thus, the successful transmission of the message would be affected. The last type of noise is psychological noise. **Psychological noise**, idiosyncrasies that occur within the speaker, interfere with the speaker's ability to express or understand the intended message. Speech apprehension and exaggerations are two examples of psychological noise that may impact successful communication.

© Kendall Hunt Publishing

Communication is shared knowledge and experiences.

As we examine Nathalie's and Chris' interaction in the cafeteria, we recognize the role each plays in the communication process and the results of their communication encounter. As we examine the process, we can describe each element. We might make the assumption that communication is **linear**, which asserts that communication is one-way and that the message carried on the channel flows from the sender to the receiver. In linear communication, there is no feedback. As we see in the case of Nathalie and Chris, this is not the way communication flows in an interpersonal communication context.

If we take the linear approach a step further and add feedback from the receiver back to the sender, the communication is

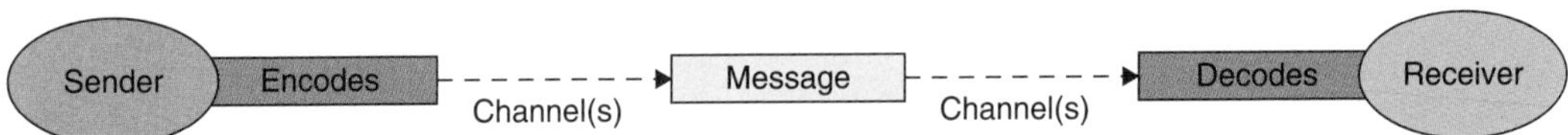

interactive. The **interactive model** operates under the assumption that once the message is received and understood by the receiver, the process is complete.

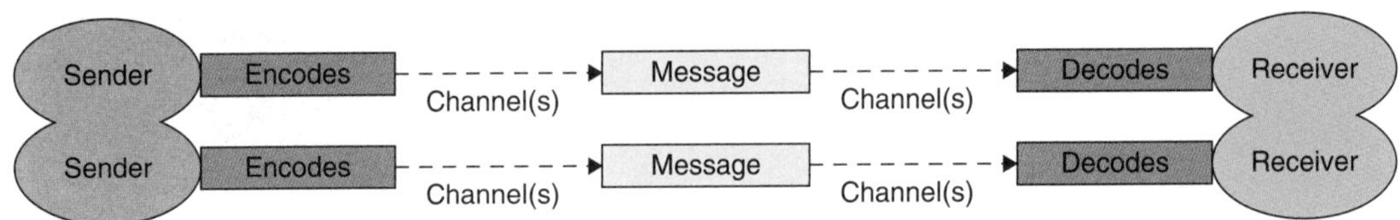

In the interactive model, once Chris suggests that Nathalie go the party and she responds negatively, "Boy, I got a GPA and scholarship to maintain and Chris states "Me too," the communication would be ended. We know that this is not true in the case of Nathalie and Chris nor is it true in most communication contexts. The **interactive model** presumes the message of the sender will match the message that is decoded by the receiver. The interactive model does not allow for misunderstanding or, in some cases, totally miss understood messages. The transactional model does.

Communication is Transactional

Communication is a **transactional** process which means the process possesses three identifiable characteristics. The first characteristic is that communication is "continuous." Communicators are constantly and simultaneously encoding and decoding messages. For example, in the case of Nathalie and Chris, even when Chris turns and walks to the door as if to terminate the information exchange, he was communicating with Nathalie. What message was he sending? How does Nathalie respond?

The second characteristic of communication as a transactional process is all "communicators play roles." We communicate with our differently from the way we communicate with our minister. Our language choice differs significantly in many cases. Our topics or subject matter may differ. Since Nathalie and Chris are involved in a relationship, the language they choose to use with each other facilitates the needs of their interpersonal relationship. For example, Chris refers to his friends as "my boys" when talking with Nathalie. His language choice is specific to the communication with Nathalie. In a different context, for example speaking to his math professor he may choose to refer to his "boys" as his "friends." Their degree of disclosure is significantly, different from the degree of disclosure that each has with their other classmates or even their instructors.

The last characteristic of the transactional theory is that "all communication has a past, present and future." As communicators, we receive and send messages based upon what has occurred in our past.

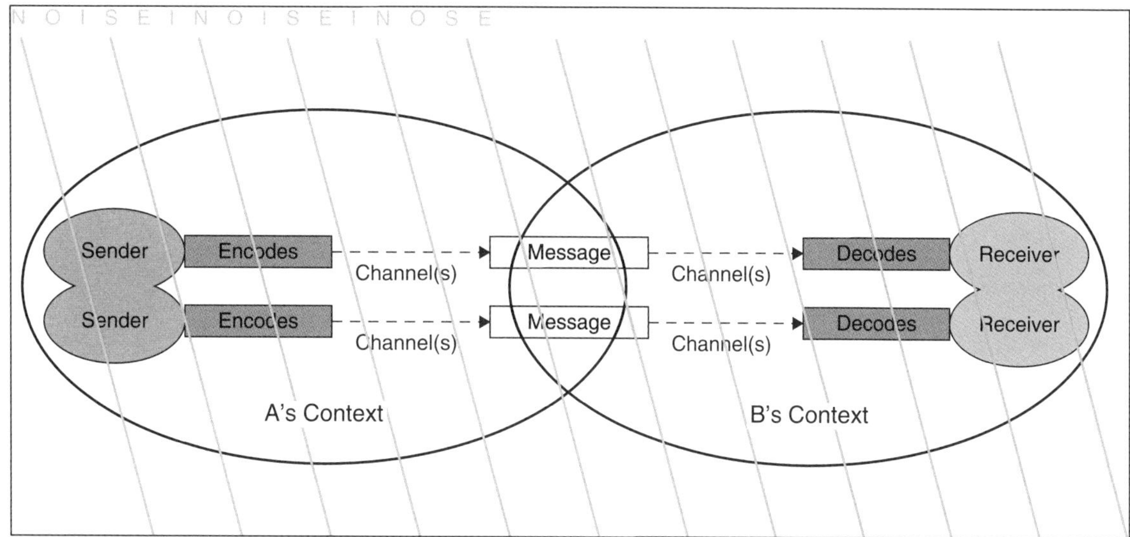

We act upon these messages based upon our experiences. Those experiences will have an impact upon how we communicate in the future.

Types of Communication

The communication context can occur within several types of communication. While the types share characteristics, they each have their own identity. Let's look at each to gain a clear understanding of the different types that are most often used: intrapersonal, interpersonal, small group, public, intercultural and computer mediated communication.

Intrapersonal Communication

Intrapersonal communication can be best described as communication within oneself. Intrapersonal communication is the ongoing dialogue that you have in your head. The alarm goes off. You sit up in the bed to think, "Man, how I would love to go back to sleep for twenty more minutes." You have just engaged in a conversation in which you are both the sender and receiver. As the sender and receiver, you are actively involved in the encoding and decoding of messages within yourself! As you encode yourself generated messages, you are continuously providing feedback. The stronger our ability as intrapersonal communicators, the stronger our ability as intrapersonal communicators, the greater understanding we have of ourselves. In essence, strong intrapersonal communication yields increased ability to recall and retain information. Strong intrapersonal communication leads to an increased ability to solve problems and make responsible decisions. In our story of Nathalie and Chris, when Chris gets up from the table and Nathalie thinks, *"Come on Nathalie. He's never asked you to chill with him before. This could be your way in there with him. And besides you are a little drained from studying and little drink may relax you,"* she is engaging in intrapersonal communication. Most importantly, as we engage in this ongoing internal processing, we increase our ability to communicate effectively with others.

Interpersonal Communication

Interpersonal or dyadic communication is an interaction between two people. Interpersonal communication occurs whenever one person willingly or unwillingly exchanges information with another. Our success in life is greatly affected by our effectiveness in interpersonal communication. From our engagement in social relationships, to our effectiveness on the job, to our successful completion of an employment interview, we are dependent upon our ability to communicate effectively one-on-one as well as to develop and maintain relationships. The majority of the college student's communication takes place within the interpersonal communication context. As a student engages in other contexts, a student will find him/herself communicating in multiple dialogues within larger groups.

Small-Group Communication

Small groups are a critical part of a student's life. If you are on the track team, a member of the editiorial board of the school newspaper, a cast member of the Christmas play at church or a member of a group of students working on a class project, you are a member of a small group. Most students prefer not to work in small groups because they believe that working in a group requires more work than working alone. This perception often times factors directly into the effectiveness of the group. The key to a positive small group interaction is to learn strategies that help you function effectively within the group to achieve a positive outcome. These essential strategies, coupled with the type of leader who takes the authoratiative role within the group, leads to a successful and positive group experience, minimizing anxiety.

Small groups are critical part of a students life.

Public Communication

You have been asked to introduce the speaker for Founder's Day at Ogden Hall. While you have made a few group presentations in your biology class, you have never even stepped on the stage of the 1800 seat Ogden Hall auditorium. Suddenly, you feel sick and break out in a sweat, and you cannot keep from shaking. You are suffering from **topophobia**, the fear of speaking in public. Studies show that people are more afraid of public speaking than dying. Yes, dying!

Truth of the matter is, all successful people will at some point engage in public communication. The success of this communication context is greatly dependent upon a speaker's ability to make a connection with the audience regardless of its size.

Public communication differs from small communication but how?

Public communication can be described as a communication context in which the membership becomes too large for more than one or two people to speak. By its nature, the audience provides nonverbal feedback to the speaker. The audience is unable to provide verbal feedback due to the numbers of the participants. This provides a greater need for the speaker to connect with the audience to convey a message by keeping the audience engaged and involved.

Good public speakers employ skills that accomplish their goals. While some public speakers demonstrate an innate talent for this communication context, most speakers develop such skills by observation and practice.

Intercultural Communication

The tragedy of 911 greatly impacted our view of culture and diversity in the field of communication. The term culture has almost as many definitions as the word communication. For communicators today, a successful relationship greatly depends on one's ability to demonstrate communication competency across cultures. For our exploration and discussion, **culture** will be referred to as shared perceptions and expectations of a group of people. As we further explore these communication patterns and expectations, our engagement with other cultures become more socially positive and, in some cases, professionally productive. Based upon the premise that culture is learned, dynamic and pervasive, we can begin to understand the role culture plays in the success of our relationships. Good communicators must develop a personal approach to maintain successful diverse interpersonal relationships. ***Communication For Today's Student*** will assist in reaching your goals with regards to culture and diversity.

Newyork is the melting pot of perceptions and expectations.

Computer Mediated Communication

There major difference between Computer Mediated Communication (CMC) and face to face communication is control. **Computer Mediated Communication** (CMC) can be described as the use of computer networks to exchange information and to facilitate the interactive sharing of information. This exchange differs from other types of communication as it occurs over a single channel, whether it is via emails, discussion groups, chat, IM, web pages or news groups. Computer Mediated Communication (CMC) best facilitates our communication goals and objectives when coupled with digital literacy. This broadens the scope of our communication and affects our ability to process and exchange information in a manner in which social and economic subjectifiers can be eliminated. So, why would today's student choose Computer Mediated Communication (CMC) over face-to-face communication? The reasons range from personal preferences to accepted social risks.

Ethics in Communication

When we communicate with individuals, we have an unspoken expectation that the information being shared with us is true. How would you feel if you had a long conversation with a friend and later discovered that everything you had been told was a lie? What would you think if you attended a seminar on increasing your finances, completed all of the steps outlined for you to follow, and discovered that your finances never increased? In each of these situations, you would more than likely be extremely disappointed or possibly hurt and angered. To avoid such situations happening to you or causing them to happen to others, it is pertinent that you practice **ethics** in your personal and professional communication.

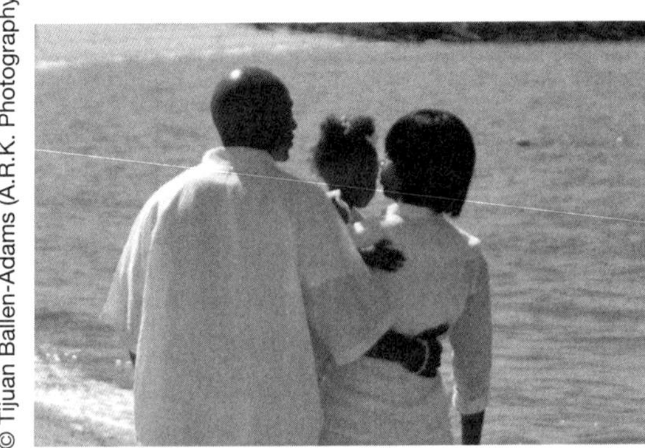

When is computer mediated communication preferred over face-to-face communication.

As you communicate with others, you must decide what to say and what not to say. You must decide whether to present factual information or fictitious information. You must decide whether to tell half of the story or the whole story. You must decide whether to tell the truth or tell a lie. You must decide whether or not to practice ethical communication. The decision to be ethical in your communication is a decision that will impact your listener(s) and, ultimately, you. It is a decision that must be made with much thought and careful consideration.

The best decision to make when it comes to ethics in communication is the decision to be ethical. As the communicator, you should want to share information that is accurate and factual with the listener, whether for personal or professional purposes. When you practice ethics in communication, those with whom you communicate will be able to trust you. When you tell your employer that you have completed a task, he or she will trust that it has been done. If you tell your friends that you will meet them, they will trust that you will be there.

From this point forward, it is important for you to take a moment before you speak and consider the ethics of what you are saying. Is the information accurate? How will it affect the listener? Should I share this information or keep it to myself? Once you begin taking ethics into consideration, you will have made one more giant step towards becoming an effective communicator.

Let's Get Started

In Chapter 1, you were introduced to the foundations of communication. We discussed the importance of studying communication and how it can affect our personal and professional lives. The communication process was defined, and we used the Communication Model to explicate the role that each element of communication plays in the process. You learned that communication is transactional. The Nathalie and Chris scenario served as our reference and guide to the explication. You were introduced to the types of communication (intrapersonal, interpersonal, small-group, public, intercultural, computer-mediated) and presented a discussion on the ethics of communication.

Moving forward through the book, you will be engaged in activities that introduce you to and familiarize you with the important components of effective communication that will be useful to you both personally and professionally.

The topic of Chapter 2, *Perception and Listening*, is how individuals process information. The chapter will cover the factors that influence perception as well as the steps to effective listening. Chapter 3, *What is the Power of Verbal and Nonverbal Communication*, will identify the differences between verbal and non-verbal messages and how each is used in the communication process. Chapters 4, 5, and 6 are all related to the role communication plays in relationships. *Interpersonal Relationships* describes the essential elements that draw people together and explains the role of emotional intelligence in communication. *Evaluating and Improving Relationships* discusses the stages of relationships as they are formed and dissolved. The chapter also addresses conflict resolution within relationships. *Intercultural Relationships* defines culture, identifies the characteristics of culture, and evaluates the impact cultural values have on interpersonal communication. Additionally, the chapter provides strategies to enhance effective interpersonal communication in diverse relationships.

The second half of the book helps to prepare you for oral presentations. In chapter 7, *Researching Your Topic*, the text offers strategies for accessing, analyzing, and using information in your speech. You are also given guidelines for the using various forms of support. *Organizing and Outlining Your Ideas*, Chapter 8, teaches you how to generate the main points of the speech and presents patterns for organizing the points. The chapter also offers guidance in planning the outline of the speech and speaker's notes. Chapter 9, *Delivery*, addresses the methods of delivery and the aspects of vocal and physical delivery.

After all of the foundational materials are presented, the next two chapters focus on two unique purposes for speaking. First, Chapter 10 addresses *Speaking to Inform* and expounds upon the types of informative speaking and the goals of informative speaking. Secondly, Chapter 11 addresses

Speaking to Persuade through a discussion of the elements of persuasion, inductive and deductive reasoning, emotion and logic. The chapter also discusses the ethics of persuasive speaking.

The last two chapters in the text deal with groups. In Chapter 12, *What are the Roles of Leadership and Power in Group Dynamics?*, the differences between leadership and power are identified. The chapter offers the six bases of power that are typical in a small group as well as ways to deal with conflict within small groups. The closing chapter, *Small Group Presentations*, presents the characteristics of small groups and the role and responsibilities of individuals within small groups. The chapter makes suggestions for presenting in a small group and identifies small group formats.

By the time you have completed reading the text and completed the related assignments, you will be equipped with all of the tools necessary to be an effective communicator in both your personal and professional lives. These tools will last a life time and contribute to your success as an individual. Now, let's get started!

Communication is important to our everyday lives.

Name____ Date_______________

Exercise 1.1 Chapter 1 – Communication for Today's Student: An Introduction

I. Good communication skills are guaranteed to make us more successful in life.

Establish a communication journal for one week which chronicles your communication experiences within the following contexts:

Intrapersonal

Interpersonal

Intercultural

Small group

Public

As you record your experiences consider the following for inclusion:

- Are the elements of communication represented in the communication experience?
- What is the channel that the message is being transmitted upon?
- Was there any noise involved and if so, what type?
- Was there anything that you would like to change about your communication experience?
- Would consider the experience positive or negative?
- How would you approach changing the outcome of that experience?

II. Choose one context to illustrate, using a cartoon format. Label the elements!

Name____ Date_______________

Exercise 1.2 Chapter 1 – Communication for Today's Student: An Introduction

The National Communication Association published a ***Credo for Commnunication Ethics*** which describes the expectations of ethical behavior. The document condemns such behavior as distortion, intimidation, coercion intolerance and hatred; while it advocates truthfulness, accuracy and honesty, freedom of expression and so on.

With a partner, document a media event in which ethical communication practices where in question according to the standards of the ***Credo***. Prepare a 2 to 3 minute speech to explain why the situation was one in which the National Communication Association would condemn or advocate based upon the Credo and why? Be sure to cite the specific principle from the ***Credo***.

2

Perception and Listening

After reading this chapter, you should be able to:

- ❒ Explain the reason humans are limited in their capacity to process information
- ❒ Distinguish between the three key perception processes
- ❒ Define the primary selectivity processes
- ❒ Describe the factors that affect the selective exposure, selective attention and selective retention processes
- ❒ Demonstrate an understanding of social identity theory
- ❒ Explain schemata and the types of information that it typically includes
- ❒ Describe the four schemata that we use to interpret communication events
- ❒ Define attribution theory and distinguish between internal and external attributions
- ❒ Explain covariation theory and the three types of information used to interpret people's behavior
- ❒ Define self-serving bias and explain how it is problematic
- ❒ Describe the fundamental attribution error
- ❒ Discuss three factors that influence our perceptions
- ❒ Distinguish between hearing and listening processes
- ❒ Identify the seven steps to effective listening

- ❒ Recall the four listening styles and identify the focus of each
- ❒ Explain the four motivations to listen and recall a potential pitfall of each
- ❒ Recognize the six common listening misbehaviors

Key Terms

perception
limited capacity processors
selection
selective exposure
biased information search
proximity
utility
reinforce
selective attention
novelty
size
concrete
selective retention
primacy and recency
organization
constructivism
schemata
prototypes
personal constructs
stereotypes
social identity theory
scripts
script theory
interpretation
attribution theory
external attribution
unintentionality
intentionality
internal attribution
covariation theory
distinctiveness
consistency
consensus
self-serving bias
fundamental attribution error
rapport talk
report talk
hearing
listening
BIG EARS
paraphrasing
positive feedback
negative feedback
dual perspective taking
noise
listening styles
people-oriented
action-oriented
content-oriented
time-oriented listening
discriminate listening
appreciative listening
comprehensive listening
evaluative listening
empathetic listening
pseudo-listening
monopolizing
disconfirming
defensive listening
selective listening
ambushing

2 Scenario

"No, no, no Chris!" Melody shouted from the back of the auditorium. "That's wrong! Can someone please kill the music? And kill the fans too!"

Chris sighed loudly as the blasting music was instantly turned off. He looked around the auditorium. People were scattered everywhere doing different jobs. They were in rehearsals for the annual charity fashion show. It was one of the biggest events of the year on campus. Student models of all races, ethnicities, sizes, and colors came out to model clothes by student designers. Every year the proceeds from the fashion show went to a charity of their choice. This year they were going toward helping rebuild houses in New Orleans in response to Hurricane Katrina.

Chris looked over at his friends who were standing in the wings of the stage and rolled his eyes. He noticed that everyone was getting tired of Melody. Chris was the only freshman in the talent show this year. He performed well due to a little bit of modeling experience he had from participating in shows back home. Because he was the only freshman, Melody was being critical of everything he did. She found herself to be the perfect critic since she had been a big time model since the age of 13. She took a break to attend college and only did jobs on holiday and summer breaks. Now that she was graduating from college in a matter of months, she was going to return to the runway. If Chris would have known about Melody and her ways, he would have steered clear of the fashion show.

Melody stomped her way towards the stage, as if she were on a runway in Paris, with her hand on her hip. Her little short-legged assistant tried to keep up with her, but her short legs were no match for Melody's long insured stems. "Chris, what did I say about your walk down the runway?" Melanie asked with obvious frustration.

"I don't know Melody," Chris replied in a monotone voice. "What did you say?"

"I said you were walking like a Neanderthal," Melody said cooly. "You look sloppy!"

"I do not look sloppy!" Chris shouted.

"Yes, you do!" Melody screamed. "I told you to walk straight and kill that limp you got going on there."

"You told me to walk with a limp, since I'm modeling street wear," Chris reminded her.

"No, I didn't!"

"Yes, you did!"

"No, I didn't!"

"Yes, you did!"

"Forget it!" Melody bellowed. She took a deep breath and mustered up a fake smile. "Look, Chris, I didn't say walk with a limp. You must not have understood what I was saying. It's ok, because I'm willing to tell you again. Take my advice; I am a runway model after all. I've modeled with the best of them. Trust me and do exactly what I say. Ok? Listen to me right now. Kill the limp!" she said. She turned on her stiletto heel and stomped back toward the back of the auditorium with her assistant running behind her. "Start from the top. Cue the music and the fans!"

Chris shook his head and walked back stage, trying to make sure he remembered everything Melody said so they could avoid any more confrontations.

In the Friends episode "The One Where Ross and Rachel Take a Break," Ross becomes frustrated by Rachel's enthusiasm for her new job. To make matters worse, Ross has also been acting jealous over Rachel's relationship with her boss, Mark. Ross tries to explain to Rachel that he wants to have a relationship with her, that he is tired of always getting her answering machine and having dates cancelled because of her work. The situation becomes a bit heated when Rachel sarcastically asks Ross if he wants her to quit her job so she can be his girlfriend full-time, with no other obligations. Rachel gets very frustrated and tells Ross that they can't keep arguing about the same thing over and over again.

Finally, Rachel suggests that maybe they should take a break. Ross understands that to mean a moment to cool off and calm down; maybe do something that will take their minds off the problem. Rachel has something else in mind: a break from the relationship.

Overview

Just like Ross and Rachel, we have all encountered situations in relationships where our perceptions have caused us to interpret messages differently than they were intended. Ross perceived Rachel's request to take a "break" to mean that she needed a temporary time-out from their discussion. In Rachel's mind, the meaning of the word "break" was much different.

Imagine a world where we could completely eliminate misunderstandings between roommates, co-workers, relationship partners, parents, children, teachers, and students. Could such a world *ever* exist? In this chapter we explore the reasons our messages are sometimes partially interpreted, completely misinterpreted, or even ignored by others. Two processes that play a key role in how we send and receive messages in our relationships are perception and listening. In the first part of this chapter we examine the process of perception, paying special attention to the relationship between elements of perception and their relationship to interpersonal communication. We will then turn our attention to the process of listening and how it impacts our interpersonal relationships. Can you recall a time when someone accused you of not listening? Perhaps you *heard* what the person said but did not really *listen* to what they were saying. In the second part of this chapter we will distinguish between the terms *hearing* and *listening,* and advance a number of ways to improve listening, an extremely important, yet often neglected, communication skill.

Do You Hear What I Hear?

Perception and listening are so closely intertwined that it is difficult to discuss one without addressing the other. As we form relationships, our perception impacts how we view the other person as well as how we interpret their messages and behaviors. In the opening scenario Ross perceived his relationship with Rachel to be solid. Rachel, on the other hand, perceived the relationship to be on rocky ground due to Ross' jealous behavior. It is not at all unusual for two people to perceive the same relationship in very different ways. Now consider the role that perception plays on your ability to listen. It should come as no surprise that if our perception differs, our listening skills will also differ. In fact, interpretation is a common factor present in both of the processes of perception and of listening. When Rachel commented that they needed a "break," Ross' perception of their relationship caused him to listen and interpret her message in a way that was very different from what Rachel intended. If you watch reality television shows such as *Survivor* or *Big Brother,* you see numerous examples of the link between perception and listening. Since these programs involve strategy, many of the players plant "seeds of doubt" in the minds of their competitors with the hope that it impairs their perception and ability to listen and interpret messages from others. Often, the winning contestant is the player who has succeeded in impairing the perception and listening skills of the competitors.

As we form relationships, our preception impacts how we view the other person as well as how we interpret their message and behaviors.

Our hope is that once you gain a better understanding of the relationship between these two concepts, you will gain a better understanding of why individuals view relationships, people, behaviors, and messages in different ways. An awareness of the impact of perception and listening in our relationships will increase the accuracy of our interpersonal communication. Let us first focus on the primary perceptual processes and examine the relationship between perception and interpersonal communication.

Perception and Interpersonal Communication

Perception can be best described as the lens through which we view the world. Just as your view of color would be altered if you were to wear a pair of glasses with blue lenses, our perception impacts our view of people, events, and behaviors. One definition of perception is that it is the process of selecting, organizing and interpreting sensory information into a coherent or lucid depiction of the world around us (Klopf 1995). Stated more simply, perception is essentially how we interpret and assign meaning to others' behaviors and messages based on our background and past experiences. The word "experience" is important in understanding the overall process of perception. Consider the role that perception has played in your college experience. Perhaps you enjoy writing and have kept a personal journal. If your English professor assigned daily journal entries in her class, you might tell others that the class was one of the most enjoyable ones you have ever taken. Based on your experience—and your love for writing and journaling—you perceived the class to be easy and enjoyable, and you looked forward to communicating with your professor during her office hours to discuss how you could improve on your writing. But suppose there is another student who has struggled with writing throughout his academic career. He might report to others that the teacher was difficult to talk with and that her assignments were unfair. Based on his perception, their conversations during office hours may have been full of criticism and confusion, and he may describe the instructor as being "uncaring" and an "impossible perfectionist." Since each student brought a unique background and set of experiences to the class, the resulting perceptions of the teacher and class were very different.

Chances are that you have learned about perception in other classes, such as psychology or sociology. Researchers from a wide range of academic fields study perceptual processes. While psychologists conducted much of the initial research in the area of perception, communication scholars have focused specifically on the impact of perception on the meanings assigned to messages. From a communication perspective, perception is important because we often define ourselves based on our perceptions of how others see us. If people respond favorably toward us, we may feel more self-assured and communicate in a more confident manner. Our perception also causes us to form impressions of others which impacts how we communicate with them. How would you feel if you approached one of your classmates at a party and she ignored you? Chances are you would perceive her to be rude and would avoid subsequent interactions with her when you see her in class or on campus. But take a moment to consider the factors that might have influenced your perception. Perhaps you, or maybe even your classmate, were nervous because you have not been to many parties on campus. Maybe your classmate did not recognize you due to the fact that there are many people in the class. There are a number of factors that could alter the perception each of you has of the interaction at the party. All of our interpersonal interactions are influenced by the perceptions we form of ourselves and others. In order to fully grasp the importance of perception, let us examine how we break down bits of information from our environment and form perceptions of ourselves and others.

Have your ever felt overwhelmed at work?

Lyrics from a song made popular by the group The Police illustrate a common problem most of us have experienced in our lifetime—being inundated with too much information. Have you ever felt overwhelmed because it seemed as though your professor disseminated too much information in one lecture? Or have you experienced problems at work because your manager gave you too many instructions, tasks or responsibilities at once? Perhaps you have returned to your apartment after being away for a few days only to find that your inbox is overflowing with email and your answering machine is filled with messages. If any of these situations seem familiar to you, you are not alone. On any given day, we encounter literally thousands of stimuli that bombard our senses and compete for our attention.

Social psychologist Robert Cialdini (2001) notes that we live in an extremely complicated society which he describes as "easily the most rapidly moving and complex that has ever existed on this planet" (7). Cialdini (2001) further states that we cannot analyze all aspects of our environment because "we haven't the time, energy or capacity for it" (7). If it is not possible to process and recall everything we see, hear, taste, touch, or smell, then how do we make sense of the world around us?

The way humans manage all of the stimuli encountered in the environment is to limit the amount and type of information taken in. This elimination process often occurs at a subconscious level. Thus, on any given day, we put limits on what we choose to see, hear, taste, touch, or smell. Because of the innate limitations in our ability to process information, humans are often described as **limited capacity processors.** Stated simply, we consciously and subconsciously make choices about the amount and type of stimuli we perceive. Think of a time when you were so focused on your homework that when your mother commented on how loud you were playing your music, you thought, "Wow, I can't even really hear it." To fully understand how people make sense of their environment, we need to take a closer look at three key perceptual processes: selection, organization and interpretation.

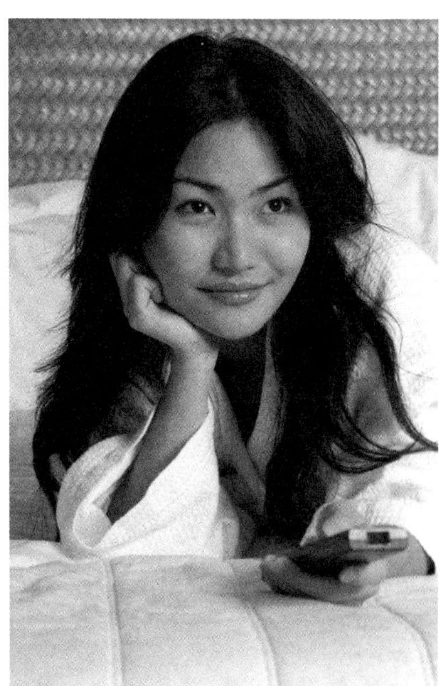
© Philip Date, 2007, Shutterstock.

It's your choice to watch television and subject yourself to shows and advertising.

Selection

The first perception process is **selection.** While you might not always be consciously aware of the process of selection, we are continually making choices about the amount and type of information that we choose to notice. Remember our earlier discussion about our ability to be limited capacity processors? It is virtually impossible to pay attention to all the things we could possibly sense at any given time. These limitations in our ability to assimilate and interpret information prevent us from "taking it all in" and so we must select certain messages or stimuli over others. These selections we make are often done in a purposeful rather than random manner (Klopf 1995). Three primary selectivity processes which impact our perception include selective exposure, selective attention, and selective retention. The next sections provide an overview of each of these processes and discuss variables that affect them.

Selective exposure refers to the choice to subject oneself to certain stimuli. Choices regarding which messages and stimuli you will subject yourself to are made each day. You choose whether to expose yourself to the messages being sent by advertisers and newscasters when you decide whether to turn on your television or radio each morning. You choose whether to subject yourself to the messages left on your answering machine or via email. Often the choice to engage in selective exposure is based on our desire to seek information or stimuli that is comfortable or familiar to us. Culture plays a key role in determining what messages or stimuli we choose to expose ourselves to and those which we avoid. Consider the fact that some people avoid communicating with those from other cultural backgrounds. They engage in selective exposure by avoiding conversations with people from different cultures. Individuals may focus on the obvious differences of race or ethnicity and assume that they do not have anything in common with people who are so dissimilar. The choice to avoid communication may cause individuals to miss learning about all the beliefs and interests that are shared. According to Fischer and his colleagues (2005), we are most likely to seek out information consistent with our beliefs, values, and attitudes and to avoid information that is viewed as inconsistent. Our propensity to seek out certain types of information and avoid others is referred to as a **biased information search** (Fischer et al. 2005). While we might not consciously be aware of this process, each day we selectively choose to associate with particular individuals or groups of people and attend to certain types of messages in a variety of contexts. Perhaps today you chose to attend your communication class rather than going out to eat lunch with a friend. The decision to attend your communication class is yet another example of selective exposure.

There are a number of factors that affect selective exposure including, among others: proximity, utility, and reinforcement. Not surprisingly, we are most likely to selectively expose ourselves to messages that are nearby, or close in proximity. In fact, proximity is the number one predictor of whether we will develop a relationship with another person (Katz and Hill 1958). Consider the relationships that you formed with those who attended your high school. Proximity impacted your ability to selectively expose yourself to those in the same school and form relationships. While the Internet has changed the way we communicate and form relationships, most people still find it difficult to form relationships and communicate with those who are not physically close to them. Second, we are most likely to expose ourselves to messages that we perceive as being useful. **Utility** refers to the perception that particular messages are immediately useful; these messages have a much greater chance of being selected than those that are not seen as useful (McCroskey and Richmond 1996). Expecting an important message from your parents will influence your choice to selectively expose yourself to your email messages. If there are several messages in your inbox, a message from friend or family member is more likely to be viewed than one from the Department of Student Services at your university. Finally, most people expose themselves to messages that are consistent with their views, or reinforce, their attitudes and beliefs (Fischer et al. 2005). Thus, if you are strongly opposed to the death penalty, you will probably not attend a lecture delivered by a professor advocating capital punishment for convicted murderers.

Once we have made the decision to place ourselves in a position to physically receive a message, we then focus on certain aspects or elements of the message. **Selective attention** refers to the decision to pay attention to certain stimuli while simultaneously ignoring others. Factors which affect selective attention often include the novelty, size, and concreteness of the stimuli. Novelty refers to the tendency to pay attention to stimuli that are novel, new, or different. Novel aspects are more likely to capture our attention than those with which we are familiar. For example, we tend to notice a friend's new hairstyle almost immediately. In the *Friends* episode discussed at the beginning of the chapter, Rachel became more aware of and paid closer attention to changes in Ross' behavior. Previously, he had been secure and confident in their relationship, but as Rachel became more focused on her career, his messages communicated a new jealousy. Another factor that affects selective attention is the size, or magnitude, of the stimuli. We are more likely to pay attention to large items, objects, or people. It probably is not completely by chance that most Chief Executive Officers in U.S. companies are at least six feet tall and that virtually every U.S. President elected since 1900 has been the taller of the two candidates. Finally, we are more likely to pay attention to information that is concrete, or well-defined, than to information which is perceived as abstract or ambiguous. Individuals have an easier time attending to messages that are clear and straightforward. For example, if a manager tells an employee to "change her attitude and behavior," but does not provide specific or concrete information about how or why the attitude or behavior is problematic, the employee is likely to ignore this message (McCroskey and Richmond 1996).

What kind of an impression do you try to make in a job interview?

Once the decision has been made to expose and attend to stimuli, the final stage in the selectivity process involves selective retention, which refers to the choice to save or delete information from one's long term memory. Two factors affecting the propensity to retain information include primacy and recency effects, and utility. Researchers have identified a range of variables which affect an individual's ability to retain information. When studying the type of information people are most likely to retain, researchers note that arguments delivered first (**primacy**) and last (**recency**) in a persuasive presentation are more likely to be recalled and to be more persuasive (Gass and Seiter 2003). As we form relationships, we are often concerned with the first or last impression that we make. It has been estimated that we form our initial impression of others during the first three to five seconds. Recall the last job interview that you attended. Careful attention was paid to your clothing and appearance to ensure that you would make a positive first impression that the interviewer would remember. However, if you tripped and spilled the contents of your portfolio as you exited the interview, the recency of the last impression may be imprinted on the interviewer's memory. A second important factor related to retention is **utility**, or usefulness. Almost all of us have heard the phrase, "use it or lose it." Essentially what this phrase implies is that if we do not apply the information we obtain, we may not retain it later. For example, many of you might have received training in cardiopulmonary resuscitation (CPR) at one time in your life. But if one of your classmates needed CPR, would you remember the steps? The same principle is true of the information and skills discussed in this text. It is our hope that by providing you with examples of concepts and information, you will see the usefulness of the strategies and become more effective in your interpersonal interactions with others.

Organization

Once we have selected information, or stimuli, we then begin the process of placing it into categories in order to make sense of it. **Organization** "refers to our need to place the perceived characteristics of something into the whole to which it seems to belong" (Klopf 1995, 51). Organization is the process by which we take the stimuli and make sense of it so that it is meaningful to us. Remember the earlier example of the classmate who ignored you at a party? Some of the stimuli that caused you to form your perception included her lack of eye contact and her failure to reciprocate your greeting. In the organization process, you take each of these stimuli (eye contact and lack of communication) and put them together to form an impression.

One theory that is useful in understanding how individuals organize information in meaningful ways is constructivism. Kelly (1970) developed the theory of **constructivism** to explain the process we use to organize and interpret experiences by applying cognitive structures labeled schemata. **Schemata** are "organized clusters of knowledge and information about particular topics" (Hockenbury and Hockenbury 2006, 265). Another way to describe schemata is as mental filing cabinets with several drawers used to help organize and process information. Schemata are the results of one's experiences and, therefore, are dynamic and often changing as we encounter new relationships and life experiences. Suppose your first romantic relationship was a disaster. The initial schema you formed to organize information about romantic relationships (which may have been obtained from television shows or movies) was likely altered to include this negative experience you encountered. But suppose your next romantic partner is incredibly thoughtful and romantic. New information is incorporated to your schema that now enables you to evaluate various aspects of romantic relationships based on both the positive and negative experiences you encountered in the past. Thus, we apply schemata to make sense of our communication experiences. More specifically, we apply four different types of schemata to interpret interpersonal encounters: prototypes, personal constructs, stereotypes, and scripts (Fiske and Taylor 1984; Kelley 1972; Reeder 1985).

Have you ever thought of your ideal romantic partner? What would he or she be like? **Prototypes** are knowledge structures which represent the most common attributes of a phenomenon. These structures are used to help organize stimuli and influence our interactions with others (Fehr and Russell 1991). Prototypes provide us with a "benchmark" that is the standard used to evaluate and categorize other examples that fall into the same category. Recall your initial encounter with someone you dated recently. It is very likely that you evaluated this individual's behaviors based on whether this person fit your "prototypical," or best, example of a relationship partner. If you were to make a list of the characteristics you desire in the "ideal" romantic partner, these preconceived ideas and expectations represent your prototype and affect how you will perceive each potential romantic partner encountered in the future. Research by Fehr and Russell (1991) supports the idea that we have prototypes about love and friendship. They conducted six different studies in an attempt to identify participants' prototypical examples of different types of love (e.g., maternal love, paternal love, friendship love, sisterly love, puppy love, infatuation, and so on) and the factors associated with love. Characteristics such as caring, helping, establishing a bond, sharing, feeling free to talk, demonstrating respect, and exhibiting closeness were all associated with perceptions of love. In a related study, Fehr (2004) examined prototypical examples of interactions which led to greater perceived intimacy in same-sex friendships. Fehr (2004) found that interaction patterns which involved increased levels of self-disclosure and emotional support were perceived by friends as being more prototypical of expectations for intimacy than other types of practical support. Prototype theory is extremely useful in shedding light on how we organize our thoughts about interpersonal communication and relationships.

Personal constructs serve to help you evaluate others and influence your interactions.

A second type of schemata is **personal constructs** which Kelly (1955; 1970; 1991) describes as bipolar dimensions of meaning used to predict and evaluate how people behave. Personal constructs have also been described as the "mental yardsticks" that we use to assess people and social situations. Several examples of personal constructs include: responsible-irresponsible, assertive-unassertive, friendly-unfriendly, intelligent-unintelligent, and forthright-guarded. Personal constructs serve as another means of evaluating others and simultaneously influence how we approach interactions. For example, if you label your co-worker as "friendly" you may smile more at this person and share more personal information than you would with another co-worker labeled as "unfriendly." Raskin (2002) notes that we monitor our personal constructs closely and keep track of how accurately they predict life circumstances. When necessary, we revise them when we perceive them as unreliable. We tend to define situations and people based on the personal constructs that we use regularly. Thus, it is possible that we might not be aware of qualities some people possess or situations that we do not access regularly (Raskin 2002).

The third type of schema we use to help us organize information is stereotypes. Stereotypes are impressions and expectations based on one's knowledge or beliefs about a specific group of people which are then applied to all individuals who are members of that group. Stereotypes greatly influence the way messages are perceived. Some researchers argue that stereotypes are often activated automatically when an individual observes a member of a group or category (Carlston 1992) and we are likely to predict how that person will behave. For example, Hamilton and Sherman (1994) note that individuals' perceptions of different racial and ethnic groups are often "planted in early childhood by influential adults in their lives" (3). Influential individuals, such as family members, and the media play an important role in shaping how we define others and how we view the world.

If you're on a sports team, you may identify more closely with other athletes.

Why do we categorize people, events, and objects? As mentioned previously, we are limited in our ability to process the sheer number of stimuli bombarding us at any given time. Thus, we identify ways to categorize and organize stimuli to enhance "cognitive efficiency," or to make information more manageable. A second explanation for our tendency to stereotype as described by Hamilton and Sherman (1994) is "categorization as self-enhancement" (6). Simply stated, we tend to evaluate those groups to which we belong more favorably than groups to which we do not belong. Recall the groups you associated with in high school. If you were a member of the student council, you may have viewed members as being strong leaders and very organized. Students who were not members of the student council may have created their own schema for evaluating its members—they may have labeled them as being "power-hungry," or aggressive. Social identity theory offers an explanation for our tendency to evaluate in-groups more positively than out-groups. According to social identity theory, an individual's self-esteem is often connected to membership or association with social groups (Hamilton and Sherman 1994; Turner 1987). In an effort to maintain a positive identity, we may overemphasize or accentuate differences between in-groups and out-groups.

Can placing people into groups or categories based on particular traits or characteristics be problematic? Absolutely! For example, individuals are often categorized based on whether they have some type of physical or mental disability. Braithwaite and her colleagues found that people without disabilities often assume that individuals with physical disabilities are helpless, while this is certainly not the case (Braithwaite and Harter 2000). They conducted a number of interviews with persons with physical disabilities and found that they often received a great deal of either unwanted or unsolicited help from persons without disabilities. This example illustrates the problem of inaccurately categorizing people. In this case, persons without disabilities inaccurately categorized persons with disabilities as helpless or needy, resulting in inappropriate "helping" behavior.

People form stereotypes about individuals based on race, culture, sex, sexual orientation, age, education, intelligence, and affiliations, among other characteristics. It is crucial that we realize that stereotypes are formed as a result of our perceptions of others and, as a result, can be accurate or inaccurate. When inaccurate or inflexible stereotypes are applied to individuals, they often divide rather than unite people. Is it possible to resist the temptation to stereotype or categorize people? While the research on changing stereotypes is not extensive, much of it is promising. Stereotyping is a normal tendency. Our desire to reduce our level of uncertainty about people and situations leads us into the stereotype "trap." We are uncomfortable in situations where we have little or no information about others, and our initial tendency is to open our schematic files in an attempt to locate any information that will help us figure out how to communicate. For example, one of the authors of your textbook is a native of West Virginia. Throughout her life, she has encountered stereotypes of people from West Virginia. When she lived in California, one of her college roommates commented, "You're nothing at all what I expected someone from West Virginia to be like!" When asked to describe her expectations, the roommate described some very negative stereotypes. The two became best friends and discovered that even though one was from Texas and the other was from West Virginia, they had more in common than they thought. If you have never communicated with a person from another culture, your first tendency may be to recall any information associated with the person's culture that you have read about or seen on television. Regardless of whether this information is accurate or inaccurate, it is often used as a "guide" for our expectations and communication. The key to overcoming the negative outcomes of stereotyping is to remain open-minded and flexible. While your tendency may be to look for something to help organize and make sense of stimuli, remember that the information used to form the stereotype may be incorrect. Fortunately, there is a growing body of scholarship which suggests that the stereotypes people form can be modified over time (Hamilton and Sherman 1994).

The last type of schema we use to organize is scripts. According to Abelson (1982), scripts are knowledge structures that guide and influence how we process information. Abelson (1982) describes scripts as an "organized bundle of expectations about an event sequence" (134). Simply stated, we adhere to a number of different scripts throughout a day, scripts that tell us what to do and say, as well as *how* to do and say it. Very often we never notice how scripted our day-to-day interactions are until someone deviates from the expected script. A comedian makes reference to the potential embarrassment caused by scripts in his description of an encounter he had when exiting a taxi cab at the airport.

Taxi Driver: Thanks! Have a nice flight!

Comedian: You too! (*then, realizing that the taxi driver is not flying*) I mean, the next time you fly somewhere.

Another scenario, a casual conversation between two co-workers at the copy machine in the workplace, illustrates the relevance of scripts to our day-to-day functioning.

Dominique: Hi Anthony!

Anthony: Hey Dominique, how are you?

Dominique: Not so good. My arthritis is acting up and it's making it impossible for me to get any work done on this report that is due at noon. Then my son's school just called to say he's not feeling well, and I can't get a hold of my sister to go pick him up at school. It's just been one thing after another.

Anthony: (*looking at his watch*) Wow, I didn't realize it was so late! Um, yeah, well, hey, nice talking to you. I've got to go!

Did Anthony respond appropriately to Dominique's explicit description of how she was feeling? Can you explain why Anthony had to go? Script theory explains Anthony's reaction to Dominique's description of her arthritis and problems with child care. According to script theory, we often interact with others in a way that could be described as "automatic" or even "mindless." Because we have repeated experience with these scripts, we are able to adhere to them in a manner described as "mindless," meaning that we are not consciously aware of the fact that we are following a script. Essentially, we rely on scripts to tell us how to proceed in situations and what to say. We enter into situations that we have been in before with a specific set of expectations and, when individuals violate our expectations by not adhering to the script, we are not sure what to do. From an interpersonal communication perspective, we use scripts to determine how to proceed during social interaction and form perceptions of others based on whether or not they are following the "script."

Interpretation

After we have selected and organized information, the final step in the perception process involves interpretation. **Interpretation** is the subjective process of making sense of our perceptions. The interpretation process is described as highly subjective because individuals' interpretations of communication events vary extensively and are influenced by a wide range of factors. The following sections serve as an overview of the dominant theory used to explain how people interpret information, discuss errors in interpretive processes, and identify factors that influence the ways we interpret information.

Are we the same? Are we twins? Are we sisters?

The dominant theory that explains how people explain their own and others' behavior is known as **attribution theory** (Heider 1958; Kelley 1967; 1971). This theory is also known as naïve psychology because people often try to connect observable behavior to unobservable causes (Littlejohn 1983). Can you recall a time when you have tried to explain a friend's unusual behavior? Perhaps she was supposed to phone you at a scheduled time, and the call never came. You may try to explain her lack of communication by theorizing that she overslept, the car broke down, or she had a fight with a significant other. All of these are causes that you have not directly observed, but they are used as potential explanations for the friend's behavior. Attribution theory is commonly applied to interpret the reasons for our own actions as well as the actions of others. According to Heider (1958) there are three basic assumptions to attribution theory: (1) that it is natural for people to attempt to establish the causes of their own and others' behavior, (2) that people assign causes for behavior systematically, and (3) that the attribution impacts the perceiver's feelings and subsequent behavior. Thus, the causes assigned to peoples' behaviors play a significant role in determining reactions to interpreted behaviors.

Maybe you visualize your friend sitting by her broken-down car as a reason she didn't call you.

According to attribution theory, people assign causes to behaviors in a fairly systematic way and typically use different types of information to make these decisions. Generally, when individuals attempt to explain behaviors, they will choose among three different explanations: the situation, unintentionality or chance, and intentionality or dispositions (Heider 1958). A person's behavior may be best explained by considering the situation and how this factor may have influenced behavior. Situational factors are often referred to as **external attributions.** For example, perhaps you are normally talkative and outgoing when in social situations. However, you go to a party with some friends and see your former relationship partner with a new "love" interest. Because you still have feelings for this person, this situation is upsetting to you, and you spend the evening moping and avoiding conversations. Hence, your behavior at the party could be best explained by situational or external attributions. The second factor typically used to explain behavior is **unintentionality** or chance, which refers to one's inability to predict whether the behaviors will be consistent in the future (Kelsey et al. 2004). For example, someone may guess several answers on a difficult test and then claim that they may or may not be able to replicate their test performance again in the future. The third factor, **intentionality,** or disposition, is also referred to as an internal attribution. **Internal attributions** are typically described as being stable or persistent and often refer to behaviors that are likely to be exhibited repeatedly across a variety of contexts (Heider 1958). If your friend Sally acts quiet and reserved in almost all situations, then you would explain her quiet and reserved demeanor at your birthday party based on internal attributions or personality traits. When attempting to explain her behavior, you might say "Sally is just that way," or tell others that she is normally very shy.

Harold Kelley (1973) also developed a prominent theory of attribution which attempts to explain how we formulate perceptions of others. Kelley's covariation theory states that we decide whether peoples' behavior is based on either internal or external factors by using three different and important types of information: distinctiveness, consensus, and consistency. In order to apply Kelley's covariation principle, we must have multiple observations of individuals to accurately explain their behavior. **Distinctiveness** refers to whether or not a person typically behaves the same way with the target, or receiver, of the behavior. When distinctiveness is high, we tend to attribute others' behavior to external causes. When distinctiveness is low, we tend to attribute others' behavior to internal causes. For example, if Professor Munhall is always pleasant and helpful toward all students, he would be exhibiting low levels of distinctiveness. In this situation, Dr. Munhall's behavior would be attributed to internal factors (e.g., he is such a caring teacher). Suppose one minute Professor Munhall snaps at Alan during class and the next minute he responds calmly to Marcus' request for clarification. In this situation, his behavior would be described as highly distinctive since he does not normally behave this way toward students. External factors would be used to explain his highly distinctive behavior (e.g., he had a bad day).

The second type of information used to attribute causes to behaviors is consistency. **Consistency** refers to whether an individual behaves the same way across contexts and at various times. For example, would the person behave the same way regardless of whether she was at a party, at work, at school, or at a bar? It is important to keep in mind that the key element here is the context or situation. When an individual acts in a highly consistent manner, we tend to attribute the individual's behavior to internal rather than external causes. Very often, we ask whether the behavior is unique or consistent in the particular context. If your friend Kaia is always loud and outgoing in social situations, and you observe her acting this way at a party, you would explain her behavior based on internal rather than external factors. That is, Kaia acted in a loud, outgoing manner because this is the way she typically behaves with most individuals and in most situations (high consistency). Conversely, if Kaia was quiet, shy, and withdrawn at the same party, you might explain her behavior by saying that the party must not have been fun (external factor) because she was acting differently than the expected behavior in social situations (low consistency).

The final factor, **consensus**, considers whether the behavior is unique to the individual or if they are behaving in the way that would be typically expected of others. We say that consensus is high when a person acts the same way that others would behave. Recall our example from the beginning of the chapter. Did Ross behave in a way that was similar to the way Joey, Chandler, or several other men would respond? The key element in this factor is the actor, or source of behavior, (as opposed to the context, which is the focus of consistency). When consensus is high, we attribute peoples' behavior to external rather than internal factors. For example, the majority of Americans say that they do not enjoy giving speeches and typically experience anxiety prior to and during the event (high consensus). Thus, we attribute Jay's speech anxiety to external (everyone is nervous about public speaking) rather than internal factors. But suppose Jay actually looks forward to the prospect of public speaking. When someone actually enjoys giving speeches (low consensus), we might explain this person's unique behavior by saying this person is highly confident and self-assured (internal factors).

Not surprisingly, we often evaluate and explain our *own* behavior using standards that are very different from those used to evaluate and explain the behavior of *others*. The two most common attribution errors people make are known as the self-serving bias and the fundamental attribution error. The self-serving bias states that we tend to manufacture, or construct, attributions which best serve our own self-interests (Hamachek 1992). For example, when we excel in school or sports, we often explain our success based on internal factors or causes. We might think "I am smart" or "I am an incredible athlete," both of which are internal attributions. The self-serving bias provides us with a viable explanation for the sources of student motivation in the classroom. Research by Gorham and her colleagues (1992) indicates that students view motivation in school as a student-owned trait or characteristic. Thus, when a student feels motivated to do well in school, he or she credits this intention to do well on internal rather than external factors. On the other hand, when a student feels unmotivated, or is unwilling to work hard in school, he or she is more likely to attribute the cause of this lack of motivation to the teacher's behavior (external attributions—the teacher did not explain the assignment clearly) rather than to the self (internal attributions). Why do we avoid taking responsibility for our poor performance, mistakes, or shortcomings? One explanation for attributing our failures to external causes is to save face. While our tendency to protect our own self-image is understandable, it is important to realize that these distorted perceptions of self are problematic. Falsely taking credit for accomplishments and blaming others (or circumstances) for our failures can lead to distorted self-images and inaccurate representations of ourselves during social interaction (Hamacheck, 1992).

The next question to ask is whether we attribute others' failures and successes to external or internal factors? A second common attribution error often made during the interpretation stage of perception is the **fundamental attribution error.** When attempting to explain others' negative behaviors, we tend to overestimate the internal factors or causes and underestimate the external factors or causes. Conversely, when attempting to explain our *own* mistakes or shortcomings, we tend to overestimate the external causes and underestimate the internal causes. For example, if you are driving to school and see someone speeding by you, you might say to your friend, "What a reckless driver," (internal attribution). However, if you are speeding down the same road the next day and that same friend asks you why you are in such a rush, you might respond, "I am late for work," or "I need to get a parking space," both of which are external attributions. Kelsey and her colleagues (2004) recently used attribution theory to investigate the explanations students provided for their college instructors' classroom "misbehaviors." Examples of teacher misbehaviors include boring lectures, unfair grading, and providing too much information. The researchers found that students were more likely to attribute their teachers' inappropriate classroom behaviors to internal causes (e.g., he doesn't care about teaching) rather than to external causes (e.g., she's had a bad day). It is important to understand and acknowledge that while the way we make sense of our own and others' behaviors is less than perfect, it greatly affects how we interact with others. To improve the way we select, organize, and interpret information, it is also essential to consider our individual differences and how these differences impact our perception.

Individual Differences and Perceptions

While there are numerous factors that affect the way we perceive information, in this section we focus on three widely researched and acknowledged variables related to perception. Three variables that have been identified by scholars as impacting perception are sex, age, and culture. We begin our discussion by considering how sex differences affect perception and communication.

Do you think men and women view the world differently? Deborah Tannen, a noted gender scholar and linguist, would answer this question with an unequivocal "Yes!" Tannen (1986; 1990; 1994) notes that men and women hold different worldviews and philosophies regarding how they are expected to act in society which evolve from early interactions with family members, peers, and society. Tannen and other gender scholars (see, for example, Wood 1999) assert that men and women are socialized differently and, as a result, develop different perceptions of the world and their place within it. For example, women often perceive the world as a place to connect and form bonds with others. Men, on the other hand, view the world as a place to assert their independence and autonomy. These differences in perceptions affect the ways that men and women approach social interactions. Tannen says that women often engage in **rapport talk** which is analogous to small talk or phatic communication, while men often exhibit **report talk** which involves discussions about facts, events, and solutions. The following scenario illustrates the difference between rapport and report talk.

Women are socialized differently and, as a result, develop different perceptions of the world and their place within it.

Elyse and Dave got a flat tire during their drive to work. As they discuss the event with colleagues, Elyse explains various details associated with the tire episode when speaking with her friends. "It was horrible! We were driving down the freeway when all of the sudden we heard a 'thump-thump' under the car. Of course, today would be the day that we left the cell phone at home on the table! Didn't you get a flat tire about a month ago, Janelle?"

Typically, other females respond by sharing their similar stories and experiences. Dave, on the other hand, would provide the details of the morning's event differently.

"We got a flat tire on Interstate 270 this morning. We didn't have a cell phone, but the car behind us pulled over and let me use their phone to call AAA."

It is important to note that not all men and women communicate this way. However, because men and women may see the world differently, it affects how they perceive themselves and others and ultimately impacts their interpersonal communication.

A second frequently studied variable that affects perceptions is age. Recall the last time you engaged in a conversation with older relatives, friends, or co-workers. Did you notice any differences in your perspectives on various issues? One student recently shared an example of a conversation held with her mother that illustrated the impact of age on perceptual differences. Because this female student does not like to cook or clean, her mother told her that "No man will want to marry her!" The daughter argued her "case" by explaining to her mother that times have changed and that women and men today often share domestic responsibilities in the home. This conversation between mother and daughter illustrates how age and experience impacts our perceptions. As we grow older, we tend to build on our diverse life experiences and our perceptions often change or, in some cases, become more firmly ingrained. Some research indicates that older individuals possess more consistent and stable attitudes and are more difficult to persuade (Alwin and Krosnick 1991). Other findings suggest that as people age they become more cognitively sophisticated and are better able to see the world from others' perspectives (Bartsch and London 2000). Thus, it is important to consider how age affects both our own and others' perceptions.

Finally, culture affects our perceptions of the world and simultaneously influences our communication with others. One reason for examining cultural differences is to learn more about how socialization in different cultures affects peoples' perceptions and behavior. For example, researchers often study perceptual and behavioral differences in individualistic and collectivistic cultures. Collectivistic cultures emphasize group harmony and concern for others. An example of a collectivistic culture is found in China. Individualistic cultures, as found in the United States, tend to value individual rights, independence, and autonomy. Members of collectivistic cultures view the world much differently than individuals from highly individualistic cultures. There are numerous research examples which illustrate the difference between individualistic and collectivistic cultural beliefs, attitudes, behaviors, and values. One interesting study explored Chinese and U.S. managerial differences in attempts to influence employees (Yukl, Fu, and McDonald 2003). According to Yukl and his colleagues, "the cross-cultural differences in rated effectiveness of tactics were consistent with cultural values and traditions" (Yukl, Fu, and McDonald 2003, 68). Chinese managers rated informal strategies and strategies that emphasized personal relations as more effective than traditional Western strategies which emphasize being direct and task oriented. Swiss and American managers perceived more direct task-oriented tactics as being more effective than informal strategies and strategies that emphasized personal relations. In another study, Miller (1984) examined the impact of culture on the fundamental attribution error. She asked children and adults in India and the U.S. to provide possible explanations for pro-social (e.g., helping someone paint their house) and anti-social behaviors (e.g., engaging in aggressive behavior). Miller's findings provide valuable insight into how factors such as age and culture impact our perception. Children in both cultures offered similar attributions for the behaviors. However, adults in the U.S. were more likely than their Indian counterparts to explain events by attributing them to individual traits. Adults from India, on the other hand, focused on situational or contextual causes as possible explanations for behaviors. It is important to remember that most of us hold more favorable perceptions of the groups we belong to than those to which we do not belong. Thus, we should be cognizant of our tendency to be favorably disposed towards people, ideas, beliefs, and concepts from our culture and our inclination to be more critical of people, ideas, and concepts from other cultural perspectives.

The Link Between Perception and Listening

By now you have a more sophisticated understanding of why some information is selected over others, how information is organized, and how messages are interpreted. Additionally, we have provided you with some information about common attribution errors that individuals make and variables that affect the process of perception. To further understand the potential implications of perception, we must consider how our different perspectives of people and messages influence and are influenced by listening. At the beginning of this chapter, we pointed out that perception and listening are closely related to one another. Our perception of others impacts both our ability and our desire to listen in social interactions.

In the *Friends* episode "The One the Morning After" Ross tries to explain to Rachel his reasons for sleeping with another woman on the same night that Rachel suggested that they take a "break" from their relationship. Ross pleads with Rachel to work through it. He tells her he can't even think of what his life would be like without her; without everything she is to him. Rachel just can't get beyond what Ross did to betray her. She tells him that he has become a completely different person to her, now that she's seen that he is capable of hurting her. Rachel believes there will never be anything he can say or do that will change the way she feels about him now.

Because her perception of Ross' commitment to their relationship has changed, so has Rachel's ability to listen to the messages he attempts to communicate. As we listen to messages communicated by others, new information is provided that may cause us to change existing perceptions or perhaps even form new ones. Listening is an essential part of effective interpersonal communication. Yet it is often understudied and underemphasized in communication courses. In the next section we make a distinction between hearing and listening, offer strategies to enhance your own listening skills, and describe the various listening styles employed by individuals.

Listening is a key element for acquiring information and developing and sustaining our relationships.

Listening

These quotations illustrate the power and functions of listening in the communication process. Listening is a key element for acquiring information and developing and sustaining our relationships. Yet, communication practitioners often refer to listening as the "forgotten" communication skill. The fact that listening skills are often neglected or undervalued is surprising since most people engage in listening more than any other type of communication activity. For example, college students report that up to 50 percent of their time is spent listening, compared to speaking (20 percent), reading (6 percent), and writing (8 percent) (Janusik and Wolvin 2006). While colleges often require classes which emphasize competence in writing and speaking, few highlight listening as an important communication skill.

Marge, it takes two to lie. One to lie and one to listen.
—*Homer Simpson*

The most basic of all human needs is the need to understand and be understood.
The best way to understand people is to listen to them.
—*Ralph Nichols*

Listening, not imitation, may be the sincerest form of flattery.
—*Dr. Joyce Brothers*

When we engage in effective listening behaviors we communicate a message that we comprehend and care about what the speaker has to say. Recall a time when you attempted to communicate with a friend or family member, only to receive a distracted response of "Yeah. Uh-huh. Mm-hmm." The lack of active listening behavior is extremely frustrating. A lack of awareness of ineffective listening behaviors has potential negative implications for both personal and professional relationships. Our goal in focusing on this topic is twofold: to assist you in understanding the listening process and to shed some light on how your own behaviors may be interpreted by others. Our hope is that after completing this chapter you will be able to evaluate your own listening skills and to implement some of our suggestions.

As stated earlier, individuals typically spend more time listening during their lifetime than any other communication activity. For many of you, this chapter will be the only formal training in appropriate and effective listening skills you will ever have. The implications of effective listening span a variety of interpersonal contexts. In the health care setting, Wanzer and her colleagues (2004) found that patients who perceived their physicians to employ effective listening skills were more satisfied with their doctor and the care provided. Research has also identified a link between one's career success and effective listening skills. Employers report that listening is a top skill sought in hiring new employees, and it plays a significant role in evaluations for promotion and incentives (AICPA 2006). As we begin our discussion of effective listening skills, it is important that we first distinguish between the concepts of "hearing" and "listening."

Gina was cooking dinner for Joni one evening after a long day at work. As she stirred the pasta sauce on the stove, she sighed, "I just don't understand why my manager doesn't see what's happening with our latest project. Half of the team is running around clueless, and I keep getting left with their messes to clean up."

Table 2.1 Daily Average Hours Devoted to Communication Activities		
Communication Activities	Total Number of Hours	Approximate Percentage of Time
Writing	1.82	8
Reading	1.40	6
Speaking	4.83	20
Listening*	5.80	24
Television*	2.12	9
Radio*	.86	4
CD/Tapes*	1.32	5
Phone*	1.87	8
Email	1.33	6
Internet	2.73	11
Total Listening Hours	11.97	50
Items marked with an * represent those activities which focus primarily on listening.		

Joni gave a half-hearted response while scanning her emails on her laptop. "Uh-huh," she said without breaking eye contact with the computer screen.

Gina stopped cooking and scolded Joni, "You never listen when I try to tell you about my day at work!"

Joni was shocked, "What do you mean? I heard every word you said!"

Gina countered, "Prove it! What did I just say?"

Joni dropped her head and apologized, realizing that while she had heard Gina talking, she hadn't really listened to a word she said.

Have you ever been involved in a situation similar to the one described above? Perhaps you have been the one who has heard the words but did not listen to what was being said. Perhaps one of the most common mistakes made in the listening process is making the assumption that hearing is the same as listening. In fact, listening and hearing are two distinct processes. **Hearing** involves the physical process of sound waves traveling into the ear canal, vibrating the ear drum and eventually sending signals to the brain. Although we often hear messages, we do not necessarily attend to them. This explains why you might be sitting in your room right now reading this text and hearing an air conditioner turn on, birds chirping outside, or friends yelling in the hallway. But while your brain has processed these sound waves, you may not have necessarily been listening for these stimuli. **Listening** not only involves the physical process of hearing, but it also involves the psychological process of attending to the stimuli, creating meaning and responding. Listening is often described as a dynamic and ongoing process in which individuals physically receive a message, employ cognitive processes to attribute meaning to the message, and provide verbal and/or nonverbal feedback to the source.

As you reflect on this definition, it should become quite apparent that listening is a highly complex process. First, listening is dynamic because it is an ongoing activity that requires an individual to be active and engaged. Unlike hearing, listening requires an individual to be mindful and aware of one's surroundings. After we physically receive the sound waves and hear the message, the next step involves employing cognitive processing to attribute meaning to the information that was received. Hopefully the steps involved in this cognitive process are familiar to you. They include: selection, organization, and interpretation. Do you recall our earlier discussion of these stages as part of the perception process? These same elements are involved in listening. We are selective in the information we expose ourselves to and attend to in the perception process; the same is true in listening. We select what sounds and messages we will listen to and which we will ignore. Have you ever encountered a mother who can carry on a phone conversation and never become distracted while children are screaming and playing in the background? The mother has selected what sounds to focus her attention on in the listening process—she has selected the message that is being received via the telephone. Just as we organize stimuli during the perception process, information is also organized as a part of the listening process. Finally, we must interpret information and assign a meaning to what we have heard while listening. The relationship between perception and listening should be even clearer—the similarities between both processes are nearly identical. The final stage of the listening process involves formulating a response, or feedback, to send to the source via verbal and/or nonverbal channels. Examples of verbal feedback may include, "You look sad," "Tell me more," or "What do you plan to do?" Some examples of nonverbal responses could include nodding your head, making eye contact, or even giving a hug.

Table 2.2	Key Strategies for Effective Listening (BIG EARS)
B	Be open and receptive to the message
I	Interpret the message
G	Give feedback
E	Engage in dual perspective
A	Adapt your listening style
R	Reduce noise
S	Store the message

To help you remember some of the key strategies involved in effective listening, remember the following acronym: **BIG EARS.** Each of these strategies is discussed in the paragraphs that follow.

Be Open to the Message. Listening is difficult enough to begin with, but when we fail to prepare ourselves to receive messages, it becomes even more so. Effective listening requires you to employ effective nonverbal listening behaviors, control message overload, and manage your preoccupations and other distractions.

© Kendall Hunt Publishing

Manage multiple preoccupations and distractions that can impair your ability to listen.

First, we need to be aware of our nonverbal listening behaviors. The next time you are sitting in class listening to a lecture, take a moment and consider the role your nonverbal behaviors play in the listening process. Do you look like you are open to receiving messages? Maintaining an open body position, engaging in eye contact, and responding to the lecture by nodding your head are all examples of nonverbal behaviors that communicate a willingness to listen.

Next, focus on ways to manage the multiple sources of information that are competing for your attention. Remember our discussion of perception and the role of selective attention and exposure? Effective listening behaviors require you to dedicate your attention to a particular message. The next time you are tempted to watch *Grey's Anatomy* while carrying on a phone conversation with your mother, think twice. One of the sources will ultimately win out over the other—will it be the television show or your mother?

Finally, identify ways to manage the multiple preoccupations and distractions that can impair your ability to listen. Look beyond superficial factors that may be hindering your ability to focus on the message. While a professor's distracting delivery style or prehistoric clothing choices may cause your attention to focus away from the lecture being delivered, these are not excuses to disregard the source's message. Remain focused on the content of the message. On average, Americans speak at a rate of 125 words per minute. However, the human brain can process more than 450 words per minute (Hilliard and Palmer 2003) and we can think at a rate of 1000–3000 words per minute (Hilliard and Palmer 2003). So what happens with all that extra time? Often we daydream or we become bored because our brain can work faster than the speaker can talk. Therefore, it is important to dedicate yourself to relating the information to existing information that you already know. While this can be challenging at times, chances are that it will prove to be extremely useful. Ask yourself questions during a conversation or lecture such as, "How will this information benefit me?" or "How will this information benefit my relationship with the source?" Being open to receiving messages is the first step to ensuring an effective listening experience.

Interpreting the Message. Interpretation refers to the cognitive processes involved in listening. Recall our discussion of the role of interpretation in perception. We pointed out that associations are often made between stimuli and things with which we are already familiar. Interpretation is also a key element in listening, and in verifying that the meaning we assigned to the message is close to that which was intended by the source. Some strategies to assist in interpretation of messages include asking questions, soliciting feedback, and requesting clarification. These strategies will help you interpret the source's message more accurately. Consider the following interaction between Maya and Raj:

Maya: I hate biology.
Raj: Why?
Maya: Well, I guess I don't hate it, but I am upset I did poorly on the first exam.
Raj: Why did you do poorly?
Maya: Because I studied the wrong chapters.
Raj: So, do you dislike the material?
Maya: Well, no, I actually enjoy the teacher and the book.
Raj: So, you like biology but you are upset you studied the wrong material?
Maya: Yes, I actually like the course; I am just mad because I know I could have received an A if I had studied the right material.

Because Raj asked Maya to provide additional information to help clarify why she hated biology he was able to interpret Maya's situation more clearly. In fact, it changed the meaning of the message entirely. Maya's initial message was that she hated biology and it turns out that she actually enjoys biology. Raj was able to accurately interpret the message because he asked questions and solicited feedback. But soliciting feedback is not the only element involved in listening. **Paraphrasing** is another useful strategy for clarifying meaning and ensuring that you have accurately interpreted a message. Paraphrasing involves restating a message in your own words to see if the meaning you assigned was similar to that which was intended. But this is still not enough. Effective listening also requires you to provide the source with feedback to communicate that you have both received and understood the message.

Give feedback. Feedback serves many purposes in the listening process. By providing feedback to the source, we are confirming that we received the message and were able to interpret and assign meaning to what was being communicated. Feedback can be either positive or negative and communicate its own message. **Positive feedback** includes verbal and nonverbal behaviors that encourage the speaker to continue communicating. Examples of positive feedback include eye contact, nods, and comments such as, "I see," and "Please continue." **Negative feedback** is often discouraging to a source. Examples of negative feedback would be disconfirming verbal

What kinds of positive feedback show that you are interested and listening?

comments such as "You are over-reacting" or "I don't know why you get so upset," or negative non-verbal responses such as avoidance of eye contact, maintaining a closed body position (e.g., crossed arms), or meaningless vocalizations such as "Um-hmm." Positive feedback communicates interest and empathy for the speaker, whereas negative feedback often results in feelings of defensiveness.

Engage in dual-perspective taking. Dual-perspective taking, or empathy, refers to the attempt to see things from the other person's point of view. The concept of empathy has been a primary focus of the listening process required of social workers and counselors. Norton (1978) explains this by theorizing that all people are part of two systems—a larger societal system and a more immediate personal system. While it is often possible to gain insight into an individual's societal system, truly understanding someone's personal system is often a more difficult task. Consider the phrase, "Put yourself in another person's shoes." Do you think it is possible to truly put yourself in another person's shoes? This would require us to be able to tap into their unique background and experiences in order to perceive things exactly as they do. But is this ever really possible? Our position is that it is not. This may help explain why we find it difficult to respond to a friend who is going through a difficult break-up. Our initial response may be to respond with a statement like, "I know exactly how you feel. I've been through dozens of broken relationships." But this is not necessarily the best response. There is a unique history to your friend's relationship that you can never truly understand. While you cannot fully put yourself in her shoes, you can communicate empathy by attempting to see things from her point of view. Dual-perspective taking requires a receiver to adapt his listening style to accommodate a variety of situations.

Empathetic listening requires an attempt to see things from your friend's point to view.

Adapt your listening style. Effective communicators are flexible in their communication style and find it easy to adjust both their speaking and listening styles, based on the unique demands of the receiver, the material, or the situation. Duran (1983) defines communicative adaptability as a cognitive and behavioral

Adapt your listening style.

"ability to perceive socio-interpersonal relationships and adapt one's interaction goals and behaviors accordingly" (320). Duran and Kelly (1988) developed the Communicative Adaptability Scale. Their scale suggests we can adapt our communication in six different ways which include: social composure (feeling relaxed in social situations), social experience (enjoying and participating socially), social confirmation (maintaining the other's social image), appropriate disclosures (adapting one's disclosures appropriately to the intimacy level of the exchange), articulation (using appropriate syntax and grammar), and wit (using humor to diffuse social tension). You can determine the extent to which you are adaptable on these six dimensions by completing the Communication Adaptability Scale on page 49.

Reduce noise. Noise refers to anything that interferes with the reception of a message. Our job as listeners is to focus on ways to reduce the noise that interferes with the reception of messages.

Oftentimes, this is easier said than done. While we are able to control some forms of physical noise that interfere with listening (e.g., cell phones or radios), other types of physical noise may be more difficult to manage (e.g., a neighbor mowing her yard). Obviously, the less noise there is, the better our chances of effectively receiving the message. Reducing psychological and physiological noise may be more difficult. Sometimes it is difficult to listen to a professor's lecture knowing that you have a big midterm exam in the class that follows, and gnawing hunger pains that begin during your 11:00 A.M. class can impair listening as well. Consider ways to manage these potential distractions and maximize listening potential—be prepared for that exam, be sure to eat something before leaving for class. Planning ahead for potential distractions to listening can ultimately assist you in receiving a message that you can store in memory for future reference.

Store the message. A final strategy in the listening process involves storing what we have received for later reference. This process involves three stages: remembering, retention, and recall. Have you ever been impressed with a doctor or a professor because they remembered, retained, and recalled your name? This is not an easy task. Nichols (1961) demonstrated that immediately after listening to a ten-minute lecture, students were only able to remember about fifty percent of what they heard. As time passes, so does our ability to remember. Nichols' study suggested that after two weeks, most listeners were only able to remember about twenty-five percent of what they had heard. The following are strategies that can be used to enhance message retention.

1. Form associations between the message and something you already know.
2. Create a visual image of the information you want to remember.
3. Create a story about what you want to remember to create links between ideas. *Suppose your mother asks you to go to the store to pick up soda, laundry detergent and paper cups. You can enhance your ability to remember the information by creating a story which links the ideas such as, "Sam dropped a paper cup full of soda on her jeans and now they need to be put in the laundry machine."*
4. Create acronyms by using the beginning letters of a list of words to assist your recall. BIG EARS is an example of this tool.
5. Rhyme or create a rhythm to organize information. Creating a song or rhyme that is unusual or humorous typically helps trigger recall.

Listing Styles

Reflecting on your own interpersonal relationships, did you ever notice that individuals have different listening styles? Or perhaps you have noticed that an individual's listening style changed when the topic changed. Have you considered your own listening style and how it may change with the person or topic? For example, with our friends we might pay more attention to their feelings and when we listen to co-workers we may be more focused on the content of the message. Research has identified four predominant listening styles (Watson, Barker, and Weaver 1995). Listening style is defined as a set of "attitudes, beliefs, and predispositions about the how, where, when, who, and what of the information reception and encoding process" (Watson, Barker, and Weaver 1995, 2). This suggests that we tend to focus our listening. We may pay more attention to a person's feelings, the structure or content, or particular delivery elements, such as time. The four listening styles are people-oriented, action-oriented, content-oriented, and time-oriented. There is no optimal listening style. Different situations call for different styles. However, it is important to understand your predominate listening style. Let us take a closer look at each of these listening styles.

People-Oriented. First, people-oriented listeners seek common interests with the speaker and are highly responsive. They are interested in the speaker's feelings and emotions. Research shows a positive relationship between the people-oriented listening style and conversational sensitivity (Chesebоro 1999). This makes sense since people-oriented listeners try to understand the speakers' perspective and therefore are more sensitive to their emotional needs. They are quick to notice slight fluctuations in tone and mood. For example, they may comment, "You really look upset," or "You smile every time you say her name." Although you must consider the individual and the situation, this style may work best when we are communicating with our friends or family about sensitive issues.

Action-Oriented. An action-oriented listener prefers error-free and concise messages. They get easily frustrated with speakers who do not clearly articulate their message in a straightforward manner. They tend to steer speakers to be organized and timely in their message delivery. They grow impatient with disorganized speakers that use ambiguous descriptions or provide unrelated details. For example, an action-oriented listener may use the phrase "Get to the point," when the speaker is telling a lengthy story or may interrupt a speaker and say, "So. . . . what did you do?" The action-oriented listening style may work best when there is little time for extra details and decisions need to be made quickly.

Content-Oriented. Unlike the people-oriented listener, the content-oriented listener focuses on the details of the message. They pick up on the facts of the story and analyze it from a critical perspective. They decipher between credible and noncredible information and ask direct questions. They try to understand the message from several perspectives. For example, they may say, "Did you ever think they did that because . . ." or "Another way to think about the situation is . . ." Because they analyze the speaker's content with a critical eye, the speaker may feel reluctant to share information because they do not want to hear alternative perspectives. Additionally, they may feel intimidated by the criticalness of content-oriented listeners since they are engaged by challenging and intellectual discussion. The content-oriented listening style works best in serious situations that call for vital decision-making.

The content-oriented listener focuses on the details of the message.

Time-Oriented. Finally, time-oriented listeners are particularly interested in brief interactions with others. They direct the length of the conversation by suggesting, "I only have a minute," or they send leave taking cues (such as walking away or looking at the clock) when they believe the speaker is taking up too much of their time. This type of listening is essential when time is a limited commodity. Usually, time is precious in the workplace. A day can be eaten up by clients, co-workers, supervisors, and other individuals needing our attention. Time-oriented individuals protect their time by expressing to others how much effort they will devote to their cause.

Gender and Cultural Differences in Listening Styles

Some researchers suggest there are gender differences when it comes to listening styles. In the mid-1980s, Booth-Butterfield reported that "males tend to hear the facts while females are more aware of the mood of the communication" (1984, 39). Just about twenty years later, researchers' findings were consistent in indicating that men score themselves higher on the content-oriented listening style and women score themselves higher on the people-oriented listening style (Sargent and Weaver 2003). In addition, Kiewitz and Weaver III (1997) found that when comparing young adults from three different countries, Germans preferred the action style, Israelis preferred the content style, and Americans preferred the people and time styles.

Although no listening style is best, it is imperative to understand your own listening style and to recognize the listening styles of others. Depending on the situation and the goals in communicating, you may need to adjust your listening style. In addition, recognizing the listening style in others will help direct your responding messages. For example, if you notice your boss is engaging in action-oriented listening style, you may want to produce a clearly articulated message. He may become irritated if you include miscellaneous information or use confusing vocabulary.

Table 2.3 Guidelines for Effective Listening
Effective listeners do their best to avoid these behaviors: 1. Calling the subject uninteresting 2. Criticizing the speaker and/or delivery 3. Getting overstimulated 4. Listening only for facts (bottom line) 5. Not taking notes or outlining everything 6. Faking attention 7. Tolerating or creating distractions 8. Tuning out difficult material 9. Letting emotional words block the message 10. Wasting the time difference between speed of speech and speed of thought
Source: Nichols, R. G., and L. A. Stevens. 1957. *Are you listening?* New York: McGraw-Hill.

From *Are You Listening?* by R.G. Nichols and L.A. Stevens.

Motivation to Listen and Potential Pitfalls

When we do anything, we have some kind of motivation, or purpose. Sometimes this motivation is driven by our goals, dreams, and interests. Other times motivation may be a result of guilt, responsibility, or shame. Consider your motive for attending school. Perhaps you are a student because you have set a goal to graduate or maybe you are motivated out of a sense of responsibility to your parents. Either way, motivation drives behavior. Have you ever considered your motivation for listening? Researchers have identified five listening motivations (Wolvin and Coakley 1988). Certain motivations for listening lend themselves to particular listening barriers. Therefore, let us examine each of these motivations independently and offer potential pitfalls for each. Table 2.3 presents some guidelines for effective listening.

In certain situations we want to discriminate between what is fact and what is an opinion.

Discriminate listening. First, we may listen for the purpose of discriminating. The purpose of **discriminate listening** is to help us understand the meaning of the message. In certain situations we want to discriminate between what is fact and what is an opinion. Or perhaps we try to discriminate between what is an emotionally-based argument and what is a logically-based argument. One example of a situation in which we might engage in discriminate listening is in the workplace when we attentively listen to how a co-worker responds to our new recommendation. Here we are trying to determine if they agree or disagree with us. Another example is engaging in listening in the classroom when the teacher suggests that portions of the lecture will be on the exam. In this example, we are discriminating between what the teacher believes is important material for the exam and what is not going to be on the exam. Furthermore, we tend to use discriminate listening when we are trying to determine whether someone is lying to us.

Potential pitfall. Often when we are trying to discriminate between messages, we selectively listen to certain stimuli while ignoring others. For example, if someone does not maintain eye contact with us, we may jump to conclusions regarding her trustworthiness. If discrimination is your motivation, it is important to *keep an open mind and attend to the entire message.*

Appreciative listening. Another motivation we have for listening is appreciative listening. The purpose of appreciative listening is for the pure enjoyment of listening to the stimuli. This may be listening to your favorite tunes on your iPod, attending the opera, a musical or the movies, or listening to the sounds of the waves crashing on the shore.

Potential pitfall. With appreciative listening it is important to be proactive. In order to be successful in appreciate listening you must *decrease noise.* You can do this by controlling distractions. For example, turn off your cell phone. Sometime you can even choose your physical environment. If you are going to the movies, you can choose a particular seat away from potentially "loud" patrons. Or you may choose to go to the movies with a partner that will not inhibit your pleasure-seeking experience by talking or asking questions throughout.

Comprehensive listening. We also may be motivated to listen in order to grasp new information. Comprehensive listening involves mindfully receiving and remembering new information. When our boss is informing us of our new job duties or a friend is telling you when they need to be picked up at the airport we are engaging in comprehensive listening. Our goal is to accurately understand the new information and be able to retain it.

Potential pitfall. Often there are several messages that the speaker is sending and it is the job of the listener to determine which messages are the most important. With comprehensive listening it is critical to *recognize the main ideas and identify supportive details.* If you are unsure, *seek feedback or paraphrase the message.* For example, you may ask, "So you are flying Southwest and you need me to pick you up at baggage claim at 10:00 P.M., correct?"

Appreciative listening is for the pure enjoyment of listening to the stimuli.

Evaluative listening. When our motivation goes beyond comprehending messages to judging messages we are engaging in evaluative listening. **Evaluative listening** involves critically assessing messages. This occurs when a salesperson is trying to persuade us to buy a product or when we listen to political speeches. We are evaluating the credibility and competency of the speaker and the message. Our goal here is to create opinions and sound judgments regarding people and information.

Potential pitfall. Prejudices and biases may interfere with our listening ability when we are motivated to listen for evaluative purposes. For example, individuals who identify with a particular political party are quick to judge the messages of an individual representing an alternative party. It is important to be **aware of your own preconceived notions** and not let that impede on your ability to effectively interpret the speaker's message.

Empathetic listening. The last motivation to listen is for empathetic reasons. The purpose of empathetic (or therapeutic) listening is to help others. For example, we may meet up with our friends to discuss their most recent romantic episodes or we may help our family members make tough financial decisions. Our goal is to provide a supportive ear and assist in uncovering alternative perspectives. Often, just by listening our friends will identify their own issues or our family members will uncover their own solutions to their problems. Other times, they may ask for suggestions or recommendations.

Potential pitfall. It is critical to distinguish if the speaker indeed wants you to be an active participant in offering solutions or if he wants you "just to listen." Sometimes we assume that solutions are being sought, but what is really wanted is someone to act as a "sounding board."

Common Listening Misbehaviors

There can be severe consequences when we choose not to listen effectively. One study found that the second most frequently occurring mistake made by education leaders deals with poor interpersonal communication skills and that the most frequent example given for this type of mistake was failure to listen (Bulach, Pickett, and Booth 1998). The perception that we are not listening may be because we lack appropriate eye contact with the speaker, we appear preoccupied or distracted with other issues, or because we do not provide the appropriate feedback. When we send these signals, the speaker interprets our behavior as not caring. This can damage internal and external business relationships. These behaviors can have severe consequences. Another study examined the top five reasons why principals lost their jobs (Davis 1997). The results of this study found that the most frequently cited response by superintendents focused on failure to communicate in ways that build positive relationships. The results of this study can be applied to situations outside of the educational setting. So, how do people communicate in ways that do not build positive relationships? This section will identify the six common listening misbehaviors.

Pseudo-listening. Pseudo-listening is when we are pretending to listen. We look like we are listening by nodding our head or providing eye contact, but we are faking our attention. This is a self-centered approach to listening. Let us be honest, when we are pseudo-listening we are not "fooling" anyone. We are not able to ask appropriate questions and we are not able to provide proper feedback.

Monopolizing. Listeners that engage in monopolizing take the focus off the speaker and redirect the conversation and attention to themselves. Often, monopolizers interrupt the speaker to try to "one up" the speaker. They may try to top his story by saying "That reminds me . . ." or "You think that is bad–let me tell you what happened to me. . . ."

Disconfirming. Listeners that deny the feelings of the speaker are sending disconfirming messages. Examples of disconfirming messages include: "You shouldn't feel bad . . ." or "Don't cry . . . there is no need to cry." This misbehavior discourages the source to continue speaking and decreases perceptions of empathy.

Defensive listening. An individual who engages in defensive listening perceives a threatening environment. Defensive communication has been defined as "that behavior which occurs when an individual perceives threat or anticipates threat in the group" (Gibb 1961, 141). Defensiveness includes "how he appears to others, how he may seem favorable, how he may win, dominate, impress, or escape punishment, and/or how he may avoid or mitigate a perceived or anticipated threat" (141). In other words, defensiveness is a process of saving "face." The issue of face is associated with people's desire to display a positive public image (Goffman 1967). An example of defensive listening is, "Don't look at me, I did not tell you to do that. . . ."

Defensive listening occurs when one perceives a threatening environment.

Selective listening. Selective listening happens when a listener focuses only on parts of the message. She takes parts of the message that she agrees with (or does not agree with) and responds to those particular parts. We reduce cognitive dissonance or psychological discomfort, screening out messages that we do not agree with, to remain cognitively "stable." For example, if we recently bought a new SUV, we may choose not to pay attention to messages suggesting that SUV's are not environmentally sound. We would, however, choose to pay attention to messages that suggest SUV vehicles rated higher on safety tests.

Ambushing. Ambushers will listen for information that they can use to attack the speaker. They are selectively and strategically listening for messages that they can use against the speaker. Often ambushers interrupt the speaker. They do not allow the speaker to complete his thought and jump to conclusions. Ambushers make assumptions and get ahead of the speaker by finishing his sentences. They are self-motivated and lack dual perspective.

Name____ Date_______________

Exercise 2.1 Chapter 2 – Perception and Listening

According to Deborah Tannen, gender scholar and linguist, men and women are socialized differently and, as a result, develop different perceptions of the world and their place within it.

Describe the difference between the manner in which *women* and *men* use language. Include in your discussion an explanation of "report talk," and "rapport talk," as describe by Deborah Tannen.

Next, recall a scene from a movie you have seen which illustrates the different ways in which men and women communicate. Highlight when rapport talk and report talk are used.

Name____ Date______________

Exercise 2.2 Chapter 2 – Perception and Listening

Movie Title: ________________________

Synopsis of Movie:

____

____

____

____

____

____

____

____

____

____

____

____

____

____

____

____

____

____

____

____

____

____

Be prepared to share your answers with the class.

3

What Is the Power of Verbal and Nonverbal Communication

After reading this chapter, you should be able to:

- ❐ Define language
- ❐ Discuss the basic principles of language
- ❐ Discuss the three models that help explain how meaning is created including the semantic triangle, Sapir-Whorf hypothesis, and the muted group theory
- ❐ Identify the strategies for using language effectively
- ❐ Describe the characteristics of nonverbal communication
- ❐ Discuss the six functions of nonverbal messages to include complementing, substituting, repeating, contradicting, regulating, and deceiving
- ❐ Discuss the types of nonverbal communication including body movement, use of space, dress and appearance and eye contact

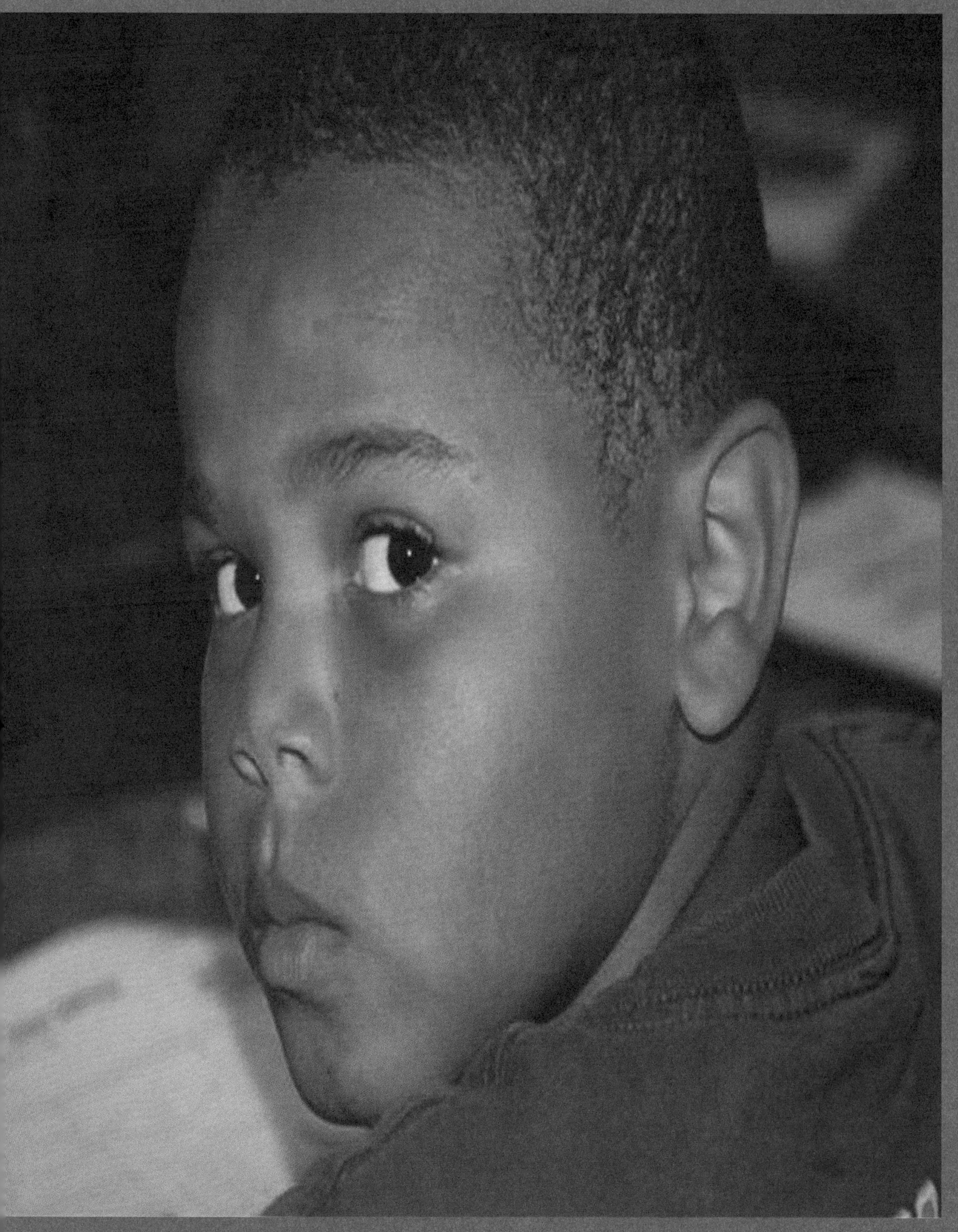

Key Terms

- language
- symbols
- grammar
- intersubjective
- meaning
- denotative meanings
- connotative meanings
- phonological rules
- syntactical rules
- semantic rules
- regulative rules
- constitutive rules
- semantic triangle
- referent
- reference
- dual perspective
- regionalisms
- jargon
- slang
- clichés
- trite words
- loaded words
- empty words
- derogatory language
- equivocal words
- kinesics
- emblem
- illustrator
- regulator
- affect display
- adaptors
- personal space
- primary territory
- secondary territory
- public territory
- intrusion of territory
- eye contact
- expectancy violations theory

3 Scenario

Chris sighed as he closed his Economics book. He had reluctantly finished studying for one of his many midterms tomorrow. He had three midterms and he felt overwhelmed. Chris rubbed his forehead and grabbed his African-American history book.

As he began to read about the Bantu tribe, he heard giggling. He looked up and his eyes fell on Samantha Washington. Samantha Washington was a young woman in his class. She had been in a few of his classes last semester and she was a cheerleader. Chris and Samantha had never talked. They didn't run in the same circles. So, Chris just admired her from afar. Samantha Washington would never notice him.

Samantha and her friends sat down, still whispering and giggling. Chris wondered what they were talking about. He shrugged it off as girl stuff. He refocused his attention on his book. After several minutes, the giggling died down, but Chris felt like someone was staring at him. He scanned his eyes around the room. Everyone in front of him had their noses in their books, studying away for their midterms. He frowned, still feeling someone staring at him. He glanced over his shoulder and found the source.

Samantha was staring at him. She was smiling at him. The thought never crossed his mind that Samantha was looking at him. But there she was, sitting across from him with her books spread out, staring at him. He smiled softly and waved. Chris' eyes widened. He looked around, wondering if she was staring at someone else. He turned back around to her and pointed to himself. She giggled a little bit and nodded. Chris' smiled a little, trying to remain cool. Chris was seldom wrong, but he was wrong in this case. Samantha Washington did notice him.

Introduction

Using words to describe magic is like using a screwdriver to cut roast beef.
—Tom Robbins, twentieth century American author

Better wise language than well-combed hair.
—Icelandic Proverb

All credibility, all good conscience, all evidence of truth come only from the senses.
—Friedrich Wilhelm Nietzsche, nineteenth century German philosopher

Eloquence is the power to translate a truth into language perfectly intelligible to the person to whom you speak.
—Ralph Waldo Emerson, nineteenth century U.S. poet, essayist

Get in touch with the way the other person feels. Feelings are 55 percent body language, 38 percent tone and 7 percent words.
—author unknown

The limits of my language means the limits of my world.
—Ludwig Wittgenstein, twentieth century philosopher

The eyes are the windows to the soul.
—Yousuf Karsh, twentieth century Canadian photographer

The difference between the right word and the almost right word is the difference between lightning and a lightning bug.
—Mark Twain, nineteenth century American author

Dialogue should simply be a sound among other sounds, just something that comes out of the mouths of people whose eyes tell the story in visual terms.
—Alfred Hitchcock, twentieth century film director

Through these quotations, you've just been exposed to the *power of verbal and nonverbal communication* to define our beliefs, expose our values, and share our experiences. The words that you use and the nonverbal behaviors that accompany them are critically important as you communicate, because they have the ability to clarify your ideas to others or to confuse them. In this chapter, you'll learn about verbal language and nonverbal communication, to discover how they are used to create shared meaning.

What Is Language?

© Kendall Hunt Publishing

Verbal language and nonverbal communication are used to create shared meaning.

So what do we know about language? Linguists estimate that there are about 5,000 to 6,000 different languages spoken in the world today; about 200 languages have a million or more native speakers. Mandarin Chinese is the most common, followed by Hindi, English, Spanish, and Bengali. However, as technology continues to shrink the communication world, English is becoming more dominant in mediated communication. According to Internet World Stats, which charts usage and population statistics, the top ten languages used in the Web are English (31% of all Internet users), Chinese (15.7%), Spanish (8.7%), Japanese (7.4%), and French and German (5% each). English is one of the official languages of the United Nation, the International Olympic Committee, in academics and in the sciences. English is also the language spoken by air traffic controllers worldwide. Yet the English that we speak in the United States is really a hybrid, using vocabulary taken from many sources, influenced by media, technology, and globalization. Let's consider what all of this means for you as you try to share meaning with others.

Language is a shared system of symbols structured in organized patterns to express thoughts and feelings. **Symbols** are arbitrary labels that we give to some idea or phenomenon. For example, the word *run* represents an action that we do, while *bottle* signifies a container for a liquid. Words are symbols, but not all symbols are words. Music, photographs, and logos are also symbols that stand for something else, as do nonverbal actions such as "OK," and "I don't know." However, in this section, we're going to focus on words as symbols. Note that the definition of language says that it's structured and shared. Languages have a *grammar* (syntax, a patterned set of rules that aid in meaning). You've learned grammar as you've been taught how to write, and it's become an unconscious part of your daily communication. Take, for example, this sentence:

The glokkish Vriks mounged oupily on the brangest Ildas.

© 2008, JupiterImages.

English is the language spoken by airline pilots and air traffic controllers all over the world.

Now, we can answer these questions:

Who did something? The Vriks mounged.
What kind of Vriks are they? Glokkish
How did they mounge? Oupily
On what did they mounge? The Ildas
What kind of Ildas are they? Brangest

You might have difficulty identifying noun, verb, adverb, and adjective, but because you know the grammar of the English language, you're still able to decipher what this sentence is telling you because of the pattern, even if the symbols themselves lack meaning for now. That leads to the next part of the definition: *symbols must be shared in order to be understood.* George Herbert Mead's Symbolic Interaction Theory asserts that meaning is **intersubjective;** that means that **meaning** *can exist only when people share common interpretations of the symbols they exchange.* So if you were given a picture of Vriks and were told that these were ancient hill people of a particular region of the country, you'd have a start at meaning!

In order to get a grasp on language, this section will uncover basic principles about language, introduce to you a few theoretical perspectives, and then will suggest language strategies to enhance your communication.

What Are the Basic Principles of Language?

There are some basic principles of language. It is arbitrary, it changes over time, it consists of denotative and connotative meanings, and it is structured by rules. Let's look at these more closely.

Arbitrary

"Language is arbitrary" means that *symbols do not have a one-to-one connection with what they represent.* What is the computer form that you use if you take a test? Is it a bubble sheet? A scantron? An opscan? Each of these names has no natural connection to that piece of paper, and it's likely that at different universities, it's called different names. Because language is arbitrary, people in groups agree on labels to use, creating private codes. That's why your organization might have specialized terms, why the military uses codes, and why your family uses nicknames that only they understand. The language that you create within that group creates group meaning and culture. The arbitrary element of language also adds to its ambiguity; meanings just aren't stable. To me, a test is the same as an exam; to you, a test might be less than an exam. If you say to me, "I'll call you later," how do I define the term later? We often fall into the trap of thinking that everyone understands us, but the reality is, it's an amazing thing that we share meaning at all!

Changes over Time

© 2008, JupiterImages.

How is your language different from your parents' and grandparents'?

Language *changes* over time in vocabulary, as well as syntax. New vocabulary is required for the latest inventions, for entertainment and leisure pursuits, for political use. In 2007, the top television buzzwords included surge and *D'oh,* while in 2006, they were *truthiness* and *wikiality*. How many of those words play a role in your culture today? Words like *cell phones* and *Internet* didn't exist fifty years ago, for example. In addition, no two people use a language in exactly the same way. Teens and young adults often use different words and phrases than their parents. The vocabulary and phrases people use may depend on where they live, their age, education level, social status, and other factors. Through our interactions, we pick up new words and phases, and then we integrate them into our communication.

Consists of Denotative and Connotative Meanings

Denotative meanings, the literal, dictionary definitions, are precise and objective. **Connotative meanings** reflect your personal, subjective definitions. They add layers of experience and emotions to meaning. Elizabeth J. Natalle examined this dichotomy in a case study of urban music, examining how our language has evolved over the years to include more negative connotation regarding talk about women as compared to talk about men. Think about *chick, sweetie, sugar pie* and *old maid,* versus stud, *hunk, playboy,* and *bachelor.* Do you get a different image? Using a study of rap music, she attempted to clarify how urban music names a particular world, creates male community, and has implications for power and gendered relationships.

A simpler way to consider denotative and connotative meanings is to examine the terms President Bush used to describe the terrorists who crashed the planes on Sept. 11, 2001. Bush's labels on that day in various locations began with "those folks who committed this act" (remarks by the president when he first heard that two planes crashed into World Trade Center) to "those responsible for these cowardly acts" (remarks by the president upon arrival at Barksdale Air Force Base) to "those who are behind these evil acts" and "the terrorists who committed these acts" (statement by the president in his address to the nation). Consider how the connotative meaning shaped the image of the perpetrators.

David K. Berlo provided several assumptions about meaning:

- Meanings are in people.
- Communication does not consist of the transmission of meanings, but of the transmission of messages.

© Cartoon Stock, www.CartoonStock.com.

- Meanings are not in the message; they are in the message users.
- Words do not mean at all; only people mean.
- People can have similar meanings only to the extent that they have had, or can anticipate having, similar experiences.
- Meanings are never fixed; as experience changes, so meanings change.
- No two people can have exactly the same meaning for anything.

These ideas echo the idea that when you use words, you need to be aware of the extent to which meaning is shared. For example, when an adoptive parent sees those "adopt a highway" locator signs, it's probable that that person sees something different than others might. "Adopt a" programs might be seen as confusing and misleading others about the term *adoption*. An adoptive parent might say that you don't adopt a road, a zoo animal, or a Cabbage Patch doll. Adoption is a means of family building, and it has a very subjective, emotional meaning. To the town official who erected the sign, it's a representation of the good work being done by some group to keep the highway clean.

Courtesy of JaxonPhotoGroup

What does this sign's language mean to you?

Structured by Rules

As we understand and use the rules of language, we begin to share meaning. Think of rules as a shared understanding of what language means, as well as an understanding of what kind of language is appropriate in various contexts. Many of the rules you use weren't consciously learned; you gathered them from interactions with other people. Some, however, were learned aspects of your culture.

Phonological rules *regulate how words sound when you pronounce them.* They help us organize language. For instance, the word lead could be used to suggest a behavior that you do (you *lead* the group to show them the way) or a kind of toxic metallic element (*lead* paint in windows is harmful to children). Do you enjoy getting a *present*, or did you *present* one to someone else? Another example of phonological rules is demonstrated by your understanding of how letters sound when they're grouped in a particular way. Take for instance the letters omb. Now put a t in front of them, and you have *tomb*. Put a c in front, and it becomes *comb*. Put a b in front, and you have *bomb*. See how the sounds shift?

The way we make singular nouns plural is also phonological. It's not as simple as adding the letter s to the end of a word. The sound changes too: dog/dogs (sounds like a *z* at the end); cook/cooks (sounds like an *ess*); bus/buses (sounds like *ess-ez*). English has many inconsistent phonological rules like these, which makes making errors quite typical, especially for nonnative English speakers.

Syntactical rules *present the arrangement of a language, how the symbols are organized.* You saw that earlier in the "glokkish Vriks" example; you're usually unaware of the syntactical rules until they're violated. In English, we put adjectives prior to most nouns: I live in a red house. In French, you live in a house red (the adjective follows the noun).

Semantic rules *govern the meaning of specific symbols.* Because words are abstractions, we need rules to tell us what they mean in particular situations. Take, for example, the headline, "School Needs to Be Aired." What does that mean? Is the school so smelly that it needs to be refreshed? Or are the needs of the school going to be broadcast or spoken in a public forum? Words can be interpreted in more than one way, and we need semantic rules to lead us to shared meaning. Although these three kinds of rules help us to pattern language, there are also rules that help us guide the entire communication event.

You can count on a close friend for comfort when you have a problem.

Regulative rules *tell us when, how, where, and with whom we can talk about certain things.* You know when it's OK to interrupt someone; you know when turn-taking is expected. You may be enrolled in classes where you are expected to express your opinion; in other classes, you know to hold your tongue. How do you feel about public displays of affection? When is it OK to correct your boss? These regulative rules help us to maintain respect, reveal information about ourselves, and interact with others.

Constitutive rules *tell us how to "count" different kinds of communication.* These rules reveal what you feel is appropriate. You know that when someone waves or blows kisses, that person is showing affection or friendliness. You know what topics you can discuss with your parents, friends, teachers, co-workers, and strangers. You have rules that reveal your expectations for communication with different people; you expect your doctor to be informative and firm with advice, and you anticipate that your friend will compliment you and empathize. As we interact with others, we begin to grasp and use the rules. For instance, when you start a new job, you take in the rules on whom to talk with, how to talk with supervisors and co-workers, and what topics are appropriate, along with the mechanics of how to talk and the meaning of job-specific words. Interestingly enough, you might not even be aware of the rules until they're broken!

How Do Theorists Describe Language and Meaning?

Can you picture a book, a pen, a laptop, and a horse? Your ability to conjure up these images means that you've been exposed to the symbols that represent them in the English language. How about the picture shown on the right? What do you see? If you said "keys," then that shows how you have acquired language; you've been taught that these things are associated with the symbol "keys." How are you able to do those connections? There are a great number of perspectives related to language, meaning, and symbols. In this section, you'll be exposed to three models that present varying perspectives on the way that meaning is created.

© Costin Cojocaru, 2008, Shutterstock.

Semantic Triangle

One of the models that demonstrate how words come to have meaning is the **semantic triangle.** Ogden and Richards suggest that a major problem with communication is that we tend to treat *words* as if they were the *thing*. As a result, we confuse the symbol for the thing or object.

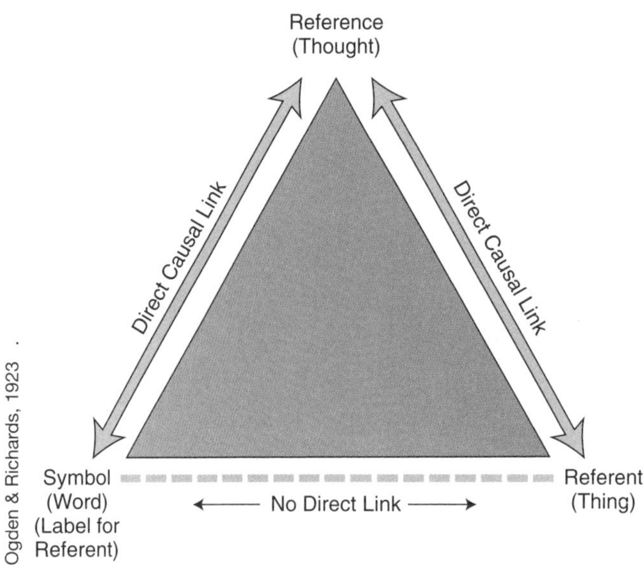

The Semantic Triangle—Ogden & Richards, 1923.

At the bottom right hand of the triangle is the **referent,** the thing that we want to communicate about that exists in reality. As we travel up the right side, we find the **reference(s)**, which consist of thoughts, experiences, and feelings about the referent. This is a causal connection; seeing the object results in those thoughts. Another causal connection exists as you travel down the left side of the triangle, to the *symbol,* or *word*. That's the label we apply to that referent.

The problem is that there is not a direct connection between a symbol and referent; it's an indirect connection, shown by the dotted line. According to this model, it's that indirect link between *referent* and *symbol* that creates the greatest potential for communication misunderstandings. We assume that others share our references, and we think that they must use the same label or symbol because of that shared state of being. A simple example should help.

A mom is teaching her son words by reading simple children's books—books about tools, farms, trucks, zoos, and dinosaurs. Usually, this reading activity happens on the front porch. One day, the mom sees the neighbor's cat sneaking up on her birdfeeders, and under her breath, she mutters something about the "stupid cat." The next day, the toddler goes off to day care, and when mom comes to pick him up, she's met by the teacher. She laughingly tells how she was reading a book about animals that day, and when she got to the page with cute kittens on it, the little boy yelled out, "Stupid cat." The embarrassed mother just learned a lesson about the semantic triangle. For her, the referent (cat) evokes images of bird-murdering, allergy-causing felines (references). She creates the label "stupid cat." (symbol). When the boy sees a picture of one, he naturally thinks that is what those things are called. Unfortunately, that's not the universal name!

You can experience the same thing: If you tell others that you own a dog, what referent do you think they apply the label to? The semantic triangle is a practical tool that helps us to understand the relationship of referent, references, and symbol, or thing, thoughts, and word. It reminds us that one word doesn't necessarily evoke the same meaning in any two people.

Sapir–Whorf Hypothesis

Another theoretical approach to language is the *Sapir–Whorf hypothesis* (also known as the theory of linguistic relativity). According to this approach, your perception of reality is determined by your thought processes, and your thought processes are limited by your language. Therefore, language shapes reality. Your culture determines your language, which, in turn, determines the way that you categorize thoughts about the world and your experiences in it. If you don't have the words to describe or explain something, then you can't really know it or talk about it.

For example, researchers Linda Perry and Deborah Ballard-Reisch suggest that existing language does not represent the reality that biological sex comes in more forms than female and male, gender identities are not neatly ascribed to one's biological sex, and sexual orientation does not fit snugly into, "I like men, I like women, I like both, I like neither," choices. They also assert that evolving new language such as the word *gendex* (representing the dynamic interplay of a person's sexual identity, sex preference, sexual orientation, and gender identity) can work against biases and discrimination. Another example is the concept of *bipolar disorder.* It used to be called manic depressive, and it refers to a mood disorder characterized by unusual shifts in a person's mood, energy, and ability to function. But if you don't know what that illness is, you might just agree with a family member who says, "You're just going through a phase." The lack of language restricts our ability to perceive the world. Reality is embedded in your language.

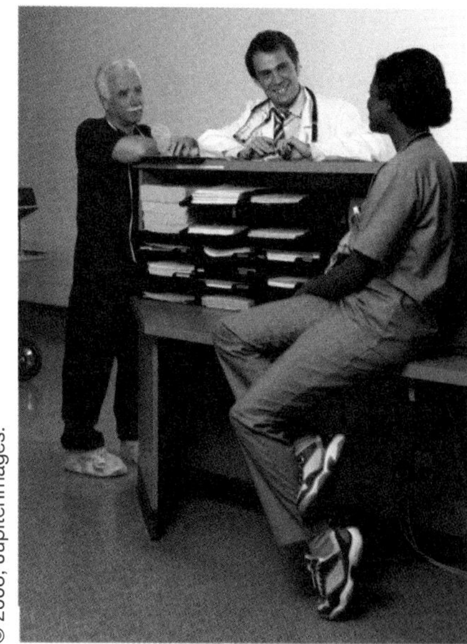

The muted group theory suggests that language serves men better than women.

Muted Group Theory

As these perspectives suggest, the *words* that you use are powerful. They have the ability to express attitudes and to represent values. Communication scholar Cheris Kramarae developed *the muted group theory* to suggest that power and status are connected, and because muted groups lack the power of appropriate language, they have no voice and receive little attention. Kramarae noted, "The language of a particular culture does not serve all its speakers, for not all speakers contribute in an equal fashion to its formulation. Women (and members of other subordinate groups) are not as free or as able as men are to say what they wish, when and where they wish, because the words and the norms for their use have been formulated by the dominant group, men." She asserts that language serves men better than women (and perhaps European Americans better than African Americans or other groups) because the European American men's experiences are named clearly in language, and the experiences of other groups (women, people with disabilities, and ethnic minorities) are not. Due to this problem with language, muted groups appear less articulate than men in public settings.

The task of muted groups is to conceptualize a thought and then scan the vocabulary that is suited to men's thinking for the best way to encode the idea. The term sexual harassment is an example. Although the act of harassment has existed for centuries, it wasn't until sex discrimination was prohibited by Title VII of the 1964 Civil Rights Act. It also took the Clarence Hill–Anita Thomas hearing in 1991 to make the term *gender discrimination* part of the popular dialogue, as the media focused attention on the workplace issue.

Because they are rendered inarticulate, muted groups are silenced in a variety of ways. Ridicule happens when the group's language is trivialized (men talk, women gab). Ritual creates dominance (the woman changes her name at the wedding ceremony but the man doesn't). Control happens as the media present some points of view and ignore others (we don't hear from the elderly or homeless). Harassment results from the control that men exert over public spaces (women get verbal threats couched as compliments when they walk down the streets). This theory affirms that as muted groups create more language to express their experiences and as all people come to have similar experiences, inequalities of language (and the power that comes with it) should change.

Each of these perspectives demonstrates how language impacts meaning. They show how we believe meaning comes into being, how we are limited by the language we possess, and how language wields power. By now, you should be sensitive to the many ways that you can miscommunicate, or at least communicate ineffectively through language choices. How can you become more sensitive to strategic language choices?

How Can I use Language Effectively?

Communication scholar Julia T. Wood says that the single most important guideline is to engage in a dual **perspective**, recognizing another person's point of view and taking that into account as you communicate. Wood suggests that you should understand both your own and another's point of view and acknowledge each when you communicate. You'll see that concept played out throughout this text; you need to consider your audience's beliefs, attitudes, and values as you create your message. Here are some strategic tips for effective language use to maintain that dual perspective.

Use Accurate Language

Make sure you are using the term correctly, and if you're unsure if the audience will understand your meaning, define it. You'll learn about defining in the chapter on informative speaking. Remember, what makes perfect sense to you may be gobbledygook to me. When the doctor tells you that you have a rather large contusion, do you know what that is?

Use Appropriate Language

Appropriate means that the language you use is suitable for the context, for the audience, for the topic, and for you. Some occasions call for more formal language (proposals to a client), while others will let slang pass (texting a friend). Some audiences expect technical language, while others need simple terms. Off-color humor might work in certain instances and with specific groups, but you probably shouldn't choose to use it at a church gathering. You need to consider if your audience utilizes regionalisms (words or phrases that are specific to one part of the country) or jargon (specialized professional language) as you speak with them.

It's important to use appropriate language for the occasion.

Your topic also can determine suitable language. Some topics call for lots of vivid language and imagery, while others are better suited to simplicity. If you are honoring your boss upon his retirement, then the topic probably calls for words that evoke appreciation and emotion. But if you're telling someone how to put together a computer table, then simple explanatory words are expected. Finally, you need to use words that are appropriate to you. You have developed your own style of language over the years; do you use the same words as your parents? Don't try to use words that just don't flow easily from your mind; it's not going to sound like you.

Use Unbiased Language

Biased language includes any language that defames a subgroup (women; people from specific ethnic, religious, or racial groups; people with disabilities) or eliminates them from consideration. Even if you would never think about using language that defames anyone else, you can fall into using language that more subtly discriminates. Sexist language is replete with this: We use the masculine pronoun (he, him) when we don't have a referent. So if you personify "the judge," "the executive," "the director," as male by using the pronoun *he*, you eliminate one whole subgroup from consideration.

The same holds true when you use the word *man* in occupational terms, when the job holders could be either male or female. Examples are fireman, policeman, garbage man, chairman; they're easily made nonsexist by saying firefighter, police officer, garbage collector, and chair or presiding officer. Finally, while the generic use of *man* (like in mankind) originally was used to denote both men and women, its meaning has become more specific to adult males. It's simple to change the word to be more inclusive: mankind becomes people or human beings; man-made becomes manufactured; the common man becomes the average person.

The Associated Press *Stylebook* has a lengthy entry on "disabled, handicapped, impaired" terminology, including when to use (and not to use) terms such *as blind, deaf, mute, wheelchair-user,* and so on. A separate entry on *retarded* says "mentally retarded" is the preferred term. The World Bank advises using *persons with disabilities and disabled people,* not handicapped.

Use appropriate labels when referring to sexual orientation. The terms *lesbians, gay men,* and *bisexuals or bisexual women and men* are preferred to the term *homosexuals* (because the emphasis on the latter is on sex, while the former all refer to the whole person, not just the sex partner he or she chooses). In general, try to find out what the people's preferences are, and be specific when applicable. For instance, if all the subjects are either Navajo or Cree, stating this is more accurate than calling them Native Americans.

Avoid Verbal Distractions

If you divert the audience from your intended meaning by using confusing words, your credibility will be lowered and your audience may become lost. The following are distractions:

- **Slang** *consists of words that are short-lived, arbitrarily changed, and often vulgar ideas.* Slang excludes people from a group. Internet slang was usually created to save keystrokes and consists of "u" for you, "r" for *are,* and "4" for for. Poker slang includes *dead man's hand* (two pair, aces, and eights); to act (make a play); and *going all* in (betting all of your chips on the hand). *Daggy* means out of fashion or uncool; *fives* means to reserve a seat.
- **Cliches** or **trite words** *have been overused and lose power or impact.* The Unicorn Hunters of Lake Superior University keeps a list of banished words that is regularly updated. In 2007, it listed words such as combined celebrity names (*Brangelina* and *Tomcat*), *awesome* (because it no longer means majestic), and *undocumented alien* (just use the word illegal).
- **Loaded words** *sound like they're describing, but they're actually revealing your attitude.* When speaking of abortion, consider the different image created by the terms *unborn child* or *fetus.* Are you *thrifty* but your friend is *cheap*? How about your brother; is he one of those *health-nuts* who is dedicated to the cult of marathoning? Colorful language is entertaining, but if it distorts the meaning or distracts the audience, then don't use it.
- **Empty words** *are overworked exaggerations.* They lose their strength because their meaning is exaggerated. How many products are advertised as *new and improved or supersized*? What exactly does that mean?
- **Derogatory language** *consists of words that are degrading or tasteless.* If you use degrading terms to refer to ethnic groups (*Polack* for a person of Polish descent; *Chink* for someone from China; Spic for an Italian) then you are guilty of verbal bigotry.
- **Equivocal words** *have more than one correct denotative meaning.* A famous example is of a nurse telling a patient that he "wouldn't be needing" the books he asked to be brought from home. Although she meant that he was going home that day and could read there, the patient took that to mean that he was near death and wouldn't have time to read. One time while evaluating a debate,

an instructor encountered students arguing the issue of the legalization of marijuana. The side arguing for the legalization used the Bible, citing chapter and verse and asserting that God created the grass and said, "The grass is good." This sent the other side into a tailspin as they tried to refute the biblical passage. This simple equivocal use of the term grass lost the debate for the opposition!

What should you take from this section on Language?

Because our language is arbitrary and evolving, it's easy to be misunderstood. You can attempt to enhance shared meaning by remembering that language is a shared system of symbols; through language, you share ideas, articulate values, transmit information, reveal experiences, and maintain relationships. Language is essential to your ability to think and to operate within the many cultures (community of meaning) that you travel through. You should be sensitive to the words you choose as you attempt to connect with others. Now let's turn our attention to the other means by which you create meaning: your nonverbal communication behaviors.

What Is Nonverbal Communication?

Pretend you are hoarse and the doctor has told you not to speak at all for the next three days. Nor can you IM or text or do any other computer-related communication. How would you do the following?

- Let your friend know that you can't hear her. Or tell her that she's talking too loudly.
- Tell your lab partner that you want him to come where you are.
- Show the teacher that you don't know the answer to the question she just asked you.
- Let a child know that he needs to settle down; his play is getting too rough.
- Tell your significant other that you're not angry, and everything is OK.
- Express disappointment over a loss by your team, which always seems to lose the lead in the last two minutes.
- Signify that you're running late and have to leave.

How hard would it be to make yourself understood? What you've just attempted to do without verbal language is present a message nonverbally. We all constantly send nonverbal messages, giving our receivers all types of cues about ourselves. An awareness of nonverbal communication is important: your nonverbal behaviors present an image of yourself to those around you. They tell others how you want to relate to them, and they may reveal emotions or feelings that you either are trying to hide or simply can't express.

In the remainder of this chapter, you will be introduced to some of the elements of the study of nonverbal communication in the hopes of creating a greater awareness of these elements of the message. You will examine *definitions* of nonverbal communication, its *functions,* and *types* of nonverbal communication. Along the way, we will provide examples and illustrations to help you understand the applications of various nonverbal behaviors and how they can be used to help you interpret the messages of other people. You should also gain some insight into how to use nonverbal behaviors to enhance your own communication.

What Is the Nature of Nonverbal Communication?

Although nonverbal communication is a complex system of behaviors and meanings, its basic definition *can be* fairly straightforward. Here are four definitions for comparison:

1. All types of communication that do not rely on words or other linguistic systems
2. Any message other than written or spoken words that conveys meaning
3. Anything in a message besides the words themselves
4. Messages expressed by nonlinguistic means

Taking these definitions and the body of related research into consideration, we propose a very simple definition: nonverbal communication is *all nonlinguistic aspects of communication.* That definition covers quite a lot of territory. Except for the actual words that we speak, *everything* else is classified as nonverbal communication. The way you move, the tone of your voice, the way you use your eyes, the way you occupy and use space, the way you dress, the shape of your body, your facial expressions, the way you smell, your hand gestures, and the way you pronounce (or mispronounce) words are all considered nonverbal communication. Some of these behaviors have meaning independent of language or other behaviors; others have meaning only when considered with what is said, the context and culture in which a communication event takes place, and the relationship between the communicators.

Maybe you're getting a hint of the richness of nonverbal expression. Without any formal training, you already are able to interpret messages that others send nonverbally. Your skill level, however, may not be as strong as you think, so keep in mind the goal of increasing strategic communication as you continue. Researchers have also been fascinated with the extent to which nonverbal communication impacts meaning, and their findings provide glimpses into the impact of nonverbals on shared

What can you say about his nonverbal communication?

meanings and culture. If nothing else, by the end of this section, you will discover that the study of nonverbal communication has come a long way since it was referred to only as *body language!*

What Are the Characteristics of Nonverbal Communication?

Ambiguous

Most nonverbal behaviors have no generally accepted meaning. Instead, the connection between the behavior and its meaning is vague or *ambiguous*, leaving understanding open to various interpretations. The meaning we apply to words is fairly specific, but the meaning we give to nonverbal communication is nonspecific. The meanings you attribute to nonverbal behaviors are heavily dependent on the relationship between you and the others you're interacting with, the nature of the communication event, the content of the words that accompanies it, and the culture in which the event takes place. For example, consider the ubiquitous "thumbs up" hand gesture. In the United States it means, "OK" or "very good." In some eastern cultures, however, it is considered an insult and an obscene hand gesture. In Great Britain, Australia, and New Zealand, it could be a signal used by hitchhikers who are thumbing a lift; it could be an OK signal; it also could be an insult signal meaning "up yours" or "sit on this" when the thumb is jerked sharply upward. In Indonesia, the thumb gesture means "good job" in response to someone who has completed an excellent job, or "delicious" when great food is tasted. In another context, if you smile at a joke, that's understood in an entirely different way than if you do it after someone misses a chair and falls to the ground. A smile could also show affection, embarrassment, or even be used to hide pain or anger. As you can see, it is possible to find several meanings for the same nonverbal behavior, and it is possible to find several nonverbal behaviors that mean the same thing.

In the United States, a thumbs-up is appropriate for celebrating.

Continuous

With verbal communication, if you stop speaking, listeners can't attribute any more meaning to your words. Nonverbal communication, by contrast, is so pervasive and complex that others can continue to gather meaning, even if you are doing absolutely nothing! The mere act of doing nothing can send a message; you might blush, stutter, wring your hands, or sweat unintentionally, causing others to react to you. You might not mean to send a message, but your lack of intention to communicate doesn't prevent other people from assigning meaning to your behavior. In addition, your appearance, the expression on your face, your posture, where (or if) you are seated, and how you use the space around you all provide information that is subject to interpretation by others.

What can you tell by this boy's expression?

Sometimes Unplanned and Unconscious

Nonverbal communication can be either unconscious or intentional, but most of our nonverbal behaviors are exhibited without much or any conscious thought. You rarely plan or think carefully about your nonverbal behaviors. When you are angry, it is naturally expressed on your face as well as elsewhere in your body. The same is true for how your voice changes when you're nervous, how your arms cross when you're feeling defensive, or how you scratch your head when you're unsure of something. These expressions and behaviors are rarely planned or structured; they just happen suddenly and without conscious thought.

Sometimes Learned and Intentional

Saying that some nonverbal behaviors are natural or occur without conscious thought doesn't mean that people are born with a complete inventory of instinctive nonverbal behaviors. Much of your nonverbal behavior is learned rather than instinctive or innate. You learn the "proper" way to sit or approach, how close to stand next to someone, how to look at others, how to use touch, all from your experiences and your culture. You have been taught their meaning through your experience in interactions with other people. As a result, you can structure some nonverbal behaviors to send intentional messages, such as disapproval when you shake your head from side to side or give a "high five" to show excitement. However, unlike the formal training you received in reading, writing, and speaking, you learned (and continue to learn) nonverbal communication in a much less formal and unceremonious way, and you use it in a much less precise way than spoken language. But *because* many of these behaviors are learned, you can actively work to improve your nonverbal skills. There is a debate as to whether unintentional nonverbal behaviors really count as communication. Since others incorporate their understanding of our nonverbals as part of shared meaning, we're going to say that intentional and unintentional nonverbals both are worth recognizing here. Our position is that it's nearly impossible not to communicate nonverbally.

More Believable than Verbal

Communication textbooks have been saying for years that, when verbal and nonverbal messages contradict each other, people typically believe the nonverbal message. Because nonverbal is more spontaneous and less conscious, we don't or can't manipulate it as easily as we can control verbal communication. When you were younger and your parents thought that you might be lying to them, they would say, "Look me in the eye and say that again." Your face was more believable to them than what you were saying verbally. Your nonverbal messages would tell them the truth. How could this be so?

Research suggests that between 65 percent and 93 percent of the meaning people attribute to messages comes from the nonverbal channel. There is a small fudge factor in those percentages, however, because the Mehrabian and Ferris study assumed up to 93 percent of meaning came from nonverbal messages in situations *where no other background information* was available. The reality is that many factors affect the meaning given to messages, including how familiar the communicators are with the language being spoken, cultural knowledge, and even individual differences in personality characteristics.

Regardless of the exact percentage of meaning that comes from the verbal or nonverbal channels, we still appear to get more meaning from the nonverbal channel. Unless you are very good at controlling all your nonverbal behaviors, your parents can probably still know when you are not telling the truth.

What Are the Functions of Nonverbal Communication?

Types of nonverbal communication will be described a little later in the chapter, but you first need to understand what part nonverbals play in the communication process. Nonverbal communication performs six general functions that add information and insight to nonverbal messages to help us create meaning. Those functions are complementing, substituting, repeating, contradicting, regulating, and deceiving.

Complementing Verbal Messages

If someone shakes your hand while saying "Congratulations" at your college graduation, the handshake gives added meaning to the verbal message. Gestures, tone of voice, facial expressions, and other nonverbal behaviors can clarify, reinforce, accent, or add to the meaning of verbal messages. For instance, if you are angry with a friend and are telling him off, pounding your hand into your fist would add depth to your meaning. These nonverbal behaviors are usually not consciously planned, but they are spontaneous reactions to the context and the verbal message.

Substituting for Verbal Messages

You can use a nonverbal message *in the place* of a verbal message. A substituting behavior can be a clear "stop" hand gesture; it can be nodding the head up and down to say yes; or it can be a shoulder shrug to indicate "I don't know." When you use this kind of gesture, you don't have to supply any verbal message for the meaning to be clear to others. However, keep in mind that your nonverbals may be interpreted differently, given what you have learned from your context and culture. As an example, someone in Japan might act in a controlled fashion, while someone from the Mideast might seem more emotional, even when both are feeling the same intensity of emotion. Your interpretation of those postures, without accompanying verbals, might lead you to the wrong conclusions.

Repeating Verbal Messages

If a stranger on your college campus asks you for directions to the administration building, you might reply, "Carty Hall is two blocks south of here." While you are delivering the verbal message, you also *repeat* the message by pointing to the south. The gesture reinforces the meaning of the verbal message and provides a clear orientation to listeners who are unfamiliar with the campus.

Nonverbal messages can substitute for verbal messages. What specific messages are being sent by the people in these photos?

Contradicting Verbal Messages

Nonverbal messages sometimes *contradict* the verbal message. It can be done by accident, such as when you say "turn right" but you point to the left. Or it could be done without thinking (unconsciously), such as when you have a sour expression on your face as you tell your former girlfriend how much you "really like" her new boyfriend. Finally, you could use planned nonverbal behaviors, such as a wink of the eye and a sarcastic tone of voice, to contradict the verbal message, "Nice hat!" A famous example of this contradiction happened in September 1960, when 70 million U.S. viewers tuned in to watch Senator John Kennedy of Massachusetts and Vice President Richard Nixon in the first-ever televised presidential debate. The so-called Great Debates were television's first attempt to offer voters a chance to see the presidential candidates "in person" and head to head. Nixon was more well known, since he had been on the political scene as senator and two-term vice president. He had made a career out of fighting communism right in the midst of the Cold War. Kennedy was a relative newcomer, having served only a brief and undistinguished time as senator; he had no foreign affairs experience. Expectations were low for Kennedy; there seemed to be a huge reputation disparity between them.

Gestures are very important in establishing speaker credibility in debates.

During the debate, their points were fairly even. But it was the visual contrast between the two men that was astounding. Nixon had seriously injured his knee, had lost weight, and had recently suffered from the flu. When the first debate came, he was underweight and pasty looking, with a murky 5:00 shadow darkening his lower face. He wore a white, poorly fitting shirt and a gray suit that nearly blended into the background set, and he refused to wear make-up, even though he was advised to do so. Kennedy supplemented his tan with make-up, wore a dark suit, and had been coached on how to sit and where to look when he wasn't speaking. Kennedy's smooth delivery made him credible, because he came off as confident, vibrant, and poised. Nixon looked tired, pasty, and uncomfortable (he sweated heavily).

Polls taken after the first debate showed that most people who listened to it on the radio felt that Nixon had won, while most who watched it on television declared Kennedy the victor. Those television viewers focused on what they saw, not what they heard.

Is there sarcasm detected in the "nice hat" comment?

Contradictory messages can be difficult for others to interpret, so it's important to monitor your nonverbal behaviors. People have a tendency to prefer the meaning of the nonverbal message when it conflicts with the verbal, so when you say turn right, you should try to point to the right. Or if you don't want your former girlfriend to know how jealous you are of her new boyfriend, try to guard against making that sour face. Most adults, however, will interpret the "Nice hat" comment as sarcasm and clearly understand the message.

Regulating the Flow of Communication

Nonverbal behaviors help us to control the verbal messages we're presenting. To prevent chaos when two are more people are engaged in conversation, we use a system of signals to indicate whose turn it is speak. Think about that. How do you know when it is appropriate for you to begin speaking in a group or in a classroom? When you're talking, no one is there saying, "Now, it's your turn." You might use tone of voice to indicate that you want to speak and silence to show that you're ready to yield the floor. If you don't want to be interrupted, you might not make eye contact with the potential interruptor. If you expect an answer, you might directly look at the other person. You probably also use nonverbals to let others know that you're trying to control their talk. Have you ever started to put your computer or lecture materials away before the professor is done speaking? You use nonverbal behavior to indicate that you want to speak, that you are finished speaking, that you want to continue speaking, or that you do not want to speak at all. The nonverbal signals include tone of voice, posture, gestures, eye contact, and other behaviors.

Deceiving Listeners

Sometimes, your nonverbal behaviors are attempts to mislead somebody or hide the truth. This deception doesn't have to be malicious or mean. If you're a poker player, you might wear sunglasses in order to shield your eyes; pupils dilate when you're excited, and you want to keep that excitement close to your vest. Sometimes, you deceive to protect yourself or the other person, like when you pat someone on the back and say, "Everything will be all right," even when you know it won't.

There are many movies based on the premise that you can learn to nonverbally behave like someone you're not in order to deceive others. In *Tootsie* (1982), Dustin Hoffman becomes the female star of a television soap opera. Robin Williams stars as *Mrs. Doubtfire* (1993), dressing as a woman so he can see his children. In *The Birdcage* (1996), Robin Williams attempts to teach Nathan Lane how to do an exaggerated John Wayne walk to disguise his effeminate stroll. *Mulan* (1998) is a young woman wanting to fight the Huns in the place of her father, so she poses as a male to join the army. Big *Momma's House* (2000) stars Martin Lawrence, who plays an FBI agent who goes undercover and dresses as a heavy-set woman. In *White Chicks* (2004) Shawn Wayans and Marlon Wayans are sibling FBI agents who must protect two cruise line heiresses from a kidnapping plot. Finally, in *The Lord of the Rings: The Return of the King* (2004), Éowyn dresses as a soldier to be allowed to fight with the men.

A great deal of research on deception has practical implications. For instance, some occupations, such as lawyers and actors, require you to act differently than you might feel. Research has found that they are more successful at deception than the rest of the general population. People who monitor themselves have been found to be more effective in hiding deception cues than are people who are not as self-aware. Just think about the last time you told someone a "white lie." Were you a little nervous? How did you show that? Did the words come easily? Did you stammer or have to search for words? When you fib, you have to weigh the consequences of being caught versus the need to fib (telling a child that Santa or the Easter Bunny exists). You have to look and act sincere and believable, even though you're churning inside. If you can look composed and natural, then you are more likely to be a successful liar. In fact, research tells us that people with a greater social skills repertoire and more communication competence will generally be more proficient, alert, confident, and expressive, and less fidgety, nervous and rigid, making them more skilled at deception than others.

Now that you see the many roles that nonverbals can play in communication, let's turn from the functions to the categories of nonverbal communication.

What Are the types of Nonverbal Communication?

Although many types of behaviors can communicate, available space and the focus of this book limit our discussion of nonverbal communication to body movement (kinesics), the use of space (proxemics), dress and appearance, and eye contact (occulesics). Vocalics, or paralanguage (the use of the voice), is covered in the chapter on delivery.

Body Movement/Kinesics

(Birdwhistell first identified kinesics, or the study of our use of the body to communicate. It includes gestures, posture, facial expressions, and other body movements. Five research themes have emerged in kinesics: the use of emblems, illustrators, regulators, affect displays, and adaptors. A brief look at all five themes will provide a good orientation to the complex ways that we can use our bodies to send messages.

Emblems. An emblem is a nonverbal behavior that has a distinct verbal referent or even a denotative definition, and it is often used to send a specific message to others. The verbal referent is typically one or two words of a short phrase. For example, the "thumbs-up" hand gesture is listed in many dictionaries and is defined as a *gesture of approval.* There is a high level of agreement about the meaning of an emblem within cultures, but not usually across cultures.

Most emblems are created with the hands, but we can create them in other ways. For example, a shoulder shrug suggests "I don't know," or a wrinkled nose indicates that "something stinks." But the emblems we are most familiar with are usually hand gestures. Try to make the gesture that goes with each of the following meanings:

- "Sit down beside me."
- "Follow me."
- "I can't hear you."
- "Be quiet!"
- "Shame on you!"
- "OK."
- "I promise."
- "What time is it?"
- "Good bye!"

In addition to everyday conversation, emblems are used by divers while under water, by police officers directing traffic, by construction workers, and by catchers, pitchers, and managers during baseball games. Don't forget the very familiar and more or less universal signal some people use to indicate displeasure with other drivers! Keep in mind, though, that the emblems you know are not always shared. The hand gesture we use for "come here," with the hand palm up with the index finger extending in and out three or four times, has a very different meaning in Latin America. It means that you are romantically interested in the person, and is considered a solicitation. Emblems can replace the verbal or reinforce it.

Bikers use emblems when manuvering in traffic.

Illustrators. An illustrator is a gesture that is used with language to emphasize, stress, or repeat what is being said. It can be used to give directions, show the size or shape of something, and give clarification. Can you imagine trying to explain to a new parent how to "burp" a baby without using illustrators? Can you give directions to the campus library with your hands in your pockets? Sure you could, but the illustrators add much meaning and clarification to your directions or instructions; they help with that function of clarifying. In a study done several years ago, speakers were found to be more persuasive when they used illustrators than when they did not. More recent research has even extended the importance of illustrators. Robert Krauss found that gestures do more than amplify or accent verbal communication.

Affect displays express emotion.

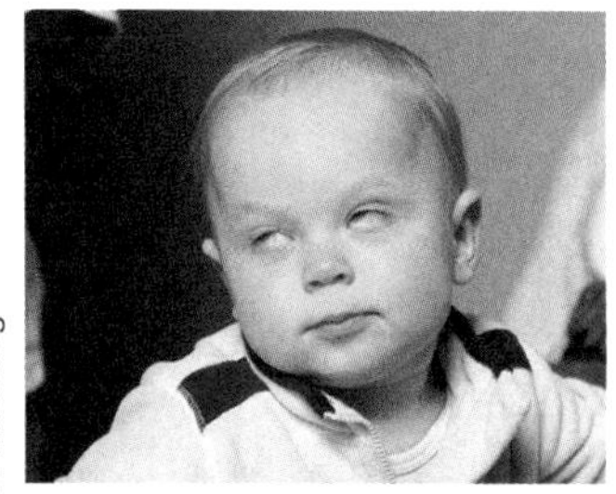

Can you make judgments about the nature and intensity of the emotions expressed on these faces?

They also help people retrieve ideas and words, such as when you try to define a term with a spatial meaning such as underneath, next to, and above, which Krauss calls *lexical retrieval*. If not done to excess, "talking with your hands" can be a very good thing!

Regulators. A regulator is a turn-taking signal that helps control the flow, the pace, and turn-taking in conversations, and you learned about their coordinating role earlier. If a group of people are talking and trying to share meaning, they must take turns speaking, and taking turns requires cooperation among the communicators. To accomplish this cooperation, along with the content of the conversation, participants must also communicate about who will speak next and when that turn will begin. Regulators help us with this task.

Weimann and Knapp and Argyle identified four categories of turn related signals in a typical conversation:

1. *Turn requesting* signals: These are used by a nonspeaker to take the floor. Nonverbal regulators used to request a turn include rapid head nods, forward leaning posture, and increased eye contact with the speaker.
2. *Turn yielding* signals: The speaker uses these to give up the floor. Nonverbal regulators used to yield a turn include increased eye contact with a nonspeaker, leaning back from a forward posture, or a sudden end to gesturing used while speaking.
3. *Turn maintenance* signals: These are used by the speaker to keep the floor (i.e., continue speaking). Nonverbal signals used to keep the turn include speaking louder or faster (increasing volume or rate of speech), continuing to gesture, or avoiding eye contact with the person requesting the turn.
4. *Back channel* signals: Nonspeaker refuses a turn that has been offered by the speaker. Nonverbal signals used to refuse a turn include nodding the head and avoiding eye contact with the person exhibiting a turn-yielding signal.

Affect displays. An **affect display** is a form of nonverbal behavior that expresses emotions. Although this behavior is most often associated with facial expressions, affect can also be expressed through posture and gestures. These behaviors cannot only express the type of emotion being experienced, but can

What do these adaptors tell you about the internal feelings of the people in the photos?

also express the intensity of the emotion. A smile suggests that you are happy. A slumped-over posture and a scowl on your face can suggest that you are unhappy, while your clinched fists and tense muscles can communicate just *how* unhappy you might be.

The emotions communicated by your face and body can affect the way you are perceived by other people. People who smile spontaneously are often considered by others to be more likable and more approachable than people who do not smile or people who just pretend to smile.

Adaptors. Adaptors are behaviors that can indicate our internal conditions or feelings to other people. We tend to use these behaviors when we become excited or anxious. Think about the kind of things that you do in communication situations when you feel nervous or excited. Do you scratch your head? Bite your nails? Play with your glasses? Rub your nose? You might not know, because most people are not aware of displaying these behaviors.

Adaptors are generally considered the least desirable type of nonverbal communication. Self-touching in this way could be a distraction to the audience, and it is often perceived as a sign of anxiety. One study found that deceivers bob their heads more often than people who tell the truth. Cultural guidelines may prohibit these behaviors, too. Wriggling your nose or having a disgusted facial look to show that you're repulsed seems to have a universal meaning.

However, in some cultures, people are socialized to mask emotional cues, and in others they're taught to emphasize them. Latin Americans will usually greet friends and relatives more personally than do Americans. Everyone hugs, including the men. Men usually also greet woman with *besitos,* meaning they touch cheeks while making a kissing noise with their lips. Women also greet other women with *besitos.* These little kisses are purely friendly and have no romantic meaning. Maslow and colleagues suggested that the anxiety displayed by adaptors can be interpreted by other communicators as a sign of deception; you are anxious because you are not being honest with the others and you fear being discovered!

Personal Distances

Hall recognized characteristic distances maintained between people in the U.S. culture, depending on their perceived relationships. The distance categories are *intimate, personal, social,* and public.

Type	Distance	Who Is Permitted/Context
Intimate Distance © 2007. Courtesy of JaxonPhotoGroup.	touching to 18 inches	**Who:** Spouses and family members, boyfriends and girlfriends, and very close friends. Context: A date with your spouse.
Personal Distance  © Kendall Hunt Publishing	18 inches to 4 feet	**Who:** Good friends and people you know well. Context: Having lunch with a good friend or co-worker.
Social Distance  © Kendall Hunt Publishing	4 feet to 12 feet	**Who:** Business associates, teachers, and people you know but with whom you have a professional but less social relationship. Context: A business meeting, small group discussion, or an employment interview.
Public Distance  © Kendall Hunt Publishing	12 feet and beyond	**Who:** A person you don't know; a stranger on the street. **Context:** Giving a presentation to a large group; walking downtown on a public sidewalk.

Relationships affect the way we use space. Based on the use of space, describe the relationships in these photos. Be specific about the nonverbal clues that indicate the relationship.

Use of Space/Proxemics

The study of proxemics is typically divided into two applications: The use of personal space and how people claim and mark territory as their own. Most of us don't even think about the impact of space on our relationships, but research has shown that your use of space can influence shared meaning and impact your relationship. Knapp and Hall found that our use of space can seriously affect our ability to achieve desired goals. Both applications can be used and managed by people to communicate fairly specific messages, and they can provide evidence to help us make judgments about person using the space.

Personal space. When you consider the idea of **personal space,** think of a small amount of portable space that you carry around with you all the time. You control who is and who is not permitted inside of that space. Permission to enter that space is granted based on the relationship you have with that person, the context of the encounter, the culture in which you live, and your own personal preferences and tolerances. For example, you would be likely to allow business and professional colleagues to be reasonably close to you; you would allow good friends to be very close to you; and you would allow romantic partners to be closer still, even to the point of touching. In addition, you might allow people that you don't know to be very close to you in the appropriate context, like a crowded elevator or a busy airport.

Sometimes we allow our personal space to be violated.

When someone enters your space without permission, you can interpret it as a lack of courtesy, or even as a threat. You will feel uncomfortable, so you can either wait for the trespasser to move out of your space, or you can move away until you feel comfortable again.

People mark their territory in many ways.

The range of personal space varies across cultures. The box describes spaces typical to the culture in the United States. If you visit the United Kingdom, you will notice that these spaces are slightly expanded; that is, the British prefer just a bit more distance between people. By contrast, many Eastern cultures, including Asia and the Middle East, prefer a smaller distance. When these cultures meet, people from the United States often feel "crowded" by people from Asian cultures, while people from Japan might think that Americans are "cold" or "stand-offish" because of the increased interpersonal distances. As you can see, there is no shortage of opportunities for misunderstanding! Burgoon suggests that we want to stay near others, but we also want to maintain some distance—think about the dilemma this causes! Try to be sensitive to cultural norms when you assign meaning to the use of personal space.

Territoriality. We also have a tendency to claim space as our own. We have just looked at personal space, which is portable space that you carry around with you. Territory, by contrast, is not mobile; it stays in one place. You can think of territory as a kind of extension of you that is projected on to space or objects. Space that you occupy or control, and objects that belong to you or that you use regularly, are all important to you. If any person not authorized by you occupies that space or touches those objects, you feel violated and threatened. To help describe this kind of attachment to places and things, we turn to Altman, who classified territory into three categories: primary, secondary, and public.

Primary territory is space or those items that you personally control. This includes personal items that only you would use, like your clothes and your toothbrush. It also includes the private spaces in your house like your bathroom and bedroom. Many people treat still other places as primary territory such as their car, their office at work, and even their refrigerator!

Secondary territory is not your private property. That is, it is not owned by you, but it is typically associated with you. Examples of secondary territory include the desk you always use in class, the seat you always sit in at the office conference table, your favorite fishing spot at the lake, or your usual table at the library.

Public territory is available to anyone, so any space that you try to claim is only temporary. You might define your space on the beach by using markers such as blankets, beach chairs, or umbrellas. Or you might spread out your books and notes at the library to claim space on a work table. Our use of the territory lasts as long as we are using it, or as long as other people respect our markers.

Most of us pay little attention to these claims of space, and we probably don't even realize that we do it. However, these claims come clearly to our attention when they are violated. It seems like there is almost nothing worse than walking into the classroom on the day of the big exam to find someone else in your seat! Sure, any seat will work just as well, but that is *your* seat where you feel most comfortable and confident. We tend to feel violated whenever any unauthorized person uses our space or touches our stuff!

Lyman and Scott identified three levels of **intrusion of territory:** violation, invasion, and contamination. A *violation* happens when your space or your stuff is used without your permission, like when a neighbor borrows one of your tools without asking first. An *invasion* occurs when an unauthorized person enters the territory that you have claimed with markers. They might move your books and notes at the library (while you were looking for a book) and take over your space at the table, or they could cut in front of you in a check-out line at the grocery store. Finally, a *contamination* occurs when space that you claim is used without your authorization, but your evidence of the use is not the presence of the user but objects left behind. For example, you arrive at your office in the morning to find cups and fast food wrappers on your desk. There is nobody in your office, but you know somebody *was* there, and he or she was eating at your desk. Territory that you claim as your own should not be used by anyone without your permission. How you respond to territory depends very much on who invaded the territory and why it was invaded, which you'll see explained in expectancy violations theory, which follows later in this chapter.

Dress/Appearance

Your appearance, along with the way you dress, influences the way other people respond to you. In some situations, your appearance can be the primary factor that determines the response of others. *Physical attractiveness,* as well as personal grooming and hygiene, weigh heavily on judgments that are made about you every day. If that's not enough pressure, along with protecting you from the environment and fulfilling cultural requirements for modesty,

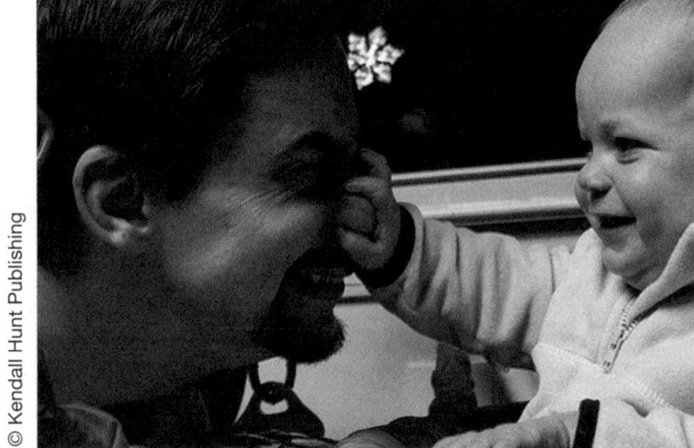

Is there ever a time when you should allow your territory to be violated?

clothing is also a potent source of nonverbal information about you. Morris tells us that clothing sends continuous signals about us and who we think we are. For example, watch the scene in the 1990 movie *Pretty Woman* when the character played by Julia Roberts first enters a "high-class" clothing store and is treated poorly by the staff. What about her appearance led to that treatment?

Among other qualities, clothing can suggest social and economic status, education, level of success, or trustworthiness and character. Morris suggests that clothing can be a cultural display and one that communicates something special about the wearer. People have a tendency to express certain values central to their belief systems that indicate the kind of people they perceive themselves to be. Katz tells us that we hold and express particular attitudes to satisfy this need and that those attitudes reflect a positive view of ourselves. Clothing and appearance are consistent with this concept. For example, if you consider yourself to be the "artistic" type, or a successful business person, or a talented athlete, your clothing choices will likely reflect that self image.

Gordon et al., suggests that clothing fulfills a number of symbolic functions:

- Traditional and religious ceremonies often involve specific clothing.
- Self-beautification (real or imagined) is often reflected in clothing.
- Clothing expresses cultural values regarding sexual identity and practice.
- Clothes differentiate roles and levels of authority.
- Clothing is used in the acquisition and display of status.

Think about the way you dress and why you make those clothing choices. What are you trying to say? Are you trying to fit in? Are you trying to identify yourself with a particular group? Are you trying to show respect for an occasion or person?

How could her tattoos impact others' perceptions?

Clothing is not the only aspect of appearance to consider. Think of the other personal choices people make with tattoos, body art, and personal grooming. What are the impacts of blue hair, black nail colors, Mohawks or dreadlocks, multiple piercing and colorful tattoos? You have the right to communicate about yourself in any way you want, but remember that if you go against cultural norms, you may be creating perceptual barriers that impede communication. Your appearance is a prime source of information that others use to make judgments about you. Try to use some care when making choices about how you should look in particular situations. You can always maintain your individuality, but you should also dress to show respect for the occasion and the people that you will be coming into contact with. If you have to give a presentation for a business group, for example, you can show your respect for the group by dressing in more formal attire. Wearing jeans with ripped out knees may say a lot about who you think you are, but wearing the suit for the business group also communicates who you think you are. You are someone who combines your own needs with a respect for the needs of other people!

Eye Movement/ Occulesics

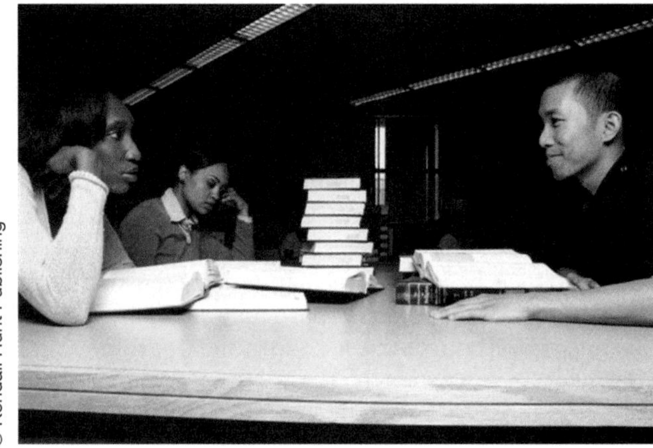

© Kendall Hunt Publishing

By making eye contact with others, you can find clues about their level of understanding and interest.

In many Western cultures, including the United States, making **eye contact** with another person is considered a sign of sincerity, caring, honesty, and sometimes power or status. Pearson found that men sometimes use eye contact to challenge others and to assert themselves. Women tend to hold eye contact more than men, regardless of the sex of the person that they're interacting with. Some Eastern cultures view eye contact with others as an impolite invasion of privacy and they especially disapprove of eye contact with a person of higher status. In another study, it was found that inner-city African-American persuaders look continually at the listener, and African American listeners tend to look away from the persuader most of the time. The opposite is true of middle-class Whites; as persuaders, they look only occasionally at the listener, and White listeners look continuously at the persuader. This could explain why the two groups could have incorrect inferences about the amount of interest the other has when they communicate.

We consider the use of eye contact to be an essential tool for achieving communication goals. In U.S. culture, how does it make you feel when someone will not make eye contact with you? Do you trust this person? Do you suspect his or her motives?

Eye contact helps us communicate in at least four ways: It can open a channel of communication, demonstrate concern, gather feedback, and moderate anxiety.

Open a communication channel. You can let others know that you would like to communicate with them by simply looking at them. A brief moment of eye contact can open a channel of communication and make other messages possible.

Demonstrate concern. Engaging other people in eye contact during conversations shows a concern for them, as well as your commitment that they understand your message. In addition, eye contact can be used to communicate liking and attraction.

Gather feedback. If you would like information about what other people are thinking, take a look at their eyes. You won't be able to read thoughts, but you can certainly find clues to indicate that they are listening, that they understand the message, and perhaps that they care about what you are saying. The old adage that speakers should look at the back wall of the room when giving a public speech is pretty bad advice; you will miss out on critical information about the frame of mind of audience members, as well as other feedback essential to achieving your goals.

Moderate anxiety. When speakers get nervous or anxious during a public presentation, they have a tendency to avoid eye contact with the listeners by either looking at the floor, the back wall of the room, or at their notes. As they continue to stare at the floor, anxiety (fear of unknown outcomes) continues to build. Occasionally, but rarely, anxiety can build to the point at which it completely takes over, and the speaker freezes. You can avoid this scenario through *careful preparation* for the event, and by allowing the listeners to provide you with support. By *establishing eye contact* with members of your audience, you will see listeners smiling at you or expressing support with their posture, head nods, or other behaviors. Not looking at the audience or conversational partners removes your opportunity to get or give supportive feedback. When others notice your anxiety, they usually want to help you. Look at the audience, feel the support and try to relax, and then refocus on your communication goals.

How Does Theory Describe Nonverbal Behavior's Impact on Relationships?

Have you ever played elevator games with strangers? You know, you enter an empty elevator and take the "power position" by the buttons. At the next floor, someone enters and either asks you to push the button for a floor or reaches in front of you to select a floor and then retreats to the opposite corner away from you. There's no further talk or eye contact. The next person who enters does the same thing, finding a corner. Everyone faces the doors, anticipates its opening, watching the numbers change as if by magic. If others enter, their volume drops to a hush, or they stop talking until they leave. Now, have you ever tried *this?* Get on an elevator and keep walking until you face the back wall. After all, that's how you entered, right? Go stand right next to the power person, real close. Keep talking real loud. Sit down on your backpack or luggage. What do you think will happen? How will others react to you?

One theory that attempts to explain the influence of nonverbal communication on meaning and relationships is **expectancy violations theory.** Judee Burgoon said that "nonverbal cues are an inherent and essential part of message creation (production) and interpretation (processing)." Expectancy violations theory (EVT) suggests that we hold expectations about the nonverbal behavior of others. It asserts that when communicative norms are violated, the violation may be perceived either favorably or unfavorably, depending on the perception that the receiver has of the violator. Burgoon's early writing on EVT integrated Hall's ideas on personal space (which you read about earlier) as a core aspect of the theory. EVT says that our *expectancies* are the thoughts and behaviors anticipated when we interact with another.

We have expectations of how others ought to think and behave. Levine says that these expectancies are a result of social norms, stereotypes, and your own personal idiosyncrasies, and these expectancies cause us to interact with others. We have both preinteractional and interactional expectations. *Preinteractional expectations* are made up of the skills and knowledge you bring to an interaction; *interactional expectations* are your skills and knowledge that let you carry out the interaction.

Another basic idea of EVT is that we learn our expectations from our cultures: You've learned what kind of touching is appropriate with whom, how to greet a stranger, and where to stand in relationship with another, for example.

Finally, EVT says that we make predictions about others based on their nonverbal behavior. So how does this work? Let's say you're standing in line at the grocery store, and the person in front of you looks at what you're about to buy and then makes eye contact with you. At first, you might be uncomfortable, thinking that the person is judging you by the way she is eyeing your groceries. If she then gives you a warm smile and points to her big pile containing the same things, you might feel a bit more comfortable. You've made predictions based on nonverbal behavior: The person is not threatening or judging you negatively.

But EVT is about *violations* of our expectations. Burgoon says that when people deviate from expectations, that deviation is judged based on the other's ability to reward us. A reward could be something as simple as a smile, friendliness, or acknowledgment of competence. This potential to reward is called *communicator reward valence,* which is the interactants' ability to reward or punish and the positive and negative characteristics they have. Someone in power, like your professor for instance, may have more communicator reward valence than a stranger, because the professor has the power of grades and probably has more credibility for you. If someone violates our expectations, these deviations cause *arousal,* an increased attention to the deviation. Cognitive arousal is mental awareness of the deviation; physical arousal involves physiological heightening. For instance, if a person stares at you, you might wonder why he's doing that (cognitive arousal) or you might start to sweat (physical arousal). Once arousal happens, threats occur. Your *threat threshold* is the tolerance you have for deviations; how threatened do you feel? Maybe you don't mind if another person stands too close; maybe you can't put up with someone staring at you. The size of your threat threshold is based on how you view the person who is deviating from your expectations; what is that other's communicator reward valence? Then you add in the *violation valence,* which consists of your positive or negative value placed towards the deviations from your expectations.

When someone violates one of your expectations (for instance, he touches you when you didn't expect it), you interpret the meaning of that violation and decide if you like it or not. If you don't like it, then the violation valence is negative; if the surprise was pleasant (even though you didn't expect it), then the violation valence is positive. The theory predicts that if a violation is ambiguous, then the communicator reward valence will influence how you interpret and evaluate the violation. If the person is someone you like, then you'll positively evaluate his violation; if you don't like him, then you'll negatively evaluate his violation. Take a simple example of how someone is dressed. On an interview, there are certain expectations of how you should look. If you go in wearing jeans and a t-shirt and the company wants its workers to wear suits, then you've violated expectancies. It's pretty likely that you don't have any power here, or any way to reward the company for hiring you. Thus, the interviewer will evaluate you negatively, feeling aroused

On an interview, you want to be positively evaluated.

that you didn't understand such a basic concept like appropriate attire. However, what if you are a highly sought-after, uniquely imaginative individual that the company has been pursuing? Your violation of the dress code might be seen positively; you're bold and creative, just like they thought. EVT is an interesting theory that focuses on what we expect nonverbally in conversations, as well as suggesting what happens when our expectations aren't met. It's very practical in applications across many contexts.

What Are the Key Points to Remember About Nonverbal Communication?

Nonverbal communication is a complex combination of behaviors that form a source of information used by other people to make sense of messages that you send. Even though much of your nonverbal behavior is spontaneous and unconscious, you should realize that it contributes a significant percentage of the meaning that people attribute to your messages. As such, you should try as hard as you can to be a good self-monitor and pay close attention to your nonverbal behaviors. However, nonverbal behavior is also a source of information for you. It can help you to more accurately interpret the communication of others, so pay attention!

Be careful to not overgeneralize the meanings of particular nonverbal cues. The specific meaning of any nonverbal behavior is typically dependent on multiple factors, including (but not limited to) culture, the relationship between the people communicating, the specific communication context, and individual characteristics of the participants. You wouldn't want others to make stereotypical assumptions about your behavior, so make sure that you don't make those same assumptions about the behavior of others. Gather as much information as possible before reaching conclusions. Sometimes a touch is just a touch!

Summary

Verbal and nonverbal communication are powerful, critically important elements in the creation of shared meaning, because they have the ability to clarify your ideas to others or to confuse them. It's not always easy to use language or nonverbal behavior correctly, because both are arbitrary and ambiguous. The relationship that words or movements have with ideas is not based on a concrete characteristic; instead, you are relying on the ability of the audience to associate your symbols with their cognitions (beliefs, attitudes, and values). You've been exposed to some theoretical explanations of how these attempts to create meaning work in our lives. We interpret language and nonverbal communication because of our particular culture, which provides a frame of reference on how to assign meaning. In order to be a competent communicator, you need to remain aware that your words aren't always understood as you mean them to be and that your nonverbal behavior can supplement or contradict those words.

Name____ Date______________

Exercise 3.1 Chapter 3 – What Is the Power of Verbal and Nonverbal Communication? This is a two part exercise.

Part One

There is power in verbal language. Language is a shared system of symbols and structures in organized patterns to express thoughts and feelings. Let's explore further the basic principles of language by identifying the following terms as they relate to how we use language.

Define the following:

Connotation reflect your personal, subjective definitions

Denotation literal, dictionary definitions that are precise and objective

Unbiased Language Use appropriate labels when using sexual orientation, and occupational

Accurate Language

Jargon Specialized professional language

Regionalism words or phrases that are specific to one part of the country

Muted Group Theory

Phonological Rules regulate how words sound when you pronounce them

Regulative Rules tell us when, how, where, and with we can talk about certain things

Semantic Rules govern the meaning of specific symbols

10/19/11

Slang consist of words that are short-lived, arbitrarily changed, and often vulgar ideas

Cliché an expression that has been overused

Loaded Words sound like they're describing, but they're actually revealing your attitude

Empty Words overworked exaggerations

Equivocal Words have more than one correct denotative meaning

Part T.wo

Write a creative and engaging scenario about Shane and Kayla using the terms you have just defined. Indicate when you use each term by placing the term in parenthesis behind the example.

The story begins......

Shane and Kayla were in Precollege at Harmony University. They met at a pool party at Harmony gym when Shane walked over to Kayla and said "Hello, my name is Shane. What's up?" (semantic rules)

"Oh, nothing. (empty words) I'm just enjoying the party. So are you a junior?", said Kayla. "No, I'm a soph—", said Shane, but before he could finish his sentence some guys in the pool started splashing water everywhere. The look of annoyance surrounded Shane's face (connotation). "Hey, guys cut it out. That's really annoying" (denotation), said Shane. "So are you doing anything tomorrow", said Shane to Kayla. "No, I've got plenty of time on my hands" (cliché), said Kayla. "Well how 'bout you and me go to the movies" (slang), said Shane. "Sure", said Kayla, and they went to see a movie the next day.

Be prepared to read your story to the class.

Name____ Date______________

Exercise 3.2 Chapter 3 – What Is the Power of Verbal and Nonverbal Communication?

Nonverbal Communication is all nonlinguistic aspects of communication. The types of nonverbal communication include: Body movement, eye messages, space and distance, dress and appearance. Give a brief definition of each. Then, visit one of the sites listed below and record examples of each as you observed the nonverbal "types" in action. Record your time and place on the sheet attached and be very specific with your observations.

Choose one site:

Student Center
Cafeteria
Local fast food restaurant
Library
A dorm lobby

Name: Michael Cox

Place: Student Center

Type of Nonverbal Behavior	*Definition*	*Observation*
Body Movement	The use of the body to communicate	guy waved to his friend
Eye contact	The connection you form with listeners through your gaze	girl made flitations look at me
Space and Distance	how space influences your relationships	people walked
Dress and Appearance	The way you dress influences people	A guy in a suit looked professional

Be prepared to share your observations with the class.

4 Interpersonal Relationships

After reading this chapter, you should be able to:

- ❒ Explain emotional intelligence and its contribution to communication effectiveness
- ❒ Clarify the interpersonal needs you are trying to meet when you seek out others
- ❒ Explain how bids and responses to bids contribute to relationship development and your role in both bidding and responding to the bids of others
- ❒ Define self-disclosure, why it's important, and how the Johari Window helps you understand how the self-disclosure process takes place
- ❒ Describe each of the essential elements that draw people together

Key Terms

Attitudes
Beliefs
Bids
Blind pane
Commitment
Compatibility
Cultural information
Emotional intelligence
Empathy
Hidden pane
Interpersonal communication
Johari Window
Open pane
Owned messages
Proximity
Psychological information
Response to a bid
Self-disclosure
Small talk
Social penetration
Sociological information
Unknown pane

4 Scenario

Music bounced off the walls as the next sorority took the stage. Carla screamed as she saw her older sister take the stage, leading off into the next step.

"Yea, that's my big sister," Carla yelled, jumping up and down with pride.

Everyone in the crowd erupted with cheers as the group struck their last pose. Carla screamed and clapped. "Come on Ariel let's go congratulate them. Did you see them Ariel?!"

"Yea, they were great," Ariel exclaimed, "Your sister got skills leading everyone off like that. I'd be so nervous."

"Well, you better get that out your system because when we pledge we'll be on that stage too!" Carla declared, walking through the crowd. She looked back at her roommate, "The ladies of that sorority are."

Carla's sentence was cut short as she walked right into someone. She lost her balance and almost plummeted to the ground, but was caught before she hit the ground. She took a deep breath. "Thanks Ariel!" Ariel felt herself being lifted from the floor.

"You're a lifesaver, and you're really strong..." Carla drifted off as she realized that the person who caught her wasn't Ariel, but a guy.

"My name isn't Ariel, but I'm glad you're ok. And thanks for the strong comment," The guy replied.

Carla smiled shyly, "Oh, I see you're not Ariel. And thanks."

"Hey, don't mention it. I should be thanking you for putting my workout to use." He chuckled, "My name is Brian by the way."

"My name is Carla," Carla introduced herself. "Once again, thanks. I'd better be off. C'mon Ariel!"

Carla grabbed Ariel's hand, but before Carla could move Brian blocked her way. "Wait before you go, here's my card. Call me sometime." Carla arched a brow, "I want to be a doctor one day. I got to be prepared, right. See you later."

Brian handed her the card and left. Ariel shook her head. "If you don't call him..."

"I'd be a total idiot," Carla finished.

Leslie Stevens's online dating service had her rate herself and her potential mate in categories ranging from sex drive to "socialistic-butterflyosity." An algorithm then calculated her compatibility with a list of matches. Leslie wanted a vegetarian boyfriend who played piano and liked folk music, and she discovered the exact match in Cody Moore—he lived in a dorm on her campus as well. Leslie began sending Cody online messages, and the next thing they knew they were having lunch together and hanging out in real life. Stevens said, "The chances of meeting Moore without the help of an online community were pretty much nil."

Online dating services have changed the way the college crowd interacts. Instead of getting to know classmates over coffee or through mutual friends, students can now access a goldmine of information about their peers—and potential mates—online.

© Kendall Hunt Publishing

Interaction with others is called interpersonal communication, and it occurs whenever one person interacts with another—usually in an informal setting. You cannot survive in society without interpersonal communication skills. They enable you to function socially and to maintain relationships important to you.

According to Clyde Lindley, director of the Center for Psychological Services, Silver Springs, Maryland, "Much research shows the importance of interpersonal relationships to well-being, happiness, and satisfaction with life." One study showed that lack of contact with others doubles the chance of getting sick or dying. In a study of college roommates, the researchers discovered that the more roommates disliked each other, the more likely they were to go to the doctor and to come down with colds and the flu. Isolation has more impact on men than on women. Men without close social ties are two to three times more likely to die earlier than men who have them.

This chapter begins by examining the big picture—how you understand and get along with others, who are you attracted to and why—and then discusses the specifics in the next two sections: talking to each other and self-disclosure. The final sections examine the essential elements of good relationships and the Internet's effect on interpersonal relationships.

Emotional Intelligence

Anyone who has taught long enough to see students mature can tell you of some who were smart in the classroom but never went anywhere and others who did not do particularly well in school but went on to have successful careers and relationships. Their success is due to what Daniel Goleman calls "emotional intelligence." Although there isn't unanimous agreement on the validity of the concept of emotional intelligence, it provides useful insights into some important aspects of interpersonal relationships. Edwin Locke, for example, argues that the concept is not a form of intelligence and is defined too broadly and inclusively to have intelligible meaning.

Being Self-Aware

Before you can deal with the emotions of others, you need to recognize your own by paying attention to how you feel. Self-awarenesss requires the ability to get a little distance from the emotion so that you can look at it without being overwhelmed by it or reacting to it too quickly. For example, if you are having an argument with someone and act on your anger, you might tell the other person that you never want to see him or her again. On the other hand, if you can recognize how angry you are feeling, you might be able to say, "Let me think about this some more and talk to you about it later."

Distancing yourself from an emotion does not mean denying it ("I shouldn't feel this way"). Rather, it's a way to articulate to yourself what you are feeling so that you can act on it appropriately.

Managing Emotions

Managing your emotions means expressing them in a manner that is appropriate to the circumstances. You may not be able to do this easily because emotions often come from below the surface of your consciousness. For example, there may have been a time that unexpected tears came to your eyes, or other times when you felt a terrible rage well up inside you.

Another emotion that gets out of control is anxiety. When anxiety is out of control, you feel so worried or so upset that it interferes with the way you function. In a university setting, for instance, most teachers have had students who have been so worried about the right way to do an assignment that they didn't do it at all or did it poorly because they were afraid to take any chances.

Managing your emotions does not mean that you should never feel angry, worried, or anxious. These emotions are all part of being human, and if you don't find a way to express them, they can result in depression or antisocial acts. *It's important that you control these emotions rather than letting them control you.*

Managing your emotions does not mean that you never feel angry, worried, or anxious. It's important that you control these emotions rather than letting them control you.

One interesting finding about emotions is that women are better than men at detecting them. In a study where men and women were shown video clips in which someone was having an emotional reaction, 80 percent of the time women were better than men at discerning the emotion.

Motivating Yourself

Motivating yourself is setting a goal and then disciplining yourself to do what you have to do to reach it. Whether you are an athlete or a writer, talent is not enough to make you win the race or get your story published. Both writers and athletes will tell you that they worked hard on many boring activities before they mastered their discipline.

Self-motivation requires resisting impulses. If you are studying for a test, for example, it might be tempting to go to the computer and chat with a friend. If you give in to this impulse, you might become so engrossed in the computer that you completely forget the test.

Some of the most fascinating research on impulse control was done on a group of four-year-old preschoolers. When a child was put into a room with a researcher, he or she was offered a marshmallow. However, the children were told that the researcher had an errand to run and that if they didn't eat the marshmallow, they would get two when the researcher returned. The researcher was gone 15 to 20 minutes—an eternity for a child. The minute he was gone, one-third of the children ate their marshmallows; the remainder found ways to distract themselves: They tried to go to sleep, they talked to themselves, or they engaged in play.

Later these same children were studied when they were teenagers. Those who waited when they were children were much better in social skills, more assertive, and better able to handle themselves in a crisis. Academically, they were far superior as students, and they scored an average of 210 points higher on SAT scores.

Other influences on motivation, according to Goleman, were positive thinking and optimism. Those who had a strong sense of self could bounce back after they had a negative experience. Rather than dwelling on the failure, they looked at ways in which they could improve.

Recognizing Emotions in Others

Empathy, the ability to recognize and share someone else's feelings, is essential to human relationships. It comes from hearing what people are really saying—both by listening to their words and by reading body language such as gestures and facial expressions, and recognizing what they mean by a particular tone of voice. When someone has the same feelings or experiences you have had, it's not difficult to feel empathy. You are really put to the test when you haven't had the other person's feelings or experiences. For example, how can you feel empathy with an African student who hasn't been home for three years and stays in the dorm over Christmas? You can feel sorry for him, and you could tell him that you would feel terrible if you couldn't go home for the holidays. However, these emotions are pity (feeling sorry for him) and sympathy (saying that you'd feel bad too), but they are not empathy because you have not shared his experience. You may go in the direction of empathy if you talk to him for a while, look at the pictures of his brothers and sisters, hear about all the delicious things his mother cooks for Christmas, and so on. Empathy is the extent to which you can sit in his place, see what he sees, and taste what he tastes.

Empathy has a strong moral dimension. Being able to recognize and share someone's distress means that you will not want to hurt him or her. Child molesters and sociopaths, for example, are people lacking in empathy. Sharing empathy with others also means that you are able to reach out and help them because when you can feel as they feel, they are no longer alone.

Handling Relationships

What are some of the characteristics of popular people you know? Chances are that they are people who are largely positive and energetic and that being with them makes you feel positive too. Most likely, they are also the people who organize others (such as the child who suggests a game), negotiate solutions when there is a problem to be solved, and generally connect with others emotionally.

Who is most popular in this picture? Is popularity their main goal?

Being popular, however, is not their only goal. People also need a sense of balance; they need to recognize their own needs and know how to fulfill them. For example, you might be popular if you are always willing to stop studying to go to a party. This, however, would not meet your own need to pass your courses.

The Importance of Emotional Intelligence to Strategic Flexibility

Self-concept is the way you think about and value yourself. The way you look at others and the world around you, and how well you understand and get along with others, have direct influence on your self-concept, just as the way you think about and value yourself influences both perception and emotional intelligence.

Perception, emotional intelligence, and self-concept have a direct bearing on strategic flexibility simply because they either enhance or impair your ability to anticipate, assess, evaluate, select, and apply your skills and behaviors. The better your perceptive skills, the more likely that your emotional intelligence is high and your self-concept is positive.

Remember the first characteristic of emotional intelligence: self-awareness. Part of maturity is recognizing that just because you have emotions doesn't necessarily mean you must act on them. Not only do you recognize your own emotions, but you understand, too, the triggers that cause them to come to the surface. As you begin to recognize your emotions and their triggers, you will learn how to manage them and to reveal the appropriate ones in given circumstances.

As you become accustomed to using the strategic flexibility framework, you develop self-control through self-discipline. It is as if you are setting mini-goals for yourself. You anticipate situations with the goal of applying the appropriate and relevant skills and behaviors. You achieve success when you maximize your communication, enhance your credibility, and not only support but achieve your intentions.

Listening to others becomes easier when you are secure in your self. Your perceptions become more accurate, and your observations of the nonverbal behavior of others and attempts to really understand them improve. In the end there is a greater chance that you will be able to handle relationships more successfully. Handling relationships is not easy, nor is it automatic. It is learned behavior, and emotional intelligence can help you establish and sustain long-term, meaningful relationships. The problem is simply that emotional intelligence often develops slowly—along with emotional maturity. If you take each of the areas of emotional intelligence, and you make them an issue before thinking about any serious relationship, you are more likely to take the necessary time.

One of our needs may be to increase our self-esteem by seeking people who will love and support us.

Personal Motivation for Interpersonal Contact

This section is divided into two parts: attractiveness and motives for interpersonal contact. In the first part we examine those elements that cause us to be attracted to others: physical attraction, perceived gain, similarities, differences, proximity, and cyberattraction. In the second, motives for interpersonal contact, we look at the interpersonal needs others fulfill: pleasure, affection, inclusion, escape, relaxation, control, health, and cybermotivation. There is no doubt that the factors in these two sections can overlap and intermingle. For example, one of our needs may be to be seen with people who are attractive, or *one of our needs may be to increase our self-esteem by seeking people who will love and support us.*

Attractiveness

Helen Fisher, a research anthropologist at Rutgers University, writes, "There is much evidence that people generally fall in love with those of the same socioeconomic and ethnic background, of roughly the same age, with the same degree of intelligence and level of education, and with a similar sense of humor and grade of attractiveness." The point is that we are attracted to people similar to ourselves. From Fisher's vantage point, all it might take is some self-examination to determine what factors would attract you to someone else.

People are attracted to one another for many reasons, but numbers count, too. Sam Roberts, in a *New York Times* article entitled "So Many Men, So Few Women," says, "If you're in your 20s, single, straight, and looking for love, the statistical odds of finding a full-time partner are better if you're a woman. Unless you're a black woman." Roberts writes, "The Census Bureau calculates that among single non-Hispanic whites in their 20s, there are 120 men for every 100 women. The comparable figures are 153 Hispanic men, 132 Asian men, and 92 black men for every 100 single women in their 20s of the same race or ethnicity."

There are many factors that make up attraction to others. Physical attraction, perceived gain, similarities, differences, and proximity are some of them. What are the likely factors at play here?

Sometimes our attraction to others can be measured by individual features, but we are more than the sum of our individual parts. What makes you more is not only what others can see, but what goes on inside you as well—your confidence, your belief in yourself, your unwillingness to put yourself down (or up). Even if you are the world's best looking and brightest, you could still ruin another person's feeling of being special in your presence, by either attacking yourself or bragging.

Every day you encounter scores of people, but most of them recede into a kind of human landscape. Occasionally, however, you think, "Hey, I would really like to get to know this person better." Of the scores of people you meet, how do you pick one whom you want to know better? What are the ingredients that make up your attraction to others?

Physical attraction. We are often attracted to others because of the way they look; we like their style and want to get to know them better. Physical attraction may be sexual attraction. In most cases, however, it goes beyond that. For adults who have had experience in the world, physical attraction usually recedes into the background as they get to know a person. Physical attraction can be a reason for getting to know someone, but it is usually not the basis for a long-term relationship.

Perceived gain. Often we are attracted to people because we think we have something to gain from associating with them. For example, a man might want a woman willing to subsume herself or to limit her ambitions to make life more congenial for him. Andrew Hacker, a political scientist at Queens College, has predicted a growing divide between the sexes because women are less willing to do this.

Professor Stephanie Coontz, a sociology professor at Evergreen State College in Washington, believes that women "have become more distrustful of marriage and men have been more likely to say marriage is an ideal state." Coontz suggests that the new equality in marriage has caused women to be more cautious—because marriage "comes with a lot of expectations about women doing the comfort-generating work." Because people's behavior about marriage has changed more in the past 30 years than in the last 3,000, according to Coontz, potential gains from relationships—especially marriage—may need to be reassessed and reevaluated.

With respect to perceived gain, "conventional wisdom is that we choose friends because of who *they* are, but it turns out that we actually love them because of the way they support who *we are*." If, indeed, this is the case, then the perceived gain is the increased self-confidence, self-assurance, poise, and composure we gain when we choose the right relationship partner.

Although Americans believe they live in a classless society, this is not true. Even colleges and universities have a social hierarchy: Private schools (especially those in the Ivy League) have the most status, while junior and community colleges have the least. Colleges that are supported by a church are in a category of their own. What does this have to do with attraction? People will usually seek out others in their own class. Sometimes, however, they are motivated to move up, and they try to blend into a higher class because the perceived awards will be greater.

Similarities. You may be attracted to someone who shares your **attitudes** and **beliefs** or seems knowledgeable about topics you find interesting and significant. Your beliefs are your convictions; your attitudes are the deeply felt beliefs that govern how you behave. When it comes to a strongly felt belief, you probably look for people who believe as you do. For example, in today's world it would be difficult for an Albanian and a Serb to be close friends—their politics have put them in opposing camps.

As adults grow older and meet more and more people, they become aware of the kinds of people they like and dislike, and they recognize the importance of compatibility. Compatibility means having similar attitudes and personality, and a liking for the same activities. For example, one couple decides to live in the city and focus on their careers rather than have a family. They like drama and excitement in their life—something the city provides. They often attend hockey and basketball games, and they spend their money on trendy clothes and eating out. Because they like the same things, their relationship is likely to last.

Differences. Although two people who have very different beliefs are unlikely to form a strong and lasting relationship, people with different personality characteristics might be attracted to each other. For example, a person who doesn't like making decisions might be attracted to a strong decision maker. Because these characteristics complement each other, they might help strengthen the relationship.

Specific interests may be so similar that they outweigh any differences. An American who runs in the Boston Marathon might have more in common with a runner from Kenya than with someone who spends every Sunday morning reading the newspaper and eating doughnuts. Association with a group might bring people together. Although a Rotary member from Indiana would have a different cultural background than a Rotary member from India, the fact that they both belong to Rotary will create a common ground for some of their interactions.

Proximity. Proximity is the close contact that occurs when people share an experience such as work, play, or school. Even when people might not otherwise have been attracted to each other, they may begin to know and like each other because they are together so much. For example, being in the same study group for a semester, sharing an office, or standing side-by-side on an assembly line are activities that place people in close proximity. Once they begin to share their lives on a day-to-day basis, they may find themselves becoming friends or even forming a romantic relationship.

Specific interests may be so similar that they outweigh any differences.

Sometimes people who are attracted to each other form a strong friendship but lose touch when they no longer have proximity. Typically, friends who move to different cities vow to stay in touch, but it is not unusual for contact to drop to a yearly holiday card. Proximity, then, is important not just for starting relationships but also for keeping them going.

Cyberattraction. When you filter out those aspects of central importance in face-to-face communication—eye contact, self-contact gestures, posture, voice pitch, intensity, stress, rhythm, and volume—the process changes. In cyberattraction, we depend on cues such as language, style, timing, speed of writing, and use of punctuation and emoticons. These form the substance of computer-mediated communication (CMC), discussed in Chapter 1.

CMC gives people an opportunity to interact without the weight of the physical-attractiveness stereotype and gives the smaller number of cues available a greater value. Partners build their stereotypical impressions of each other based on the language content of CMC messages. One researcher has found evidence that CMC groups gradually increase their impression development to a level approaching that of face-to-face groups, but the process takes longer because the cues are fewer.

What are the specific cues of attractiveness in the cyberworld? First, you need to engage in an attentive and sensitive process of negotiation. The negotiation needs to be both intriguing and enticing. Second, you need to simulate proximity by the shared use of a particular tool such as a chat room or newsgroup, and frequent contact is essential. Third, because people are attracted to someone they believe has attitudes similar to their own, because it is difficult and time consuming to learn how people think about multiple issues online, and because there is no way to compare someone's attitudes with their self-presentation (what people can see for themselves), there must be, according to one researcher, a strategic management of the similarity of perceptions.

The fourth cue of attractiveness in the cyberworld is that you need to attract attention and show interest, usually with flatteries and verbal or multimedia compliments, such as virtual flowers. The fifth cue is humor. Humor is easily expressed in typed text, and those who excel at it increase their score on the interpersonal attraction scale.

One of the most important cues to online attractiveness, the sixth, is a certain level of intimacy, or self-disclosure. Because you have no nonverbal cues on which to rely, and because online partners may be relative strangers, the degree of self-disclosure depends on inferring how the other person feels and how to pursue the relationship further. Anonymity often allows, even encourages, less inhibited behavior and opening oneself to another with little or no fear of losing face.

Motives for Interpersonal Communication

In Daniel Goleman's book, *Social Intelligence* (Bantam, 2006), he claims that the brain is wired for sociability and connectedness—for altruism, compassion, concern, and rapport. In his words, "We are wired to connect. Neuroscience has discovered that our brain's very design makes it sociable, inexorably drawn into an intimate brain-to-brain linkup whenever we engage with another person."

The point of Goleman's book is that although everyone has needs that will vary with personality and moods, and that when we seek out others, we are trying to meet one or more of our interpersonal needs—pleasure, affection, inclusion, escape, relaxation, control, health, or cybermotivation—there is something much deeper—very extensive circuitry—that has established a biological need to interact. Let's briefly examine these other interpersonal needs for seeking out others.

Everyone has needs that will vary with personality and moods. When you seek out others, you are trying to meet one or more of the following interpersonal needs: pleasure, affection, inclusion, escape, relaxation, control, health, and cybermotivation.

Pleasure. We engage in a lot of interpersonal communication because it's fun. You chat online or gossip on the telephone with your best friend; you sit around and argue about sports teams with your buddies; you stop at the student center to have coffee, but also in the hope of meeting someone you know.

Affection. Whether it is expressed nonverbally (hugging, touching) or verbally ("I'm really glad you called me today"), affection is important to human happiness.

© 2009. Courtesy of JaxonPhotoGroup.

Affection is important to human happiness.

Unlike inclusion, affection is a one-to-one emotion.

Inclusion. Inclusion—involvement with others—is one of the most powerful human needs. Although nearly everyone has had the experience of being excluded, most people have had more experiences of being included. You may eat with a certain group at the cafeteria, go to parties at friends' houses, or join a club at the university. Belonging in this way is important to everyone's sense of well-being.

Escape. At one time or another, we all engage in interpersonal communication to try to avoid the jobs we are supposed to do. For example, before you begin writing your term paper, you decide to wander down the hall of your dorm to talk to a friend. A new form of escape is escape by computer. Chat rooms, e-mail, and surfing the Internet are particularly popular and enable you to escape without even going anywhere.

Relaxation. You often talk to your friends or families to relax and unwind from the activities of the day. You might sit with co-workers during a break, spend a few minutes with your spouse after work, or go out with a group of friends on the weekend.

Control. In a broad sense control means being able to make choices.

In the best relationships, the persons try to share control, which may change due to circumstances. For example, a couple we know moved to a new place where the wife had to commute two hours a day. This meant that she was not home to cook the evening meal, so her husband had to do it. He took control by reorganizing the kitchen to his liking—a legitimate action since he was now the main cook.

Researchers have found that people who have control over their own lives are healthier both mentally and physically. Students learn better when teachers give them some independence, and workers feel better about their jobs when they can make some decisions about how their work should be done. People who have the sense that they are in control of their lives are meeting one of their deepest needs.

Health. Research shows that people with strong social ties live longer than those who are isolated. If you have a romantic partner, frequent contact with friends and family, or involvement with volunteer or religious organizations, the social support systems you form assist you in keeping heart rate, hypertension, and stress hormones under control. Lonely people often view the world as threatening, and although they want to be connected, they both expect negative responses and engage in self-protective behaviors that are self-defeating. Experts advise lonely people to join a local club or organization just because of the health-protective effects.

Cybermotivation. In computer-mediated communication, there is often considerably less anxiety than in real-life interactions. There is usually increased motivation because engaging in CMC is entertaining and exciting. In addition, CMC can bolster self-esteem, and you can self-disclose with little possibility of losing face. There is anonymity if you want it, and an opportunity to be who you want to be as well. The high levels of affiliation and trust often result in higher levels of self-disclosure, associated with our having a heightened sense of who we are when communicating via CMC.

Talking to Each Other

Roles, Relationships, and Communication

All relationships are governed by the roles that the participants expect each other to play. Sometimes these roles are tightly defined; other times the participants have the flexibility to define them.

Often the roles you know best are those that are the most traditionally defined such as teacher and parent. Even though the people who work in these roles might want more flexibility than is allowed by traditional definitions, they often feel social pressure to conform to traditional roles and thus to traditional behavior.

Usually at the beginning of a relationship with someone your own age, you can choose the roles you want to play. Friends, for example, often decide on the role they will play within a friendship. Once the relationship is established, role expectations become fixed and friends expect each other to react in certain ways.

A critical question in a marriage is whether you want to play the role your father or mother played. If you don't, how will you set out to define your own role? Sherod Miller, a psychologist, says that once the partners give up old roles—the ones that were based on gender—they have to work out new ones: a process that leads to negotiating every aspect of their lives, especially when the first baby arrives.

Other psychologists who have studied marriage found that the most successful marriages are ones where the male partners listen to their female partners rather than reacting defensively to complaints and criticism. A husband's willingness to listen shows that he understands and respects his wife's needs, and when this occurs, there is a much better chance of marital stability.

As well as roles for your intimate relationships, there are roles for all aspects of your life and communication that work best in each of them. Your job is to find out which communication works best for all the roles you play. You will see, then, that much of your success in playing a role will depend on how well you communicate in that role.

Beginning Conversations: The Art of Small Talk

Have you ever felt nervous about entering a classroom where you didn't know any of the students? In many new social situations you might feel uneasy. You may wonder whether you will be able to begin a conversation and whether you will find people you like and, just as important, people who like you. The uncertainty you are feeling will probably be shared by other people in the room. How do you go about reducing it?

When most people begin conversations, they engage in small talk—social conversation about unimportant topics that allows a person to maintain contact without making a deep commitment. There are all sorts of conventions in small talk. Scholars who have studied conversation have found that it follows a routine that varies only slightly. Figure 4.1 shows this conversation pattern.

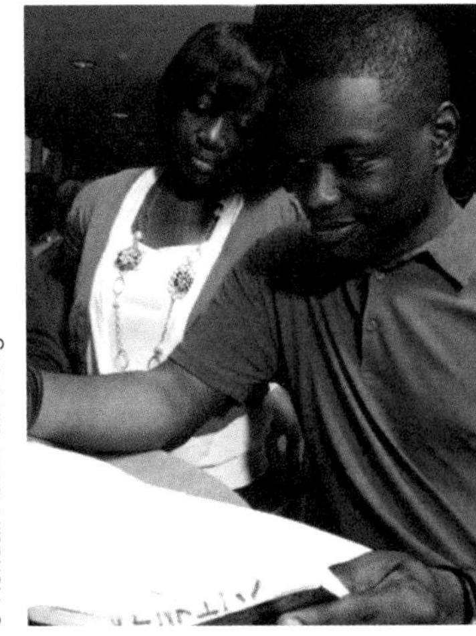

When most people begin conversations, they engage in small talk.

If you follow this figure from top to bottom, you will see how conversations begin, progress and end, in the sections that are numbered, there is some variation people may speak about one or more of these topics.

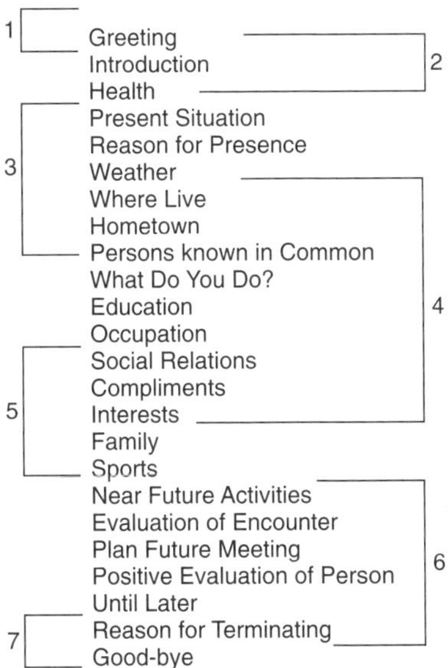

Figure 4.1 How People Begin Conversations

As you can see in this figure, many of the conversational responses are based on questions, some to find out information, others to establish common ground. Other questions are asked just to fill time or to be sociable. Since most people like answering questions about themselves, they are flattered when someone shows interest in them.

Dianna Booher, a business communications consultant, offers the following tips for beginning conversations:

- *Introduce yourself in a way that gives the other person a way to respond to you.* This approach will uncover what the two of you have in common, and it will probably lead to subjects for conversation. Here, for example, is how a person who was much younger than most of the guests at the university president's party introduced himself: "Hi, I'm Jim Dolan, and I'm the student member of the Board of Trustees at the university."
- *Give people a way to remember your name.*
- *Personalize your greeting.* If you know something about the person, try to work it into your greeting. For example, "I liked the presentation you made in class last week."

Booher also suggests that when you end the conversation, you do it as gracefully as possible. "Excuse me, I've enjoyed talking to you" is a short and graceful ending.

Because small-talk topics and questions are socially sanctioned, they create a safe meeting ground. They provide you with a chance to establish who you are with others. They also permit you to find out more about yourself through the eyes of others. Although you don't give away a lot of personal information in small talk, the image you give to others and the image you receive of them will let you know whether you want to see them again.

Bids and the Bidding Process

If you knew specifically what it was that holds relationships together, and you knew that it was within your control, would you change the way you conducted yourself in your interpersonal relationships? What holds relationships together are bids and the bidding process. A bid, according to John Gottman and his team of relationships researchers, "can be a question, a gesture, a look, a touch—any single expression that says, 'I want to feel connected to you.' A response to a bid is just that—a positive or negative answer to somebody's request for emotional connection." See Figure 4.2.

What determines your ability to bid and to respond to bids? Some people are likely to be better at bids and responses than others. There are three major influences at work. First, it may be a function of the way people's brains process feelings. Second, it may be a function of the way emotions were handled in the homes where people grew up. And third, it may be a function of people's emotional communication skills. These three influences can be complex, interacting variables. Despite their influence, however, sometimes just knowing what ingredients can influence a relationship, or just

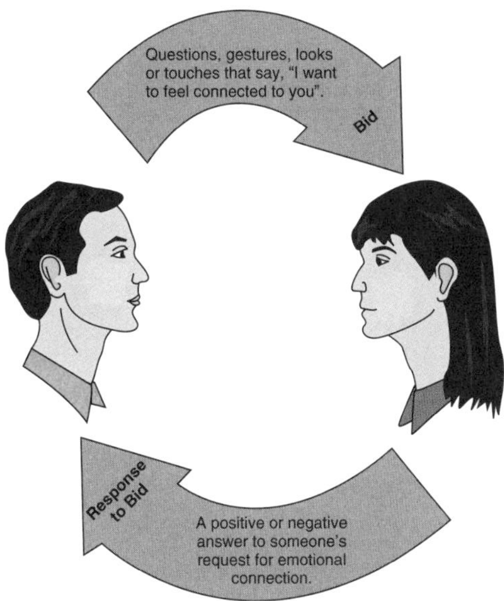

Figure 4.2 Bids and Responses to Bids

knowing specifically what you can do to make a relationship you cherish a success, is enough. Placing bids and responding to bids is a skill that can be learned, practiced, and mastered.

© Kendall Hunt Publishing

Some people are likely to be better at bids and responses than others.

How do bids contribute to relationship development? In successful relationships, bids for emotional connection are responded to positively. Bids from either relationship partner are neither ignored nor dismissed, whether they are simple or mundane. It is the simple and mundane bids that weave the fabric that forms the backdrop for all future bids. Many come nonverbally and include vocalizing, affiliating gestures (like opening a door or offering a place to sit), playful touching, facial expressions, or affectionate touching. Sure, some bids may be unseen, unheard, or overlooked just as some may be sent in a subtle, camouflaged, confused, or nonspecific manner. It is the overall pattern of behavior that is important, not necessarily any single, solitary bid. Remember, in most positive relationships thousands of bids take place daily.

Each encounter in a relationship is made up of many smaller exchanges—bids and responses to those bids. These exchanges of emotional information will either strengthen or weaken the connections between people, and these connections form the fabric we referred to earlier. Here, in the first example, the response to the bid is negative. In the next, the response is positive:

Hey, Chris. Did you get that class report finished?
Would you stop nagging at me? You sound just like my mother!

Would you get me a soda while you're up?
No problem. Do you want anything else?

The point is not the content, and the point has nothing to do with timing or circumstances. The point is that a positive response to a bid typically leads to continued interaction, and the chances for a successful relationship become better and better. And the reverse is just as clear. Negative responses to bids will shut down communication. Bids cease, and the relationship terminates.

How can you encourage bids? How can you make certain you respond positively to the bids of others if you choose to do so? Gottman and his researchers discuss six common sense ways to encourage and reinforce the bids of others. These are outlined in Figure 4.3.

Owned Messages

An owned message (also known as an I-message, as coined by Thomas Gordon) is "*an acknowledgment of subjectivity by a message-sender through the use of first-person-singular terms* (I, me, my, mine). 'Responsible' communicators are those who 'own' their thoughts and feelings by employing these pronouns."

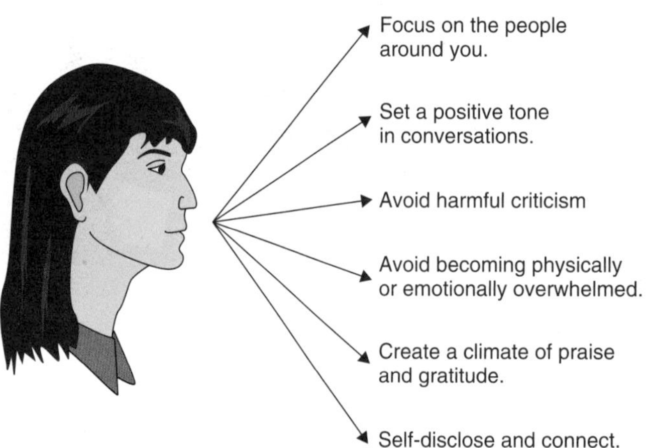
Focus on the people around you.
Set a positive tone in conversations.
Avoid harmful criticism
Avoid becoming physically or emotionally overwhelmed.
Create a climate of praise and gratitude.
Self-disclose and connect.

Figure 4.3 How to Encourage Bids

Owned messages tend to provoke less interpersonal defensiveness than you-messages, and they are useful for conveying negative information. Some simple examples of owned and unowned messages will demonstrate the difference. To say "You make me mad" is an example of an unowned message (a you-message) and, as is obvious, has the potential for creating defensiveness in another person. To say "I'm feeling angry" is an example of owning a message and is less likely to create defensiveness.

Gordon said owned messages can be called "responsibility messages" because those who send them are taking responsibility for their own inner condition (listening to *themselves*) and assuming responsibility for being open enough to share their assessment of themselves with others. In addition, they leave the responsibility for the other person's behavior with them.

What does an I-message look like? Gordon suggests a behavior/feelings/effects formula for constructing I-messages.

1. A description by the one concerned of the other's unacceptable (disruptive) behavior.
2. The feelings of the one concerned in reaction to the other's unacceptable behavior.
3. An explanation of how the other's behavior interferes with the one concerned's ability to answer his or her own needs.

Example: "Jennifer, when you leave things everywhere (1) I get frustrated (2) because I cannot do what I have to do (3)."

Remember as you use owned messages, any given behavior can be an asset or a liability, depending on the goal or situation. Interpersonal skills are competent when communicators employ them sensitively and sensibly according to the requirements of a particular social setting. Using owned messages is a skill that is generally perceived to be competent across contexts. It can increase your sense of control and responsibility, and control and responsibility are issues that are basic and paramount to interpersonal competence.

Self-Disclosure: Important Talk

To communicate who you are to other people, you have to engage in self-disclosure—a process in which one person tells another person something he or she would not reveal to just anyone.

The Importance of Self-Disclosure

Social penetration is the process of increasing both disclosure and intimacy in a relationship, and it is one of the most widely studied processes in relational development. The theory is that relationships become more intimate over time as partners disclose more and more information about themselves. When partners in a relationship are motivated, and when they exert the extra effort necessary not just to continue their relationship but to permit its growth, the relationship necessarily undergoes certain qualitative changes. Partners experience an additional sense of connectedness. At the same time, writes one researcher, "communicative transactions become increasingly interpersonal."

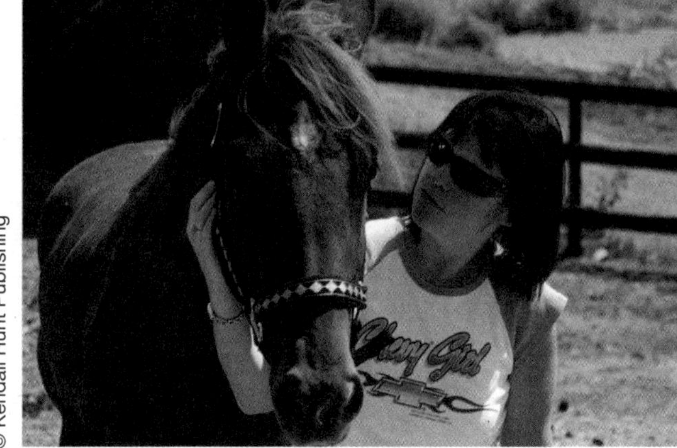

A strong sense of self leads to stronger interpersonal relationships.

Whether you want to encourage a relationship, hold it at the same level, or back off often depends on the information you get during the process of self-disclosure. Gerald Miller and his communication-research colleagues state that there are three kinds of information. The first kind is cultural information, which tells us about a person's most generally shared cultural attributes such as language, shared values, beliefs, and ideologies. Information at this level is as shallow and impersonal as is a greeting or good-bye. Knowing it allows you to perform acceptably in most social situations, but it is not very helpful when it comes to relationships.

The second kind of information is sociological and tells you something about others' social groups and roles. This level of communication allows you to be successful communicating with your doctor, dentist, lawyer, or hair stylist. You know something about their roles and affiliations, but you know relatively little about the person separate from his or her role.

Telling a secret might be one form of self-disclosure.

The third kind of information is psychological, which is the most specific and intimate because it allows you to know individual traits, feelings, attitudes, and important personal data. This is the type of information on which most of your predictions about relationships will be based.

It is through self-disclosure, then, that you meet someone who believes the way you do—that you discover a common interest, for example, which you can pursue in greater depth because both of you have some background and information to share. Such a partner is likely to react to situations and events the way you would, and you trust him or her enough to reveal even more about yourself.

Self-disclosure is important to relationships in other ways as well. You use it in the process of reciprocity: When someone discloses with you, your tendency is to self-disclose in return. You use self-disclosure for self-clarification—to clarify beliefs, opinions, thoughts, attitudes, and problems: "I thought you understood I was only kidding." You use it for identity management in attempts to make yourself more attractive: "I'm using a new fragrance; did you notice?" You use it for social control when revealing information may increase your control over the situation or a person: "I was given the authority to lead this group, and I think we should all stick to our agenda."

The Process of Self-Disclosure

One way to look at how the self-disclosure process operates was developed by Joseph Luft and Harry Ingham. Combining their first names, they labeled their model the **Johari Window** (see Figure 4.4). It is through the feedback process that you see yourself as others see you and others learn, too, how you see them. For example, giving and receiving feedback tells others how their behavior affects you, how you feel, and what you perceive just as it is a reaction by others, usually in terms of their feelings and perceptions, telling you how your behavior affects them. Because of the importance of this concept—self-disclosure—understanding the panes in the Johari Window offers a way to picture the entire process of giving and receiving feedback and, as necessary, make adjustments when relationships call for it.

The "Free to self and others" area—the **open pane**—includes information about yourself that you are willing to communicate, as well as information you are unable to hide (such as a blush when you are embarrassed). When students meet for the first time in a class, they follow the instructor's suggestion

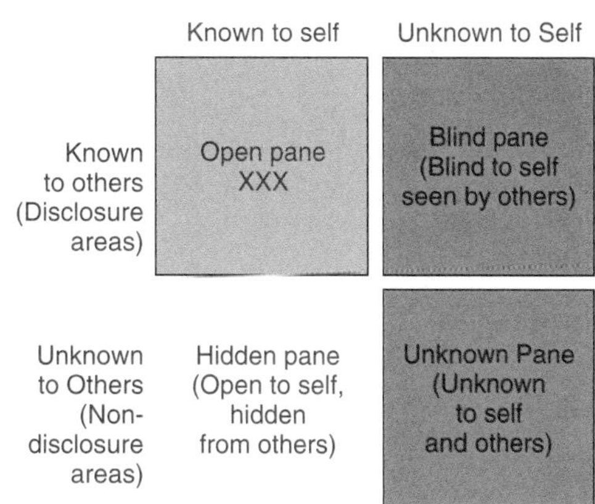

Figure 4.4 The Johari Window

and introduce themselves. Most of them stick to bare essentials: their names, where they come from, and their majors. When people do not know one another very well, the open pane is smaller than when they have become better acquainted.

The area labeled "Blind to self, seen by others"—the **blind pane**—is a kind of accidental disclosure area: There are certain things you do not know about yourself that others know about you. For example, when you interact in a group, group members will learn about you from your verbal cues, mannerisms, the way you say things, or the style in which you relate to others. They may know that you always look away from people when you talk to them, or they may find out that you always clear your throat before you speak.

The **hidden pane**—self-knowledge hidden from others—is a deliberate nondisclosure area; there are certain things you know about yourself that you do not want known, so you deliberately conceal them from others. Most people hide things that might evoke disapproval from those they love and admire: "I was a teenage shoplifter"; "I don't know how to read very well." Others keep certain areas hidden from one person but open to another: A young woman tells her best friend, but not her mother, that her grades are low because she seldom studies.

The **unknown pane** is a nondisclosure area; it provides no possibility of disclosure because it is unknown to the self or to others. This pane represents all the parts of you that are not yet revealed, such as your intrapersonal dynamics, childhood memories, latent potentialities, and unrecognized resources.

The disclosure and nondisclosure areas vary from one relationship to another, and they change all the time in the same relationship. Figure 4.5 shows how the Johari Window might look in a close

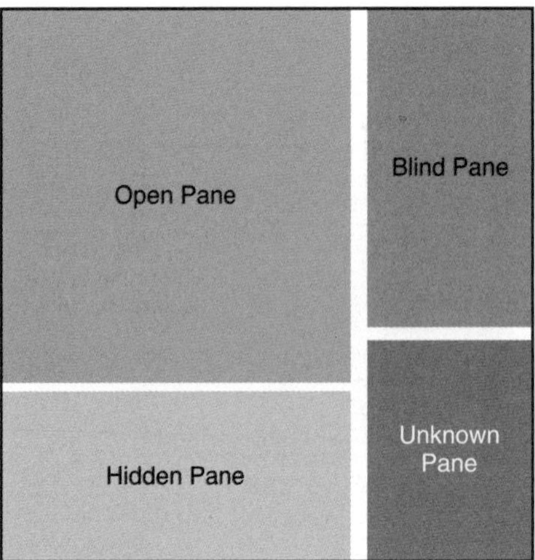

Figure 4.5 The Johari Window after a Relationship Has Developed

relationship. The open pane becomes much larger because a person is likely to disclose more. When disclosure increases, people not only reveal more information about themselves but also are likely to discover things about themselves that they had not known before. If you apply the Johari Window to each of your relationships, you will find that the panes are different sizes in each one. In other words, you are likely to be more self-disclosing in some relationships than you are in others.

Self-Disclosure and Intimacy: Rewards and Fears

Self-disclosure is the most rewarding when it leads to greater intimacy. Only intimate relationships give you a chance to really be yourself, to share who you are with another person. This kind of intimacy can be found in romantic relationships and among family members and close friends. One study has found that both men and women are willing to self-disclose to about the same degree.

Although in this chapter we take the position that self-disclosure is very important if you are going to have deep and satisfying relationships, we also acknowledge that many people fear the consequences of revealing themselves to another.

By telling someone you are vulnerable, you open yourself up to attack.

Fear of having your faults exposed. Self-disclosure in a relationship may lead to communicating that you are not perfect and exposing things from your past that you would rather keep hidden. Once your fears, anxieties, or weaknesses are known to another person, that person could tell them to others or use them against you.

Fear that your partner will become your critic. By telling someone you are vulnerable, you open yourself to attack. A wife, for example, tells her husband how bad she felt when she wasn't invited to the senior prom. One day when they are having a fight, he says, "Don't tell me how much people like you. You didn't even get invited to the prom!"

Fear of losing your individuality. Some people feel that if they reveal too much, they lose their sense of self, that there are private things that only they should know. This might be especially true during the years when teenagers are trying to gain autonomy from their families. Part of being autonomous is making decisions on your own and not telling everything to your parents.

Fear of being abandoned. Sometimes one partner is afraid that if the other knows something about him or her, he or she will be abandoned. For example, someone might not want to tell another about his struggle with alcoholism for fear that the other person will no longer love, accept, or want him.

When Should Self-Disclosure Occur?

Disclosure should occur only in relationships that are important to you. People who do not know you very well are likely to feel uncomfortable if you tell them too much about yourself too soon. Wait until you have some signs that a relationship has the possibility of developing further. For example, if someone seeks you out to invite you to go out with him or her, after three or four times this is a sign that the person wants the relationship to develop.

For disclosure to work, both parties must be involved in it. If one person does all the disclosing and the other party just sits back and listens, disclosure is not likely to continue. Remember that disclosure means taking a risk. You will never know how another person will respond to your openness until you give it a try. To avoid getting hurt, try testing the water before you plunge in. One way of doing this is to talk about a subject in general terms and see how the other person reacts before you talk about your own experience with it.

Finally, examine your own motives for self-disclosure. Why do you want the other person to know this information? Will it really enhance the relationship, or can it do harm? All of us have some secrets that we should probably keep to ourselves. Sharing them may cause injury or make the other person lose trust in us. Although some secrets are a burden to keep, it may serve the interest of the relationship to do so. Those in relationships who believe in full and complete disclosure with partners risk the possibility of damage and even loss.

Essential Elements of Good Relationships

Once you have begun using bids, owned messages, and self-disclosure, a relationship has truly begun and you need to "grow" it. Here, we will look at elements that draw people together: verbal skills, emotional expressiveness, conversational focus, nonverbal analysis, conversational encouragement, care and appreciation, commitment, and adaptation.

Verbal Skills

Partners in good relationships must have ongoing conversations, or dialogues, about the relationship itself. They must be able to search together for ways of reducing conflict, to discuss expectations they have of each other, and to explore anything else that might affect the relationship. In her article "Finding Real Love," Cary Barbor ends by saying, "Learning how best to communicate with each other and treat one another will help us enjoy loving, lasting relationships."

Not only do females begin talking earlier than males, on most national assessment tests they score well ahead of males in reading and writing, and many more major in English, comparative literature, and foreign languages than men. To make certain the playing field remains level, males may need to apply themselves more when it comes to verbal skills, because for partners to continue in a relationship, they must find mutually beneficial ways of communicating. Also, males need to alter their perception of relationships as stable, static commodities that never need discussion or reexamination.

Emotional Expressiveness

Gottman noted that your ability to bid and to respond to bids depends on the way your brain processes feelings, the way emotions were handled in your home, and your emotional communication skills. Christina Hoff Sommers claims that females' verbal skills "may be responsible for their superior emotional expressiveness." Her claim is supported by Daniel Goleman in *Emotional Intelligence* who says, "Because girls develop language more quickly than do boys, this leads them to be more experienced at articulating their feelings and more skilled than boys at using words to explore and substitute for emotional reactions such as physical fights." Not only are females more expressive and responsive to others, they "invite others into conversations." Once again, to level the playing field, males need to improve their ability at emotional expressiveness.

Achieving emotional expressiveness may require discussing points of conflict. This is particularly important if relationships are to be successful. Some people are conditioned to stay away from conflict. Childhood messages such as "Hold your tongue" and "I don't ever want to hear you talk that way again" lead us to believe that it's wrong to say words that other people do not want to hear. As adults, however, we have to recondition ourselves to discuss areas of conflict: Withdrawing from or avoiding conflict is too harmful to relationships.

Conversational Focus

A third factor likely to affect your ability to handle relationships is what you choose to talk about. Sommers claims that "Males, whether young or old, are less interested than females in talking about feelings and personal relationships." Researchers at Northwestern University analyzed the conversational focus of college students gathered around a cafeteria table. They discovered that 56 percent of the women's targets were intimates, close

Males are less interested than females in talking about feelings and personal relationships.

friends, boyfriends, and family members, but only 25 percent of the conversational focus of men was friends and relatives. When researchers simultaneously presented male and female college students with two images on a stereoscope, one of an object, the other of a person, male subjects more often saw the object while female subjects more often saw the person. Males need to increase their focus on feelings and relationships—to not only make their feelings know, but to make other people, especially their relationship partner, know how they feel about them and about their relationship.

Nonverbal Analysis

A fourth factor that will affect your ability to handle relationships is your ability to read between the lines, to analyze the nonverbal cues of the other person. Dozens of experiments confirm "that women are much better than men at judging emotions based on the expression on a stranger's face." Not only are women better at observing the nonverbal cues of others, they also "tend to give obvious visual and vocal clues to signal they are following what others say and are interested in it." Clues might include nodding their heads, smiling, establishing eye contact, and offering responsive gestures. Males need to increase their sensitivity to nonverbal cues. Because they are not conditioned to be as observant in this area, they need to be especially vigilant and aware.

Conversational Encouragement

Often, men listen to others without showing their feelings; they keep their responses and feelings to themselves, as noted in the section on emotional expressiveness. This can be interpreted as an unwillingness to listen or lack of interest. Women, on the other hand, encourage others to continue talking using listening noises such as "um, hmmm," "yes," "that's interesting," "so," "and," and so forth. They are encouragers, and these vocalizations not only reveal they are listening and interested, but they also prompt others to continue talking and to elaborate on their ideas.

Roger Axtell, in his book *Do's and Taboos Around the World for Women in Business*, quotes Kathi Seifert, group president of North American personal care products for the Kimberly-Clark Corporation, who says, "Women are naturally more caring, nurturing, and better listeners. They like to help and to respond to people's needs." Shmuley Boteach, dean of the L'Chaim Society, which hosts world figures and diplomats and concentrates on values-based leadership, says women "when speaking to their husbands, . . . stop talking in midsentence because they know they are not being listened to. They feel like a piece of furniture, and this experience of being ignored is a denial of their value. Their spirit is crushed." Fein and Schneider, in *The Rules for Marriage*, write "Learn how to listen without interrupting or offering advice, so that you can understand your spouse's perspective on things." Men need to open up more, show their feelings, listen better, and reveal their responses. It may help, too, if men view conversations as Mary Boone describes them: "The purpose of a conversation is not to *agree* with each other, it's to learn from each other on both an intellectual and emotional level."

Care and Appreciation

Scholars have found that people consistently use ways to communicate whether they want to have a relationship with a person or whether they want to avoid him or her. The approach people use most often to foster a relationship is expressing *caring and appreciation* for the other person. Typical remarks might be, "We had such a good time last night, I would like to see you again," or "I am so glad that we are friends"—bids expressing "I want to feel connected to you." The second most used technique is giving *compliments:* "That was such a funny joke you told last night," or "You look great today"—more bids seeking connection. The third technique they use is engaging in *self-disclosure*—(also a bid) telling someone something about themselves that they wouldn't tell most people: "I felt so bad when I failed the test," or "I really like her; I wish she would pay some attention to me."

Commitment

All relationships need **commitment**—a strong desire by both parties for the relationship to continue and a willingness of both parties to take responsibility for the problems that occur in the relationship. Trying to force a partner to make a commitment, however, is a waste of time, claims Adrienne Burgess, in an article "I Vow to Thee" in the *Guardian.* She says, "Not only does it (commitment) provide no guarantees, but it also causes resentment and hostility, which undermines any loving feelings. In relationships with a real future, therefore, commitment usually develops at much the same rate on both sides. But promises of commitment are meaningless in the long-term, too—commitment isn't an act of will (while we can promise to stay with someone physically, we can't promise the same emotionally), and isn't something we do in any active sense. Commitment is a spin-off from other things: how satisfied we are with our relationship; whether we see a viable alternative to it; and whether moving on would cause us to lose important investments (time, money, shared property, and children)."

All relationships have some kind of commitment as their foundation, but sometimes the partners to the commitment have different expectations. *Unconditional* commitments are those in which you commit yourself to another regardless of what may happen. [Marriage vows are often cited as examples of unconditional commitments; however, with divorce rates hovering around 50 percent,] it is clear that nearly one out of every two couples who accept the unconditional commitment do not fulfill it. *Conditional* commitments set forth the conditions of the commitment and carry with them the implication of

Marriage vows are often cited as examples of unconditional commitments; however, with divorce rates hovering around 50 percent.

"only if." "I will commit to you only if I do not find something better in the meantime," or "I will commit to you only if something extraordinary doesn't happen."

Although commitments are important and reassuring, it is perhaps better to accept them for what they are worth, based on the trust and faith in the person making the commitment and with hope for a positive future. However, it is best to prepare for the fact that most commitments are conditional, and it is unlikely that all conditions will be, or even could be, revealed or even known. Of course marriage should be an unconditional commitment, but we live in a transient society where planned obsolescence, endless technological advances, and instant millionaires guarantee a rapid and regular turnover of products, information, and fortunes; why should we expect relationships, including marriages, to be anything other than of short duration? Dreams, faith, optimism, visualizations, and confidence are all fine, but they really don't prepare you for a realistic conditional future. Only you can do that.

Adaptation

The time and effort dedicated to supporting, encouraging, and nurturing relationships—even well-established ones—must be spent in both introspection (the act of contemplating one's mental processes and emotional state in the relationship) and communication. Introspection and communication within relationships are foreign to conventional masculinity.

Verbal skills, emotional expressiveness, conversational focus, nonverbal analysis, conversational encouragement, care and appreciation, and commitment are tools that help hold relationships together. You need to speak, listen, negotiate, stay on course, and hold your relationship in warm regard. But if you can't adapt and adjust your skills and behaviors to the changes that occur, as introspection and communication will help you to do, these tools are useless. "After years of research," says one writer, "it turns out that what makes for highly adaptive people is their capacity to adapt."

The Internet and Interpersonal Relationships

MySpace, Facebook, and other social networking sites (there are hundreds) are the digital equivalent of hanging out at the mall. Students load the sites with photos, news about music groups, and detailed profiles of their likes and dislikes, and use them for blogging. Building a profile taps into students' desires for self-expression. Social networking sites are all about sharing, connecting, and community, and they have exploded in popularity because people want to state their case and talk about their lives. Like instant messaging and chat rooms before it, social networking has become a powerful way for people to communicate via the Web and another place for people to spend their time online.

How popular is the Internet for sharing, connecting, and maintaining a community? Michigan State University Professor Nicole Ellison and her colleagues studied how college students used Facebook and reports, "Checking Facebook is routine. When [students] first get on the computer, they check their e-mail. They log on to instant messaging. They check their Facebook."

There is another reason, too, for the popularity of MySpace or Facebook: "If you go to college," writes Susan Lipkins, an adolescent psychologist in Port Washington, New York, "and you don't have a full bunch of people on your MySpace or Facebook, then it's implying that there's something wrong with you. Listing your buddies and your friends is a way of establishing yourself, of feeling connected and feeling like you're accepted."

Perhaps a new definition of "friends" is needed—for example, "cyberfriends." Michael Bugeja, director of the Greenlee School of Journalism and Communication at Iowa State University and author of *Interpersonal Divide: The Search for Community in a Technological Age.* (Oxford University Press, 2005), says that real friends can never be replaced by online ones. "Friending," writes Bugeja, "really appeals to the ego, where friendships appeal to the conscience." Cyberfriends are social contacts, but those friends could develop into "more substantive" relationships, Bugeja says.

When you consider the amount of time students use cell phones, text-messaging, computers, video games, and instant messaging, the total amount of media content students are exposed to each day has, obviously, gone up. Because of multitasking, they are packing that content "into an average of six and a half hours a day, including three hours watching television, nearly two hours listening to music, more than an hour on the computer outside of homework. . ., and just under an hour playing video games." In his book *Conversation: A History of a Declining Art* (Yale University Press, 2006), Stephen Miller states that the proliferation of devices like iPods and use of the Internet have encouraged insularity. People on the go prefer communicating by text message, and something as antiquated as face-to-face interaction with someone you don't know can be irritating.

When face-to-face interactions become uncomfortable, employers and communications experts get anxious. Although this generation may be technologically savvier, will they be able to have a professional discussion? Sonya Hamlin, author of *How to Talk So People Listen: Connecting in Today's Workplace* (Harper Paperbacks, 1989), says students are losing natural, human, instinctive skills. "They're not listening," Hamlin writes. "With IM, you can reread six times before deciding how to answer. There's no improvisation, none of the spontaneity of phone banter or a face-to-face chat. Talk is a euphemism. We do it now in quotes."

There is no doubt that some students have turned text messaging into the meat and potatoes of their social interaction, according to Amanda Pressner in her article, "Can Love Blossom in a Text Message?" There is a gender difference in the way men and women use messaging to manage their relationships. Women use it to foster emotional interaction, and although both sexes will revise plans, break dates, or end relationships through text, Simeon Yates of Sheffield Hallam University, in research presented at the International Pragmatics Association, says, "Men are a lot more likely to do so." Why? Because text gets the point across "without a lengthy and uncomfortable explanation."

There are five basic levels of safety in using MySpace or any of the other social networking sites, according to Kevin and Dale Farnham in their book *MySpace Safety* (How-To Primers, 2006). The first is not to talk to strangers, and the second is not to post provocative pictures, comments, or blog entries. Even pictures you post can be altered or broadcast in ways you may not be happy about. What people are often unaware of is that whatever you say or post may be sending a message to people you don't know who may interpret it in ways you don't expect. A post, once posted, can never be retrieved; even when deleted, older versions can still exist on others' computers. Many people can see your page including your parents, teachers, the police, the college you are attending or may attend, or employers.

The third basic level of safety is never to post information that identifies you: your full name, Social Security number, where you live, your cell phone number, where you go to school or go for fun. This includes not mentioning sports teams or clubs you support. Never reveal your daily schedule, upcoming events you plan to attend, or where you hang out. Fourth, where possible, use the settings provided to limit who can view your information and posts. Fifth, and finally, use your brain. Think about the potential impact of what you are typing into the computer and onto the Net. If it's information designed just for a particular friend or friends, send it via e-mail. Thinking before you publicly post is wise for any public communication.

The Internet has proven its value in interpersonal relationships. Look at the benefits that cell phones, text messaging, computers with e-mail and instant messaging capabilities, and social networking sites provide in keeping families and friends in touch, even though spread over wide geographical areas. The Internet can affirm, reinforce, and assist in not just establishing but also maintaining good relationships.

Summary

Interpersonal communication, or one-to-one communication, is necessary for you to function in society. It helps you connect with others and develop empathy, and it contributes to your mental and physical health. Emotional intelligence is made up of being aware of your feelings, managing your emotions, motivating yourself, recognizing emotions in others, and handling relationships. All these have a direct bearing on strategic flexibility.

Strategic flexibility benefits from the contributions of perception, self-concept, and emotional intelligence because together these factors promote self-control, assist in managing emotions, and foster effective listening. They help you maximize your communication, enhance your credibility, and accomplish your intentions—all factors that make your use of the strategic flexibility format both more likely and more effective.

The ingredients that make up your attraction to others include physical attraction, perceived gain, similarities, differences, and proximity. In cyberattraction, those communicating depend on cues such as language, style, timing, speed of writing, and use of punctuation and emotions.

The motives for seeking out interpersonal relationships are pleasure, affection (warm emotional attachments with others), inclusion (involvement with others), escape, relaxation, control (getting others to do as you want them to or being able to make choices in your life), health, and cybermotivation. Cybermotivation involves less anxiety, entertainment, excitement, unwinding, forgetting about daily problems such as school and work, privacy, complete availability, relieving boredom, bolstering self-esteem, anonymity if you want it, and high levels of self-disclosure.

Relationships with others are governed by the roles you are expected to play. Small talk is an instrument of communication that renders people attractive. To engage in small talk plan ahead, ask open-ended questions, share feelings and information, and reconnect via your past.

Bids and the bidding process are the glue that holds relationships together. Bids can be questions, gestures, looks, or touches, and responses to bids are positive or negative answers to somebody's request for emotional connection. Owned messages are acknowledgments of subjectivity by message senders through the use of first-person singular terms. Their value is that they provoke less interpersonal defensiveness than you-messages.

Self-disclosure is the process of communicating oneself to another person, telling another who you are and what you are feeling. It can be understood through the Johari Window, which has four panes: open, blind, hidden, and unknown. As relationships develop and disclosure increases, the open pane gets larger.

The essential elements of good relationships include verbal skills, emotional expressiveness, conversational focus, nonverbal analysis, conversational encouragement, care and appreciation, commitment, and adaptation.

For many, the Internet serves as a valuable, important, and worthwhile form of communication because it promotes healthy communication and interaction; allows a strong support system; facilitates the social integration of otherwise marginalized people; reduces the costs of communication; increases the numbers of social contacts; offers opportunities for communication on an international level; and loosens social restrictions. The Internet affirms, reinforces, and assists in maintaining effective interpersonal relationships.

Name____ Date_______________

Exercises 4.1 Chapter 4 – Interpersonal Relationships

The Johari Window was developed by Joseph Luft and Harry Ingham as way of explaining and understanding the process of disclosure. For this assignment, you will *CONSTRUCT* the Johari Window. This visual exercise will allow you to understand the process of self-disclosure and self-perception.

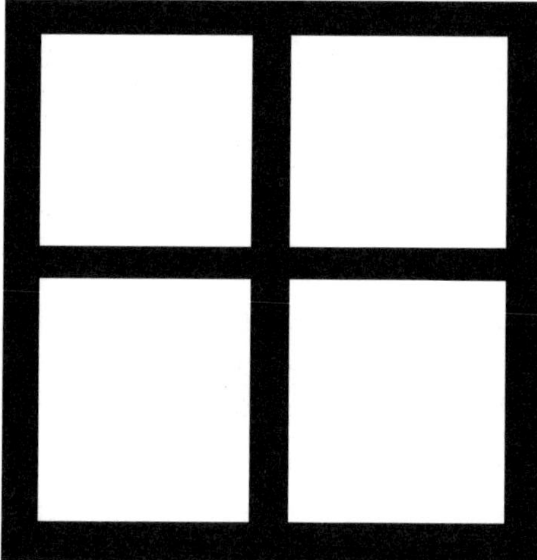

This assignment will either be constructed manually or digitally. In order to construct the Johari Window digitally, Microsoft Office or Adobe Office Suite programs can be used to design this project. Manually: Using a piece of poster board or cardboard, plywood etc., construct the background for the Johari Window. Use four sheets of 8 1/2 x 11 paper to make the (four) panes for the background. Label all parts. Use a 2 or 3 dimensional object that illustrates each pane and adhere the object to the pane in additional to labeling the pane. The object should personify the criteria for the pane. Make sure you label the horizontal (x) and vertical axis (y) on the window. Please write your name on the back of the board. In addition, make sure your images are good color representatives for each panel. You will be evaluated on your use of creativity.

Supplies Required:

Foamboard, Poster board, or Cardboard
Arts and Crafts supplies

5

Evaluating and Improving Relationships

After reading this chapter, you should be able to:

- ❒ Describe the stages of relationships coming together and coming apart
- ❒ Explain the essential, broad questions that need to be resolved before embarking on a serious relationship
- ❒ Clarify the different negative influences (six big issues) likely to come your way in an interpersonal relationship and how you might approach them
- ❒ Define defensive communication, explain how to avoid it, and distinguish between good and bad criticism
- ❒ List and explain the steps in conflict resolution and the roles that culture, gender, and power play

Key Terms

Aggressive talk
Assertiveness
Avoidance
Complaint
Conflict resolution
Costs
Criticism
Defensive communication
Empathy
Evaluative statements
Extrinsic costs
Extrinsic rewards
Indirect aggression
Instrumental costs
Instrumental rewards
Intrinsic costs
Intrinsic rewards
Regrettable talk
Rewards

5 Scenario

Carla bit her lip nervously as she sat on the bench in front of the waterfront. It was two in the morning, and she had a big math test in the morning, but she came as soon as Brian texted her.

Meet me at the waterfront n 10mins.
- BRIAN

She wondered what he wanted to talk about. She hoped everything was ok. For the past three months things had drastically changed between them. Carla met Brian at a step show on campus. He was sweet and very friendly. At first she was a little intimidated because he was a popular senior, but after a few weeks of talking on the phone and meeting in the cafeteria for lunch, Carla felt completely comfortable with him. So it came as no surprise to anyone that they started dating. Brian proved to be the perfect boyfriend. He met her after class for lunch and dinner; they studied together, and spent hours talking and spending time with each other. Brian was the first boy Carla ever loved, and that's why it was painful to witness this change in their relationship. As of late, Brian couldn't meet for dinner or spend that much time with her. At first, Carla thought it was because he was traveling around interviewing for medical school, but she sensed it was something else.

"Hey Carla." Carla was so deep in her thoughts she didn't even see Brian standing over her.

She smiled weakly, "Hey."

Brian sat down on the bench next to her. Carla was a little surprised by his appearance. His clothes were a little dingy, and he looked upset. He took her hand in his and leaned over and kissed her forehead. "How have you've been?"

"Not good," Carla answered truthfully. "I've been worried about you. Where have you been Brian?"

"I'm sor-"

“I’ve been calling you and texting you,” Carla stammered. “I have even been telling your roommate to tell you I’ve been looking for you.”

“Carla I know.”

“You know!” Carla yelled, standing to her feet. “Have you been ignoring me!?”

“Carla!” Brian yelled loudly, causing Carla to jump. Brian shook his head and closed his eyes. “Baby please, please sit down.”

Carla sat down, staring at him. Brian was always such a soft-spoken person. He never raised his voice. He never had the need to. Brian licked his lips before continuing, “Carla I’ve been under so much stress.”

Carla took his hand and rubbed it, “I know.”

“Shh, let me finish Carla,” Brian urged. “I’ve been busy with these interviews for school. Well, at my John Hopkins interview I ran into an old friend of mine, Samantha. We met at young doctors program back in high school,” Brian said. “We had a thing.”

Carla’s hold on Brian’s hand loosened, “Samantha?”

“We had dinner one night, and we reflected on old times. I ended up staying another week there. And all these old feelings came back.”

Carla threw Brian’s hand back into his lap, “What are you saying?”

“Carla, I wasn’t planning on falling in love with her,” Brian said, reaching for Carla.

Carla’s eyes widened. She swore she heard her heart break in her chest. “You’re in love with her?” Brian leaned back on the bench and said nothing. Carla nodded. As she wiped her tears, she felt the roughness. She looked down at the innocent promise ring that Brian brought her last winter. The ring was obsolete now. The promise the ring symbolized was now broken. Carla wiggled the ring off and dropped it in Brian’s palm, where her hand once rested.

“Here, hopefully you can keep your promise to her. Bye Brian.” And with that Carla walked away.

When Vicki Vance left for school, she thought she had found the love of her life. Kent was popular, good looking, athletic, and deeply in love with her. Everyone who knew them, knew they were meant to be together—a "match made in heaven" they would say.

Vicki wanted to pursue politics, and she needed a political science major with a communication minor to make it possible. She was looking forward to her undergraduate education because she thought the challenge would be both inspiring and exciting.

Kent did not want to go to college; he didn't do well in high school, and he found reading, studying, and learning dull and boring. His close friends were not planning to further their education, and he liked hanging out with his friends and working at the local department store.

Things between Vicki and Kent were great when Vicki first left for college, but staying in touch with Kent was tough because he didn't like using the Internet, never called just to say "hi," and didn't believe in writing letters. Kent was jealous of Vicki and all the male contacts she had made at school. He resented her continued education, and the tension was magnified when she discussed her classes, assignments, professors, and campus activities. Every time Vicki went home she noticed the distance between them had widened; consequently she went home less and less.

Vicki met Mark in her first political science class, when she had to borrow a pen from him to take notes. Mark would walk her from class, wait for her before class, and always select a seat next to hers in lecture. Soon they were hanging out together, and through their many discussions they discovered they had several similar interests and goals.

Vicki was feeling torn. She had known Kent for nearly four years. They were close, and she knew it would hurt him deeply if she even talked about Mark, much less told Kent they should try to cool their relationship. She felt she had to keep quiet, hope that things would change in some way, and wait for Kent either to find someone else or realize that their relationship was over. Vicki didn't like her decision. She had no guts, and she didn't like that. But she didn't want to hurt Kent.

It would be wonderful if, once relationships were formed, they remained healthy, happy, and rewarding for both partners. Unfortunately, this is not true. If you look at the divorce statistics alone you realize that many relationships don't last, but the fact that 50 percent of marriages end in divorce is *not* true either. By the 5th year of marriage, 10 percent end in divorce; by the 10th year, another 10 percent (or 20 percent cumulatively) end in divorce; another 10 percent end in divorce by the 18th year (30 percent cumulatively), and by 50 years, another 10 percent (or 40 percent cumulatively). These statistics vary by state, by region within states, and by religious affiliation, race, culture, and co-culture, too. Most marriages that fail, however, do so before the partners reach their mid-40s.

Partners often cite a number of reasons for their failed marriages, and these relate to failed relationships of any kind: poor communication, financial problems, lack of commitment, a dramatic change in priorities, and infidelity. Other reasons include failed expectations or unmet needs; addictions and substance abuse; physical, sexual, or emotional abuse; and lack of conflict resolution skills.

Five factors destroy relationships between young people:

1. The partners fail to anticipate differences resulting from diverse cultural backgrounds, family experiences, and gender.
2. They buy into the notion of a "fifty-fifty" relationship, honestly expecting their partner to meet them halfway.
3. They have been taught that humankind is basically good; therefore they fail to anticipate the conflict that will occur when either of two self-centered partners demands his or her own way.
4. They fail to cope with life's trials. Instead of standing together through hard times, they blame each other or think something is wrong with their partner and the way he or she handles difficulties.
5. They have a fantasy view of love. They quickly feel stuck with an unloving partner and become deceived into believing the next one will be better.

The purpose of this chapter is to discuss some of the ways to evaluate and improve relationships. We will first look at the stages of a relationship—both coming together and coming apart—which will help you better understand where a relationship is, especially if it is in one of the declining stages. We discuss some of the questions that need to be asked in evaluating relationships: questions to ask about yourself, your partner, rewards and costs, and relationship roles. In the section titled "Improving Relationships," we look at aggressive talk, regrettable talk, criticism and complaints, avoidance, defensive communication, resolving conflicts, and the communication strategies you can use in each case. We end the chapter by assessing and evaluating relationships established on the Internet.

Not all relationships are positive and should be saved. Some are highly resistant to any kind of alteration; thus, sometimes any kind of change that either partner attempts will fail.

Just one clarifying comment on the notion of a fifty-fifty relationship mentioned earlier: Often, couples honestly expect their relationship partner to meet them halfway. This is a fantasy. If you have no intention of committing yourself 100 percent to a relationship—on both an initial and an ongoing level—it is unlikely you will be successful. Fifty-fifty is unrealistic simply because when either partner cannot or fails to hold up his or her end of the bargain—which often happens when *any* other commitments come into play (like work or children)—the relationship fails.

The Stages of a Relationship

All relationships go through predictable stages as they grow and develop whether they are between romantic couples, friends, business partners, or roommates. Identifying the stages of a relationship and the attributes, stumbling blocks, and joys of each stage can help you negotiate it and the future with more success. The information is useful both to evaluation—do you like where you are, and is it bringing the rewards you want?—and to improvement—what can I do differently to achieve the goals I want?

Most relationships begin with superficial communication; then, if the people like each other, they take steps to see each other again. Mark L. Knapp, a writer and researcher who focuses on relationships, has found that relationships develop along rather predictable lines. He describes five stages in which relationships come together and another five in which they fall apart. Each stage is characterized by certain kinds of communication. Let's begin with a relationship that is coming together, using the example of Vicki and Kent.

Coming Together

Stage 1: Initiating

There are numerous stumbling blocks when people want to initiate a relationship. The *initiating* stage is characterized by nervousness, caution, and a degree of hesitation, but these are healthy stumbling blocks since engaging in the initiaring stage hears some risks, the primary one being rejection. The specific suggestions in the last chapter regarding small talk, conversation starters, and bids and responses to bids should be of some help at this early stage.

The joys of entering the initiating stage are enormous.

The joys of entering the initiating stage are enormous. It is like beginning any new adventure where the outcome is unknown, but the trip can make it all worthwhile. Joys, of course, include happiness or just finding a friend (companion, soulmate, intimate, confidante, playmate, kindred spirit, buddy, pal, chum, homeboy, homegirl, or colleague). Sometimes just the boost to your self-esteem is sufficient.

Michael Leviric and Hara Estroff Marano, in an article titled "Why 1 Hate Beauty," explain the importance of beauty in the initiating stage. They claim that "In the world of abstract logic, marriage is looked on as a basic matching problem with statistical underpinnings in game theory." They state, "Logic says that everybody wants to do as well as they possibly can in selecting a life partner. And when people apply varied criteria for choosing a mate, everybody ends up with a partner with whom they are more or less satisfied. Not everybody gets his or her No. 1 choice, but everybody winds up reasonably content."

Vicki and Kent were introduced by friends on both sides who not only knew they were perfect for each other but told them so. The buildup was so great, both knew the reality couldn't match the hype. Although Vicki didn't like Kent at first (she thought he was a showoff), he was a great dancer, and having a male friend who loved to dance was something Vicki found attractive. Often, first impressions tell you whether the other person is interesting enough for you to pursue a relationship. For Vicki and Kent, it was all the small talk and the bids and responses to bids that started to draw them together—even though the first impression may not have predicted movement to the next stage.

Stage 2: Experimenting

In the *experimenting stage*, people make a conscious effort to seek out common interests and experiences. They experiment by expressing their ideas, attitudes, and values and seeing how the other person reacts. For example, someone with strong feelings about the equality of all races might express an opinion to see whether the other person agrees or disagrees.

The stumbling blocks in stage 2 are fewer. Perhaps the biggest one is the length of time experimenting can take. Talking with someone superficially at school, work, church, or in a chat room can last for years. This is healthy because so many people do not take the time to get to really know another person, and decisions about moving to the next stage often occur without sufficient knowledge and understanding. Thus, it is good to draw out this stage. Most relationships never go beyond this stage and, it seems, many that did perhaps should not have—especially when no foundation for proceeding had been established.

The joy of stage 2 is that everything is generally pleasant, relaxed, and uncritical, although still a bit uncertain. Stage 2 is rewarding, too, if you like getting to know someone else: seeking common ground, testing the waters with self-disclosure, and providing personal histories. Vicki went through this stage with Kent, and it went on and on simply because dancing and talking together served their purposes early in the relationship, and, particularly, because Vicki was not especially impressed with him early on. Kent would tell Vicki about his family, upbringing, interests, and hobbies, but Vicki was reluctant to open up as much for some time.

Between Vicki and Mark, things were quite different. When Mark waited after class to walk her across campus, the two of them covered more territory getting to know each other in that first meeting than Vicki and Kent did in weeks. They not only found they had common interests and values, but they both decided they wanted to talk even more. Vicki and Mark engaged in an equal amount of self-disclosure. The connectedness and comfort they experienced with each other led them to going for coffee after class, meeting outside class to eat together, and going to campus events together. It was as if stage 1, initiating, was defined and completed when Vicki asked Mark for a pen, and Mark gave her his extra one.

Many relationships stay at this particular stage—the participants enjoy the level of the relationship but show no desire to pursue it further.

Stage 3: Intensifying

There are many joys associated with the *intensifying stage*. Vicki and Mark have discovered that they like each other quite a lot. They spend more time with each other because they are happy, loving, and warm. They listen to each other's iPods and spend free time together. Not only do they enjoy each other's company, but closeness is both wanted and needed, so they hold hands, kiss, and hug. They start to open up to each other—telling each other private things about their families and friends. They talk about their moral values. They also begin to share their frustrations, imperfections, and prejudices.

In the intensifying stage, closeness is wanted and needed.

Other things happen in the relationship. Vicki and Mark call each other by nicknames; they develop a "shorthand" way of speaking; they have jokes that no one else understands. Their conversations begin to reveal shared assumptions and expectations. Trust becomes important. They believe that if either one tells the other a secret, it will stay between them. They start to make expressions of commitment such as making plans together: "Let's go to Ocean City to work next summer." Expressions of commitment include buying gifts for each other or doing favors without being asked. They also start engaging in some gentle challenges of each other: "Do you really believe that, or are you just saying it?" Openness has its risks in the intensifying stage. Self-disclosure makes the relationship strong, but it also makes the participants more vulnerable to each other.

This is likely to be the only stumbling block—vulnerability. The key here is trust, and it underscores the value of the "getting-to-know-you" stages of initiating and experimenting. Trust often takes time to develop. When trust is secure, there is less chance of being wounded, injured, or attacked because of a breach of trust: Lack of fidelity, lying, or the sharing of personal information with others outside the relationship are breaches of trust and can cause deep wounds that are difficult to overcome.

Stage 4: Integrating

Vicki and Mark have reached the *integrating stage*—the point at which their individual personalities are beginning to merge. People expect to see them together, and they are unhappy when apart. If people see just one of them, they ask about the other. The friendship has taken on a specialness. They do most things together and reflect about their common experiences—the things they do together and have a lot of the same friends; their friends assume that if they invite one, they should invite the other. Each of them is able to predict and explain the behavior of the other. They feel like one person.

This is where the problem occurred between Vicki and Kent. Their relationship had already reached stage 4, integrating, before she left for college and before she met Mark. She and Kent had developed a deep and important relationship and suddenly, without warning, Mark entered the picture. Vicki and Mark have not reached this stage; however, given what has already occurred in their relationship, it seems as if it won't be very long. Those who reach this stage are usually best friends, couples, or parents and children. It is at this stage—if it hasn't happened before—that partners meet one another's family and friends.

Stage 5: Bonding

The last coming-together stage of a relationship is *bonding*. At this point, the participants make some sort of commitment that announces their relationship to those around them. An announcement of an engagement or marriage would be an example of bonding. In other cases, such as those between friends, the bonding agreement might be less formal—for example, agreeing to room together. Whatever form it takes, bonding makes it more difficult for either party to break away from the relationship. Therefore, it is a step taken when the participants have some sort of long-term commitment to their relationship.

Bonding occurs in nonromantic relationships as well. For example, good friends become best friends often because of some especially meaningful (good or bad) "bonding" experience. Dorm roommates are often randomly assigned, but nonromantic apartment mates, who must depend on each other for bill paying, housekeeping, amenities, and the like, are more likely to be successful if they've reached a bonded relationship before moving in together. Partners in business, in the police, or in the military—where success, reputation, and even survival depend on close bonding with and trusting of each other—each know exactly what to expect from the other in critical situations. This same kind of bonding can occur between dancers and ice skaters as well. Although there are times when you may want to believe it isn't so, sex on its own, or a "one-night stand" with a virtual stranger, is not bonding.

Advancing from Stage 1 to Stage 5

The five coming-together stages build on one another (see Figure 5.1). For a relationship to advance to the next stage, both parties must want the change to occur. Because most of us have only limited

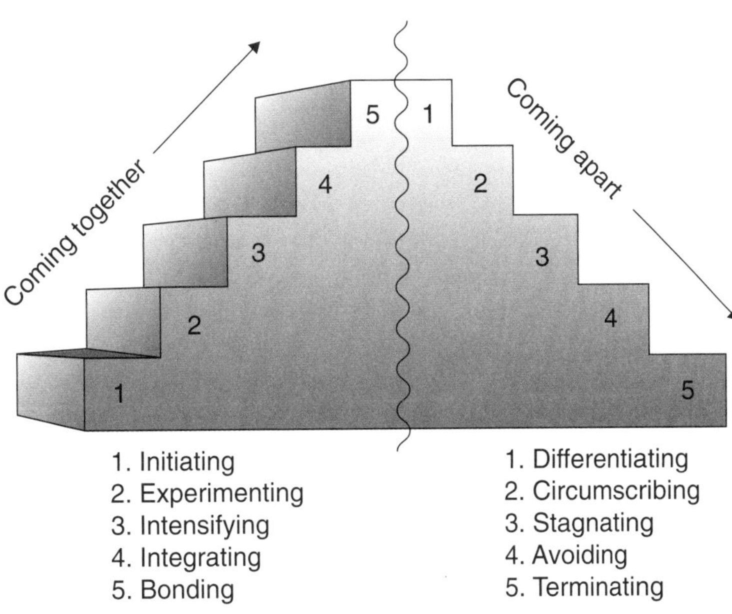

Figure 5.1 The Stages of a Relationship

time and energy for intense relationships, we are willing to let most of our relationships remain at the second or third stage. The first three stages permit us to become involved in friendship and to carry out normal social activities. The fourth and fifth stages, integrating and bonding, demand much more energy and commitment—they are reserved for very special relationships.

Bonding makes it more difficult for either party to break away from the relationship.

Notice that, for the most part, in the coming-together stages, the joys both partners experience outweigh the stumbling blocks that occur. In all stages you have five choices: to continue moving forward, to stagnate, to slow down, to go backward, or to exit. Since stage 3 is the first in which there is self-disclosure, moving from stage 2 to stage 3 is particularly sensitive. If one person opens up too quickly, the other might feel so uncomfortable that he or she will be unwilling to go on to a new stage in the relationship.

Coming Apart

For a relationship to continue, the participants must grow and change together. If they cannot do this in ways that are satisfying to both of them, the relationship will come apart. Although it is more satisfying to look at relationships coming together, we all know that relationships also fail. Relationships that are failing can also be described in five stages—stages that reverse the process of coming together. Notice as you read about each stage that stumbling blocks have eliminated any joy that was there.

Stage 1: Differentiating

Time has passed, and Vicki and Mark have been married for over a year. The first months were a little rocky, but now serious problems are beginning to emerge. Vicki likes to go out several nights each week; Mark wants to stay home. Mark likes to cook new and exotic food; Vicki wants to eat meat and potatoes. Even their love for movies is causing conflict: Vicki wants to see them as soon as they open; Mark wants to wait until they are released as DVDs so that they can watch them at home.

Vicki and Mark have entered the *differentiating stage*. The interdependence of their courting stage is no longer so attractive. Now they are beginning to focus on how different they are, and much of their conversation is about their differences rather than their similarities. There is noticeable arguing, with talk about being incompatible.

To some extent, the differentiating stage is a healthy phase that most couples experience. Many work out their differences by being autonomous sometimes and interdependent other times. For example,

Vicki and Mark go together to family gatherings and to parties. However, when Mark goes hunting, Vicki goes shopping.

The differences the two recognized and tolerated during the stages of coming together become focal points for discussion and argument. They can be worked out if they are not too great.

The most visible sign of differentiating is conflict. But differentiating can take place without conflict. Even if nothing specific is bothering the couple, they may discover, as they mature and find new interests, that they have less and less to talk about. Vicki, for example, reads the newspaper every day and follows world events. Mark, on the other hand, gets his news from the Internet and finds it too depressing to talk about. Each experiences slight loneliness because the two of them are no longer as close as a couple, and regarding the relationship itself, there is some confusion and inadequacy creeping in. Where is the relationship going? How long can it go on like this? Am I at fault? These are a few of the questions that one or the other partner may be considering; usually they are internalized and never expressed at this stage.

Stage 2: Circumscribing

When a relationship begins to fall apart, less and less information is exchanged. It seems better to stay away from points of conflict in the relationship in order to avoid a full-scale fight. Thus this is called the *circumscribing stage.*

Now conversation is superficial; everyday matters are discussed: "Your mail is on the desk." "Did I get any telephone calls?" "Do you want some popcorn?" The number of interactions is decreased, the depth of discussions is reduced, and the duration of each conversation is shortened. Because communication is constricted, the relationship is constricted.

Most people who find themselves in this stage try to resolve their problems by discussing the relationship itself. In response, the negative turn in the relationship might change. For example, Mark could go out to a movie with Vicki, and Vicki could agree to try some different food. In other cases, discussion about the relationship might reveal greater differences between the participants. In such cases, discussion about the relationship leads to even more conflict, so the participants limit discussion to "safe" topics. Vicki and Mark, for instance, stay away from the topic of having children because they know they will fight about it.

Often, people at this stage pursue different activities. Sometimes, too, they act aloof from each other. These experiences reveal coldness and distance. With respect to each other, partners are uncaring, and one or the other may become depressed or frustrated, feeling unloved and misunderstood.

Persons who are in this stage often cover up their relationship problems. Although they might reveal problems to very close friends, in social situations they give the appearance of being committed to each other. They create a social or public face—in essence, a mask.

Stage 3: Stagnating

The *stagnating stage* is a time of inactivity. The relationship has no chance to grow, and when the partners communicate, they talk like strangers. The subject of the relationship itself is now off limits. Rather than try to resolve the conflict, the partners are more likely to think, "Why bother to talk? We'll just fight, and things will get even worse"; thus, for self-protection, they give short answers to questions.

How long this stage lasts depends on many things. If Vicki and Mark lead busy lives and just come home to sleep, they might go on in this stage for months or even years. However, if Mark stays home and broods about the relationship, he may look for some kind of resolution to their conflict. Most couples whose relationship reaches this stage feel a lot of pain. The partners may find it hard to separate and may hold on to the hope that they can still work things out. Either partner at this stage may feel unwanted, scared, bored, and sentimental.

Stage 4: Avoiding

The *avoiding stage* involves physical separation. The parties avoid face-to-face interaction. They are not interested in spending time together, in building any kind of relationship, or in establishing any communication channels.

This stage is usually characterized by unfriendliness, hostility, and antagonism. Sometimes the cues are subtle: "I only have a minute. I have an appointment." They can also be direct and forceful: "Don't call me anymore" or "I'm sorry, I just don't want to see you." Often, responses are "I don't care" and "I don't know." If communication occurs, it covers general matters only; there is no talk about the relationship.

In relationships where physical separation is impossible, the participants may act as if the other person does not exist. Partners eat in silence, stay busy, and, if possible, spend a lot of time away. Each one carries on his or her activities in a separate room and avoids any kind of interaction. In the case of Vicki and Mark, Vicki might sleep in the bedroom and Mark on the living room couch. Often, partners feel some sense of nervousness, as well as helplessness and annoyance.

Stage 5: Terminating

In the *terminating stage*, the participants find a way to bring the relationship to an end. Differences are emphasized, and communication is difficult and awkward. Each party is preparing for life without the other. They may talk about staying in touch and discuss what went wrong. A goal at this stage may be to divide up their belongings. There are feelings of unhappiness, but these are accompanied by a sense of relief. Often one partner is lonely or scared because of having to face life alone again.

Some relationships cannot be entirely terminated. Partners who have children might terminate their relationship with each other as marriage partners but decide to continue in some kind of relationship as parents to the children. The more amicably this can be done, the better it is for the children involved. Partners might set down a list of rules that will govern the new relationship. When the termination is a divorce, the court is the one that establishes the rules.

Sociologist Diane Vaughan has studied the patterns that occur when a relationship is about to end. She says that one member of the couple, realizing he or she is unhappy, begins the process of ending the relationship. This person typically begins by finding alternatives—often in the form of a transitional person. Although the transitional person might be a romantic interest, the person could also be a minister, a therapist, or a good friend. When one partner begins to find satisfaction elsewhere, the couple's relationship becomes less endurable. At this point the dissatisfied person lets the other know of his or her discontent through body language and words.

Finally the time comes when the dissatisfied person lets the partner know that he or she wants to end the relationship. The partner typically feels betrayed, hurt, and shocked—and is often unprepared. Vaughan says that during the breakup, both partners suffer emotional pain and go through the same stages of disengagement: the process just happens at different times for each of them.

Evaluating Relationships: Asking the Right Questions

One reason many relationships fail is simply that people seldom take the time to ask the essential questions—especially the questions that should be asked *before* embarking on a serious relationship. It is true, of course, that some of us begin a relationship with no intention of its becoming serious and then discover it has evolved to that level without a decision ever being made. Perhaps some of the questions in this section will help you if this happens.

Our purpose is not to destroy spontaneity, surprise, and discovery, but to deal with some of the broad issues that often lead relationships to fail. When these are resolved to your satisfaction, and you have taken all the necessary precautions that would predict a satisfactory future partner, there will be plenty of room for spontaneity, surprise, and discovery.

Some of us begin a relationship with no intention of its becoming serious and then discover it has evolved to that level without a decision ever being made.

Ask Yourself Questions

There are three questions to ask yourself. The first has to do with fear of commitment. Are you concerned about the idea of forever? Do you fear you could make a mistake in the person you choose? Do you fear a loss of your freedom or autonomy? Are you afraid of a bad marriage—like your parents, for instance? Do you fear you would be a bad mate?

Antoinette Coleman, in her online newsletter *The Art of Intimacy*, states that "If you answered yes to any of these, it would be a good idea to begin working to understand where these feelings come from. Once you understand them better, you can choose to address them." It may simply be that you are not ready to make any long-term commitment, and you know at this point in your life that you just need more time, or more emotional growth.

The second question is about fear of forming a relationship with another person. How many dating experiences have you had? Do you tend to rush into relationships, or do you move them along with thought and careful decision making? Can you live with out a partner? Can you envision yourself in the immediate future with a partner? Do you really know and like yourself? Do you believe you could have a successful relationship?

The third question asks about making a commitment to *this* particular relationship and to *this* particular person. Is there a genuine connection? Do you have a vague feeling that something is missing? What is the quality of your intimate relating—*not* how often or how good the sex is, but how open, sharing, and real your interactions are with each other. Does it seem that the two of you are just killing time? Does your partner want what you want? Do you seem to be inconsistent in your level of contact and affection? Is your partner still not over a past relationship? Do you (and does your partner) really know what you want?

Ask Questions about Your Partner

Let's say that through frequent contact and increased levels of self-disclosure you have discovered a potential relationship partner, but you don't know whether this partner is even ready for a relationship. What questions should you ask yourself to determine a partner's readiness? Six are absolutely essential:

1. Is this person able to communicate with you openly and honestly?
2. Does this person appear to have a strong self-concept?
3. Is this person aware of the time and effort required to have a long-term, loving relationship?
4. Is this person willing to put forth the necessary time and effort along with you to make a long-term, loving relationship possible?
5. Does this person see the commitment necessary for a long-term, loving relationship as *more than simply fifty-fifty?*
6. Is this person prepared—as you are—to make a relationship partner his or her *first* priority, after himself or herself, in life?

If the answer to any of these questions is "no," then this partner is probably not for you.

Here is a key point: Entering into a relationship hoping that the other person will change, or thinking that you will change the other person, "is not a solid foundation for a loving, committed relationship. In most cases, with rare exceptions, you are wasting your time." Instead, get into the habit of looking for what you can love and appreciate about your partner, rather than how he or she needs to change or be fixed, and it will change the whole dynamic of your relationship.

Ask Questions about Rewards and Costs

In Chapter 4 we introduced a small portion of Altman and Taylor's social penetration theory. Their theory is based on social exchange—the idea that relationships are sustained when they are relatively rewarding and discontinued when they are relatively costly. Rewards are the pleasures that result from being in a relationship. Costs are the problems. The essential question is, "Do the rewards outweigh the costs?" or, phrased a bit differently, "Are you willing to live with the costs considering the strength of the rewards?" When you know your relationship partner well—see the Consider. This box—it is easier to weigh rewards and costs.

Altman and Taylor listed three types of rewards and costs: extrinsic, intrinsic, and instrumental. **Extrinsic** means outside the relationship. **Intrinsic** means within the relationship. **Instrumental** refers to the basic exchange of goods and services. To make sense of these, let's put them into the context of a relationship you have that has not yet progressed to the level of sexual intimacy. Whether or not you want to take it to that level depends on weighing the rewards and costs.

Extrinsic rewards: You like the people your partner has introduced you to and the friends he or she hangs out with.
Intrinsic rewards: You appreciate the attention, warmth, and affection you gain from being in the relationship.
Instrumental rewards: You know that if you decide to raise the current level of intimacy, one of the rewards when you move in with your partner (which you have already discussed) is that you will share both the rent and the furniture.
Extrinsic costs: You are not going to have as much time for your friends, and you are going to have to share them with your partner.
Intrinsic costs: Not only will you feel obligated to return the attention, warmth, and affection you are receiving—probably at an increased level if the level of intimacy increases—but you will also spend time listening, communicating, and self-disclosing.
Instrumental costs: You will have to share your belongings.

Now it is up to you. Often, it is good to actually list the rewards and costs honestly not just so you can compare them but so that you can think about them specifically and over time.

Mira Kirshenbaum, a therapist who works with families and couples, holds that since the dynamics of a relationship are constantly shifting, it is better to ask questions about the relationship that go right to the heart of it. For example, she maintains that the answer to a question like the following will tell a lot about a relationship: "Does it seem to you that your partner generally and consistently blocks your attempts to bring up topics or raise questions, particularly about things you care about?"

Ask Questions about Roles

Roles are important simply because to be happy and content in a relationship, both parties must be satisfied with the roles and expectations. Roles may evolve naturally and spontaneously for males, but for females, they must be discussed and negotiated.

One of the questions we asked students in interpersonal-communication classes had to do with relationship expectations: "What role do you expect to play in any future intimate relationship you have?" Sometimes students referred to the roles their parents played, sometimes they offered a politically correct response such as, "That would have to be worked out with my future partner," and sometimes a few would take the traditional stance that males were the breadwinners and females the homemaker raising the kids. Most female students wanted to play a role equal to that of their partner and have an equal say in how roles would be determined.

In successful relationships, the participants have usually worked out their roles and expectations. But circumstances change through the course of a relationship, and if the communication channels are not available and open, unexpected problems can occur down the road.

Consider an example. Doug and Rita had never directly discussed roles; things were essentially equal. Then unexpectedly Rita found herself pregnant, but Doug and Rita never stopped to talk about how their roles would change once the baby was born. Who was going to take care of the baby during the day? Were there going to be any changes in school commitments or workloads, and who was going to make changes if necessary? Who was going to get up at night when the baby cried? Who would adjust his or her schedule if the baby became sick?

There is no way to ask all the questions that will prepare you for changes likely to occur in relationships. There are, however, some questions you could ask while dating that might give you important information about how your partner views relationship roles. For example, "What do you want in a wife (or husband)?" Many women think males want a maid—a wife who stays home, cooks, cleans, and isn't too smart; however, many males *say* they want, more than anything else, a capable, assertive, happy partner, not just a housekeeper. On the other hand, some men think women want a partner who is a big, burly, hairy, handsome "he-man" with money. Most women, however, want a loving, gentle, warm, caring, intelligent, capable, self-confident man who is willing to stand up for his beliefs.

Some other key questions might be, "Who do you think should be responsible for financially supporting the family?" or, a related question, "Who do you think should be responsible for caring for the house and family?" "If you were the husband of a working woman, would you be willing to do an equal share of the housework and child care?" "What determines who will be the boss in a marriage?" "Do you think it's necessary for a couple to be roughly equal in ability in love, in neediness, and in education to have an egalitarian [equal] relationship?"

Both men and women are likely to know how their partner would want them to respond. In the period of infatuation and, often in the early stages of a loving relationship, partners want to please each other. That is sufficient grounds for observing the behaviors of possible future partners to see whether what they say is supported by activities with which you agree—that is, that there are no mixed messages.

Can you ask "too many questions"? Never. Just don't act as though it's an interview. Spread them out over a sufficient amount of time, work them in among other thoughts and feelings, and remember a key point: Often men do not want to open up, share feelings, or even communicate. Accept this as a signal. Do you want to have a long-term relationship in which there is little or no communication?

Improving Relationships: Using Communication Strategies

Negative influences are a natural and expected part of relationships. It is not the frequency of their occurrence; it is how carefully, delicately, and respectfully they are resolved to *both* partners' satisfaction that is important. All the motivation and willingness to communicate, assertiveness training, owned messages, and listening and communication skills in the world cannot prevent relationships from becoming fertile ground for silence and stonewalling, for anger and frustration, or for just plain hard times. No speech, article, book, or expert can protect you from the range of painful emotions that make you human. The greater the number of skills and behaviors you have in your toolbox, however, the greater the likelihood that you will be able to face and resolve all the negative influences that come your way. This is where your ability in and use of strategic flexibility has its real payoffs—not just in holding your relationships together (the big picture), but in satisfactorily resolving all those daily, nuisance-type issues that seem to provoke and keep you in a negative frame of mind.

In this section we will look at six of the big issues: aggressive talk and aggression, regrettable talk, criticism and complaints, avoidance, and defensive communication. In the final sections of this chapter we will focus on resolving conflicts and the role of the Internet.

Aggressive Talk and Aggression

Aggressive talk is talk that attacks a person's self-concept with the intent of inflicting psychological pain. This kind of talk includes disparaging words such as *nigger, faggot*, and *slut*, and phrases such as "You are so stupid," or "You are an inconsiderate idiot." Aggressive talk makes recipients feel inadequate, embarrassed, or angry, and because of the impact it has on receivers, it is seldom justified. Not only does aggression breed aggression, but it can escalate, and verbal aggression can quickly lead to physical aggression. People who can control verbal aggression are those who can recognize their anger and control it when it occurs—usually by giving themselves a cooling-off period.

When aggressive talk leads to aggression—an unprovoked attack—in relationships, often the relationship is doomed. People tempted to use verbal aggression should be aware that such actions can destroy relationships.

A more subtle act, and one we are often not aware of committing, is **indirect aggression** (sometimes called *passive aggression*)—when aggression is a mental act (usually characterized by manipulation, scheming, cunning, deviousness, or conniving). People who use this form of communication often feel powerless, and they respond in the only way they can, by doing something to thwart the person in power. For example, if your mother asked you to clean the kitchen, and you did a poor job so that she would never ask you again, you are using passive aggression. Or, if you were forced to go to college, and you flunked all your courses just to show your parents their decision was wrong.

It is difficult to deal with those who are aggressive, and if the acts of aggression are excessive, uncontrolled, or frequent, it may be necessary to seek professional assistance—for you, your partner, or the two of you together.

If your goal is to deal with the aggressive talk of a partner, your first step is to make every effort to see the situation *from his or her point of view:* with empathy. When the time is appropriate—usually *not* immediately after the aggressive talk has occurred because emotions have been triggered and normal conversation may not take place—you might begin a conversation by asking your partner to explain his or her point of view. Encourage him or her to talk about underlying assumptions, beliefs, or background factors that may have led to the behavior you are upset about. Summarize the person's words and *emotions* from his or her point of view (so that he or she agrees you understand it). Understanding the other's situation, point of view, and reasons for beliefs and behavior is usually the major task to accomplish.

If it is impossible to have this kind of conversation, it might be helpful for you to imagine a scenario that will allow you to defuse your anger. Or you may interpret your partner's aggressive talk as a legitimate need to take care of himself or herself. If you can focus on evidence from the present or past that proves he or she loves you and is not trying to hurt you, it is easier to forgive the behavior, forget about it, and move on.

Regrettable Talk

Regrettable talk is talk you regretted after saying it. You invited someone to help you move into a new place, and he tells you he has just been diagnosed with cancer and will be in the hospital. Of course you couldn't have known that, but you are now embarrassed for having asked him. Regrettable talk might have hurt someone, or it may have shared a secret you were not supposed to tell.

Mark Knapp, Laura Stafford, and John Daly, all communication researchers, studied regrettable words. They discovered that 75 percent of regrettable words fell into five categories. The most common was the blunder—forgetting someone's name or getting it wrong, or asking "How's your mother?" and hearing the reply "She died." The next category was direct attack—a generalized criticism of the other person or of his or her family or friends. The third was negative group references, which often contained racial or ethnic slurs. The fourth involved direct and specific criticism, such as "You never clean house," or "Don't go out with that guy; he's a sleazeball!" The fifth category—revealing or explaining too much—included telling secrets or reporting hurtful things said by others.

When people were asked why they had made the remark in the first place, the most common response was, "I was stupid. I just wasn't thinking." Some said their remarks were selfish—intended to meet their own needs rather than the other person's. Others admitted to having bad intentions. They deliberately set out to harm the other person. On a less negative level, people said that they were trying to be nice but the words just slipped out. Some people said that they were trying to be funny or to tease the other person, and the words were taken in the wrong way.

How did the people who were the objects of the regrettable words respond? Most often they felt hurt. Many got angry or made a sarcastic reply. Some hung up the phone, walked away, or changed the subject. Others were able to dismiss the statement or to laugh about it. When the speaker acknowledged the error, the listener often helped to "cover" the incident by offering an explanation or justification.

One of the most interesting aspects of this study addressed whether regrettable words had a negative impact on the relationship. Of the respondents, 30 percent said there was a long-term negative change, 39 percent said there was no change in the relationship at all, and 16 percent said that the change was positive—for example, "In the long run. I think our relationship is stronger since it happened."

Criticism and Complaints

Most people experience anger from time to time in close relationships. Anger does not have to destroy a relationship: University of Michigan researchers found that the average couple has one serious fight a month and several small ones. John Gottman, psychologist at the University of Washington, found that anger is not the most destructive emotion in a marriage, since both happy and miserable couples fight. He calls the real demoris "the Four Horsemen of the Apocalypse"—criticism, contempt, defensiveness, and stonewalling.

Most people experience anger from time to time in close relationships. Anger doesn't have to destroy relationships. It is *how* people fight that makes the difference.

Experts agree that it's *how* partners fight that makes the difference. The most effective kind of anger is that which expresses one's own feelings while conveying concern for one's partner. Since most anger begins with a complaint or criticism, let's look at the most effective way to express it.

Criticism is a negative evaluation of a person for something he or she has done or the way he or she is. In more distant relationships, criticism usually originates from a higher status person and is directed toward one with lower status. If the participants are equals, such as friends or a couple, criticism could come from either partner.

Researchers have discovered that criticism has five targets: appearance (body, clothing, smell, posture, and accessories); performance (carrying out a motor, intellectual, or creative skill); personhood (personality, goodness, or general ability); relationship style (dealing with others); and decisions and attitudes (opinions, plans, or lifestyle). They found that the target of most criticism is performance, followed by relationship style, appearance, and general personhood.

The researchers also looked at what the recipients perceived as "good" and "bad" criticism. Most of the study's respondents believed that those who did not know them very well didn't have the right to criticize them. They were much more likely to identify criticism as bad if it was given in front of others rather than privately.

Criticism was labeled "bad" if it contained negative language (profanity or judgmental labels such as "stupid jerk") or if it was stated harshly by screaming or yelling. It was better received if it was specific and gave details on how to improve ("If you are going to be home after midnight, please call and let me know where you are"). Criticism was considered good if the person who made it also offered to assist in making the change or if its receiver could see how it would be in his or her best interest to change ("If you called me when you are going to be late, I wouldn't be so upset once you got home"). Finally, good criticism places negative remarks into a broad positive context ("If you called, it would reduce a lot of tension and anxiety in our relationship").

A complaint is an expression of dissatisfaction with some behavior, attitude, belief, or characteristic of a partner or of someone else. A complaint differs from criticism in that it is not necessarily directed at any specific person.

In studies of complaints between partners, researchers found that, as with criticism, some responses to complaints were more useful than others. First, when complaints are trivial, they can probably be ignored. "This spaghetti is overcooked," or "Why do I have to be the only one to shovel the snow?" are trivial complaints. Second, a complaint should not be directed at anyone specifically. When you say, "Why doesn't anyone ever close doors?" you are not pointing to any one person, so the guilty party can change his or her behavior without losing face. Third, a complaint should be softened or toned down so that the complainer can express his or her frustration or dissatisfaction without provoking a big argument. Fourth, if the complaint is serious, the partners should discuss it and try to arrive at a solution or a compromise before the complaint turns into a serious conflict.

The most useful communication strategy for dealing with criticism is to use owned messages, as discussed in Chapter 4. Rebecca Cline and Bonnie Johnson's research emphasized the importance of making the careful language choices that owned messages require. People react negatively and defensively when conversation is filled with you-messages such as "You always blame others for your problems," or "You need to have the last word, don't you?"

Avoidance

Many people who are in unsatisfying relationships try to dodge any discussion of their problems. Some people use silence; others change the subject if their partners try to begin a discussion. Often people who refrain from discussing relationships are trying to avoid any kind of conflict. The downside of avoidance—refusing to deal with conflict or painful issues—is that unless the problem is discussed, it probably will not go away.

The best communication strategy to use with respect to avoidance is a combination of owned messages—"I need to deal with the conflict we're having. I cannot continue avoiding talking about it, because it eats away at me and makes me angry"— and assertiveness. Assertiveness is taking the responsibility of expressing needs, thoughts, and feelings in a direct, clear manner. "I know you think that if we don't talk about it, it will just go away, but I know it's going to come up again. I want to talk about it right now [assertiveness]."

Defensive Communication

Defensive communication occurs when one partner tries to defend himself or herself against the remarks or behavior of the other. The problem with defensive communication is that we are so busy defending ourselves that we cannot listen to what the other person is saying. Also, defending ourselves is dealing with past behavior; it gives us no chance to think about resolving the problem.

Table 5-1 Categories of Defensive and Supportive Behavior

Defensive Climate	Supportive Climate
1. Evaluation	1. Description
2. Control	2. Problem solving
3. Strategy	3. Spontaneity
4. Neutrality	4. Empathy
5. Superiority	5. Equality
6. Certainty	6. Provisionalism

How can we avoid defensive communication? A researcher, in a classic article, came up with six categories of defensive communication and supportive strategies to counter each of them (see Table 5-1). Consider the supportive response in each instance, as communication strategies.

www.mhhe.com/hybels9e
For an example of defensive communication view clip, "Defensive Communication."

Evaluation versus description Evaluative statements involve a judgment. If the judgment is negative, the person you are speaking to is likely to react defensively. If you tell your roommate, "It is inconsiderate of you to slam the door when I am trying to sleep," he might respond, "It's inconsiderate of you to snore every night when I am trying to sleep." On the other hand, if you tell your roommate, "I had trouble sleeping last night because I woke up when I heard the door slam," he is much more likely to do something about the problem. Since you have merely described the problem, the message is not as threatening.

Control versus problem solving People who consistently attempt to exert control believe that they are always right and that no other opinion (or even fact) is worth listening to.

Others tend to respond negatively if they think someone is trying to control them. For example, if you are working on a class project with a classmate and you begin by taking charge and telling him or her what to do, you will probably be resented. A better approach is for you and your classmate to engage in problem solving together. The same applies to close relationships. If conflict arises and you decide what should be done ("I'll take the car and you take the bicycle"), your partner is not likely to respond positively. It is better to discuss the options together.

Strategy versus spontaneity Often strategy is little more than manipulation. Rather than openly asking people to do something, you try to manipulate them into doing what you want by using strategies such as making them feel guilty or ashamed. A statement that begins "If you love me, you will . . ." is always manipulative. A better approach is to express your honest feelings spontaneously: "I am feeling overwhelmed with all the planning I have to do for the party. Will you help me out today?"

Neutrality versus empathy If you receive a low grade on a paper and are feeling bad about it, you don't want your friend to say, "Maybe the teacher was right. Let's look at both sides." When feelings are high, no one wants a neutral, objective response. What is needed is for the other person to show empathy—the ability to recognize and identify with our feelings. An empathic response to a poor grade in a course might be, "You must feel bad. You studied hard for that class."

Superiority versus equality People who always take charge of situations seem to imply that they are the only ones qualified to do so. Even if we have a position that is superior to someone else's, people will react less defensively if we do not communicate this superiority. An attitude of equality—"Let's tackle this problem together"—produces much less defensive behavior.

Certainty versus Provisionalism Don't confuse people who are confident and secure with people who think they are always right. Confident and secure people may hold strong opinions; they are likely, however, to make many provisional statements that permit another point of view to be expressed. For example, someone might say, "I feel strongly on this subject, but I would be interested in hearing what you have to say."

Avoiding Defensive Communication: A Practical Example

Although we have discussed each of the six defensive categories separately, in most communication situations several of them appear simultaneously. You can see how this works in the following situations:

© Kendall Hunt Publishing

Avoid defensive communication for happier relationships.

A Defensive Dialogue

Boss: You're an hour late. If you're going to work here, you have to be on time. (superiority, control)
Employee: My car wouldn't start.
Boss: That's no reason to be late. (certainty, evaluation) You should have called. (evaluation)
Employee: I tried, but ...
Boss: When work starts at 8 A.M., you must be here at 8 A.M. (superiority, control) If you can't make it, you should look for another job. (superiority, control, certainty) If you're late again, don't bother coming to work. (superiority, control, strategy)

This dialogue leaves the employee feeling defensive, angry, and unable to say anything. Let's take a look at how it might have gone if the boss had been more willing to listen:

A Supportive Dialogue

Boss: You're an hour late. What happened? (description, equality)
Employee: My car wouldn't start.
Boss: Weren't you near a phone? (still no evaluation)
Employee: Every time I tried to call, the line was busy. I finally decided that it would be faster to walk here than to keep trying to call.

Boss: When people don't get here on time, I always worry that we're going to fall behind schedule. (spontaneity) Wasn't there any way of letting me know what happened? (problem solving)

Employee: Yeah. I guess I panicked. I should have asked my sister to keep trying to call to let you know what happened. If it ever happens again, that's what I'll do.

Boss: Good. Now let's get to work. There's a lot of catching up to do.

Dealing with Rejection

It is because your drive to connect with others is so deeply embedded in your DNA that disappointment when you fail to connect or from the departure of a loved one is among the most stressful of all experiences. Research has shown that being ditched by your best friend is as threatening to your well-being as touching a hot stove.

How can you successfully cope with rejection? The first technique for successfully coping with rejection is to *avoid self-defeating assumptions*. Often, the first response to rejection is to let it become an indictment of your life. It may cause you to believe it is an indication of a basic flaw or shortcoming in your personality. Rejection by a partner, for example, may make you feel unlovable by anyone.

The second technique for successfully coping with rejection is *don't magnify its impact*. Rejection often triggers a negative mindset that suggests it is a forecast of your future. The point isn't to minimize its impact, it is to assess it realistically within the perspective of your life. Look, for example, where you have been, where you are, and where you hope to go in the future. Perhaps your rejection isn't as significant as it currently seems without this broader perspective.

Rejection can create a self-fulfilling prophecy if, indeed, you believe you are a reject and then behave in ways that prove your prophecy. If you enter future relationships believing that you are not good enough, incapable of sustaining a relationship, or unworthy of another's love and affection, your attitude is likely to stimulate behaviors that may prompt another rejection. Just remember that a rejection in the past is not a predictor of rejection in the future.

Rejections hurt, but the third technique for dealing with them successfully is *don't let them compromise or derail your dreams*. It is true that you can retreat from the possibility of future rejections, but by doing so you may miss new opportunities and challenges. These new opportunities and challenges may yield pleasure, great happiness, and tremendous success. Think how you might look back and regret your behavior if retreating from the possibility of future rejections was the course of action you decided upon.

The fourth and final technique for successfully dealing with rejection is to *learn from them*. If there is helpful feedback, listen to it. If you have time for self-reflection, engage in it. If you see little to change, persevere. Your best course of action may be to deal with it, learn from it, forgive, if necessary, forget about it, and move on. Move on to improving future relationships that matter and have consequence.

Resolving Conflict

In their book, *Interpersonal Conflict* (McGraw-Hill, 2007), William Wilmot and Joyce Hocker define conflict as "an expressed struggle between at least two parties who perceive incompatible goals, scarce resources, and interference from others in achieving their goals." Conflict is expressed through your communication when you feel your goals and those of another are contradictory, you are both competing for similar and yet scarce resources, or you perceive interference from the other person in trying to get what you want.

When you are in conflict and have decided that nothing will be served by avoidance or aggression, the option left open to you is conflict resolution—negotiation, to find a solution to the conflict. If the conflict has occurred because of a perception of incompatible goals, you negotiate to determine how you can both reach your goals. For the negotiation to be considered successful, both you and the other person must be satisfied and feel that you have come out ahead. This is referred to as *win-win negotiating.*

Culture, gender, and power play roles in conflict.

Culture, gender, and power play roles in conflict. Culture plays a role because perceptions, expectations, behaviors, and communication patterns are rooted in culture. Often, when cultures are better understood, conflict prevention and resolution becomes more effective. Gender is framed in a cultural context, and research shows that in some circumstances there are gender differences to conflict. For example, in laboratory exercises, "men will often exhibit dominating and competitive behavior and women exhibit avoidant and compromising behavior." Wilmot and Hocker cite Deborah Tannen's research when they write, "Women are more likely to avoid conflict. Men are more likely than women to take control of the conversation to lead it in the direction they want. However, they expect their (female) conversational partners to mount some resistance to this effort, as men would be likely to do. Women often remain in the 'listening' role rather than 'lecturing,' which puts them at a disadvantage in having their voices heard."

Power plays a major role in conflict as well. Perceived differences in power can lead to antagonism. "People feel passionately about power—who has it, who ought to have more or less, how people misuse power, and how justified they feel in trying to gain more power for themselves." Conflicts involving power do not have to be destructive. Constructive conflict management almost always depends on a search for power with others.

Deborah Wieder-Hatfield, a researcher in this area, has suggested a useful model for resolving conflict. In this model, each individual looks at the conflict intrapersonally. Then the partners get together to work out the problem.

In the first stage, *intrapersonal evaluation*, each person analyzes the problem alone. This analysis is accomplished through a series of questions: How do I feel about this problem? How can I describe the other person's behavior? What are the facts?

In the second stage, the parties in the conflict get together to work out an *interpersonal definition* of the problem. It is important that both parties believe there is a problem and can define what it is. In this stage, it is important that each person listen carefully and check the accuracy of what he or she has heard by paraphrasing what was said. The same is true for feelings. At the end of this stage, both partners should agree on the facts of the problem.

In the third stage, the partners should discuss *shared goals*. Still focusing on the problem, the individuals should ask, "What are my needs and desires?" and "What are your needs and desires?" Then they should work to see whether their needs and goals overlap.

At the fourth stage, the partners must come up with *possible solutions* to the problem. Here it is useful to create as long a list as possible. Then each individual can eliminate solutions he or she considers unacceptable.

In the fifth stage, the partners move on to *weighing goals against solutions*. Some compromises are inevitable at this stage. The solutions may not be entirely satisfactory to either party, but they are a compromise that both hope they can live with. Negotiators would label this a win-win solution.

Since all resolutions are easier to make than to keep, the last stage of the process is to *evaluate the solution* after some time has passed. Did the solution work? Does it need to be changed? Should it be discussed again at a later date? As we mentioned earlier, it is not easy to change human behavior. When partners work to resolve conflict, even when they come up with good solutions there is likely to be some backsliding. It therefore makes good sense to give partners a chance to live up to their resolutions. Letting time pass before both negotiators are held accountable helps achieve this goal.

Gottman, from all of his research on couples, says that happy couples have a different way of relating to each other during disputes. Partners make frequent "repair attempts," reaching out to each other in an effort to prevent negativity from getting out of control in the midst of conflict. Humor, too, is often part of a successful repair attempt. If partners can work together and appreciate the best in each other, they learn to cope with the problems that are part of every relationship. Partners must learn to love each other not just for what they have in common but for things that make them complementary as well.

The Bottom Line

The Institute for American Values conducted a study whose results bear directly on the discussions in this chapter. Their research countered what they labeled the "divorce assumption"—that most people assume that a person stuck in a bad marriage has two choices: stay married and miserable or get a divorce and become happier. The study found no evidence that unhappily married adults who divorced were typically any happier than unhappily married people who stayed married.

Two-thirds of unhappily married spouses who stayed married reported that their marriages were happy five years later. Those in the most unhappy marriages reported the most dramatic turnarounds. These unhappy partners had endured serious problems, including alcoholism, infidelity, verbal abuse, emotional neglect, depression, illness, and work and money troubles. The study found three principal techniques for their recovery; those in unhappy unions of any kind can learn something about what it takes to improve relationships.

The first technique is *endurance*. Many couples, the study found, did not so much solve their problems as transcend them—they simply and stubbornly outlasted their problems. By taking one day at a time and pushing through their difficulties, the unhappy spouses said in their focus groups, many sources of conflict and distress eased—whether it was financial problems, job reversals, depression, child problems, even infidelity.

Unhappy partners find other ways to improve their overall contentment, even if they could not markedly improve their marital happiness.

The second technique is *work ethic*. Unhappy spouses actively worked to solve problems, change behavior, and improve communication. They tackled their problems by arranging for more private time with one another, seeking counseling, receiving help from in-laws or other relatives, consulting clergy or secular counselors, and even by threatening divorce and consulting divorce attorneys.

The third technique was *personal happiness*. In these cases, the unhappy partners found other ways to improve their overall contentment, even if they could not markedly improve their marital happiness. That is, they improved their own happiness and built, for themselves, a good and happy life, despite a mediocre marriage.

The bottom line to improving relationship happiness proved to be *commitment*—having a positive attitude toward the relationship. Unhappy partners minimized the importance of difficulties they couldn't resolve, and they actively worked to belittle and downplay the attractiveness of alternatives to their current relationship.

The Internet and Evaluating and Improving Relationships

When you are using the Internet, and when your goal is to evaluate an online relationship, the key is to move slowly. The potential for lies, deceit, half-truths, hidden agendas, and misunderstandings is real, and they are more likely to reveal themselves over time simply because people have difficulty being on their best behavior for a long period. What are the red flags to look for?

Does the other person avoid direct answers to questions about issues that are important to you?
Does the other person make demeaning or disrespectful comments about you or other people?
Is there any inconsistency in basic information? For example, do the answers about marital status, children, employment, and location appear consistent? How about the information on age, appearance, education, and career?
Is the other person pushing too quickly for an in-person meeting or avoiding phone contact?
Is he or she engaging in overly sexy conversation right from the start?
Is the other person asking for money?

Ask direct questions when you find an inconsistency. Do the answers make sense? If you don't get direct answers, how are the questions declined? If you attempt to dig deeper, which is your right, mature people may respectfully ask you to back off, tell you that you are frightening them, or let you know that your questions are premature. These responses let you know the other person knows, first, how to be respectful and, second, how to take care of himself or herself.

There are seven tips for making the transition from virtual to real world smooth and safe:

1. *Don't give our personal information.* If someone asks for a phone number, get theirs, and call back from a pay phone. Don't tell where you live or work, or what you do.
   Gather as much information about the other person as possible, but stop communicating with anyone who pressures you for personal information or who in any way attempts to trick you into revealing it.
2. *Move slowly.* This not only helps you assess the other person by looking for odd behavior or inconsistencies, but it also allows you to find out whether the other person is indeed who he or she says. One of the problems with online communication is the ease of self-disclosure. You share too much of yourself too quickly, thinking it will make you close, but intimacy is cultivated over time.
3. *Use caution.* Careful, thoughtful decisions yield better relationship results. Trust builds gradually. Pay attention, and look for the red flags.
4. *Be honest.* If you are realistic about your own claims, you will have little anxiety about trying to control and manage your information. Exaggeration is often difficult to explain if you decide to meet later. Be yourself.

5. *Request a photo*. Request photos, not just a single photo. Not only does this give you an idea of a person's appearance, but when you have several images in several settings—like casual, formal, indoor, and outdoors—you have contexts in which to place verbal comments. When you hear excuses about why you can't see photos, consider that the person may have something to hide.
6. *Chat on the phone*. After using the Internet—or along with it—the telephone is the next step. It is another way to find out about a person's communication and social skills, and with the addition of all the vocal cues—volume, pitch, rate, tone, and quality—and the elements of enthusiasm, force, and variety, you begin to form a better, bigger picture of the other person.
7. *Meet only when you are ready*. When you are ready, you can choose whether to pursue the relationship in the offline world. No matter what level of online intimacy was attained, you can still decide not to meet offline. Even if you decide to arrange a meeting, you have the right to change your mind.

If you should decide to meet in person, meet in daylight in a safe, public place where other people will be present. Always tell a friend where you are going and when you will return, and provide your own transportation. If you feel unsafe or uncomfortable, leave.

Summary

The most important relationships in our lives go through five stages as they are coming together: initiating, experimenting, intensifying, integrating, and bonding. Relationships that remain superficial go through only the first or second stage. When relationships come apart, they also go through five stages: differentiating, circumscribing, stagnating, avoiding, and terminating.

In evaluating relationships, ask yourself questions about commitment, forming a relationship with another person, and making a commitment to a specific relationship and particular person. Next, you need to ask yourself questions about your partner. Following that, ask yourself questions about rewards and costs and, finally, ask yourself questions about roles.

To improve relationships you are likely to have to deal with aggressive talk and aggression, regretable talk, criticism and complaints, avoidance, defensive communication, conflict, and rejection. There are no universal, all-encompassing, always successful ways for dealing with each of these areas; however, it should be clear that the better you are at applying the strategic flexibility framework, the better you will be at revealing empathy, using owned messages, and displaying assertiveness when necessary.

The bottom line was revealed in a study by the Institute for American Values and the techniques the survey uncovered that unhappy couples use to recover. The first is endurance; simply outlast the problems. The second is work ethic; put forth effort to solve problems, change behavior, and improve communication. The third is personal happiness; find other ways to improve your overall contentment. All of these techniques require commitment—a positive attitude toward relationships.

There are several ways to evaluate online relationships. We looked at red flags, tips for making the transition from online to real life smooth and safe, and suggestions for meeting in person.

Name____ Date______________

Exercise 5.1 Chapter 5 – Evaluating and Improving Relationships

Stages of a Relationship

According to Marc L. Knapp, writer and researcher, relationships are in a constant state of change. Relationships are either coming together or coming apart. Relationships require attention and maintenance. They require servicing. In order to have a long lasting and healthy relationship, it is important to recognize and identify each stage.

You and a partner will identify the stages of a relationship, both coming apart and coming together. Then, identify a popular song that you have heard and that you have on your MP3 player in which the lyrics reflect each stage. Bring your players to class and be certain you can explain and support your selections.

Name: ____________________

Place: ____________________

Identify and Cite the Song		
Coming together	*Definition*	*Song Title*
Initiating		
Experimenting		
Intensifying		
Integrating		
Bonding		

Coming Apart	*Definition*	*Song Title*
Differentiating		
Circumscribing		
Stagnating		
Avoiding		
Terminating		

Supplies Required:

MP3 Player (loaded)

MP3 Speakers

6

Intercultural Relationships

After reading this chapter, you should be able to:

- ❐ Understand three reasons for studying the impact of diversity on interpersonal relationships
- ❐ Increase awareness of four basic core concepts: knowledge, understanding, acceptance, and skills
- ❐ Define culture
- ❐ Differentiate the co-cultural categories of ethnicity, race, region, and social class
- ❐ Identify three characteristics of culture
- ❐ Discuss factors which affect our perceptions of others: needs, beliefs, values, and attitudes
- ❐ Identify three steps in the process of forming stereotypes
- ❐ Recognize how stereotypes and prejudice influence interpersonal relationships
- ❐ Describe three forms of prejudice
- ❐ Explain the three functions that prejudices fulfill in our interpersonal relationships

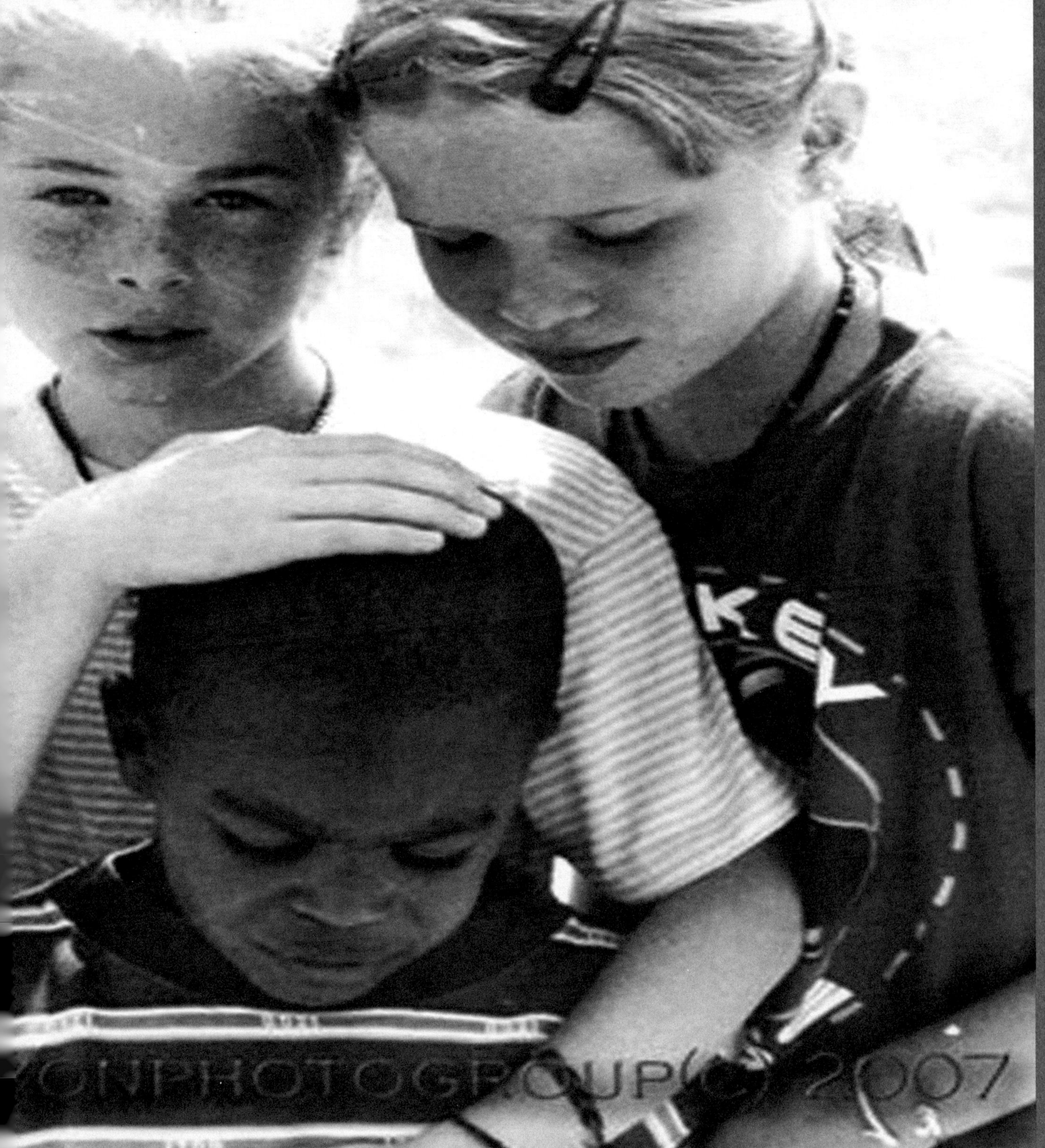
ONPHOTOGROUP(C) 2007

- ❒ Evaluate the impact of Hofstede's four dimensions of cultural values on interpersonal communication
- ❒ Recognize five strategies to enhance effective interpersonal communication in diverse relationships

Key Terms

knowledge
uncertainty reduction theory (URT)
passive strategies
active strategies
interactive strategies
self-disclosure
understanding
acceptance
ethnocentrism
skills
culture
diversity
socialization
ethnicity
race
regional differences
social class
homophily
explicit learning
implicit learning
perception
personal orientation system
needs
beliefs
values
attitudes
stereotyping
racial profiling
prejudice
racism
race
ageism
sexism
verbal abuse
discrimination
violence
acceptance
high/low context cultures
individualism/collectivism
power distance
masculine/feminine cultures
uncertainty avoidance

6 Scenario

"Wow, what are these photos of?" Chris asked his roommate, as he looked in his photo album.

This semester Chris was paired with a new roommate. His new roommate was an exchange student from Hong Kong, named Lee. For the past two weeks, Chris had been helping Lee make a smooth transition to life on campus. After sharing with Lee about his family and traditions, Chris started learning about Lee's.

"Those are photos of the Chinese New Year in Hong Kong," Lee said, as he peered at the photos.

"Oh cool. This looks fun. How do you celebrate it with your family?" Chris asked. "Is it like our New Year?"

Lee plopped down on his bed. "Not really. Before the holiday, we clean the entire house. We get rid of everything that reminds us of the old year."

"That's sounds refreshing," Chris said. "It's like starting the year off with a clean slate."

"Exactly," Lee continued, "then my mother buys red envelopes and fresh fruit, like oranges and tangerines for the house. We all get new sets of clothes and we prepare dinner. Then, on New Year's Eve all of our family comes over and eat dinner. We pay our respect to the Gods and open all the doors at midnight to let go of the past year."

As Lee went on, Chris thought about how different their cultures' were. He realized that even though we are all people, we all have different ideas, traditions, and ways a life. But with understanding, we can respect and appreciate each other's cultures.

On July 28, 2006, actor Mel Gibson was pulled over while speeding on Pacific Coast Highway in Malibu, California. As officers were questioning Gibson, he began yelling at them, making anti-Semitic and sexist comments toward the arresting officers.

In October 2006, *Grey's Anatomy* actor Isaiah Washington got into a fight with fellow actor Patrick Dempsey over an alleged gay slur that Washington made about their colleague, T. R. Knight. Even though the incident eventually faded from the spotlight, Washington publicly made an anti-gay comment at the 2007 Golden Globe awards a few months later as he attempted to defend his earlier actions to members of the press.

In November 2006, *Seinfeld* actor Michael Richards erupted into a series of racial epithets targeted toward two African American men attending his performance at the Laugh Factory in Los Angeles. Richards claimed that he was angry at the men for heckling him and allegedly disturbing his comedy routine.

What causes individuals to engage in such negative behavior? Why do people exchange such hurtful words and actions? One reason may be the inability to engage in effective interpersonal communication with those who are different. We make decisions on how to communicate with others based on our beliefs, our values, and our attitudes. As a result, if our beliefs or attitudes toward another individual or group are negative, our communication with them may be negative as well. Why is it that some people fear and apprehend communication with diverse others instead of embracing differences as the added "spice" of interpersonal relationships? In this chapter we will explore a variety of concepts that help explain how our attitudes, beliefs, and values both shape and are shaped by our interactions with others.

Overview

Throughout this text, we have discussed various aspects of interpersonal communication and the roles they play in initiating and sustaining relationships. As we approach the end of the journey of exploring the specifics of interpersonal communication, we would be remiss if we failed to discuss the one variable that *all* interpersonal relationships have in common—they are comprised of diverse individuals. Typically, discussions of diversity focus on things that we can see: race, ethnicity, and gender being the most commonly identified elements when defining diversity. Focusing attention on the obvious differences *may*

Relationships are comprised of individuals who are diverse in many ways.

cause us to fail to recognize that cultural attitudes, values, and norms also play a role in our interpersonal relationships. These are only a few of the less apparent factors that create challenges for relational partners when trying to achieve shared meaning. Consider friends who get upset with one another simply because they differ in their beliefs of how to spend their first weekend out of school. One might want to hang out with family members who were visiting from out of town instead of going out to the exclusive "Summer Kickoff Party" at the hot new nightclub that the other friend had received an exclusive invitation to attend. Differing values for family relationships and friendships contribute to the diversity encountered in this relationship. Maybe you have had a difficult time getting a teacher to understand that your questions are not intended to "challenge his authority," but are attempts to better understand the information being presented in class.

Diversity comes in many shapes and forms. While knowledge of the traditional views of cultural diversity can help you to understand the challenges you may encounter in your own relationships, it is important to focus on the source of many of our communication behaviors and to understand how cultural perceptions impact our view of relationships and communication. We can use the analogy of a coach and a team to understand the influence of diversity on interpersonal relationships and the role communication plays in the process. A good coach would not send a team out on the playing field without preparing them for the game. Plays are taught and rehearsed; team members know what to expect from one another. Practice sessions are conducted so that these preferred ways of acting and reacting can be learned and refined. Sure, there are times when the game plan does not work as planned. The coach and team may become frustrated. They regroup, communicate, and develop an alternate plan. However, if the team continues to run exactly the same play every single game, the chances for success will be slim. Becoming a competent communicator across cultures requires you to develop a similar game plan. You need to be aware of the characteristics that can lead to misunderstandings when communicating with people from diverse backgrounds. Knowing that each person's communication is guided by his unique set of values, beliefs, and attitudes will prepare you for differences in your approaches to conversations. Just as a team needs to study plays, people need to study and understand the various elements that create confusion and miscommunication in cross-cultural encounters. This chapter will help you to develop a personal game plan for becoming a competent communicator in diverse interpersonal relationships. Four core concepts which are essential to enhancing competence include: knowledge, understanding, skills, and acceptance. Let us examine each of these concepts more closely.

The Impact of Cultural Diversity on Interpersonal Relationships

As buzz words such as "diversity" and "cultural sensitivity" continue to permeate discussions regarding relationships in the workplace, the classroom, and our personal lives, there is a need to increase the understanding of both diversity and communication, and their influence on personal

Now more than ever, we have opportunities to form relationships with many different people.

relationships. This is an extremely exciting time in our history. Changes in political and social policy, evolving demographics, and technological advances have provided us with vast opportunities for forming relationships with diverse others. Three specific reasons for exploring the impact of cultural diversity on communication in interpersonal relationships are (1) increased awareness of self, (2) appreciation for technological transformations, and (3) understanding of demographic transitions.

Understanding the Self

Perhaps the simplest and most overlooked reason for studying the impact of diversity on our relationships is the opportunity it provides for exploring and understanding our own cultural background and identity. By delving into the cultural factors which influence communication patterns, we begin to gain an awareness of our own reasons for thinking and behaving as we do.

> A woman had lived in a small town with a population of 350 all of her life. The population was entirely Caucasian, and the overwhelming majority was Methodist and middle-class. Upon moving to a large metropolitan area, she found the challenges of understanding the cultural differences to be phenomenal. Her knowledge of initiating relationships was limited to experiences in a small, cohesive community. Shortly after moving into her new apartment, she encountered her next door neighbor struggling to bring several bags of groceries from the parking lot to the building. While introducing herself, she attempted to take a couple of bags from her neighbor's car. She was quickly told that her assistance was not needed. She discussed the incident with a roommate. The roommate pointed out, "You have to understand that people in large cities don't just walk up and help one another. Don't be offended. City folks just don't trust people as easily as people you're accustomed to." As she found the first few weeks in the city to be frustrating, her focus was on how "strange" other people were, not on understanding how her own cultural background influenced her perceptions and expectations of others' behavior.

When considering the impact they have on our identity formation, our first instinct may be to focus on interactions with family members and peers. Communication with significant others plays a large role in shaping our sense of self. However, it is essential that we examine the role that culture has played in the process as well. After all, it is likely that the rules and expectations that our family and friends have for our communication behaviors are derived from cultural expectations. Many unspoken guidelines are within different cultural influences.

Technological Transformations

© Tad Denson, 2007, Shutterstock.

How have cell phones impacted the way we communicate?

In the 1960s, Marshall McLuhan introduced the notion of a "global village" (McLuhan and Powers 1989). He predicted that mass media and technology would bring the world closer together, a notion considered to be farfetched at that time. But a quick inventory of today's technologies, which provide opportunities for forming diverse relationships, reveals that McLuhan's vision was quite accurate. Airline travel, television, cell phones, and the Internet are just a few of the technologies that have changed the way we communicate. Humans now have the capability to travel around the world in a matter of hours, simultaneously view events as they occur in other cities and countries, and concurrently interact with persons from around the globe.

Opportunities provided by technology for forming relationships with diverse persons have increased exponentially over the past twenty years. A 2005 survey revealed that nearly 1 billion people worldwide have access to the Internet (http://www.internetworldstats.com/america.htm). In the United States alone, nearly 250 million people use the World Wide Web to find information and to form relationships with others. Teenagers are forming and maintaining relationships via the computer at increasing rates due to social networking sites such as MySpace and Facebook. Some schools encourage students to communicate with intercultural email partners in a variety of subject areas. Internet chat rooms and discussion boards enable individuals to form friendships with others from almost anywhere. An examination of one teen chat site revealed that there were students communicating with one another from seven different states as well as from Canada, Great Britain, and Puerto Rico. As corporate America expands its boundaries to include many overseas partners, work teams will be comprised of members from diverse cultures. People come to the workplace with diverse beliefs, experiences, and expectations about the role of communication in relationships at work. Gergen (1991) emphasizes the fact that new technology has eliminated the barriers of space and time which previously inhibited relationships from forming with diverse individuals. Technology provides opportunities to communicate with persons who come from backgrounds entirely different than our own. Understanding the factors that influence communication will enhance our appreciation of these opportunities.

Influence of Demographic Transitions

© Kendall Hunt Publishing

The demographic composition of the United States will continue to change and become more diverse.

Over the past twenty years, the demographic composition of the United States has changed dramatically. And predictions for the twenty-first century indicate that the life expectancy of the population will be longer and that the racial and ethnic composition will be more diverse than ever. Medical advancements have extended the life expectancy of Americans. Immigration patterns have changed dramatically since the 1960s, before then most immigrants came primarily from European countries. Today, nearly ninety percent of immigrants arrive from Latin American and Asian nations. By the middle of the twenty-first century, the majority of the U.S. population will be comprised of today's racial and ethnic minorities. Over the past decade, the number of interracial and interdenominational marriages has increased, and the U.S. workplace has seen a shift from the predominance of white male employees to a more diverse workforce that is also comprised of women and racial and ethnic groups. Opportunities to expand our linguistic, political, and social knowledge abound.

However, not all intercultural encounters are viewed as opportunities. While these demographic shifts create opportunities for diverse relationships, it is important to recognize that they present communication challenges as well. Some intercultural encounters are approached with fear and apprehension. Uncertainty about other individuals creates tension. In July 2005, a series of bombs exploded on subways and a bus in London. Since that time, reporters have pointed to the mistrust, misunderstanding, and fear that have caused members of this city (which once prided itself on its racial, ethnic, and religious diversity), to be more cautious in their interactions with others.

Consequences of changing demographics are being felt in many social institutions. Schools are faced with issues such as bilingualism, differences in learning styles, and challenges of conflict among diverse groups. The Los Angeles school system reported that more than 100 different languages were spoken in classrooms across the county. Yet language is only one piece of a cultural code to be deciphered; other factors include understanding the perceptions and motivations that influence relationships in the home culture. Administrators at Taylor County High School in

Georgia were faced with the challenge of how to address a group of students who wanted to host a "white-only" prom:

> Even after schools were integrated in the South, many rural areas still held separate proms for blacks and whites, and Taylor County High School was no exception. The first integrated prom in 31 years was organized by the school's Junior class because they collectively decided they all wanted to be together as a complete group. Every year before that, students and their parents planned separate dances. The proms weren't organized by the school itself, as school officials were concerned about potential interracial dating issues. The year after the first integrated prom, a small group of white students announced that they also wanted a separate dance. One of the students who had initiated the integrated dance said she was bitterly disappointed to hear that some students wanted to go back to the old ways after they had succeeded in bringing about such a change in the school.

Now more than ever, relationship success depends on the ability to demonstrate communication competence across cultures. Achieving communication competence is the ultimate goal in our interpersonal relationships. When the source and receiver are from diverse backgrounds and have unique expectations of communication, this goal may be perceived as difficult to achieve.

Communication Competence: Four Core Concepts

Knowledge

Knowledge refers to the theoretical principles and concepts that explain behaviors occurring within a specific communication context. In other words, increasing your knowledge of communication theories and the concepts used to explain the challenges faced in intercultural relationships will enhance your ability to understand and accept those differences. In addition, knowledge will enhance your interpersonal skills when communicating with diverse others. You have already increased your knowledge base as a result of reading this textbook up to this point. Each of the concepts and theories that have been introduced has enhanced your understanding of the factors that impact communication in interpersonal relationships. Throughout this chapter we will take a second look at some of the theories introduced earlier in the text that have direct implications for intercultural encounters.

Uncertainty reduction theory. Berger and Calabrese's **uncertainty reduction theory** (URT) helps us understand how knowledge can assist us in forming effective interpersonal relationships by predicting the attitudes, behaviors, and emotions of others. As we initiate new relationships, our goal is to reduce our level of uncertainty about the other person (Berger and Calabrese 1975). When crossing cultural lines, alleviating this ambiguity becomes a bit trickier. For example, the notion of what constitutes acceptable disclosures in interpersonal relationships in the U.S. might differ from what is considered proper in other cultures. Is it acceptable to ask about another person's occupation? About her family? How does the other person view status differentials and what rules does he or she adopt for communicating with someone of different status? Berger (1979) identified three primary communication strategies used to reduce uncertainty in relationships. These are: **passive strategies, active strategies,** and **interactive strategies.**

Passive strategies typically involve observation and social comparison. We observe members of other cultures and make assessments as to the differences that exist. When one of your authors arrived in Hong Kong to teach summer classes, she did not speak Chinese. She spent many hours during her first weekend there sitting at the busy harbor, browsing through shopping areas, and walking around campus to observe how people interacted with one another. Through her observations, she learned the cultural rules for personal space, noticed styles of dress and forms of nonverbal greetings, and became familiar with the protocol for communication between students and teachers on campus.

Active strategies require us to engage in interactions with others to learn additional information about the other person. Suppose your professor assigns you to have weekly conversations with an international partner during the semester. Prior to your first meeting, you may decide to ask other international students what they know about your conversation partner's culture, or you may go online and participate in chat rooms that have members from the conversation partner's culture.

Interactive strategies typically involve a face-to-face encounter between two individuals to reduce uncertainty. Typically, partners engage in **self-disclosure** as a means of sharing information about themselves with others. When examining cultural differences in disclosure, it was found that American college students disclose about a much wider range of topics, and to more people outside the family, whereas college students in Korea self-disclose mostly to immediate family members (Ishii, Thomas and Klopf 1993). Consider the following example:

> Alicia was excited to learn that she had been selected to live with an international student in the dorm during her freshmen year. She had been fortunate enough to travel with her parents on business trips to various countries for the past several years and found learning about other cultures to be fascinating. Her new roommate, Kyon, was from Korea. As they were unpacking their things, Alicia told Kyon about her hometown, her summer vacation to Hilton Head Island, and about all of her friends from high school who were attending their college. She shared how frightened she was about the first day of classes, and she laughed as she told Kyon how she had taken her schedule and walked around campus to locate her classrooms for the first day of class. Eventually, Alicia noticed that she had been doing all the talking, so she began asking Kyon questions. While Kyon was willing to discuss the classes she would be taking and the plane trip from Korea, she seemed reluctant to talk about her family, friends, or even her fears about starting college.

Without knowledge of cultural differences in communication styles, Alicia may have become easily frustrated by Kyon's lack of disclosure. After all, in the United States it is common to engage in question-asking and self-disclosure to reduce our uncertainty about others. But understanding that expectations for self-disclosure in Korea are different from those held by Americans will help alleviate the potential frustration and hurt feelings that could occur otherwise.

Knowledge of one's own culture is learned. Cultures teach their members preferred perceptual and communication patterns just as a coach teaches a team the plays. Beginning at a very young age, this learning process instills knowledge about the culture's accepted behaviors. As children enter kindergarten in the U.S., they learn that they need to raise their hand to ask a question in class and to listen quietly while the teacher is speaking. Communication is the channel for teaching these lessons. Members of a culture practice the preferred behaviors and, if they deviate from the endorsed mannerisms they will probably find that they are unsuccessful in their communication. Consider the following example:

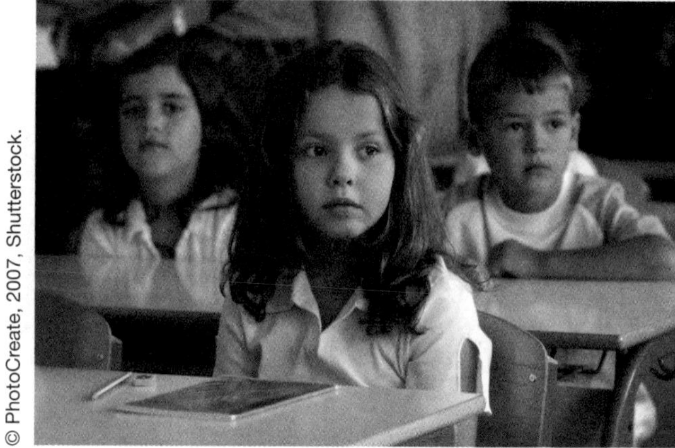

Young children learn quickly that listening quietly to the teacher is the accepted behavior for school.

> A student from Ethiopia shared this story about his experiences in American classrooms. During his high school years, he lost class participation points because of his unwillingness to speak out in class. While he was confused about his low grade, he did not approach the teacher and ask for clarification. Rather, he accepted the teacher's evaluation of his performance. However, what the teacher did not know was that in his culture students are not active participants in class. The teacher is viewed as the authority and the students are expected to listen and learn. Further, to question a teacher's authority would be viewed as extremely disrespectful.

As we engage in relationships with diverse persons, the knowledge of what constitutes competent communication behaviors is learned. Recent articles have focused on the need for cultural and social knowledge among U.S. armed service workers (McFate 2005; McFate and Jackson 2005). As U.S. military personnel travel overseas for service, it is important that they have a solid understanding of the cultural beliefs and norms that are expected. While the mission of the troops may be to restore order, respect for cultural expectations must still be demonstrated. Even the simple act of eating and drinking could be perceived as being offensive without proper knowledge of cultural norms. Soldiers training for duty in Iraq need to understand that members of Muslim cultures do not eat or drink during the day during the month of Ramadan. By refraining from eating or drinking in front of members of the Muslim culture during this period, U.S. soldiers can display respect for the Muslim culture. Studying the role of values, beliefs, attitudes, and needs in shaping and sustaining relationships can be invaluable. New knowledge can remove some of the barriers that can create communication challenges in relationships with diverse people. But knowledge in and of itself is insufficient for achieving competence. We also need to gain an understanding of why others communicate the way they do.

Understanding

Understanding involves applying knowledge to specific situations in an attempt to explain the behaviors that are occurring. While you may know how uncertainty reduction theory (URT) is defined, it is important to gain an understanding of how it impacts a particular interaction. Understanding involves exploring the roots, or sources of communication, rather than simply explaining the behavior. Imagine this scenario. You attend the funeral of the mother of your close friend who is Jewish. At the end of the ceremony, Jewish tradition calls for friends and family members to shovel dirt onto the coffin, but you are not aware of this tradition. This act makes you extremely uncomfortable, and you decide not to participate in the tradition; you end up offending your friend. Knowledge of the Jewish cultural customs would have assisted you in understanding the negative reaction that resulted from your refusal to participate in the ceremony.

As the twenty-first century opens, the cultural composition of the United States is becoming increasingly diverse. A recent Associated Press news article suggests that the term "minority" may no longer be an accurate descriptor for various U.S. co-cultures (http://www.diversityinc.com/public/16722 print.cfm). Non-Latino whites currently encompass less than fifty percent of the population of Texas, and it is predicted that more than one-third of all Americans will soon live in a state where groups formerly considered minority groups will outnumber Caucasians. Changes in demographics provide more opportunities for individuals to interact with individuals who are from diverse cultural backgrounds. Consider the various relationship contexts we have discussed in this text. The chances are greater than ever before that you will form relationships with teachers, physicians, and co-workers who are from diverse backgrounds.

Broadening our understanding of diversity to understand the influence of a variety of elements such as race, ethnicity, language differences, and religious beliefs is essential for relationship success. In many classrooms across the U.S., Caucasians are no longer the majority. On the surface, twenty-five students may appear to be similar, based on their racial or ethnic status, but it is quite possible that there are twenty-five different cultural backgrounds represented. One aspect of their diverse backgrounds may be seen in the language that is spoken in each of their homes. Nearly seventeen percent of elementary and secondary school students speak a language other than English in their homes (http://www.census.gov/prod/2004pubs/04statab/educ.pdf). Even where racial and ethnic diversity may be minimal, students come from different geographical locations and religious backgrounds and are impacted by their unique family backgrounds. Understanding how each of these elements impacts individual decisions to communicate in relationships is essential. For example, Jack was confused when he saw his friend Adam place a rock on the grave of a close friend who had recently passed away after a car accident. He did notunderstand that

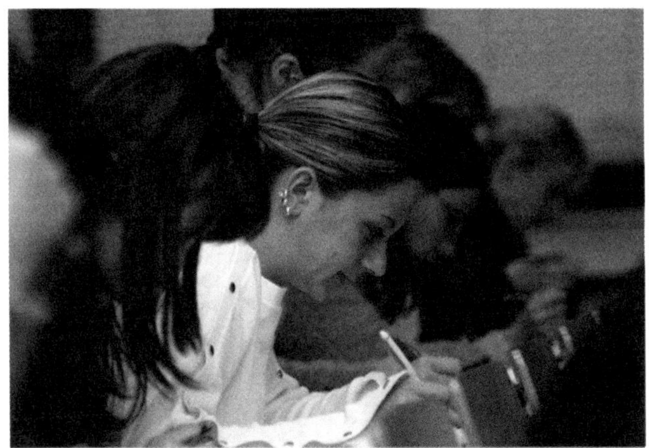

A room full of students appearing to be similar on the surface could have many different cultural backgrounds.

Adam's behavior was guided by an old Jewish custom of placing a rock on a loved one's grave as a sign of respect. According to tradition, the rocks were originally used as a way to mark gravesites. As more people visited the site, they added rocks to demonstrate how many people loved and respected the person.

It is important to understand that what works in one relationship may not work in all. Consider our earlier example of the coach and his team. Just as it would be ineffective to run the same play over and over again in a game, communicating with diverse persons in the same manner would not result in satisfying relationships. While this chapter will assist you in building knowledge and understanding of communication differences, acceptance of differences is also key to interpersonal success.

Acceptance

Acceptance refers to our awareness of the feelings and emotions involved in diverse approaches to relationships and communication. It encompasses our willingness to understand the behavior of others. Accepting differences in behavior enables us to be less judgmental and to reject ethnocentric thinking. **Ethnocentrism** refers to the tendency to perceive our own ways of behaving and thinking as being correct, or acceptable, and judging the behaviors of others as being "strange," incorrect, or inferior. Challenges in our interactions are often attributed to external, rather than cultural factors. Consider two co-workers who attempt to influence one another on a project on which they are collaborating. Joe tries to persuade Maynae by directly disagreeing with her proposal and engaging in assertive communication. Maynae's cultural background is one that values saving face. Thus, she avoids directly disagreeing with Joe—rather, she nods her head and proceeds with the project as she planned. Both of them end up frustrated. Joe cannot understand why Maynae did not follow their game plan. Had she not nodded her head and agreed with him? Joe attributes Maynae's actions to her shyness. Maynae is frustrated by Joe's confusion. Did he not understand that she did not want to embarrass him in front of their colleagues? She deduces that he must be in a bad mood and was not paying attention. As they continue to disagree about how to proceed with the project, they attribute the communication difficulty to the other person's mood or to shyness, both reasons being external to cultural factors. In reality, they may have diverse cultural expectations for how to influence others.

Skills

We have discussed many of the specific skills that are central to interpersonal communication throughout this text. **Skills** are the specific communication behaviors which contribute to competent and effective interpersonal communication. Effective listening, assertiveness, responsiveness, nonverbal sensitivity, language comprehension, and conflict management are only a few of the many skills required when interacting in diverse relationships. It is important to note that there is a difference between knowing how to communicate effectively across cultures, and actually being able to engage in the appropriate behaviors. You might understand that the Chinese culture values silence, but because you are an extremely talkative person and are ineffective in practicing silence you may be perceived as being rude when interacting with members of the Chinese culture. While language is an important skill to enhance communication competence, practicing nonverbal skills can also assist in producing effective interpersonal encounters. For example, when dining with friends from Japan, it is appropriate to make loud slurping sounds while eating a meal. The act of slurping is a behavior that is considered to be a compliment to the cook in Japan as it communicates that the food is delicious. But what if you feel very uncomfortable and do not know how to demonstrate the proper slurping behavior because you have never been encouraged to do so? Remaining silent while eating is perceived as an insult in these cultures, but your lack of slurping skills inhibit your ability to communicate your appreciation for the meal.

Culture and Diversity Defined

Culture has been defined by scholars in a number of different ways. In fact, one book identified more than 200 different definitions of culture (Kroeber and Kluckhohn 1952). In the fifty years since these definitions were compiled, attention to the increasing diversity of our world has prompted scholars to create even more. Anthropologists have broadly defined culture as being comprised of perceptions, behaviors, and evaluations. This definition was expanded to include shared ideas of a group which incorporates ethical standards as well as other intellectual components. Other researchers have adopted a descriptive approach to explaining culture. Their definitions include characteristics such as knowledge, morals, beliefs, customs, art, music, law, and values. In this text, we define culture as shared perceptions which shape the communication patterns and expectations of a group of people.

Diversity refers to the unique qualities or characteristics that distinguish individuals and groups from one another. The following is a list of characteristics that contribute to diversity in our interpersonal relationships.

- Age
- Educational background
- Ethnicity
- Family status
- Gender
- Income
- Military experience
- National, regional, or other geographical areas of origin
- Ownership of property and assets
- Physical and mental ability
- Race
- Sexual orientation
- Social class
- Spiritual practice
- Work experience

Diversity takes into consideration specific elements that have tremendous potential for our relationships. Consider the characteristics that you share with your closest friend. Chances are that you formed a relationship based on similarities in some of the areas listed above. Perhaps you are close in age and have similar educational backgrounds. Stop for a moment and consider the relationship implications when there are differences across these characteristics. A couple with different spiritual backgrounds may need to negotiate whose religious beliefs will be followed in raising their children. A daughter who is a lesbian may find it difficult communicating her feelings about her relationship with her heterosexual parents. Or a soldier may be challenged to convey his beliefs about war and his value of freedom with his friends back home who have not served in the military. When considering the many characteristics of diversity, it is easy to see why many relationships encounter stumbling blocks as individuals attempt to navigate differences in knowledge, experiences, beliefs, and values.

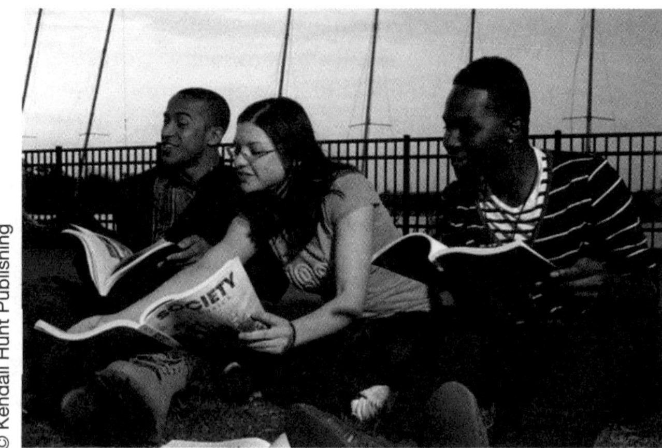

What characteristics do close friends share?

One of the first steps in becoming competent in our relationships involves recognizing the unique characteristics that each relationship partner possesses. Our culture shapes our perception and society teaches us the preferred ways of behaving. The American value for democracy is shared by many members of this country. Beginning in elementary school, we are taught the meaning of democracy. As we grow up, we see people defending their rights to free speech. Thus, our culture begins shaping our perceptions at a very young age. Perception influences and forms our values, beliefs, and attitudes. These shared perceptions are both consciously taught and unconsciously learned. **Socialization** refers to the process of learning about one's cultural norms and expectations. This is critical for an individual to become a functioning member of society. Sources of socialization include parents, peers, teachers, celebrities, political leaders, workplace colleagues, educational materials, and mass media. Perceptions are highly individualized, so much so that we may not realize that others see things differently. It may be easy to overlook the impact that diversity has on our communication patterns.

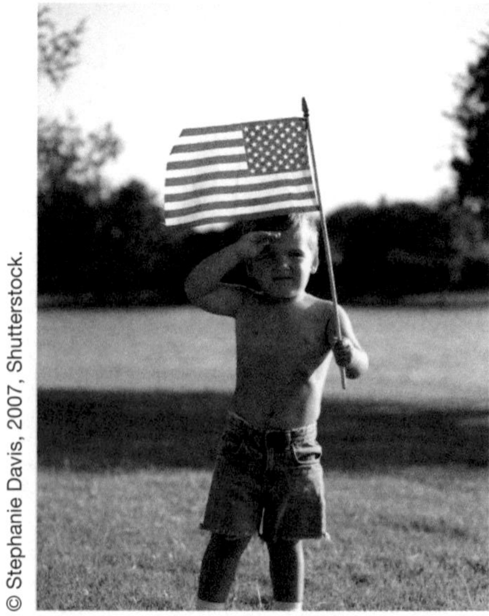

Americans typically learn to value democracy at a young age.

Communication behaviors are often unique to a culture, allowing us to easily identify members of various cultural groups. For example, an employee from Georgia assigned to work on a project with a team from Ohio is likely to be identified by her accent. Forms of address, such as when a child refers to an adult as "Miss Sarah," may also indicate a southern background. Culture is not only reflected in our behavior, it also influences our expectations. We form assumptions about how individuals should behave and what we should expect in our relationships with them. Japan is considered to be a collectivistic culture which values and encourages the accomplishments of groups over individual achievement. A student from Japan may experience difficulty in the U.S. where individualism is valued. He may be uncomfortable in situations where he is "singled out" for his individual academic achievements, preferring to be acknowledged with his class.

While we each have diverse characteristics that make us unique, we also share some aspects in common with other members of our larger culture. These shared characteristics allow us to identify with various groups and help shape our identity.

Co-cultures within the United States

Within the larger cultural context, numerous co-cultures exist, each distinguishable by unique characteristics. It is important to note that individuals are members of more than one co-culture. Consider this. An employee may claim membership as a member of the organization, in addition to being an adult, male, African-American Texan with Republican views, and of the Methodist faith. A total of seven co-cultures are claimed. Multiple memberships may contribute to confusion and miscommunication that occurs in relationships. Suppose you assume that because a teammate on your soccer team likes sports, she would not be interested in classical music or the theatre. As you pass a poster announcing the upcoming cultural arts series on your campus, you make some negative comments about people who attend musical and theatrical events. What you do not know is that your teammate has been a student of classical music since a young age, and that her mother is a trained opera singer. While this scenario is an extremely simplified example, assuming that membership in one group precludes an individual from having interests in other groups can lead to embarrassing situations that can impact relationships. Some examples of co-cultural classifications follow.

Ethnicity

While the terms "race" and "ethnicity" have often been used synonymously, these two categories are unique. **Ethnicity** refers to the common heritage, or background, shared by a group of people. Categories may be established to identify the culture from which one's ancestors came. These include Irish-American, Polish-American, or Mexican-American. While there has been some debate over the connotations associated with the labeling of some of these groups, the intention of naming is simply for identification purposes.

Race

Race is the term used to refer to genetically inherited biological characteristics such as hair texture and color, eye shape, skin color, and facial structure. Terms used to describe different racial categories include Caucasian, African American, and Asian. One situation which impacts our classification of groups results from the increasing number of intercultural marriages and relationships. Previously there were no categories on the U.S. census form to allow individuals to indicate their identification with more than one racial classification. This changed on the 2000 census with the addition of the category "other" to allow citizens to report their racial identification. As a result, individuals can now identify themselves as members of multiple racial groups rather than being restricted to only one racial identity.

Regional Differences

Within a given culture, speech patterns, attitudes, and values may differ significantly depending on the geographic location that an individual calls home. Northern Germans express values which are quite different from those of southern Germans. Those who reside in northern Brazil communicate using nonverbal gestures which are unrecognizable to those from southern Brazil. Accents within a culture also vary depending on the geographic region. Japanese spoken in Okinawa takes on different tones when spoken in Tokyo. English spoken by those who live in the Amish region of Pennsylvania is used differently by Texans. Dodd (1998) observed a variety of **regional differences** in communication styles within the boundaries of the United States. These include variety in the amount of animation, perceived openness, informal rapport, and rate of speech delivery. Even when examining the values of urban versus rural cultures, differences in values are obvious. Rural cultures appear to approach decisions more cautiously and simplistically. Members of urban cultures are more willing to take risks and reach decisions more quickly.

Social Class

Cultures often find that members stratify themselves on the basis of educational, occupational, or financial backgrounds, resulting in classifications and status differentials. Those whose careers produce high financial gain are usually awarded greater power and status in the American culture. Other cultures are more concerned with the amount of education that a person has completed. Stratification often occurs on the basis of homophily, the idea that we choose to be with people who are

When we initiate relationships, we choose to be with people who share our common interests.

similar to us. Thus, when initiating relationships, we seek out those in similar careers, with similar educational experiences, and of similar financial status.

In some cultures, it is possible to move from one social class category to another. For example, a person in the U.S. can easily move from one category to another as a result of their economic or educational status. Graduating from college may enable a person to gain a more prestigious job, and thereby allow him to achieve a higher social standing. Other cultures adhere to a philosophy of ascribed roles in society; an individual is born into a particular social class and there is nothing that can be done to warrant movement to a higher level. The caste system in India is one that restricts members from gaining social status. Relationships in these cultures are restricted to those who are in the same social class.

Characterisics of Culture

In the next sections we explain the three primary characteristics of culture: 1) it is learned, 2) it is dynamic, and 3) it is pervasive.

Culture Is Learned

The preferred ways of behaving as a member of a society are learned at a young age. Consider the learning experiences of children. Adults teach them how to say words, which foods can be eaten with the fingers and which should be eaten with utensils, and songs and rituals that are part of the culture. They may be taught that profanity is not acceptable and they are rewarded for saying the Pledge of Allegiance. Children are even taught biases and prejudices. Expectations about the nature of relationships and communication are also learned at a young age. For example, in the United States it is viewed as unacceptable for male friends to hold hands. In some Arab cultures it is not uncommon to see two men engage in this behavior. Society teaches us the behaviors that are accepted by most members of the culture, and, at the same time, instills within us a response mechanism for reacting to violations of cultural norms.

What is acceptable behavior in a culture is learned both explicitly and implicitly. Explicit learning involves actual instructions regarding the preferred way of behaving. A school may print a brochure that specifies the dress code that is required of all students, or a teacher may instruct students to raise their hand before speaking in class. In our families, we learn expectations for communication in relationships. For example, a young girl whose mother has experienced negative relationships with former spouses might be taught to "never trust men" and may find it difficult to engage in disclosure and to form relationships with males. Implicit learning occurs via observation. We are not directly told what behaviors are preferred; rather they are learned by observing others. Our choices of what to wear for a first date or the first day of work are influenced by observing what others wear or by what we have learned from the media. We learn the preferred ways of dressing so as to be accepted by our peers.

Culture Is Dynamic

Over time, events occur that cause change; cultures do not remain static. Consider changes in relationships that occurred after the events of September 11th. In the days and months following the tragedy, people reported that they engaged in more frequent communication with friends and family members. People were more willing to engage in open expressions of affection. Cultures and their members also change as a result of "borrowing" aspects from other cultures. It is quite common to open a fashion magazine and see examples of trends being borrowed from other cultures. For example, many stores and catalogues showcase Asian-inspired t-shirts and jewelry that include Chinese or Japanese writing. It is also quite common to see clothing adopting cultural styles such as the recent style of women in the U.S. wearing kimono style dresses.

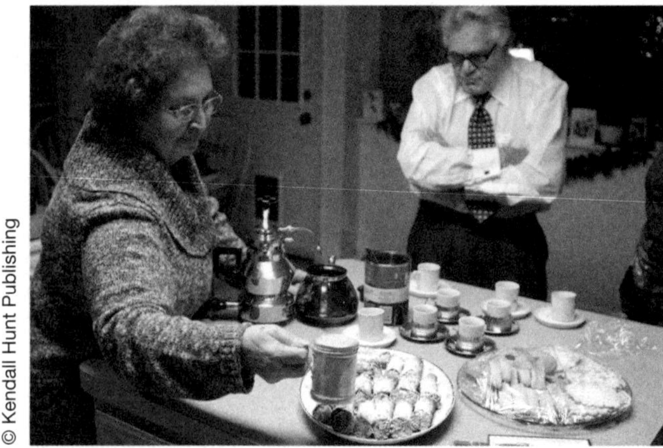

Not all cultures embrace change.

Depending on a culture's approach to uncertainty, the encouragement and acceptance of change may occur at different rates. Within the last decade, change has occurred at a rapid rate within the United States. Technological advances make some computers obsolete a year or two after purchase. Food and exercise trends also appear to go through changes as new diet fads are constantly introduced to the culture. In 2003, the Atkins diet gained popularity in the United States and carbohydrates were declared to be taboo. Not only did people begin to alter their dietary habits, restaurants altered their menus by designing and promoting dishes that were "Atkins-friendly." Eventually, doctors began questioning the health issues associated with the Atkins diet, and in 2005, the U.S. Department of Agriculture revised the traditional food pyramid to include six dimensions recommended for a healthy diet. Not only do cultures change with regard to food and clothing styles, but popular culture also undergoes transitions. The popularity of television shows change as new shows are introduced. What is "hot" one season may be "out" the next.

While you may initially question what impact these changes in various cultural aspects has on our interpersonal relationships, consider the amount of time we spend discussing aspects of culture with others. Friends gather around the water cooler and in dorm rooms to discuss the previous night's episode of Survivor or Desperate Housewives. They analyze the reasons for changes in the cafeteria menu to accommodate society's low carb trend. Changes in our culture provide many topics for discussion and debate in our personal relationships. However, not all cultures embrace change. In fact, some cultures are reluctant to implement change. For example, Germany scores high on uncertainty avoidance. This high score is reflective of the culture's reluctance to change as well as the desire to have strict rules and guidelines in place to maintain order. Some countries, such as Argentina, may find that their members adopt similar religious beliefs. When the majority of a culture's members practice the same religion, there is very little uncertainty about the beliefs held by individuals.

Culture Is Pervasive

Culture is everywhere. Take a moment and look around you. Chances are that you see numerous examples of your culture's influence with one simple glance. Is there a computer on your desk? Perhaps there are posters, photos, or artwork on the walls. Is there a television turned on or music playing? Maybe you are on campus and there are other students nearby. Take a look at the style of their clothes and listen to the words that they are saying to one another. Each of these things demonstrates the pervasive nature of culture. It surrounds us—in fact, we cannot escape the influence of our culture. If one were to adopt a descriptive definition of culture, this prevalence could be seen as influencing everything: our expectations for relationships, the clothing we wear, the language we speak, the food we choose, and even our daily schedules. Culture is represented not only in our material possessions, but also in the values, beliefs, and attitudes that comprise our personal orientation system. It shapes virtually every aspect of our lives and influences our thoughts and actions. Culture also affects how we initiate and maintain our interpersonal relationships. In many European cultures, it is common for teenagers to go out on large "group" dates, while females in Australia may ask out males and offer to split the cost of a date. In China and Japan, dating is typically reserved for those who are older, typically in their twenties. Dating was discouraged in India until recently. Families were expected to introduce couples and help them get to know one another socially in preparation for marriage. While online dating has grown in popularity in the U.S. and many European countries, this method of initiating romantic relationships would be frowned upon in cultures that view dating as a time for getting to know one's potential future in-laws.

Culture surrounds our lives and its influence is everywhere.

By taking a moment to consider the impact that culture has on our lives, it becomes clear that culture and communication are inseparable. Our verbal and nonverbal messages are shaped by our culture's influence, and we learn about our culture through the messages we receive from others. Given the level of influence that culture and communication have on one another, it should come as no surprise that the diversity that exists among members of a culture impacts the relationships that they form with one another.

How Diversity Impacts Interpersonal Relationships

Think about the first day in a new school or at a new job. Consider some of the thoughts that may go through your mind. Probably many expectations are formed about the people you see as you walk through the door. Some of the differences may be visible simply by looking at the other person, such as their gender, race, or age. In addition, many "hidden" differences also exist, such as their beliefs, values, and attitudes. Once the realization sets in that we are expected to communicate with someone whose cultural makeup is likely different from our own, we quickly search for any information, or cues, to help us make sense of how to interact in the particular situation. The process which helps us to organize the stimuli that bombards us in a potential communication encounter is known as perception.

In Chapter Two, we defined perception as the process of selecting, organizing, and interpreting stimuli into something that makes sense or is meaningful. Our perception causes us to view relationships and communicate in ways that are potentially different from the ways of others. The perception process may be explained in this way. Think about all the possible things that you could identify by using all five of your senses. Consider all the possible things that you could see, touch, feel, taste, and smell. Literally hundreds of stimuli compete for your attention at a given time! It would be virtually impossible to perceive all of the stimuli at the same time, so we pick and choose which things to pay attention to and ignore the others. Because individuals are selective in what they pay attention to and how they interpret it, each person forms their own perception of behaviors and events. As a result, we each have our own unique view of the world.

The role of selective interpretation was also discussed in Chapter Two. Because of our cultural influences, we may assign different meanings to behaviors. If we do not take the time or make the effort to see what is truly behind our interpretation, serious barriers to effective communication may occur. Imagine the reaction of a teacher who traveled to Hong Kong and, at a celebration dinner, was presented with an appetizer of chicken feet! She perceived the consumption of chicken feet to be disgusting, and her nonverbal behavior of wrinkling her nose and her refusal of the appetizer offended her hosts. The teacher regretted her reaction of obvious disgust, especially after she considered the fact that individuals of other cultures might view her favorite food (a cheeseburger), as disgusting due to their perception of the cow being sacred.

Personal Orientation System

Each individual has a set of predispositions which serves as a guide for thoughts, actions, and behaviors. These predispositions are comprised of one's needs, beliefs, values, and attitudes and are commonly referred to as one's personal orientation system. Communication plans and relationship expectations are developed and organized based on these characteristics. Many of the components of the personal orientation system are learned within the cultural context. Messages are transmitted from parents, teachers, and friends who teach the younger members of society to perceive certain actions as good or bad, fair or unfair. For example, Chinese children are taught to value history and tradition, and stories of the past are viewed as lessons to guide their behavior. Children in the U.S. tend to view stories of the past as entertaining, but instead of following tradition, they are encouraged to find new and innovative ways of doing things. When faced with decisions regarding the proper way to respond in situations, our needs, beliefs, values, and attitudes assist us in guiding our perception of a situation.

Needs

All individuals have needs, strong feelings of discomfort or desire which motivate them to achieve satisfaction or comfort. A strong relationship exists between needs and interpersonal communication, with communication serving as the primary mechanism through which we satisfy needs. If a student needs to have an assignment explained more clearly, he or she must communicate that need to the instructor. If an employee needs assistance in obtaining a copy of a company report, communication with the human resources director or with a supervisor can satisfy the need.

Everyone has a need to love and be loved.

Maslow's hierarchy of needs (1954) organizes the needs which humans must fulfill. A hierarchical structure helps us to understand the importance and priority of having some needs achieved before others. At the most basic level are the physiological needs of humans. These include the need for food, clothing, and shelter. While most cultures are able to devote adequate attention to meeting these needs, others cannot. The next level includes safety needs. Individuals possess a motivation to feel safe and secure in their surroundings. However, cultures differ in their methods for satisfying this need. At the middle of the hierarchy are affection needs. Schutz (1958) identified three basic needs across cultures: affection, control, and inclusion. We have a need to love and to be loved. Esteem needs are located at the next level of Maslow's hierarchy. Humans have a need to feel good about themselves. Interpersonal communication with others is one mechanism for meeting this need. Things that cultural members say and do impact the fulfillment of these needs. At the highest level of Maslow's hierarchy is self-actualization. This level is achieved when an individual feels that he or she has accomplished all that can be achieved in a lifetime. As the U.S. Army's motto implies, self-actualization is fulfilled when an individual feels that the goal "be all that you can be" has been met.

When applying Maslow's hierarchy to our interpersonal relationships, it becomes apparent that communication is the mechanism through which we meet some of our most basic needs, as well as fulfilling higher levels of need. Communication is the key to understanding individuals' needs and in comprehending the value placed on need fulfillment. Understanding what needs individuals have and their importance enables us to interact more effectively and to avoid misunderstandings. While one person may have a need for power and status, another may possess a strong need for friendship and affection. The intensity with which each of these needs is experienced may cause these two people to interact in very different ways.

Beliefs

A second component of culture which guides our thoughts and behaviors is our belief system. Beliefs are an important part of understanding our interactions with diverse others because they not only influence our conscious reactions to situations, but dominate our subconscious thoughts as well. We are constantly influenced by our beliefs. They are our personal convictions regarding the truth or existence of things. Through our interpersonal communication, we form beliefs about ourselves and our relationships. Based on positive interactions with your family members and teachers, you may believe that you are destined to succeed in college. Less supportive interactions might result in the belief that you will accomplish very little in life. Ultimately, these beliefs impact our communication with others. The formation of the central substance of our belief system begins at a very early age and continues to evolve as we grow and form relationships with others.

When crossing cultural borders, an examination of the beliefs possessed by a culture's members yields some fascinating differences. People from Malaysia believe that it is bad luck to touch someone on the top of the head as it is believed to be the location of the center for spiritual energy. Hawaiians possess a number of beliefs about the messages indicated by the appearance of a rainbow. Consider the superstitious beliefs held by members of the American culture. Walking under a ladder, having a black cat cross your path, and the groom seeing the bride on the wedding day prior to the ceremony are all believed to be signs of bad luck. Our beliefs impact our interpersonal communication.

Because most people do not question social institutions, many of the beliefs of a culture are perpetuated from generation to generation without any thought being given to the reasons for the existence of the beliefs. Some individuals have reported that reactions to their questioning of beliefs have been so negative that they feared rejection in their relationships and simply adopted the accepted beliefs into their own personal orientation system.

Values

Values serve as the guide for an individual's behavior. They dictate what we should and should not do. Kluckhohn (1951) describes values as a personal philosophy, either explicitly or implicitly expressed, that influences the choice of alternative actions which may be available to an individual. This definition highlights the relationship between values and communication in that values are communicated both explicitly and implicitly through our behaviors. The majority of our actions are reflective of the values which are firmly established in our personal orientation system.

Friendships are often the most valued things in peoples' lives.

Values are often communicated explicitly through verbal communication. Some cultural values are evident in the proverbs shared among people. "A stitch in time saves nine" communicates the value placed on addressing issues or problems when they are small rather than waiting until they grow bigger. Practicality and being satisfied with what you have is expressed in the proverb, "A bird in the hand is worth two in the bush." The Swedish proverb, "Friendship doubles our joy and divides our grief" describes the value placed on friendships. In his book, *A Pirate Looks at Fifty*, Jimmy Buffett communicates his value for family relationships and friendships when he states, "I have always looked at life as a voyage, mostly wonderful, sometimes frightening. In my family and friends I have discovered treasure more valuable than gold."

Nonverbal communication may be a more subtle means for communicating values. Many Asian cultures practice the custom of giving a gift to demonstrate the value for reciprocity and friendship. It is not unusual for students to offer their teachers gifts in exchange for the lessons that are learned. In the American culture, many teachers would be extremely uncomfortable accepting these gifts, resulting in confusion in the student-teacher relationship, possibly making subsequent interactions uncomfortable. It is important to gain an understanding not only of the values held by a culture's members, but also the ways in which individuals communicate these values. By doing so, misunderstandings may be avoided.

Attitudes: Stereotyping and Prejudice

Throughout our lives, each of us develops learned predispositions to respond in favorable or unfavorable ways toward people or objects. These tendencies are known as **attitudes**. A primary goal of this chapter is to assist you in identifying your responses to differences as well as to help you to understand your internal orientations guiding these reactions. If ever we interpret another's cultural customs or actions as being wrong or offensive, it is important to understand our own attitudes and how our culture has influenced their formation. Failure to understand these tendencies can result in irrational attitude formation, producing negative results in interpersonal relationships with diverse others. Two attitude formations to avoid are stereotypes and prejudices.

Stereotyping. Stereotyping results from the inability to see and appreciate the uniqueness of individuals. When generalizations about a group are made and are then attributed to any individuals who either associate with, or are members of, the group, the process of **stereotyping** is evolving. Three steps have been identified in the process of stereotyping.

The first step involves categorizing a group of people based on observable characteristics that they have in common. An international student from Scotland commented that she thought that all Americans would be like the people she saw on Beverly Hills 90210—tan, attractive, and extremely materialistic. As a result, she reported that she was initially apprehensive about forming relationships with many of her American classmates and socialized mainly with other international students.

The second step involves assigning characteristics to a group of people. An example of this step would be a popular magazine characterizing mothers who are employed outside the home as being less dedicated to their children.

Finally, we apply those characteristics to any individual that is a member of that group. An example would be the teacher who assumes that a student-athlete is not serious about academic studies. Following the events of 9/11, some members of Arab cultures have reported that they have been subjected to racial profiling. **Racial profiling** occurs when law enforcement or other officials use race as a basis for investigating a person of criminal involvement. This is a result of applying the single characteristic of race in determining whether a person should be viewed as threatening.

While stereotyping can be irrational, it is actually quite normal. Because humans are uncomfortable with uncertainty, stereotyping enables us to make predictions about our potential interactions with others. In order to become more competent in our interactions with diverse others, it is important to realize that stereotypes *can* and *do* impact our perceptions and our communication.

Prejudice. Another form of attitude which involves negative reactions toward a group of people based on inflexible and inaccurate assumptions is commonly known as **prejudice.** In essence, prejudice involves "pre-judging" individuals. Some of the most common forms of prejudice in the U.S. include racism, sexism, and ageism.

Racism. Racism refers to prejudice against an individual or group based on their racial composition. **Race** is a term used to refer to inherited biological characteristics such as skin color, eye color, hair texture, and facial structure.

In her 1995 film entitled *Blue Eyed*, Jane Elliott shares with viewers a diversity training session conducted with adults of various racial and ethnic backgrounds in Kansas City. Blue-eyed members of the group are told that they are inferior to the rest of the group simply based on their eye color. As the film unfolds, it is amazing to watch the confusion, mistrust, lack of confidence, and fear of communication that emerges among members of the group. Elliott explains that while some may consider her decision to discriminate simply on the basis of eye color to be irrational, it is not much different than choosing to treat someone differently on the basis of skin color. She points out that the chemical which produces eye color is the same one that produces skin color.

In our culture, some people assume that senior citizens are incapable of making contributions to society and can be considered helpless.

Ageism. Negative communication toward persons based on their age is referred to as **ageism**. In our culture, some people assume that senior citizens are incapable of making contributions to society and can be considered helpless. In 1967, Congress passed the ADEA (Age Discrimination in Employment Act) to protect older workers against age discrimination. According to the law, an employer cannot replace an employee over the age of forty with a younger person if the current employer is able to satisfactorily perform her or his job. Sue Sewell, age fifty-one, expresses her frustration of ageism in the workplace:

> "Society is missing out on the talent and a wealth of experience of the older worker. I have recently returned to the workplace after a spell at home and have noticed that some younger workers and management are not tolerant of the older worker. I think the older worker is stereotyped as being slow and less likely to be able to pick up new ideas and be able to use new technology. I, like many others in my age bracket, cannot give up work as we have mortgages, bills to pay, and dependents to support. I actually also enjoy being out in the world of work; it makes me feel more a part of society. If the retirement age is to be 70 and beyond as is being mooted at present, then we must have more opportunities for people to be employed whatever their age." (http://www.maturityworks.co.uk/uploads/files/matwrksreport.qxd1.pdf)

Ageism is also communicated when negative prejudices are harbored by adults against teenagers based on the attitude that teens are rude and unruly. While some equate college students on Spring Break with partying and drinking, recent programs have been developed on college campuses to provide students with opportunities to complete community service projects during their break from studies. In 2006, thousands of college students traveled to post-Hurricane Katrina Mississippi and New Orleans and spent their Spring Break vacations assisting in the clean-up process.

Sexism. Sexism refers to negative communication directed toward persons of a particular sex. In the United States, sexist attitudes have traditionally been directed toward females. As a result, females have experienced discrimination in the workplace and in other walks of life. While stories of sexism frequently focus on the prejudices against females, men also are subject to sexist behaviors. Consider the father who stays at home and raises the children. As he shops for groceries with the children in the cart or plays with them at the park on a sunny weekday afternoon, he may hear a comment such as, "It's so nice that he's babysitting the children!" Not surprisingly, he may become offended because it is assumed that he is not capable of being the primary caregiver for his children.

Communicating Prejudice

There are three primary means for communicating prejudice. Verbal abuse refers to the process of engaging in comments or jokes that are insulting or demeaning to a targeted group. Consider the impressions that we form of people as a result of their negative verbal behaviors toward others. The racist comments made by *Seinfeld's* Michael Richards may have caused some Kramer fans to question their positive attitudes toward the actor. **Discrimination** involves denying an individual or group of people their rights. While prejudice involves negative cognitions, or thoughts, discrimination is displayed when behaviors are used to express one's negative cognitions. Typically, discrimination is expressed through negative verbal comments made toward a group or an individual, with physical avoidance being the ultimate goal. The most severe form of prejudice is violence. On April 29, 1992, the verdict in the trial involving the 1991 beating of Rodney King by four Los Angeles police officers was read. Only one of the four officers was found guilty of using excessive force; the others were cleared of all charges against them. As word of the verdict was spread, riots erupted throughout Los Angeles. During the next three days, television viewers witnessed physical attacks, arson, and looting throughout the city. In the end, more than 4,000 people were injured, more than fifty were killed, and the city suffered over $1 billion in damages. This violence demonstrates the potentially extreme outcome of prejudice.

Fortunately, a 2004 study of 2,000 teens conducted by Teenage Research Unlimited (TRU) in Illinois points to changing trends among young Americans. Nearly sixty percent of teenagers reported that they have close friends of different races. Friendships of diverse religious or political beliefs and economic backgrounds are also prominent among today's teens. TRU President Michael Wood summarized the changing views of this generation as, "Teens still prefer to hang out with peers who share common ground with them. But that no longer means that their friends have to necessarily *look* the part. It's all about attitudes and actions—about who you are and what you do, not what you are" (http://www.teenresearch.com/PRview .cfm?edit_id=278.) Additional research points to the benefits of multicultural interactions that occur among college students. A 1997 study found that college students who have frequent interactions with students of different racial backgrounds and engage

Teens prefer to have friends who share their interests, regardless of their backgrounds.

in positive discussions about race and ethnicity tend to have a higher self-concept and report that they are more satisfied with college (Smith and Associates, 1997).

Functions of Prejudice

While prejudice is often based on false, irrational, and inflexible generalizations, it is often considered "normal." Why do individuals form prejudice? Three primary reasons for forming prejudice have been identified.

Acceptance. Acceptance is when a person communicates negative feelings toward a particular group in order to fit in within a desired group. An example of this is when a fraternity member expresses hatred for another fraternity's members. When asked why he has these strong feelings, the only reason offered is "because all Alpha Betas dislike them."

Defend the ego. Another reason for communicating prejudice is to defend the ego. By expressing negative feelings and attitudes toward a group of people, individuals create a scapegoat for their own misfortunes. An employee was overheard expressing his prejudice against women being selected for administrative positions. Upon further questioning, he admitted that he did not actually harbor any ill feelings toward women supervisors. Rather, he was frustrated by the fact that a woman had been offered the position rather than him.

Provide information. A final reason for prejudice is to provide information. As was stated earlier, humans have a need to reduce uncertainty. Unfortunately, many individuals form prejudice as a means for forming knowledge about a group of people with whom little or no contact has been made. Recall our earlier example of the student from Scotland who was reluctant to interact with American students because of the stereotypes formed as a result of watching *Beverly Hills 90210*. Because limited information was available, the student experienced high levels of uncertainty about how to interact with American college students. Prejudices were formed as a means to reduce the level of uncertainty and to provide a framework for building expectations. By forming these negative predispositions, an information base was constructed on which to form expectations about potential interactions.

Cultural Value Orientations

To understand the values shared by a culture's members, a number of scholars have developed models for studying value orientations. These models pose questions designed to measure the intensity with which a culture's members value specific characteristics.

Kluckhohn and Strodbeck (1961) developed one of the first models of cultural value orientation, and it is still being used in research today. Questions are designed to gain insight into such perceptions regarding relationships between humans and humans and nature. Sample questions include:

- What is the basic nature of human beings? Are they inherently evil and incapable of being trusted, or do most humans have a good heart?

- How are social relationships organized? Are relationships viewed as being hierarchical with divisions of power? Or should equal rights be present in all social relationships?

Hall's model of cultural values (1976) represents a continuum of characteristics associated with high-context and low-context cultures. These differences are characterized by distinct differences in communication styles. Cultures which fall at the low-context end of the continuum exhibit high verbal tendencies. This style is associated with a direct approach and verbal expressiveness. A philosophy of "say what you mean" is embraced. High-context cultures, on the other hand, prefer a more indirect style; cues about the intended message are interpreted through nonverbal channels. Whereas persons from a low-context culture expect messages to be direct, those from a high-context culture search the environment for cues. Rather than asking a person whether he or she is happy, high-context cultures would infer these feelings from other cues such as posture, facial expressions, and disposition. Consider the difficulties experienced by a couple who have different cultural backgrounds:

> Alec was confused. He and Miki had been living together for the past year and were engaged to be married in a few months. One evening, Miki was silent as they ate dinner. He knew something was upsetting her, but she kept insisting that things were fine. Miki was extremely frustrated as well. Why did Alec always insist that she tell him what was wrong? Did she always have to put her feelings into words? Why couldn't Alec be more in tune with her nonverbal behaviors and understand that things were not quite right?

This example illustrates the difference between the influence of the low-context approach of the U.S. on Alec's behavior and the high-context approach of Miki's Japanese upbringing. Miki expects Alec to be more aware of the messages that are being communicated via nonverbal channels, while Alec expects Miki to say what is bothering her.

A final model of cultural values is presented by Hofstede (1980). Four dimensions of values were identified by examining the attitudes of employees in more than forty cultures. These dimensions include individualism/collectivism, power distance, masculinity/femininity, and uncertainty avoidance.

Individualism/collectivism describes the relationship between the individual and the groups to which he or she belongs.

Individualism/collectivism. Individualism/ collectivism describes the relationship between the individual and the groups to which he or she belongs. Individualistic cultures, such as in the United States, focus on individual accomplishments and achievements. **Collectivism,** or value and concern for the group, is the primary value of many Asian cultures. Consider the cultural differences portrayed in the automobile manufacturing plant in the film *Gung Ho*. Asian managers took great pride in their work as their performance ultimately reflected on their group. They did not dream of taking time off for personal reasons. The American workers, on the other hand, whose behaviors reflected individualism, placed their individual needs over those of the company. Employees would take time off to be at the birth of a child or to keep a medical appointment. These differences in the values of the group versus the self had disastrous outcomes, with the company facing the risk of closing as a result of conflicting cultural values.

Power distance. Power distance refers to the distribution of power in personal relationships as well as within organizations. Low power distance cultures have a flat structure with most individuals being viewed as equals. The tendency to show favoritism to individuals based on their age, status, or gender is minimized. High power cultures are depicted by a tall hierarchical structure with distinct status differences. Imagine the frustration experienced by a young intercultural couple who had been married for only a few months. The husband, who was Hispanic, was raised in a culture that places the man as the head of the household (high power distance). His wife, who was raised by a single working mother in New York City, valued her independence. The power differential in her family of origin was low, thus she anticipated that her husband would view her as an equal partner in their relationship. As a result of their differing values for status and power based on their roles as husband and wife, the couple experienced many arguments.

Masculine/feminine. Prevalence of masculine and feminine traits in a culture characterizes Hofstede's (1980) dimensions of masculinity and femininity. Masculine cultures demonstrate a preference for assertiveness, ambition, and achievement. Characteristics of responsiveness, nurturance, and cooperation are associated with cultures at the feminine end of this dimension. Gender roles in these cultures are perceived to be more equal. Cultures such as those found in Japan and Mexico exhibit more masculine tendencies, while those found in Brazil, Sweden, and Taiwan are more feminine.

Uncertainty avoidance. Uncertainty avoidance refers to the willingness of a culture to approach or to avoid change. Cultures high in uncertainty avoidance demonstrate a preference for avoiding change. They embrace tradition and order. China and Germany are examples of countries with cultures that avoid uncertainty and embrace tradition. Cultures low in uncertainty avoidance welcome the possibility of change and are more willing to take risks. The United States and Finland are more open to change and are more tolerant of taking risks and adopting new and innovative approaches.

Cultures low in uncertainty avoidance welcome the possibility of change and are more willing to take risks.

Understanding these dimensions can provide cues as to which values are promoted among members of a culture. This information is useful for determining the appropriate methods to approach interpersonal communication and for providing valuable information that assists in checking the accuracy of one's perceptions.

Suggestions for Successful Interpersonal Relationships with Diverse Others

As shown throughout this chapter, perceptions can be faulty. But there are strategies which can enhance accuracy in perception. Each of the suggestions below involves understanding and practicing better interpersonal communication.

- Engage in careful listening and clear communication. Focus on listening for what is really being said, not what you want to hear. Be clear and explicit in your communication. Refrain from using slang or idioms.
- Refrain from judging people based on observable differences such as race, ethnicity, or gender.
- Do not misjudge people based on verbal (e.g., accent or grammar) or nonverbal differences.
- Be patient with yourself. Remember that becoming an effective cross-cultural communicator requires skills and knowledge. It takes time to practice those skills. You may make mistakes, but there are lessons to be learned from those faux pas.
- Practice patience with others. Cultural influences are powerful, and making the transition from one culture's way of thinking and behaving to another's takes time.
- Check for understanding. Do not be afraid to ask for clarification or to ensure that you understood what was being communicated. One simple question now can save offending someone later.

Summary

Throughout this chapter we have discussed the prevalence of diversity in all of our interpersonal relationships. While diversity is most frequently identified based on observable characteristics such as race, ethnicity, or sex, it is important to consider additional variables that influence our communication choices as we interact with others. Individual beliefs, attitudes, and values have a significant impact on the messages we send as well as on our reactions to the messages that we receive. At this point we would like to reiterate the importance of studying and understanding the impact of cultural diversity on our interpersonal interactions—by taking a moment to enhance your own knowledge and skills, you are better equipped to understand the reasons underlying your own communication preferences as well as the communication choices of others.

Name____ Date_______________

Exercises 6.1 Chapter 6 – Intercultural Relationships

Let's begin this exercise on culture by brainstorming the titles of movies that have issues of cultures as their subject matter. We learned that we study culture and diversity and their impact on interpersonal relationships for three reasons: 1) to increase awareness of self, 2) application for technological transformations and 3) understanding of demographics transitions. To gain a better understanding of culture and the benefits of diversity, let's prepare the following exercise with a partner.

I. Write a brief synopsis of the movie, *CRASH* or any familiar movie whose primary subject matter involves the issue of culture.

A. Identify two (2) examples of cultures.

B. Identify the co-cultures.

II. Define the Barriers and give an example from the movie that illustrates each.

Barriers	Definition	Illustration from Movie
Ethnocentricism		
Stereotyping		
Prejudice		
Racism		
Discrimination		

III. We deal with issues of culture based upon our values, attitudes, and beliefs. Define each. Describe how each has an impact upon the intercultural communication in the movie that you chose.

	Definition	**Description**
Needs		
Values		
Attitudes		
Beliefs		

7

Researching Your Topic

After reading this chapter, you should be able to:

- ❐ Develop a research strategy
- ❐ Explain the factors in establishing speaker and message credibility
- ❐ Analyze the audience
- ❐ Locate print and online resources
- ❐ Cite sources within a speech
- ❐ Identify forms of support
- ❐ Demonstrate an understanding of the guidelines for citing sources
- ❐ Establish legitimacy of sources located on the web
- ❐ Explain the five functions of support

Key Terms

Analogies
biographical sources
examples
facts
figurative analogies
general encyclopedias
government documents
journals
literal analogies
magazines
message credibility
newspapers
opinions
paraphrase
primary sources
quotations
research
secondary sources
speaker credibility
specialize encyclopedias
statistical sources
statistics
support material
testimony

7 Scenario

Katherine sighed deeply as she sat down at the library computer. She pulled out the directions for her assignment and read them under her breath. Instantly, she began regretting the decision she made on doing a speech on religion. She really didn't know too much about the topic.

"Hey sweetheart is everything ok over here?" Katherine looked up to see a friendly elderly librarian standing over her.

"Um, I'm fine," Katherine smiled weakly before returning her gaze to the computer.

"You don't seem fine," the lady continued, "My name is Mrs. Flowers. What's your name?"

"Katherine," she answered softly.

"So what seems to be the problem, and I know there is one," Mrs. Flowers asked, pulling up a chair and sitting down.

"Well, I have to do this speech for my oral communication class, and me being who I am, I picked a topic that would challenge me."

"Hmm that sounds like a good plan," Mrs. Flowers commented. "Picking something that's challenging is good sign of character."

"Well, right now I see that it was all a big mistake because I don't know where to start to look up information," Katherine huffed. "I'll probably receive my first "F" on this assignment."

"Oh no!" Mrs. Flowers shook her head, "We won't have a pity party. We'll get through this. After all, everything is right under your fingertips."

"Excuse me?" Katherine frowned.

"Honey slide over that keyboard," Mrs. Flowers smiled. "First," said Mrs. Flowers, "we are going to develop a research strategy." Katherine looked puzzled. "Then, we're going to . . . ."

Within the hour Mrs. Flowers showed Katherine how to research her to topic for her speech by using print and online resources. Katherine smiled as Mrs. Flowers stood to her feet. "Mrs. Flowers, thank you so much!"

"No problem sweetie. I told you we'd get through. Are you all set?"

Katherine nodded, "Yes ma'am. Once again, thank you."

"No problem sweetie. I'll be at my desk if you need me."

As Mrs. Flowers walked away, Katherine smiled down at her research. She just knew her speech was going to be great.

Each speaker faces multiple decisions during the speech development process. Sometimes beginning speakers find selecting a topic to be the most difficult aspect of the process. You may feel relief when your instructor approves the topic you have chosen, but your work has just begun. After choosing a topic and developing the general and specific purposes of your speech, it is time for research and to develop appropriate supporting material. Credibility is crucial. To a large extent, your listeners will evaluate your speech on the amount and relevance of research conducted and the types of supporting material used. The extent to which a speaker is perceived as a competent spokesperson is considered **speaker credibility.** A person's background, set of ethics, and delivery are all part of speaker credibility. **Message credibility,** on the other hand, is the extent to which the speech is considered to be factual and well supported through documentation (Fleshler, Ilardo, and Demoretcky 1974). It is this second type of credibility that is the focus of this chapter. Through research, one can find sufficient, relevant, and timely supporting material which will enhance a speaker's message credibility.

We live in an information society that produces far more information than we can use. Books are added to library collections on a regular basis, new information is found quarterly in journals, weekly in magazines, and daily in newspapers. Computers give us access to innumerable websites and ever larger databases. As a result of this galaxy of available information, one of your most important jobs will be to decide what is relevant and what is not, what you should incorporate into your speech and what you should discard. Setting limits on your own research requires that you stay focused on your specific purpose. Do what is required to give an effective presentation; do not allow yourself to be led down an interesting, but unrelated, path.

With all the information available on the computer, it's a big job to decide what material to use and what to discard.

Research is the raw material that forms the foundation of your speech. It gives you the tools you need to expand your specific purpose into a full-length presentation. The raw material may include interviewing experts on your topic and locating print and web-based information. The result of this process is your knowledge of the topic.

Often, research can lead you to deliver a slightly different type of speech than you expected. As facts emerge, you may expand your speech in one place, streamline it in another, and take it apart to accommodate new information. Ultimately, you will piece it together in its final form.

The research process alone is not sufficient. You must determine how to use it most effectively. **Supporting material** is the information used in a particular way to make your case. For example, if you were preparing a speech to inform your class on services available in your community for individuals who are categorized as low income, your *research process* may lead you to an organization that specializes in debt consolidation, another that offers free or low-cost medical care, an agency that gives out food for low-income individuals, and a organization that supplies children with free school supplies. As you develop your speech, one of your points might be that "a variety of services are available in our community." For *supporting material*, these agencies provide *examples* of available services. As the types of supporting material can be quite varied, you must determine what is most suited to the topic and to your listeners.

Develop a Research Strategy

Instructors rarely say, "Go! Prepare an informative speech." Instead, they establish parameters regarding topics, length of speech, minimum number of sources, and types of sources. What is the minimum number of sources required? How many different sources do you need? If you use three different issues of *Newsweek*, do they count as one source or as three? Can you use information from 1980 or 1990, or did your instructor say all material needs to be no more than five years old? Do you need both print and online sources? Does online access to a magazine count as a print source? Can you use all types of print sources? Does your instructor allow you to count an interview as a source? Can you use your family or yourself as a source? Before you begin to research your topic, make sure you know the constraints of the assignment as specified by your instructor.

Before you begin your topic research, make sure you know the parameters of the speech assignment.

The outline at the beginning of this chapter identifies aspects of the research strategy. Supporting material will be discussed later in the chapter. Specifically, in developing your research strategy, you need to address the following aspects.

1. Analyze the audience
   (What are the needs, interests, and knowledge level of my audience?)
2. Assess your knowledge/skill
   (What knowledge or skill do I have in relation to this topic?)
3. Search print and online resources
   (Based on available resources, where and what will I find the most useful?)

4. Interview, if appropriate
   (Will this speech be helped by interviewing someone with personal knowledge or expertise about this topic?)

Each of these aspects can be viewed as stages. The following section provides a look at each of these stages in greater detail.

1. Start (and End) with an Audience Analysis

Throughout this book we stress the importance of connecting with your audience. Before you determine the general or specific purpose for your speech, consider your audience's needs. As explained in the previous chapter, a careful audience analysis gives you information about who they are and what they value. Understanding your audience helps you develop specific questions that can be answered as you follow your search strategy. For example, suppose you were planning an informative speech explaining prenuptial agreements. You may have some general questions about the topic, such as the following:

When do most people get married?
What are the statistics on the number of marriages and divorces each year?
Who benefits financially and who suffers as a result of a divorce?
What happens to property in divorce?
How expensive is an agreement?
Can people draw up the agreement without legal counsel?

To construct an effective speech that achieves its specific purpose, whether it is informative or persuasive, think about your specifixc audience. So, if you are working on a speech about prenuptial agreements, consider additional questions such as:

Considering the age of my audience, how much do they know about prenuptial agreements?
What do most people think about prenuptial agreements?
What might be this audience's greatest areas of concern or interest regarding the topic?

Answering the more specific questions related to your audience helps you to determine the depth and breadth of information needed to answer your more general questions. By developing questions based on your understanding of the needs of your audience, you can increase the likelihood of establishing an effective speaker-audience connection. Reflect again on your audience *after* you have gathered information to determine whether or not you have collected enough material and if it is the right type of material to meet your audience's needs and interests.

2. Assess Your Own Knowledge and Skills

Some students find topic selection difficult because they think they have nothing to offer or the class will not be interested. Upon reflection, however, you may find you have unique experiences or you have knowledge that others do not. Perhaps you were an exchange student, so you have had firsthand experience of another culture. Maybe you were raised by parents who spoke a different language, and you know what it is like to be bilingual. Maybe you live with an unusual disease.

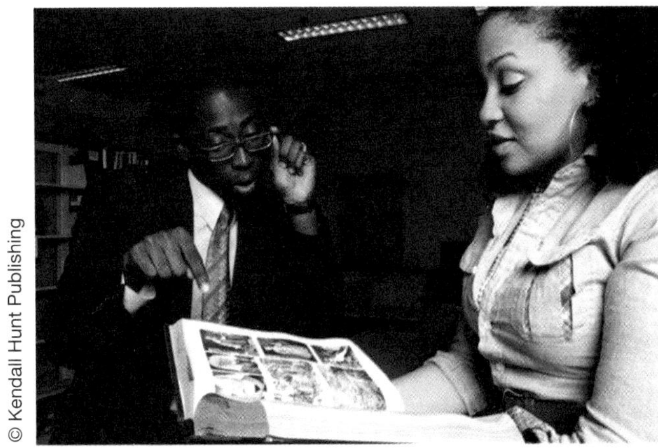

Do you have unique knowledge that would make an interesting speech topic?

Start your research process by assessing your own knowledge and skills. Most likely, you have direct knowledge or experience related to several topics. Your family may own a monument shop or a restaurant, and you grew up exposed to issues related to these professions. Maybe by the time you started college, you held one or more jobs, joined a political club, pursued hobbies like video games, or played sports such as soccer or rugby. You may know more about Jackie Chan movies than anyone on campus, or you may play disk golf. Examining your unique experiences or varied interests is a logical starting point for developing a speech.

Having personal knowledge or experience can make an impact on your audience. A student with Type I diabetes can speak credibly on what it is like to take daily injections and deal with the consequences of both low and high blood sugar. A student who works as a barista at the local coffee shop can demonstrate how to make a good shot of espresso. CAUTION: Remember the phrase, "Too much knowledge may be dangerous." Sometimes students want to share every detail with the audience, and that information can become tedious or overwhelming.

3. Search Print and Online Resources

Once you have assessed your own knowledge or skills, it is time to search print and online resources for other supporting material. The computer provides a rich playing field that also complicates our lives. We have more choices, but we have to work harder to sift through them.

Your search may result in more questions, including the following: What information is most essential to this topic? What will have the greatest impact? How much background do I need to give? Utilizing a variety of sources is advantageous for a variety of reasons; different sources focus on research, philosophy, or current events. They may be part of a daily publication, or are contained within a one-time publication. Sources target different audiences. We suggest you examine and evaluate materials from various sources to select materials that will help you most.

Avoid wasting valuable time floating aimlessly in cyberspace or walking around the library. Instead, if you need direction, *ask a librarian*. Librarians are experts in finding both print and online information efficiently, and they can show you how to use the library's newest search engines and databases. With new online and print resources being added daily, using the expertise of a librarian can make your job as a researcher much easier.

If you are new to campus, and your instructor has not arranged a library tour for your class, consider taking a workshop on using the library. Your library's home page is helpful. Most college libraries belong to a "live chat" consortium on the web, where students may contact a librarian twenty-four hours a day. Also, you can try the Library of Congress online Ask-a-Librarian Service at www.loc.gov and click on "Ask a librarian."

Narrow your focus It is natural to start with a broad topic. But as you search, the information you find will help you move to a more focused topic, enabling you to define—and refine—the approach you take to your speech. Say you are interested in giving an informative speech about the use of performance enhancement drugs in sports. You need to narrow your topic, but you are not quite sure what aspects to consider. Choose a search engine, such as Google, Yahoo!, AltaVista, or Excite.

Librarians are experts in finding information efficiently to help save research time.

Try conducting a **key-word search** on Google for "drugs in sports." This is very general. The key-word search leads you to a list of records which are weighted in order of amount of user access. You may have more than a million records or "hits" from which to choose. Look for valid subject headings, and search more deeply than the first three or four records listed.

Results of the key-word search lead you to many possibilities, including "anabolic steroids." You find a website that addresses topics such as what they are, how they work, who uses them, how prevalent they are, the different types, drugs banned by the NCAA, and medical uses. Now you have other areas to pursue. Decide what aspects you want to cover that are relevant to the audience and can be discussed effectively within the given time constraints. Perhaps you are interested in who uses them, so you enter "Who uses anabolic steroids?" This leads you to a website on uses and abuses of steroids. You know you need to define what anabolic steroids are and to find out how they are used and abused. You can continue your research by examining both print and online resources for these specific aspects of performance enhancement drugs. Now you can develop a specific purpose statement and search for information to support it.

As you search for information, keep three aspects of research in mind: First, recognize the distinction between primary and secondary sources. **Primary sources** include firsthand accounts such as diaries, journals, and letters, as well as statistics, speeches, and interviews. They are records of events as they are first described. **Secondary sources** generally provide an analysis, an explanation, or a restatement of a primary source. If the U.S. Surgeon General issues a report on the dangers of smoking, the report itself (available from the U.S. Surgeon General's Office) is the primary source; newspaper and magazine articles about the report are secondary source material.

JaxonPhotoGroup

Evaluating and using information appropriately is as important as finding it.

Second, there is a relationship between the length of your speech and the amount of time you must spend in research. Many students learn the hard way that five minutes of research will not suffice for a five-minute speech. Conventional wisdom suggests that for every one minute of speaking time, there is an hour of preparation needed. Whatever the length of the speech, you have to spend time uncovering facts and building a strong foundation of support.

Third, finding information is not enough; you must also be able to evaluate it (relevance, reliability, and so on), and utilize it in the most appropriate way in order to achieve your specific purpose. For example, your audience analysis may suggest that specific statistics are necessary to convince your audience. On the other hand, perhaps personal or expert testimony will be most persuasive. Overall, developing a research strategy is one of the most useful things you will learn in college.

Specific library resources In addition to providing access to computers for online searches, each library houses a variety of research materials, including books, reference materials, newspapers, magazines, journals, and government documents. Microfilm, specifically for archived newspapers may still be available, but the government has stopped producing microfiche. If information is not housed in your library, you can electronically extend your search far beyond your campus or community library through interlibrary loan. It may take two weeks or longer to process requests, so planning is especially important when relying on interlibrary loan.

Each library is different. One may not have the same databases or reference materials as another. Some libraries are depositories for your state, and it may be one of a few that receives state documents automatically.

Books. Historically, libraries have been most noted for their collection of books. Many universities have several libraries so students may access the large volume of books in general collections, archived collections, and specific collections. Using the library catalog is essential. Most libraries today have online computer catalogs, which contain records of all materials the library owns. In addition to identifying what books are available and where to find them, an online catalog will also indicate whether a particular book is checked out and when it is due back. Keep in mind that the library groups books by subject, so as you look in the stacks for a particular book, it makes sense to peruse surrounding books for additional resources.

General reference resources may be helpful as you begin your search for material.

General reference materials. At the beginning of your search, it may be helpful to start with one or more general reference resources, including encyclopedias, dictionaries, biographical sources, and statistical sources. Most likely, your time spent with these materials will be short, but these resources can provide you with basic facts and definitions.

Unlike some of our experiences in primary school, seldom does a student's research start and end with the encyclopedia. The *World Book Encyclopedia* is helpful if you are unfamiliar with a topic or concept. It can provide facts that are concise as well as easy to read and understand. Encyclopedias are either general or specialized. **General encyclopedias** (e.g., *The Encyclopedia Americana* and *Encyclopedia Britannica*) cover a wide range of topics in a broad manner. In contrast, **specialized encyclopedias,** such as the *Encyclopedia of Religion*, and the *International Encyclopedia of the Social Sciences*, focus on particular areas of knowledge in more detail. Over the last decade, there has been an explosion of discipline-specific encyclopedias. Articles in both general and specialized encyclopedias often contain bibliographies that lead you to additional sources.

Although encyclopedias are helpful as a basic resource, they generally are not accepted as main sources for class speeches. Use them to lead to other information. CAUTION: Do not fall into Wikipedia's web of easy access and understanding. Its legitimacy is questionable. Stephen Colbert, host of the TV show *The Colbert Report*, asked his viewers to log on to the entry "elephants" on Wikipedia.com to report that the elephant population in Africa "has tripled in the last six months." This online encyclopedia noted a spike in inaccurate entries shortly after the show aired. Most instructors discourage use of this online resource.

During your research, you may consult a dictionary when you encounter an unfamiliar word or term. They also provide information on pronunciation, spelling, word division, usage, and etymology (the origins and development of words). As with encyclopedias, dictionaries are classified as either general or specialized. It is likely you have used some general dictionaries such as the *American Heritage Dictionary* or the *Random House College Dictionary*. The dictionary is also just a click away. You might try

Merriam-Webster Online (www.m-w.com). Specialized dictionaries cover words associated with a specific subject or discipline, as in the following: *The American Political Dictionary, Black's Law Dictionary, Harvard Dictionary of Scientific and Technical Terms*, and *Webster's Sports Dictionary*. Many disciplines use their own specialized terminology that is more extensive and focused, and those definitions are found in their journals and books. CAUTION: Check with your instructor before beginning your speech with, "According to Webster's dictionary, the word ______ means . . ." As Harris (2002) notes in his book, *Using Sources Effectively*, "Generally speaking, starting with a dictionary definition not only lacks creativity but it may not be helpful if the definition is too general or vague" (35).

Biographical sources. Biographical sources, which are international, national, or specialized, provide information on an individual's education, accomplishments, and professional activities. This information is useful when evaluating someone's credibility and reliability. A biographical index indicates sources of biographical information in books and journals whereas a biographical dictionary lists and describes the accomplishments of notable people. If you are looking for a brief background of a well-known person, consult the biographical dictionary first. If you need an in-depth profile of a lesser-known person, the biographical index is the better source. Some examples of these sources are Author Biographies Master Index, Biography Index, the New York Times Index, Dictionary of American Biography, European Authors, World Authors, and Dictionary of American Scholars.

Statistical sources. When used correctly, statistics can provide powerful support. Facts and statistics give authority and credibility to research. Many federal agencies produce and distribute information electronically. The *American Statistics Index* (ASI) includes both an index and abstracts of statistical information published by the federal government. Try also the *Index to International Statistics* (IIS) and the *Statistical Abstract of the United States*. The online source LexisNexis touts itself as providing "authoritative legal, news, public records and business information" (www.lexisnexis.com).

Magazines, newspapers, and journals. Magazines (also known as periodicals) and newspapers provide the most recent print information. Once you identify ideas that connect with the needs of your audience, you can look for specific information in magazines and newspapers. General indexes cover such popular magazines and newspapers such as *Time*, *Newsweek*, *U.S. News & World Report*, the *New York Times*, and the *Chicago Tribune*. The *Readers' Guide to Periodical Literature* is an index available online as well as in print form. Other popular indexes include: the *New York Times Index*, *Wall Street Journal*, *Christian Science Monitor*, *Los Angeles Times*, *The Education Index*, *Humanities Index*, *Public Affairs Information Service Bulletin*, *Social Sciences and Humanities Index*, and *Social Sciences Index*.

Newspapers and magazines can be distinquished from journals in many ways. First, the frequency of distribution is different. While newspapers can be accessed daily, and magazines are either weekly or monthly, journals are usually quarterly publications. Second, authors of articles in newspapers and magazines are generally paid by their publisher, whereas authors of journal articles (usually referred to as "researchers" rather than "authors") are generally experts in their particular fields, and have submitted their article(s) on a competitive, reviewed basis. In general, the more prestigious the journal, the more difficult it is to get an article printed in it. Journals may have editorials or book reviews, but they generally focus on qualitative and quantitative research conducted by professionals—doctors, professors, lawyers, and so on. Third, magazines and newspapers are written for general audiences, whereas journal articles are written for a specific audience; an example would be faculty or graduate students interested in communication apprehension. Many journals can be accessed online, but not all are available electronically.

Fourth, and very importantly, journals focus on original, qualitative, and quantitative research. Much of the content in a journal is considered to be a primary source because it reports findings from research conducted by the author.

Government documents. Government documents are prepared by agencies, bureaus, and departments that monitor the affairs and activities of the nation. Documents are issued by the Office of the President, the U.S. Congress, the departments of Commerce, Agriculture, Education, Navy and Army, Indian Affairs, the Veterans' Administration, the Food and Drug Administration, and the FBI.

Through the U.S. Government Printing Office (GPO) one can find unique, authoritative, and timely materials, including detailed census data, vital statistics, congressional papers and reports, presidential documents, military reports, and impact statements on energy, the environment, and pollution. Consult the Monthly Catalog of United States Government Publications, which is available online.

Online research As stated earlier, your librarian can lead you to a variety of material. An enormous amount of databases exist, and one can approach web research in many ways. Without help of some kind, looking for information on the web is like upending the library in a football field and being given a pen light to search for information. The librarian can at least provide you with stadium lights.

If you're unfamiliar with online databases, ask the librarian for assistance.

Consider using online databases such as InfoTrac and EBSCO. According to InfoTrac College Edition's website (infotrac. thomsonlearning.com), more than 20 million articles from nearly 6,000 sources are available to you. The advantage of using this resource is that you may access cross-disciplinary, reliable, full-length articles. It is free of advertising and available twenty-four hours a day. EBSCO (www.ebsco.com) offers a similar service, and claims to be the most widely used online resource, with access to over 100 databases, and thousands of e-journals. By the time this book is printed, it is a sure bet that even more databases will be available.

Web evaluation criteria Many students will start their research online. Computers are in dorm rooms, dorm halls, academic buildings, and the library. It may take only a few steps to access one. While there is nothing inherently wrong with this, we urge you to proceed with caution. Evaluating the credibility of your online resources is critical. The quantity of information available via the Internet is colossal, and includes highly respected research as well as pure fiction presented as fact. Seek information from competent, qualified sources and avoid information from uninformed individuals with little or no credentials. Ultimately, you are held accountable for the quality and credibility of the sources you use.

As you access each website, it is important to evaluate its legitimacy as a source for your speech. Radford and his colleagues (2006) identify five web evaluation criteria that serve as useful standards for evaluating online information.

1. **Authority.** Authority relates to the concept of credibility. As we know, virtually anyone can become a web publisher. A website that passes this first test contains information provided by an individual, group, or organization known to have expertise in the area.

Questions to guide evaluation include the following:

- What toe of group put up the site? (Educational institution? Government agency? Individual? Commercial business? Organization)
- Can you identify the author(s)? (What is the organization or who is the person repsonsible for the information?)
- What are the credentials of those repsonsible?

2. **Accuracy.** A website that is accurate is reliable and error-free. One aspect of accuracy is timeliness. If the last time the site was updated was two years ago and the site is discussing a bill before the legislature, then it is no longer accurate. One assumes more accuracy when it is clear that information is scrutinized in some way before being placed on the web. Accuracy is clearly related to authority, since the sites with greater authority are most likely to have mechanisms for determining how something becomes "site-worthy."

Questions to guide evaluation include the following:

- Is the information accurate?
- Does the information confirm or contradict what is found in printed sources?
- Are references given to the sources of information?

3. **Objectivity.** The extent to which website material is presented without bias or distortion relates to objectivity. As you examine the material, you want to determine if it is presented as opinion or fact.

Questions to guide evaluation include the following:

- What is the age level of the intended audience? (Adults? Teenagers? Children?)
- Is the information on the site factual or an expression of opinion?
- Is the author controversial? A known conservative? A known liberal?
- What are the author's credentials?

4. **Coverage.** Coverage refers to the depth and breadth of the material. It may be difficult to determine who the site is targeting. As a result, material may be too general or too specific. Determine if it meets your needs or if critical information is missing.

Questions to guide evaluation include the following:

- What is the intended purpose of the site? (Educational? Informational? Commercial? Recreational?)
- Who is the intended audience (General public? Scholars? Students? Professionals?)
- Is information common knowledge? Too basic? Too technical?
- Does information include multiple aspects of the issue or concern?

5. **Currency.** Currency refers to the timeliness of the material. Some websites exist that have never been updated. Information may be no longer valid or useful. If you look for "Most popular books of the year," and find a site from 2003, that information is no longer current or relevant. Looking at birth rates or literacy rates from the past would not produce relevant information if you are looking for the most recent information.

Questions to guide evaluation include the following:

- When was the site created?
- Is the material recent?
- Is the website updated?

It's easy to access computer resources, but make sure you carefully evaluate the material you find.

When using these five criteria to evaluate your online information, remember that *all* criteria should be met, not just one or two of the above. Accurate and current information must also be objective. If critical information is missing (coverage), no matter how accurate and current the information is, it should be eliminated as a source.

4. Interview, If Appropriate

Interviews are useful if you want information too new to be found in published sources or if you want to give your listeners the views of an expert. By talking to an expert, you can clarify questions and fill in knowledge gaps, and you may learn more about a subject than you expected. In the process, you also gather opinions based on years of experience.

Look around your campus and community. You will find experts who can tell you as much as you need to know about thousands of subjects. You can get opinions about the stock market, the effect of different types of running shoes on the development of shin splints, race relations, No Child Left Behind legislation, ethanol, water or air pollution, or curbside recycling.

If you decide to interview one or more people, we offer the following four suggestions:

Contact the person well in advance. Remember, *you* are the one who needs the information. Do not think that leaving one voice message is the extent of your responsibility. You may have to make several attempts to contact the person. Schedule a date and time to interview that leaves you with ample time to prepare your speech.

Prepare questions in advance. Make sure you know what topics need to be covered and what information needs to be clarified.

Develop questions in a logical order. One question should lead naturally to another. Place the most important questions at the top to guarantee that they will be answered before your time is up.

Stay within the agreed time frame. If you promise the interview will take no longer than a half hour, keep your word, if at all possible. Do not say, "It'll just take a minute," when you need at least fifteen minutes. Build in a little time to ask unplanned questions, questions based on the interviewee's answers or for clarification.

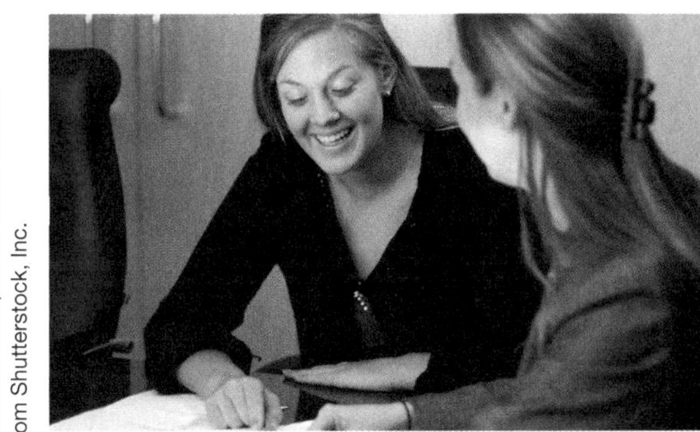

When you conduct an interview, make sure your questions develop in a logical order to get the information you need.

After reading this section on research, hopefully you are aware that it involves a significant time commitment. It is never too early to start thinking about your next speech topic and where you might find sources. Explore a variety of resources. Ask for help from your instructor or the librarian. Make sure you know the constraints of the assignment.

Citing Sources in Your Speech

Any research included in your speech needs to be cited appropriately in order to give due credit. If you interviewed someone, your audience should know the person's name, credentials, and when and where you spoke with him or her. If you use information from a website, the audience should know the name of the website and when you accessed it. For print information, the audience generally needs to know the author, date, and type of publication. Your credibility is connected to your source citation.

Expert sources and timely information add to your credibility. Essentially, all research used in your speech needs to be cited. Otherwise, you have committed an act of plagiarism. Following are ways to cite sources in your speech. *Consult with your instructor,* however, as he or she may have specific concerns.

Example 1

Correct source citation. In their 1995 book on family communication, researchers Yerby, Buerkel-Rothfuss and Bochner argue that it is difficult to understand family behavior "without an adequate description of the historical, physical, emotional, and relational context in which it occurs."

Incorrect source citation. Researchers on family communication argue that it is difficult to understand family behavior without an adequate description of the historical, physical, emotional, and relational context in which it occurs.

Explanation. We need the date to evaluate the timeliness of the material. We need to know that this information was found in a book, as opposed to a television show, a newspaper, magazine, or other source. We need the authors' names so we know who wrote the information, and so we can find the book.

Example 2

Correct source citation. According to a personal interview last week with Diane Ruyle, principal of Danube High School, fewer students are choosing vocational classes than they were ten years ago.

Incorrect source citation. According to Diane Ruyle, fewer students are choosing vocational classes.

Explanation. We need to know why the person cited Diane Ruyle. As a principal, she ought to be able to provide accurate information regarding course selection. Adding "than they were ten years ago" gives the listener a comparison basis.

Example 3

Correct source citation. According to an Associated Press article published in the *New York Times* on August 9, 2007, "unlike in South Carolina, state laws in Iowa and New Hampshire require officials there to hold the first caucus and primary in the nation, respectively."

Incorrect source citation. "Unlike in South Carolina, state laws in Iowa and New Hampshire require officials there to hold the first caucus and primary in the nation, respectively."

Explanation. First, if this is published information, it should be cited. Second, most of us do not know these facts, a citation is necessary. Otherwise, the speaker could be making this up. The date provided allows us to look up the source and shows us that the information is timely. No author was identified, and since Associated Press articles can be found in many newspapers, it is important to note this was found in the *New York Times*.

Example 4

Correct source citation. According to the current American Diabetes Association website, "Cholesterol is carried through the body in two kinds of bundles called lipoproteins—low-density lipoproteins and high-density lipoproteins. It's important to have healthy levels of both."

Incorrect source citation. Cholesterol is carried through the body in two kinds of bundles called lipoproteins—low-density lipoproteins and high-density lipoproteins. It's important to have healthy levels of both.

Explanation. This information is not common knowledge, so it should be cited. Many different organizations might include such information on their website, so it is important to note that it came from the American Diabetes Association (ADA). An audience would infer that the ADA is a credible organization regarding this topic. Using the word "current" suggests that one could find that information today on the ADA website, which reinforces the timeliness of the material.

In summary, remember that you *do not* need to cite sources when you are reporting your own original ideas or discussing ideas that are commonly held. You *must* cite sources when you are quoting directly or paraphrasing (restating or summarizing a source's ideas in your own words). You must also cite the source of an illustration, diagram, or graph. Providing the date of publication, date of website access, credentials of the source, and/or type of publication where applicable will allow the listener to evaluate the credibility of the information.

Supporting Your Speech

Imagine a chef with a piece of steak, some cauliflower, and rice, the main ingredients for a dinner special. What the chef does with these raw materials will influence the response of the consumers. The chef decides whether to grill, broil, bake, steam, or fry. Different spices can be used for different results. Numerous possibilities exist.

The research you have gathered for your speech can be viewed as the raw material. Now you need to figure out how to organize and present the material in the most effective way for your audience. This is where the concept of supporting material applies.

Supporting material gives substance to your assertions. If you say that *Casablanca* is the best movie ever produced in Hollywood, you are stating your opinion. If you cite a film critic's essay that notes it is the best movie ever, then your statement has more weight. You may also be able to find data that indicates how well the movie did, and a public opinion poll that had it ranked as the top movie. These different resources provide support. Just about anything that supports a speaker's idea can be considered supporting material.

When developing your speech, you also have many decisions to make. Consider the following example:

Your public speaking professor has just given your class an assignment to deliver an informative speech on the problem of shoplifting. These two versions are among those presented:

> **Version 1:**
> Shoplifting is an enormous problem for American retailers, who lose billions of dollars each year to customer theft. Not unexpectedly, retailers pass the cost of shoplifting onto consumers, which means that people like you and me pay dearly for the crimes of others.

Shoplifting is increasingly becoming a middle-class crime. Experts tell us that many people shoplift just for kicks—for the thrill of defying authority and for the excitement of getting away with something that is against the law. Whatever the reason, one in fifteen Americans is guilty of this crime.

Version 2:
Imagine walking up to a store owner once a year and giving that person $300 without getting anything in return. Could you afford that? Would you want to do that? Yet that's what happens. Every year, the average American family of four forks over $300 to make amends for the crimes of shoplifters.

Shoplifting is a big cost to big business. According to recent statistics from the National Association for the Prevention of Shoplifting, people who walk out of stores without first stopping at the cash register take with them more than $13 billion annually. That's more than $25 million per day. Their website claims that one out of eleven of us is guilty of this crime. To bring this figure uncomfortably close to home, that's at least two students in each of your classes.

Interestingly, shoplifting is no longer a poor person's crime. Hard as it is to imagine, many shoplifters can well afford to buy what they steal. Wynona Ryder received a great deal of unwanted press when she shoplifted $5,000 worth of merchandise at a Beverly Hills store in 2001.

Why do middle- and upper-income people steal? According to psychiatrist James Spikes, quoted in a recent *Ms.* magazine, shoplifters are "defying authority. They're saying, 'The hell with them. I'll do it anyway . . . . I can get away with it . . . .'" Psychologist Stanton Samenow, quoted in the July issue of *Life* magazine, agrees:

"Shoplifters will not accept life as it is; they want to take shortcuts. They do it for kicks" (Sawyer, Glenn Dowling 1988).

Although both versions say essentially the same thing, they are not equally effective. The difference is in the supporting materials.

Five Functions of Support

Support should strengthen your speech in five ways. Comparing Version 1 with Version 2 will help illustrate the value of supporting material.

1. *Support is specific.*
   Version 2 gives listeners more details than Version 1. We learn, for example, how much shoplifting costs each of us as well as the financial burden retailers must carry.
2. *Support helps to clarify ideas.*
   We learn much more about the reasons for shoplifting from Version 2. This clarification—from the mouths of experts—reduces the risk of misunderstanding.
3. *Support adds weight.*
   The use of credible statistics and expert opinion adds support to the second version's main points. This type of support convinces listeners by building a body of evidence that may be

difficult to deny. The testimonies of Drs. Spikes and Samenow are convincing because they are authoritative. We believe what they say far more than we do unattributed facts.

Effective support is used to develop the message you send..

4. *Support is appropriate to your audience.*
   Perhaps the most important difference between these two versions is Verssion 2's attempt to gear the supporting material to the audience. It is a rare college student who would not care about a $300 overcharge or who cannot relate to the presence of two possible shoplifters in each class. Also, movie star Wynona Ryder's shoplifting is noted in Version 2. Students are familiar with her name, but college students would not be as familiar with an older famous person who has shoplifted, such as Bess Myerson, winner of Miss America in 1945 and actress on several television shows in the 1960s.
5. *Support creates interest.*
   Although Version 1 provides information, it arouses little or no interest. Listeners have a hard time caring about the problem or becoming emotionally or intellectually involved. Version 2, on the other hand, creates interest through the use of meaningful statistics, quotations, and an example. When used properly, supporting materials can transform ordinary details into a memorable presentation.

Effective support is used to develop the message you send to your listeners. It is through this message that communication takes place between speaker and audience. In public speaking, you cannot separate the act of speaking from the message the speaker delivers. Supporting your message is one of your most important tasks as you develop your speech.

Forms of Support

Effective speeches generally rely on multiple forms of support. To give your speech greater weight and authority, at least five forms of support can be used. These include facts, statistics, examples, testimony, and analogies. Each of these forms of support will be discussed, and guidelines for using them will be presented.

Facts Nothing undermines a presentation faster than too few facts. **Facts** are pieces of information that are verifiable and irrefutable. **Opinions** are points of view that may or may not be supported in fact. Too often, speakers confuse fact and opinion when adding supporting material to a speech. For example, while it is a fact that Forest Whitaker won the 2007 Academy Award for Best Actor, it is opinion to state that he is the best actor in Hollywood.

Facts serve at least three different purposes:

1. *Facts clarify your main point.*
   They remove ambiguity, making it more likely that the message you send is the message your audience will receive.
2. *Facts indicate your knowledge of the subject.*
   Rather than say, "The League of Women Voters has been around for a long time," report, "The League of Women Voters was founded in 1919." Your audience wants to know that you have researched the topic and can discuss specifics about your topic.
3. *Facts define.*
   Facts provide needed definitions that may explain new concepts. If you are delivering a speech on "functional illiteracy," you may define the term in the following way:

> While an illiterate adult has no ability to read, write, or compute, relatively few Americans fall into this category. However, some 27 million Americans can't read, write, compute, speak, or listen effectively enough to function in society. They cannot read street signs, write out a check, apply for a job or ask a government bureaucrat about a Social Security check they never received. Although they may have minimal communications skills, for all intents and purposes, they are isolated from the rest of society. These people are considered functionally illiterate.

Include facts that will clarify the concepts you are describing in your speech.

In the above example, you anticipated the potential confusion between the terms "illiteracy" and "functional illiteracy," and you differentiated between these terms. While you defined this term for your public speaking class, if your audience was comprised of literacy coaches, this would not be necessary.

Guidelines for using facts **Carefully determine the number of facts to use.** Too few facts will reveal that you spent little time researching, while too many may overwhelm your listeners. Sometimes, students want to impress their audience, or at least their instructor, with the amount of research completed for a particular speech. The desire to include all information may result in a "data dump," where facts are given in a steady stream with little or no connection to the speech or to each other. This results in an overload of information that is difficult to process.

To be effective, the number and complexity of your facts must be closely tied to the needs of your listeners. A speech to a group of hikers on poison ivy prevention may include practical issues such as identifying the plant and recognizing, treating, and avoiding the rash. However, if you are delivering a speech on the same subject to a group of medical students, a detailed explanation of the body's biochemical response to the plant is probably more relevant.

Make sure your meanings are clear. If you use words or phrases that have different meanings to you than they do to members of your audience, the impact of your speech is lessened. Misunderstandings occur when your audience attributes meanings to terms you did not intend. Think about the following words: success, liberal, conservative, patriot, happiness, good, bad, and smart. Collectively, we do not agree on the meanings of these words. One person may define success in terms of material wealth, while another may think of it in terms of family relationships, job satisfaction, and good health. When it is essential that your audience understand the meaning you intend, take the time to define it carefully as you speak.

Define terms when they are first introduced. The first time you use a term that requires an explanation, define it so that your meaning is clear. If you are talking about the advantages of belonging to a health maintenance organization, define the term the first time it is used.

Statistics The second form of supporting material is **statistics**: the collection, analysis, interpretation, and presentation of information in numerical form. Statistics give us the information necessary to understand the magnitude of issues and to compare and contrast different points. Basic measures include the mean, median, and mode, which are generally referred to as descriptive statistics, because they allow us to discuss a set of numbers easily. The **mean** is calculated by adding all the numbers in a group and dividing by the number of items. It is the most widely used statistical measure. The **median** measures the middle score in the group. That is, half the values fall above it and half fall below. The **mode** is the value that occurs most frequently.

But statistics can be misleading. For example, if one were to examine the National League Baseball (NLB) salaries for 2005, one would find the average, or mean, salary for those players was $2,585,804 (http://asp.usatoday.com/sports/baseball/salaries). However, the highest salary went to San Francisco Giant's Barry Bonds who earned $22 million. Meanwhile, the median salary for all NLB players was $800,000. This means that half of the 439 players received more than $800,000 and half received less than that. In addition, the mode was $316,000. Twenty-six players received this amount. In this case, simply discussing these three statistical measures is not helpful, unless you want to make the point that salaries are not consistent. It might make more sense to discuss the range of salaries or look at a particular group of players' salaries. When using statistics in your speech, it is important to understand what they mean.

Guidelines for using statistics **Be precise.** Make sure you understand the statistics before including them in your speech. Consider the difference between the following statements.

> A 2-percent decrease was shown in the rate of economic growth, as measured by the gross national product, compared to the same period last year.
> The gross national product dropped by 2 percent compared to the same period last year.

In the first case, the statistic refers to a drop in the rate of growth—it tells us that the economy is growing at a slower pace but that it is still ahead of last year—while in the second, it refers to an actual drop in the gross national product in comparison to the previous year. These statements say two very different things.

It is critical that you not misinterpret statistics when analyzing the data. If you have questions, refer to a basic statistics text or another source that further explains the data.

Avoid using too many statistics. Too many statistics will confuse and bore your audience and blunt the impact of your most important statistical points. Save your statistics for the places in your speech where they will make the most impact.

Round off your numbers. Is it important for your audience to know that, according to the Census Bureau's daily population projection on March 3, 2006, the U.S. population reached 298,228,575? The figure will have greater impact—and your audience will be more likely to remember it—if you round it off to "more than 298,000,000."

Cite your sources. Because statistics are rarely remembered for very long, it is easy for speakers to misquote and misuse them—often in a calculated way for their own ends. As an ethical speaker, you need to make sure your statistics are correct and you need to quote your sources. For example, if you were talking about the history of Girl Scout cookies, you could mention that during peak production of Girl Scout cookies, according to the Little Brownie Bakery website (www.littlebrowniebakers.com), one of two bakers for the Girl Scouts, 1,050,000 pounds of flour a week are used in production.

Use visual aids to express statistics. Statistics become especially meaningful to listeners when they are presented in visual form. Visual presentations of statistics free you from the need to repeat a litany of numbers that listeners will probably never remember. Instead, by transforming these numbers into visual presentations, you can highlight only the most important points, allowing your listeners to refer to the remaining statistics at any time. For example, in a speech extolling the virtues of graduate school, a graph displaying average salaries by degrees earned would be helpful. (See Figure 7.1).

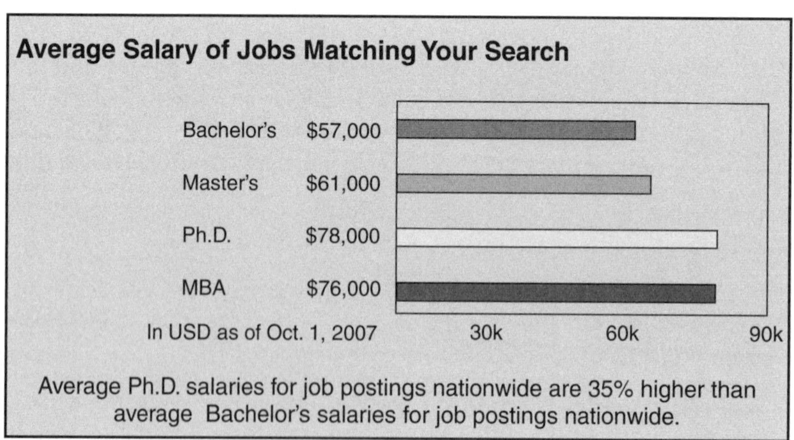

Figure 7.1 A bar graph can be used to clearly illustrate differences in values.

Examples Examples enliven speeches in a way that no other form of supporting material can. Grounding material in the specifics of everyday life has the power to create an empathic bond between speaker and audience, a bond strong enough to tie listeners to a speech and the speaker even after the example is complete.

Examples can be brief or extended, real or hypothetical, and narrative. Although examples differ in length, factual base, and source, their effectiveness lies in the extent to which they support the speaker's core idea.

Examples are brief or extended. Brief examples are short illustrations that clarify a general statement. If you made the following assertion: "Americans are more modest than Europeans," you could support it by using brief examples, such as, "If you take a walk on the beach in Italy or France, you should not be surprised to find women sunbathing topless. Also, many European countries, such as Sweden and Germany, have public saunas that are enjoyed by men and women—who are in the same sauna, sitting naked on their towels." Brief examples can be used effectively throughout a speech. Your decision to use them will depend on many factors, including the needs of your audience, the nature of your material, and your approach.

Extended examples are longer and richer in detail than brief examples. They are used most effectively to build images and to create a lasting impression on the audience, as can been seen in the following excerpt from a speech in 2006 given by Steven Darimont, candidate for sheriff in Coles County, Illinois. When making the point that money is spent unnecessarily on jail food, he stated:

> "Our food budget alone is at $140,000 and we will go over that by $12–15,000 this year. The sheriff has requested that (amount) be raised (an additional) $20,000, to $160,000 next year. The inmates currently get three hot meals a day. An example of this is breakfast: scrambled eggs, toast with butter and jelly, cold cereal with milk, hash browns, fruit, and juice. The Department of Corrections mandates only one hot meal per day, yet we feed three hot meals."

Providing more detail about the budget and the ample food choices creates a greater impact on the listener rather than saying, "We provide three hot meals a day, and we're going over budget."

Because of their impact, extended examples should not be overused or used at inappropriate points. As with other forms of support, they should be reserved for the points at which they will have the greatest effect: in clarifying the message, persuading listeners to your point of view, or establishing a speaker-audience relationship.

Examples are real or hypothetical. Sometimes the best examples are real, and come from your personal experience. By revealing parts of your life that relate to your speech topic, you provide convincing evidence and, at the same time, potentially create a powerful bond between you and your audience. Consider the student who has watched her mother die from lung cancer. The experience of hearing about the diagnosis, discussing treatment possibilities, and making final arrangements while her mother was alive can have a powerful effect on the audience. The words and emotion have great impact because the situation is real, not hypothetical, and the speaker provides a sense of reality to the topic.

At times, it suits the speaker's purpose to create a fictional example, rather than a real example, to make a point. Although these examples are not based on facts, the circumstances they describe are often realistic and thus effective.

As an educator and school administrator for more than twenty years, I have witnessed many transitions in the evolution of public education. I have also witnessed the effect that misguided politicians can have on the state of our educational process. I welcome the opportunity to share with you, using the case study method, how one such initiative *No Child Left Behind Act of 2001* affected the life of one disadvantaged student. The *No Child Left Behind Act of 2001* was based on the belief that by setting high standards and measurable goals, we can improve an individual's performance. As I share with you the case of Dwayne Jefferson, you can draw your own conclusion as to the success of this controversial initiative.

Dwayne Jefferson was a fourteen year old who attended school in a rural area in a southern town. He came from a single family home in which the mother worked two jobs to support him and his five brothers and sisters. Dwayne had below level reading scores since the first grade because there was no parent at home to assist him with homework and to encourage him to read. In lieu of a babysitter at an early age, Dwayne's mother enrolled him in an afternoon intramural basketball program in which he excelled. At the end of the final game of the season, the local high school basketball coach approached Dwayne to congratulate him on an excellent game. Never being recognized as a good student, Dwayne was excited that the coach recognized his talent on the basketball court and that he could excel in some aspect of his life. After congratulating Dwayne, the coach asked if he would be interested in joining the local high school basketball team in the fall since he would be entering high school in the next academic year. Dwayne shrugged his shoulders and said, "Sure, I'd like that." After taking Dwayne's phone number, the coach told him that if he worked hard and stayed out of trouble, he would have a great career, and by his senior year he would be on his way to play at a reputable college.

At the end of that school year, Dwayne's mother received a letter from the school guidance counselor stating that the school regretted to inform her that Dwayne had not scored high enough on the standardized reading test to matriculate from middle school to high school. Dwayne's mother asked the high school guidance counselor about her son's options. Her questions included: What programs have been put in place so that my son can continue his education with other students of his age? What assistance can I request to ensure that Dwayne receives the required score next year? Finally and most importunately, his mother asked, why haven't measures been taken prior to a test of this magnitude to ensure Dwayne was successful?

Needless to say, the case of Dwayne Jefferson is not uncommon. Early that fall Dwayne received a call from the basketball coach at the local high school. Unfortunately, Dwayne had only bad news to give the coach about his anticipated participation on the team. As you can imagine, the case of Dwayne Jefferson brings to the forefront many of the criticisms of the *No Child Left Behind Act of 2001,* from the allegation of "gaming" the system to illuminating the "problems" with standardized tests, the program has faced an uphill battle.

Hypothetical examples are useful when you want to exaggerate a point as the educator did. They are also useful when you cannot find a factual illustration for your speech. To be effective, they must be tied in some way to the point you are trying to illustrate.

It is important that your listeners know when you are using a hypothetical example and when you are not. Avoid confusion by introducing these examples in a direct way. You might start out by saying, "Imagine that you live next door to a college professor we'll call Dr. Supple," or "Let's talk about a hypothetical mother on welfare named Alice."

Examples can be in narrative form. Narratives are stories within a speech, anecdotes that create visual images in listeners' minds. In many ways, they take extended examples a step further by involving listeners in a tale that captures attention and makes a point—a story connected to the speaker's core idea. Many listeners love a good story, and when the speech is over, the narrative is what they remember.

Imagine Laura, a person who has traveled significantly, giving an informative speech on "The art of shopping outside the United States: Bartering made simple." She might include the following:

> My husband and I were in Morocco shopping with my mother and my aunt. They stopped to speak with a shop owner about carpets and my husband and I went on. About forty-five minutes later, we walked by to see them STILL speaking with the shop owner. Now, though, all three were seated, and they were drinking hot, mint tea. We approached the shopkeeper and introduced ourselves. He proceeded to tell us how different my mother and aunt were from most American women. He said that American women will ask the price of something, and he'll throw out some high price. Then the women will offer a significantly lower price. He rejects that but comes down on his original high price. The American women, usually, will accept his second price, no matter how high! Not these women! My mom and aunt bartered back and forth with the shopkeeper about the price, never giving in! The shopkeeper said he really enjoyed negotiating with them; that they were both friendly **and** insistent. They didn't back down easily, and, according to the shopkeeper, they ended up paying a reasonable price for their carpet.

By their nature, narratives demand that listeners take an active part in linking the story to the speaker's main point. The story moves from beginning to middle, to end. Even if the speaker supplies the link after the narrative, audience members still make the connections themselves as they listen.

A narrative can be used anywhere in a speech. No matter where it is placed, it assumes great importance to listeners as they become involved with the details. Through the narrative, speakers can establish a closeness with the audience that may continue even after the story is over.

Guidelines for using examples Examples add interest and impact. They should be representative because examples support your core idea only when they accurately represent the situation. No matter the type of example you use as supporting material, the following three guidelines will help you choose examples for your speeches:

Use examples frequently. Examples are often the lifeblood of a speech. Use them to make your points—but only in appropriate places. When using examples to prove a point, more than one example generally is needed.

Use only the amount of detail necessary. To make your examples work, you want to use only the amount of detail necessary for your audience and no more. The detail you provide in examples should be based on the needs of your audience. If your listeners are familiar with a topic, you can simply mention what the audience already knows. Interspersing long examples with short ones varies the pace and detail of your discussion.

Use examples to explain new concepts. Difficult concepts become easier to handle when you clarify them with examples. Keep in mind that although you may be comfortable with the complexities of a topic, your listeners might be hearing these complexities for the first time. Appropriate examples can mean the difference between communicating with or losing your audience.

Testimony The word testimony may conjure a vision of witnesses in a court of law giving sworn statements to a judge and jury, adding credibility to a case. In public speaking, testimony has nothing to do with the law, but it has everything to do with credibility. When you cite the words of others, either directly or through paraphrasing, you are attempting, in effect, to strengthen your position by telling your audience that people with special knowledge support your position or take your side. Testimony can cite either experience or opinion. Also, short quotations may be an effective way to provide testimony.

In order to be effective, however, testimony needs to be used in its proper context. Purposefully distorting the testimony of an expert to suit the needs of your speech is misleading and unethical. Be honest to your source as well as your audience.

Experience as testimony. Experience may be the most credible choice in some cases because someone was "on the scene." For example, hundreds of thousands of individuals were directly affected by hurricane Katrina. A student writer for the University of Texas at Austin newspaper interviewed Lorraine Brown about her personal experience during hurricane Katrina. The following account was printed in the September 6, 2005 issue of *The Daily Texan*.

> At 5 a.m. on Monday, after floodwaters breached the New Orleans levees, Brown awoke to find water seeping into her house. 'I saw the water on my kitchen floor, and I picked up a mop and started mopping. But then I looked out the window and saw that the water was already up to here,' she said, holding her hand at her waist.

Lorraine Brown's experience as one of the survivors of the hurricane provides vivid imagery that helps the listener recognize the terror that many experienced.

It is possible to use your own testimony when you are an expert. If you are writing a speech on what it is like to recover from a spinal cord injury, use your own expert testimony if you have suffered this injury. Similarly, if you are talking about the advantages and problems of being a female lifeguard, cite your own testimony if you are female and have spent summers saving lives at the beach. When you do not have the background necessary to convince your audience, use the testimony of those who do.

Opinion as testimony. In some circumstances, the opinion of a recognized authority may provide the credibility needed to strengthen your argument or prove a point. Jimmy Carter, former president and winner of the Nobel Peace Prize in 2002, is an outspoken critic of the Iraqi War. At a news conference in July 2005, CBS News quoted him as saying, "I thought then, and I think now, that the invasion of Iraq was unnecessary and unjust. And I think the premises on which it was launched were false" (www.cbsnews.com). While he is clearly stating an opinion, Carter carries a certain amount of credibility because of his previous position as president of the United States and as a Nobel Peace Prize winner.

Short quotations. A short quotation is a form of testimony, but its purpose is often different. Frequently, short quotations are used to set the tone for a speech, to provide humor, or to make important points more memorable. If you were receiving the MVP award for football at your high school or college, you might start out with something like this:

> "Wow. I'm reminded of John Madden's words when he was inducted into the Pro Football Hall of Fame in 2006, 'And right now, I don't have, I got like numb, you know, a tingle from the bottom of my toes to the top of my head.' Yep. That's exactly how I feel."

Shown here making a statement after receiving the Nobel Peace Prize, Jimmy Carter's opinions carry credibility because of his past accomplishments.

Madden's quote is not the most articulate or insightful comment, but it certainly expressed the emotion the football player was feeling, and this quote would set an engaging tone for an acceptance speech.

Sometimes quotations are too long or too complicated to present verbatim. You can choose to cite the source but paraphrase the message. Instead of quoting the following description of the effect crack cocaine has on the body, it might be more effective to paraphrase.

Quote:

> According to Dr. Mark S. Gold, nationally known expert on cocaine abuse, founder of the 800-COCAINE helpline, and author of *The Facts About Drugs and Alcohol*, "as an anesthetic, cocaine blocks the conduction of electrical impulses within the nerve cells involved in sensory transmissions, primarily pain. The body's motor impulses, those that control muscle function, for example, are not affected by low-dose use

of cocaine. In this way cocaine creates a deadening blockage (known as a differential block) of pain, without interfering with body movement" (Gold 1986, 36).

Paraphrase: According to Dr. Mark S. Gold, nationally known expert on cocaine abuse,

founder of the 800-COCAINE helpline and author of *The Facts About Drugs and Alcohol*, cocaine blocks pain without interfering with body movement.

The second version is more effective when speaking to a lay audience who knows little about medicine, while the former is appropriate for an audience of science students or physicians.

Guidelines for using testimony **Use only recognizable or credible testimony and quotations.** At a time when media exposure is so pervasive, it is easy to find someone who will support your point of view. Before citing a person as an authoritative source, be sure that he or she is an expert. If you are giving a speech on the greatest movies ever produced, it would make sense to quote Roger Ebert, film critic and author of numerous books on the subject of film. However, he would not be the proper choice for a speech on the joys of collecting and trading baseball cards.

As you review expert testimony, keep in mind that the more research you do, the more opinions you will find. Ultimately, your choice should be guided by relevance and credibility of the source. The fact that you quote Supreme Court Justice Sandra Day O'Connor in a speech on affirmative action is as important as the quote itself.

Choose unbiased experts. How effective is the following testimony if its source is the *owner* of the Oakland Athletics?

There is no team in baseball as complete as the Athletics. The team has better pitching, fielding, hitting, and base running than any of its competitors in the National or American League.

If the same quote came from a baseball writer for *Sports Illustrated* you would probably believe it more. Thus, when choosing expert testimony, bear in mind that opinions shaped by self-interest are less valuable, from the point of view of your audience, than those motivated by the merits of the issues.

Identify the source. Not all names of your experts will be recognizable, so it is important to tell your audience

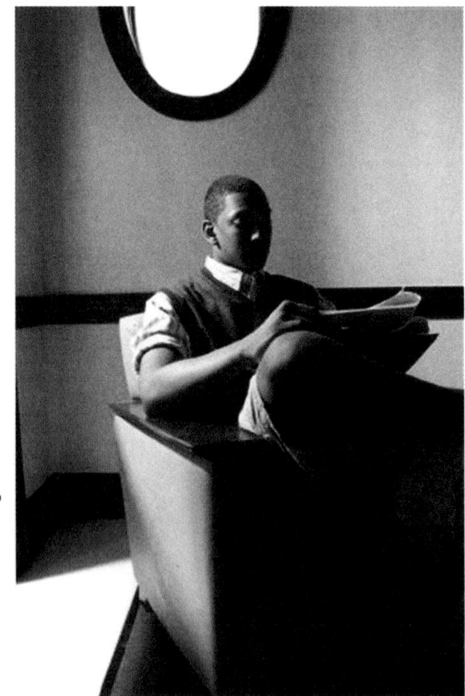

As you review expert testimony, keep in mind that the more research you do, the more opinions you wiil find.

why they are qualified to give testimony. If you are cautioning overseas travelers to avoid tourist scams, the following expert testimony provides support:

> According to Rick Steves, travelers should be wary of "The 'helpful' local: Thieves posing as concerned locals will warn you to store your wallet safely—and then steal it after they see where you stash it. Some thieves put out tacks and ambush drivers with their "assistance" in changing the tire. Others hang out at subway ticket machines eager to "help" the bewildered tourist buy tickets with a pile of quickly disappearing foreign cash" (www.ricksteves.com).

Without knowing anything about Rick Steves, your readers will have no reason to trust this advice. However, if you state his credentials first, you can establish the credibility of your expert. So instead, the speaker could start begin with, "According to Rick Steves, host and producer of the popular public television series *Rick Steves' Europe* and best-selling author of thirty European travel books, travelers should be wary of. . ."

Develop techniques to signal the beginning and ending of each quotation. Your audience may not know when a quote begins or ends. Some speakers prefer to preface quotations with the words, "And I quote" and to end quotations with the phrase, "end quote." Other speakers indicate the presence of quotations through pauses immediately before and immediately after the quotation or through a slight change of pace or inflection. It may be a good idea to use both techniques in your speech to satisfy your listeners' need for variety. Just do not make quotation signs with your fingers!

Analogies At times, the most effective form of supporting material is the analogy, which points out similarities between what we know and understand and what we do not know or cannot accept. Analogies fall into two separate categories: figurative and literal. **Figurative analogies** draw comparisons between things that are distinctly different in an attempt to clarify a concept or persuade. Biology professor and world-renowned environmentalist Paul Erlich uses an analogy of a globe holding and draining water to explain the problem of the world population explosion. The following is an excerpt from a speech delivered to the First National Congress on Optimum Population and Environment, June 9, 1970:

> As a model of the world demographic situation, think of the world as a globe, and think of a faucet being turned on into that globe as being the equivalent of the birth rate, the input into the population. Think of that drain at the base of that globe—water pouring out—as being the equivalent to the output, the death rate of the population. At the time of the Agricultural Revolution, the faucet was turned on full blast; there was a very high birth rate. The drain was wide open; there was a high death rate. There was very little water in the globe, very few people in the population—only above five million. When the Agricultural Revolution took place, we began to plug the drain, cut down the death rate, and the globe began to fill up.

This analogy is effective because it helps the audience understand the population explosion. It explains the nature of the problem in a clear, graphic way. Listener understanding comes not from the presentation of new facts (these facts were presented elsewhere in the speech) but from a simple comparison. When dealing with difficult or emotionally charged concepts, listeners benefit from this type of comparative supporting material.

Keep in mind that although figurative analogies may be helpful, they usually do not serve as sufficient proof in a persuasive argument. Erlich, for example, must back his analogy with facts, statistics, examples, and quotations to persuade his listeners that his analogy is accurate—that we are indeed in the midst of a population crisis.

A **literal analogy** compares like things from similar classes, such as a game of professional football with a game of college football. If, for example, you are delivering a speech to inform your classmates about Russia's involvement in the war in Afghanistan, the following literal analogy might be helpful:

> The war in Afghanistan was the former Soviet Union's Vietnam. Both wars were unwinnable from the start. Neither the Vietnamese nor the Afghans would tolerate foreign domination. Acting with the determination of the Biblical David, they waged a struggle against the Goliaths of Russia and the United States. In large part, the winning weapon in both wars was the collective might of village peasants who were determined to rid their countries of the Superpowers—no matter the odds.

Literal analogies serve as proof when the aspects or concepts compared are similar. When similarities are weak, the proof fails. The analogy, "As Rome fell because of moral decay, so will the United States," is valid only if the United States and Rome have similar economic and social systems, types of governments, and so on. The fewer the similarities between the United States and Rome, the weaker the proof.

Guidelines for using analogies **Use analogies to build the power of your argument.** Analogies convince through comparison to something the audience already knows. It is psychologically comforting to your listeners to hear new ideas expressed in a familiar context. The result is greater understanding and possible acceptance of your point of view.

Be certain the analogy is clear. Even when the concept of your analogy is solid, if the points of comparison are not effectively carried through from beginning to end, the analogy will fail. Your analogy must be as consistent and complete as in the following example:

In political campaigns, opponents square off against one another in an attempt to land the winning blow. Although after a close and grueling campaign that resembles a ten-round bout, one candidate may succeed by finding a soft spot in his opponent's record, the fight is hardly over. Even while the downed opponent is flat against the mat, the victor turns to the public and tells yet another distortion of the truth. "My opponent," he says, "never had a chance." Clearly, politicians and prize fighters share one goal in common: to knock their opponents senseless and to make the public believe that they did it with ease.

Avoid using too many analogies. A single effective analogy can communicate your point. Do not diminish its force by including several in a short presentation.

Summary

Research gives you the tools you need to support your thesis statement. A solid research base increases your credibility. To begin your research strategy, assess your personal knowledge and skills. Then look for print and online resources. The librarian can lead you to valuable sources within the physical library as well as online. You may need to look up information in encyclopedias, dictionaries, books, newspapers, magazines, journal articles, and government documents. When using online resources, it is important to use website evaluation criteria and to question accuracy, authority, objectivity, coverage, and currency.

Supporting materials buttress the main points of your speech and make you a more credible speaker. Among the most important forms of support are facts—verifiable information. Facts clarify your main points, indicate knowledge of your subject, and serve as definitions. Opinions differ from facts in that they cannot be verified. Statistical support involves the presentation of information in numerical form. Because statistics are easily manipulated, it is important to analyze carefully the data you present.

Five different types of examples are commonly used as forms of support. Brief examples are short illustrations that clarify a general statement. Extended examples are used to create lasting images. Narratives are stories within a speech that are linked to the speaker's main idea. Hypothetical examples are fictional examples used to make a point. Personal examples are anecdotes related to your topic that come from your own life.

When you use testimony quotations, you cite the words of others to increase the credibility of your message. Your sources gain expertise through experience and authority. Analogies focus on the similarities between the familiar and unfamiliar. Figurative analogies compare things that are different, while liberal analogies compare things from similar classes. Literal analogies can often be used as proof.

Name____ Date_______________

Exercises 7.1 Chapter 7 – Researching Your Topic

Effective support is used to develop the message you send to your listeners. Support should strengthen your speech in five ways:

- Support is specific.
- Support helps to clarify ideas.
- Support adds weight.
- Support is appropriate to your audience.
- Support creates interest.

Using a topic of your choice, fictionalize an example of support that demonstrates your ability to develop support that is *specific*, that is *clear*, *weighty*, *appropriate* and *interesting*. For example,

Topic: Water Sports

Support: According to Charles A. Hubbard's book, *The Ocean is Your Playground*, jet skiing is the most dangerous water activity for youth.

Does this support meet our five criteria?

Now develop your own examples. Be prepared to share your topics and your support with the class.

8

Organizing and Outlining Your Ideas

After reading this chapter, you should be able to:

- ❑ Explain the four step process for organizing a speech
- ❑ Demonstrate an understanding of generating a list of ideas consistent with the goals of a speech
- ❑ Determine the best pattern to utilize when organizing the main points of a speech
- ❑ Demonstrate the correct use of transitions in a speech
- ❑ Demonstrate the correct use of internal previews and summaries
- ❑ Describe the process of constructing the planning and key word outlines
- ❑ Discuss the guidelines for constructing speakers notes

Key Terms

Body
Brainstorming
Cause and effect
Chronological organization
Conclusion
Equality pattern
Internal previews
Internal summaries
Introduction
Key word outline
Main points
Organization
Past-present-future
Planning outline
Primacy effect
Problem solution organization
Progressive pattern
Recency effect
Spatial organization
Speakers notes
Specific purpose
Step by step
Strongest point pattern
Thesis statement
Topical organization
Transitions
Transitional sentences

8 Scenario

"In conclusion, we all can live and coexist together if we take the time to fully understand each otherís cultures. Thank you." Chris exhaled and wiped the perspiration from his forehead.

"Slow down, Chris," Nathalie said as she handed him his bottled water. "It's not a race."

"Man, I'm really nervous about this speech." Chris sat down in the desk beside her.

"I know you are. That's why I suggested we practice in the classroom where youíll be giving the speech." Nathalie smiled, "Pretty genius, huh?"

"Very," Chris replied, far from amused.

He was too nervous to appreciate Nathalie's attempts at settling his nerves. His last two speeches in his oral communication class had been informal. He was allowed to discuss a range of topics about himself and subjects of which he was fully aware. This was his first formal speech. He had to conduct research and construct an outline that included all of the main points of his speech.

"What are you so nervous about Chris?" Nathalie asked. "From what I see, you followed every direction your teacher gave and you followed the process that was outlined in the textbook. You have plenty of reliable books and online sources; you even have a living source. Lee helped you with all of the research, since the culture you're discussing is his."

"Yes, I guess you're right" Chris sighed before taking a sip of his water.

"Now, all we have to do is make sure you feel cool and confident in front of your audience," Nathalie said. "Let's do your speech again and this time pace yourself and make eye contact."

"Can I try to imagine my audience in their underwear?" he smirked as he walked to the front of the class.

"Do your speech, Chris," Nathalie replied as she rolled her eyes. Now she was the one who wasn't amused.

The **organization of ideas** in public speaking refers to the placement of lines of reasoning and supporting materials in a pattern that helps to achieve your specific purpose. Following a consistent pattern of organization helps listeners pay attention to your message. An organized speech with connected main points helps you maintain a clear focus that leads listeners to a logical conclusion. An organized speech flows smoothly and clearly, from introduction through body to conclusion.

Your introduction and conclusion support the body of your speech. The **introduction** should capture your audience's attention and indicate your intent, and the **conclusion** reinforces your message and brings your speech to a close. The **body** includes your main points and supporting material that supports your specific purpose and thesis statement. The introduction and conclusion are important, but audiences expect you to spend the most time and effort amplifying your main points.

It is easy to detect disorganized speakers. Their presentations ramble from topic to topic as they struggle to connect ideas. As a listener, you may be confused about what the speaker is trying to communicate. In the following example, a disorganized speaker addresses an audience on the topic of addictions:

> People in America spend billions of dollars a year going to the movies. College students alone spend $368 million on movie tickets (Martindale, 2009). There are all types of movies to see. You can choose drama, science fiction, comedy, thriller, musical, documentary, and action. Each type of movie has a different audience. Overall, American movies-no matter what type-are ruining our society.
>
> Before I discuss how movies are ruing our society, I want to talk about the fact that we celebrate the very things that are ruining us. There are many awards shows that are dedicated to movies. You have the Oscars, the SAG Awards, the MTV Movie Awards, and the Emmys which deal with television movies. These awards shows give out trophies to people for portraying characters that are immoral and participate in illegal activities. Most of the movies that get awards have a lot of violence in them, and even those movies that are funny include politically incorrect material that no one should be laughing about. Despite the poor quality of the content of today's movies, awards are still being given out.
>
> If the economy is as bad as the government says, then where do people get the money to go to the movies so much? It seems to me that everyone must not be suffering from the bad economy. Those who have money to go to these immoral movies are probably the ones who are getting their money illegally like the people in the movies they watch. Instead of wasting money on movies, they should do something helpful to society like make donations to organizations that help the homeless and feed the hungry.
>
> College students are the last group of people that need to spend so much money on movies. They are impressionable and likely to believe a lot of the fiction that they see at the theater. They might even try to copy some of the things that they see, thinking they can get away with it because the people in the movie did. This is not good. The focus of a college student should be on getting an education. I'm not saying that they should not have a life outside of school, but that life doesn't need to be the imaginary life of a movie character.

Listening to this speech is like watching a ping-pong ball bounce aimlessly across a table. You never know where the speaker will land next or what direction the speech will take. If your ideas are organized, however, you will help your audience follow and understand your message.

Organizing the Body of Your Speech

The body of your speech should flow from your introduction. Therefore, reflect first on your specific purpose and **thesis statement.** Since your specific purpose is a statement of intent and your thesis statement identifies the main ideas of your speech, referring to them as you determine your main points will help prevent misdirection. For example, consider a speech discussing how family pets help children with psychological problems. You might develop the following:

> Specific purpose: *To explain to my class how pets can provide unexpected psychological benefits for children with emotional problems by helping to bolster their self-esteem.*
> Thesis statement: *A close relationship with a family pet can help children with emotional problems feel better about themselves, help therapists build rapport with difficult-to-reach patients, and encourage the development of important social skills.*

Your thesis statement indicates your speech will address self-esteem, rapport with therapists, and the development of social skills. This suggests that there are many peripheral topics you will *exclude*, such as the type of pet, pet grooming tips, medical advances in the treatment of feline leukemia, how to choose a kennel when you go on vacation, and so on.

1. Select Your Main Points

Organizing the body of your speech involves a *four-step process: selecting the main points, supporting the main points, choosing the best organizational pattern, and creating unity throughout the speech.* Before you think about organizing your speech, you need to decide which points are essential. They must relate to your specific purpose and thesis statement. An audience analysis should help direct you in terms of what points you need to make and the extent to which you need to support them.

Usually you should limit your main points to no fewer than two and not more than five. If you add more, you are likely to confuse your listeners.

Based on your research, spend some time brainstorming to generate ideas for your speech.

Generate and Cluster Ideas

With your specific purpose and thesis statement clearly in mind, your next step is to generate a list of ideas consistent with the goals of your speech without critical evaluation initially. This stage is commonly known as **brainstorming.** Based on your research, write down ideas as they occur to you, using phrases or sentences. For purposes of illustration, consider the following:

> Specific Purpose: *To describe to my class the causes, symptoms, and treatment of shyness.*
> Thesis Statement: *Shyness, which is an anxiety response in social situations that limits social interactions, may respond to appropriate treatment.*

Your brainstorming process for the topic of shyness might result in a list of possible main points that include, but are clearly not limited to, the following: symptoms of shyness, shyness and heredity, shyness as an anxiety response, physical and psychological indications of shyness, number of people affected by shyness, shyness and self-esteem, how to handle a job interview if you are shy, treatment for shyness, and what to do when your date is shy.

Upon reflection, you may realize that several of these points overlap, and others do not relate as much to your thesis statement and should be discarded. So, you make the following list of six possible important points: Symptoms of shyness, causes of shyness, treatment for shyness, number of people affected by shyness, shyness as an anxiety response, and shyness and self-esteem.

With six being too many main points to develop, you decide that "shyness as an anxiety response" describes a symptom of shyness and that "shyness and self-esteem" describes a cause. You decide that a discussion of the number of people affected by shyness belongs in your introduction. Your final list of main points may look like this: symptoms of shyness, causes of shyness, treatment for shyness.

Through this process, you transformed a random list into a focused list of idea clusters reflecting broad areas of your speech. Your main points should be mutually exclusive; each point should be distinct. In addition, each point should be important in expressing your thesis statement.

2. Support Your Main Points

After selecting your main points, use the supporting material you gathered to strengthen each main point. Fitting each piece of research into its appropriate place may seem like completing a complex jigsaw puzzle. Patterns must be matched, rational links must be formed, and common sense must prevail. When you finish, each subpoint should be an extension of the point it supports. If the connection seems forced, reconsider the match. Here, for example, is one way to develop the three main points of the speech on shyness. As you sit at your computer, you can expand phrases into sentences. So for now, you can begin to think in terms of the language of your speech.

> **Main Point 1:** *The symptoms of shyness fall into two categories: those that can be seen and those that are felt.*

- Objective symptoms (symptoms that can be seen) make it apparent to others that you are suffering from shyness. These include blushing, dry mouth, cold clammy hands, trembling hands and knocking knees, excessive sweating, an unsettled stomach, and belligerence.

- According to psychologist Philip Zimbardo, many shy people never develop the social skills necessary to deal with difficult situations (symptoms that are felt).
- They may experience embarrassment, feelings of inferiority or inadequacy, feelings of self-consciousnes, a desire to flee, and generalized anxiety. They overreact by becoming argumentative.
- Internal symptoms make the experience horrible for the sufferer.

Main Point 2: R*ecent research has focused on three potential causes of shyness.*

- Heredity seems to play a large part.
- Psychologists at Yale and Harvard have found that ten to fifteen percent of all children are shy from birth.—Dr. Jerome Kagan of Harvard found that shy children are wary and withdrawn even with people they know.
- Shyness is also the result of faulty learning that lowers self-esteem instead of boosting self-confidence.
  - When parents criticize a child's ability or appearance or fail to praise the child's success, they plant the seeds of shyness by lowering self-esteem.
  - Older siblings may destroy a child's self-image through bullying and belittlement.
- Shyness is also attributable to poor social skills, due to never having learned how to interact with others, which leaves shy people in an uncomfortable position.

Main Point 3: *Shyness is not necessarily a life sentence; treatment is possible and so is change.*

- a survey of 10,000 adults, Stanford University researchers found that forty percent said that they had been shy in the past but no longer suffered from the problem.
- People who are extremely shy may benefit from professional therapy offered by psychiatrists and psychologists.

As you weave together your main points and support, your speech should grow in substance and strength. It will be clear to your listeners that you have something to say and that you are saying it in an organized way.

3. Choose the Best Pattern for Organizing Your Main Points

The way you organize your main points depends on your specific purpose and thesis statement, the type of material you are presenting, and the needs of your audience. As you develop your main points, you need to consider what you want to emphasize. Assuming you have established three main points, you need to choose your emphasis. You have three options. First, you may choose the **equality pattern**, which involves giving equal time to each point. This means that you will spend approximately the same time on each point as you deliver your speech. If the body of your speech was nine minutes long, each point would take about three minutes to develop.

A second option is to use a **progressive pattern**, which involves using your least important point first and your most important point last. If you choose to emphasize one point over another, the nine minutes of the body might be broken up into approximately one and a half minutes on the first point, three minutes on the second point, and four and a half minutes on the third point.

Your third option is to follow the **strongest point pattern.** In this case, your first point would take about four and a half minutes, the second point would be given about three minutes, and your final point would take approximately one and a half minutes.

The pattern you choose depends on your topic and audience. The equality pattern makes sense if you have three main points you think are equally strong and important. Some people believe that the progressive pattern is most effective, suggesting it is the first point listeners will be most likely to remember. This concept is known as the **primacy effect.** Others believe in the strongest point pattern, suggesting it is your last point listeners will remember most. This is the **recency effect.** There is general agreement, however, that your strongest argument, or the aspect you want to emphasize most strongly does *not* go in the middle of your main points.

In addition to organizing your main points by emphasis, it is important to have an overall organizational framework. A speaker has many choices in terms of how to organize his or her speech, but based on the specific purpose statement, one pattern of organization is generally more appropriate than the others. The five effective patterns of organization we will cover are chronological, topic, spatial, causal, and problem-solution.

In an informative speech on civil rights, you would likely include information about Rosa Parks' contributions to the cause.

Chronological Organization

In a chronological speech, information is focused on relationships in time. Events are presented in the order in which they occur. When developing your speech chronologically, you can choose to organize your ideas by starting at the beginning and moving to the present, then looking to the future, or going step-by-step.

To show how different organizational patterns affect the content and emphasis of a speech, we will choose a topic, establish different purposes for speaking, and show how the presentation differs when the organizational pattern is changed.

> Topic: *The civil rights movement.*
> Specific Purpose: *To inform my audience of college students about certain crucial events that occurred in the civil rights movement between 1954 and 2007.*

Thesis statement: *The civil rights movement made dramatic progress from 1954 to 2007 as can be seen in events that occurred, legislature passed, and politicial involvement of African Americans.*

In an informative speech on the civil rights movement, the speaker could include the following events:

1. The 1954 U.S. Supreme Court decision (Brown vs. Board of Education) made school segregation unconstitutional.
2. In 1955, Rosa Parks refused to give her seat to a white rider on a bus in Montgomery, Alabama. African Americans boycotted city buses for a year, and the courts ruled bus segregation unconstitutional.
3. In 1964, Congress passed sweeping civil rights law.
4. In 1984, the Reverend Jesse Jackson ran for president and became of powerful spokesperson at the Democratic National Convention.
5. In 2005, Edgar Ray Killen, member of the KKK and the ringleader of murdering civil rights activists Goodman, Chaney, and Swerner is convicted of manslaughter on the forty-first anniversary of the crimes.
6. In 2007, U.S. Senator Barack Obama easily became a leading contender for the Democratic nomination as a candidate for the presidency.

To be consistent, every event you analyze must be woven into the existing chronological outline.

Past-Present-Future Chronological order can also be used to construct a past-present-future organizational pattern. For example, if you were talking about the women's movement, you might have three points. First, you note that before the movement for women's equality, women's opportunities in the workplace were limited. Then you purport that today, greater opportunity is a reality, but women must cope with the dual responsibilities of career and home. Finally, you point out that you look forward to greater awareness from corporate America of women's dual roles and to accommodations that make the lives of working women easier. Using a past-present-future order allows a speaker to provide perspective for a topic or issue that has relevant history and future direction or potential.

Step-by-Step Chronological patterns can be used to describe the steps in a process. Here is a step-by-step description of how college texts are produced. Like the other patterns, the process shows a movement in time:

Step 1: *The author, having gathered permissions for use of copyrighted material, delivers a manuscript to the publisher.*
Step 2: *The manuscript is edited, a design and cover are chosen, photos are selected, and illustrations are drawn.*
Step 3: *The edited manuscript is sent to a compositor for typesetting and set in galley and page proof form.*
Step 4: *The final proof stage is released to the printing plant where the book is printed and bound.*

Spatial Organization

In speeches organized according to a spatial pattern, the sequence of ideas moves from one physical point to another—from London to Istanbul, from basement to attic, from end zone to end zone. To be effective, your speech must follow a consistent directional path. If you are presenting a new marketing strategy to the company sales force, you can arrange your presentation by geographic regions—first the East, then the South, then the Midwest, and finally, the West. If, after completing the pattern, you begin talking about your plans for Boston, your listeners will be confused.

Using space as the organizational key, our speech on civil rights takes the following form. Although the central topic is the same, the pattern of organization is tied to a different specific purpose and core idea:

Specific Purpose: *To inform my audience of college students how the civil rights movement spread across the nation.*
Thesis Statement: *The civil rights movement spread from the cities and rural areas of the South to the inner-city ghettos of the North and West.*

1. In places like Selma and Montgomery, AL and Nashville, TN, white brutality led to civil rights boycotts and protests.
2. Angry African Americans, pent up and hopeless in inner-city ghettos, rioted in Harlem, Newark, Chicago, and Detroit.
3. Riots took place in the Los Angeles ghetto of Watts, resulting in many deaths, far more arrests, and enormous losses from arson and looting.
4. In our 21st century we can easily see that African-Americans have become highly visible leaders in business, politics, education and religion, but the civil rights movement is still active, addressing issues of inequality and violence against minorities.

Cause and Effect

You may find that the most logical and effective way to organize is to arrange your main points into causes and effects. Here are the main points of our speech on civil rights arranged in a cause and effect pattern:

Specific Purpose: *To inform my audience of college students how the suffering experienced by African Americans in the 1950s and 1960s created the environment for social change.*
Thesis Statement: *Racial discrimination in America during the 1950s and 1960s made sweeping social change inevitable.*

Through the 1950s and early 1960s, discrimination prevented African Americans from using public accommodations, being educated with whites, riding in the front of buses, exercising their constitutional right to vote, being hired by corporations, and working for equal pay.

This pattern of discrimination resulted in landmark Supreme Court cases such as Brown vs. Board of Education, which declared separate but equal schools unconstitutional; the hugely successful march on Washington in 1963; and the passage in 1964 of the Civil Rights Act. With the cause and effect organizational pattern, the speaker can focus specifically on why something happened and what the consequences of the event or action were.

Persuasive speeches often present an audience with a problem and examine potential solutions.

Problem-Solution Organization

A common strategy, especially in persuasive speeches, is to present an audience with a problem and then examine one or more likely solutions. For example, in a classroom speech, one student described a serious safety problem for women students walking alone on campus after dark. He cited incidents in which women were attacked and robbed and described unlit areas along campus walkways where the attacks had taken place. Next, he turned to a series of proposals to eliminate, or at least minimize, the problem. His proposals included a new escort service, sponsored and maintained by various campus organizations, the installation of halogen lights along dark campus walks, and the trimming of bushes where muggers could hide.

Occasionally, speakers choose to present the solution before the problem. Had this student done so, he would have identified how to provide effective security before he explained why these solutions were necessary. Many audiences have trouble with this type of reversal because they find it hard to accept solutions when they are not familiar with the problems that brought them about.

Let us turn, once again, to our speech on civil rights, this time arranging the material in a problem-solution pattern.

> Specific Purpose: *To persuade my audience of college students that, although the civil rights movement has reduced racial discrimination in many areas, the movement must continue to press for equality in education and employment.*
> Thesis Statement: *The civil rights movement in America must remain strong and active because discriminatory patterns still exist in education and employment.*

Problem: Discrimination in education and employment has perpetuated a culture of poverty and joblessness for millions of African Americans who remain second-class citizens despite the gains of the civil rights movement.

Solution: Joblessness, and the poverty that results from it, must be addressed through job training programs and by continuing to pressure corporations to hire minorities through affirmative action programs.

Here, the goal is to persuade an audience that a problem still exists and to have listeners agree about how it can be effectively handled.

Topical Organization

The most frequently used organizational system is not tied to time or space, problem or solution, or cause or effect, but, instead, to the unique needs of your topic. The nature and scope of your topic dictate the pattern of your approach.

Working within the confines of your topic, you determine a workable pattern. If you are delivering an after-dinner humorous speech on the responses of children to their first week of preschool, you can arrange your topics according to their level of humor. For example:

1. The *school supplies* preschoolers think are necessary to survive at school.
2. The *behavior of youngsters at school* when they do not get their own way.
3. Children's stories of *their lives at home.*
4. *The reasons children believe their parents send them to school.*

These topics relate to children and their first week at school, but there is no identifiable chronological pattern, so topical order makes sense. When organizing topically, think about how to link and order topics. Transitions can help the audience understand the connections and will be discussed in the following section.

The following example shows how a speech on the civil rights movement might be treated using a topical organizational pattern.

Specific Purpose: *To inform my audience of college students about how the emergence of African American leaders in American politics and government influences the struggle for civil rights in our county.*

Thesis Statement: *The movement for civil rights is being waged from within the political establishment, and African Americans are achieving key positions in politics and in government.*

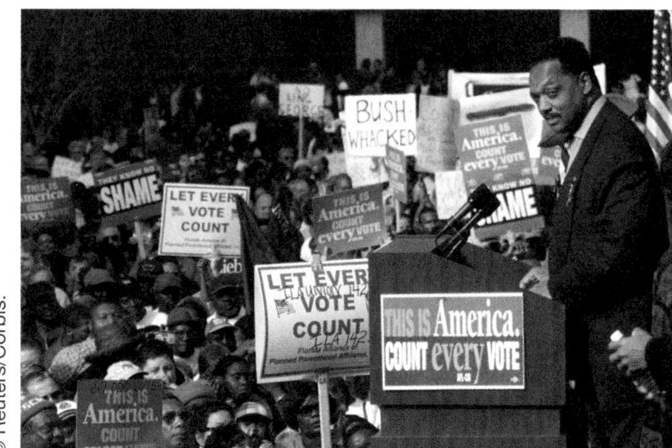

Jesse Jackson's key role as a leader in the Democratic party could be a main point in a topical organizational pattern speech on civil rights.

- Jesse Jackson became a leader in the Democratic party and succeeded in working within the system to register tens of thousands of African Americans to vote.
- Clarence Dinkins served as Mayor of New York City from 1990–1993.
- Clarence Thomas was appointed to the U.S. Supreme Court by President George H. W. Bush in 1991, and in 2004 President George W. Bush appointed Condoleezza Rice to be secretary of state for the United States.

4. Create Unity Through Connections

Without connections, your main points may be difficult to follow. Your audience may wonder what you are trying to say and why you have tried to connect ideas that do not seem to have any relationship with each other. To establish the necessary connections, use transitions, internal previews, and internal summaries.

Transitions

Transitions are the verbal bridges between ideas. They are words, phrases, or sentences that tell your audience how ideas relate. Transitions are critical because they clarify the direction of your speech by giving your audience a means to follow your organization. With only one opportunity to hear your remarks, listeners depend on transitions to make sense of your ideas.

It helps to think of transitions as verbal signposts that signal the organization and structure of your speech. Here are several examples:

> *"The first proposal I would like to discuss. . ."*
> This tells listeners that several more ideas will follow.
> *"Now that we've finished looking at the past, let's move to the future."*
> These words indicate a movement in time.
> *"Next, I'll turn from a discussion of the problems to a discussion of the solutions."*
> This tells your listeners that you are following a problem-solution approach.
> *"On the other hand, many people believe. . .*
> Here you signal an opposing viewpoint.

The following is a list of common transitional words and the speaker's purpose in using them.

Internal Previews and Summaries

Internal previews are extended transitions that tell the audience, in general terms, what you will say next. These are frequently used in the body of the speech to outline in advance the details of a main point. Here are two examples:

Speaker's Purpose	Suggested Transitional Words
To define:	*that is to say; according to; in other words*
To explain:	*for example; specifically*
To add:	*furthermore; also; in addition; likewise*
To change direction:	*although; on the other hand; conversely*
To show both sides:	*nevertheless; equally*
To contrast:	*but; still; on the contrary*
To indicate cause:	*because; for this reason; since; on account of*
To summarize:	*recapping; finally; in retrospect; summing up*
To conclude:	*in conclusion; therefore; and so; finally*
(Makay and Fetzger 1984, 68)	

- I am going to talk about the orientation you can expect to receive during your first few days on the job, including a tour of the plant, a one-on-one meeting with your supervisor, and a second meeting with the personnel director, who will explain the benefits and responsibilities of working for our corporation.
- Now that I've shown you that "junk" is the appropriate word to describe junk bonds, we will turn to an analysis of three secure financial instruments: bank certificates of deposit, Treasury bonds, and high quality corporate paper.

In the second example, the speaker combines a transition linking the material previously examined with the material to come with an internal preview. Previews are especially helpful when your main point is long and complex. They give listeners a set of expectations for what they will hear next. Use them whenever it is necessary to set the stage for your ideas (Turner 1970, 24–39).

Internal summaries follow a main point and act as reminders. Summaries are especially useful if you are trying to clarify or emphasize what you have just said, as is shown in the following two examples:

- In short, the American family today is not what it was forty years ago. As we have seen, with the majority of women working outside the home and with divorce and remarriage bringing stepchildren into the family picture, the traditional family—made up of a working father, a nonworking mother, and 2.3 kids—may be a thing of the past.
- In sum, the job market seems to be easing for health care professionals, including nurses, aides, medical technicians, physical therapists, and hospital administrators.

When summaries are combined with previews, they emphasize your previous point and make connections to the point to follow:

> In sum, it is my view that cigarette advertising should not be targeted specifically at minority communities. As we have seen, R. J. Reynolds test-marketed a cigarette for African Americans known as "Uptown," only to see it come under a barrage of criticism. What is fair advertising for cigarette makers? We will discuss that next.

Organization plays an important role in effective communication. The principles rhetoricians developed five centuries ago about the internal arrangement of ideas in public speaking have been tested by time and continue to be valid. Internal previews and summaries help the speaker create meaning with the audience by reinforcing the message and identifying what is coming next. Keep in mind that audience members do not have the opportunity to replay or to stop for clarification. Using transitions, previews, and internal summaries are tools a speaker can use to facilitate understanding and reduce the potential for misunderstanding (Clarke 1963, 23–27; Daniels and Whitman 1981, 147–160).

Constructing an Outline and Speaker's Notes

Presenting your ideas in an organized way requires a carefully constructed planning outline and a keyword outline to be used as speaker's notes. Both forms are critical to your success as an extemporaneous speaker—one who relies on notes rather than a written manuscript. Your outline is your diagram connecting the information you want to communicate in a rational, consistent way. It enables you to assemble the pieces of the information so that the puzzle makes sense to you and communicates your intended meaning to your audience. Think of outlining as a process of layering ideas on paper so that every statement supports your thesis. It is a time-consuming process, but one that will pay off in a skillful, confident presentation (Sprague and Stuart 1992, 92).

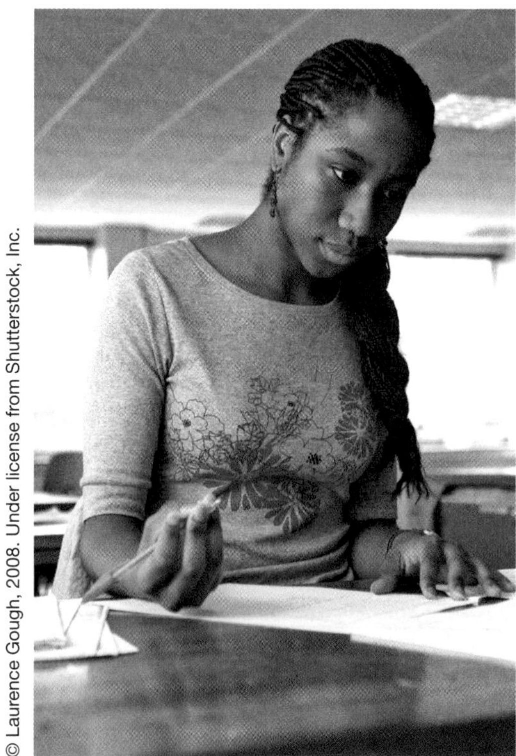

What information would you include in your planning outline?

Be familiar with the criteria for each speech assignment. Each instructor has his or her own requirements. Some may want to see your planning outline and speaker's notes while others may not. Instead of a planning outline, your instructor may ask you to turn in a full-sentence outline that includes points, subpoints, source citation, and reference page, but excludes statements about transitions or speech flow. The following discussion is designed to help you develop and, by extension, deliver, an effective speech. Your instructor will have specific ideas about the outline and note cards.

The Planning Outline

The planning outline, also known as the full-content outline, includes most of the information you will present in your speech. It does not include every word you plan to say, but gives you the flexibility required in extemporaneous speaking.

When developing a planning outline, it is important to use a traditional outline format that allows you to see the interconnections among ideas—how some points are subordinate to others and how main ideas connect. In a traditional outline, roman numerals label the speech's main ideas. Subordinate points are labeled with letters and numbers.

The proper positioning of the main and subordinate points with reference to the left margin is critical, for it provides a visual picture of the way your speech is organized. Be consistent with your indentation. The main points are along the left margin, and each sub-point is indented. Each sub-sub-point is indented under the sub-point. This visual image presents a hierarchy that expresses the internal logic of your ideas.

The outline labels (introduction, body, conclusion) remind the speaker to give each section appropriate attention, focusing on the objectives of each section. These labels should be written in the left-hand margin of your outline.

The following "boilerplate" suggests the format for a speech.

Name:
Specific purpose:
Thesis statement:

Title of Speech

Introduction

I. Capture attention and focus on topic
II. Set tone and establish credibility
III. Preview main points

Body

I. First main point
    A. First subordinate (sub-) point to explain first main point
        1. First sub-point/supporting material for first sub-point

a. Sub-point that provides greater details or explanations
b. Sub-point that provides more details, examples, or explanations to clarify and explain
2. Second sub-point/supporting material for first sub-point
B. Second subordinate (sub-) point to explain first main point
1. First sub-point/supporting material for second sub-point
2. Second sub-point/supporting material for second sub-point
a. Sub-point that provides greater details or explanations
b. Sub-point that provides more details, examples, or explanations to clarify and explain

II. Second main point
A. First subordinate (sub-) point to explain second main point
1. First sub-point/supporting material for first sub-point
a. Sub-point that provides greater details or explanations
b. Sub-point that provides more details, examples, or explanations to clarify and explain
2. Second sub-point/supporting material for first sub-point
B. Second subordinate (sub-) point to explain second main point
1. First sub-point/supporting material for second sub-point
2. Second sub-point/supporting material for second sub-point

III. Third main point
A. First subordinate (sub-) point to explain third main point
B. Second subordinate point to explain third main point
1. First sub-point/supporting material for second sub-point
2. Second subpoint/supporting material for second sub-point

Conclusion

I. Summary of main points
II. Relate to audience
III. Provide closure/final thought

References (on separate sheet)

Notice the particulars:

1. Your name, the specific purpose, thesis statement, and title of your speech are all found at the top of the page.
2. Each section (introduction, body, and conclusion) is labeled.
3. Each section begins with the Roman numeral "I."
4. Each level has at least two points. So if you have "I," minimally, you will see a "II." If you have an "A," minimally, you will see a "B." You should never have just one point or sub-point.
5. Each point is not developed identically. In some cases, there are sub-points and sub-sub-points. One point may need more development than another point.

A well-constructed planning outline ensures a coherent, well-thought-out speech. Using full sentences defines your ideas and guides your choice of language. Phrases and incomplete sentences will not state your points fluently, nor will they help you think in terms of the subtle interrelationships among ideas, transitions, and word choice.

Check with your instructor to see if you should have a regular planning outline or a full-sentence outline. A full-sentence outline requires that each point have one full-sentence. This means no sentence fragments, and no more than one sentence per point.

Include at the end of your planning outline a reference page listing all the sources used to prepare your speech, including books, magazines, journals, newspaper articles, videos, speeches, and interviews. If you are unfamiliar with documentation requirements, check the style guide preferred by your instructor, such as the *American Psychological Association (APA) Publication Manual* (online access at www.apastyle.apa.org), and the *Modern Literature Association (MLA) Handbook for Writers of Research Papers* (online access at www.mla.org).

Check with your instructor to see how detailed your source citation should be in the outline. Check to see if you should include last name, credentials, type of book (or magazine, journal, web page, etc.), year/date of publication?

Transitional sentences are valuable additions to your planning outline. They are needed when you move from the introduction to the body to the conclusion of the speech. They also link various main points within the body and serve as internal previews and summaries. Put these sentences in parentheses between the points being linked and try to use the language you may actually speak. When appropriate, include internal summaries and previews of material yet to come.

Here is an example of a planning outline that includes transitional sentences.

Speaker's name: *Jim Doe*
Specific Purpose: *To provide a solution to the problem that marriageable young men outnumber marriageable young women.*
Thesis Statement: *Because there are far more unmarried men in their twenties than there are women in the same age group, young men often find it harder to meet eligible partners.*

Title of Speech: *Young women take control of the marriage pool*

Introduction

I. It wasn't that long ago that sociologists were telling us that there were far more women of marriageable age than men.
   A. A report issued by the University of California at Berkeley told us that if we tried to match each woman born in 1950 with a man three years older, we would have millions of women left over.
   B. Neil G. Bennett, Patricia H. Craig, and David E. Bloom, researchers at Yale, predicted a lifetime of singlehood for college-educated women who postponed marriage into their thirties and forties.

II. New data from the U.S. Census Bureau suggests this trend has reversed itself for people in their twenties.
    A. For every five single young women in their twenties, there are now six single young men.
    B. Young women now have the advantage.

(Transition): Since I already see the men in my audience squirming and the women smiling, you must realize that the implications of this demographic shift are enormous. Because there are far more unmarried men in their twenties than there are women in the same age group, young men today find it harder to meet eligible partners.

We will look at the problem men face from a number of different perspectives, including loneliness, pressure from corporations to marry, and the growing rivalry between older and younger men for the same women. At the end of the speech, we will examine some possible solutions.

Body

I. Before we begin, let's take a closer look at the hard data from the Bureau of Census.
    A. About twenty years ago there were 19.9 million men and 20.4 million women in their early twenties.
    B. However, there also were about 2.3 million more unmarried men in their twenties than unmarried women in the same age group.
        1. In part, this statistic is explained by the fact that women tend to marry older men, thus removing themselves from the marriage pool.
        2. Since the number of births in the United States fell by an average of 1.7 percent a year between 1957 and 1975, the men born in any given year outnumber the women born in the years that follow, making it even more difficult for men to find a mate.

II. The result is that an increasing number of young men find themselves without a date on Saturday night.
    A. These men are lonely.
    B. Young male college graduates also feel the pressure to marry in order to get the right job in corporate America.
        1. According to career consultants, many corporations view unmarried men in their thirties as oddballs.
        2. Corporations expect their young male managers to marry by the age of thirty.
    C. Young men resent older men who date younger women.
        1. According to William Beer, the deputy chairman of the sociology department at New York's Brooklyn College, young men feel that these older men are "poaching."
        2. Older men claim they are just following a traditional pattern.

(Transition): Why are younger women attracted to older men, especially with a glut of younger men to choose from?

III. Older men are perceived as more sophisticated.
    A. They have had more time to explore the world and their personal interests.

   B. "The older men that I have met have done so much after college . . . that I haven't done," said Martha Catherine Dagenhart, then a senior at the University of North Carolina at Chapel Hill.

IV. Older men have more money.
   A. A thirty-year-old man may have worked eight years longer than a twenty-two-year-old college graduate.
   B. Many older men have money in the bank.

V. Older men are perceived as more powerful.
   A. An attractive woman in her twenties may be willing to have a relationship with a man in his forties if he's achieved a certain status in society.
      1. Often an executive will marry an assistant who sees him as a powerful person.
      2. Film stars and other major celebrities or prominence find themselves with women much younger then they are because of the power or status that goes with being a famous entertainer.
   B. Many older men cultivate an image of power and influence.

(Transition): Now that we've examined the extent and implications of this phenomenon and looked at the reasons young women are attracted to older men, let's look at what eligible bachelors in their twenties can do.

Conclusion

I. One solution to this problem is that young men in their twenties date older women.
   A. Unmarried women over thirty still outnumber men in the same age group.
   B. Women have traditionally dated older men, so demographic realities may force men to consider doing the same.

II. Men can be less selective in their choice of mates.
   A. An "I'm not willing to settle" attitude may leave many men without a companion.
   B. Turning to the Internet is currently popular, in part because of the difficulty men may have in initiating a relationship with someone they do not know.

III. Men must learn to accept the fact that they no longer have a ready supply of eligible partners—a fact older women have struggled with for years.

References

Bradsher, K. *For every five young women, six young men. New York Times, (1990, January 17), pp. C1 and C10.*

Bradsher, K. *Young men pressed to wed for success. New York Times, (1989, December 13), pp. C1 and C12.*

Too late for Prince Charming? (1986, June 2). Newsweek, June 2, 54–61.

A Brief Analysis of the Planning Outline

When applying a real topic to the boilerplate provided earlier, it is easy to see how the process unfolds. Note how transitions work, moving the speaker from the introduction of the speech to the body, from one main point to the next and, finally, from the body of the speech to the conclusion.

Remember, although the word "transition" appears in the outline, it is not stated in your speech. Transitions help connect listeners in a personal way to the subject being discussed. It also provides the thesis statement and previews the main points of the speech.

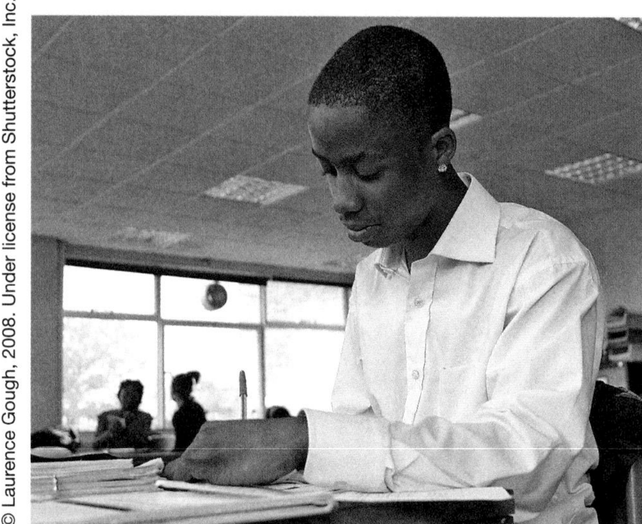

Include only the necessary information in your speaker's notes to remind you of your planned points.

Notice that quotes are written word for word in the outline. Also, note the preview that is included at the end of the transition from introduction to body. Once stated, the audience will know the main ideas you will present.

As the outline proceeds from the first- to the second- to the third-level headings, the specificity of details increase. The planning outline moves from the general to the specific.

Speaker's Notes

Speaker's notes are an abbreviated key-word outline, lacking much of the detail of the planning outline. They function as a reminder of what you plan to say and the order in which you plan to say it. Speaker's notes follow exactly the pattern of your planning outline, but in a condensed format.

Follow the same indentation pattern you used in your planning outline to indicate your points and subpoints. Include notations for the introduction, body, and conclusion and indicate transitions. It is helpful to include suggestions for an effective delivery. Remind yourself to slow down, gesture, pause, use visual aids, and so on. This will be helpful during your speech, especially if you experience speech tension.

Guidelines for constructing speaker's notes

1. ***Avoid overloading your outline.*** Many speakers feel that the more information they have in front of them, the better prepared they will be to deliver their speech. The opposite is usually

true. Speakers who load themselves with too many details are torn between focusing on their audience and focusing on their notes. Too often, as they bob their heads up and down, they lose their place.

2. ***Include only necessary information.*** You need just enough information to remind you of your planned points. At times, of course, you must be certain of your facts and your words, such as when you quote an authority or present complex statistical data. In these cases, include all the information you need in your speaker's notes. Long quotes or lists of statistics can be placed on separate index cards or sheets of paper.
3. ***Reduce your sentences to key phrases.*** Instead of writing: "The American Medical Association, an interest group for doctors, has lobbied against socialized medicine;" write: "The AMA and socialized medicine." Your notes should serve as a stimulus for what you are going to say. If you only need a few words to remind you, then use them. For example, a speaker who had directed several high school musicals planned to discuss the various aspects of directing a high school musical. Her speaker's notes could include the key words "casting," "blocking," "choreography," "singing," and "acting." Little else would be needed, since she can define and/ or describe these aspects of directing. However, under the key word "casting," she might include "when to cast," and "how to cast." Relevant quotes or perhaps a reference to a dramatic story would be included in the notes as well.
4. ***Include transitions, but in an abbreviated form.*** If you included each transition, your notes would be too long, and you would have too much written on them. Look at one of the transitions from the previous speech about men and marriage:

(Transition): Since I already see the men in my audience squirming and the women smiling, you must realize that the implications of this demographic shift are enormous. Because there are far more unmarried men in their twenties than there are women in the same age group, young men today find it harder to meet eligible partners.

We will look at the problem men face from a number of different perspectives, including loneliness, pressure to marry from corporations, and the growing rivalry between older and younger men for the same women. At the end of the speech, we will examine some possible solutions.

Instead of these two paragraphs, your speaker's notes might look like this:

Men squirming/women smiling
More unmarried men than women
Problems: loneliness, pressure to marry, growing rivalry

If you practice your speech, these words should suffice as notes. Abbreviate in a way that makes sense to you. Each person will have his or her own version of shorthand.

5. ***Notes must be legible.*** Your notes are useless if you cannot read them. Because you will be looking up and down at your notes as you speak, you must be able to find your place with ease at any point. Do not reduce your planning outline to 8-point and paste it to note cards. If you can type your notes, make sure they eare 14-point or larger. If you write your notes, take the time to write

legibly. Think about this: You may have spent several hours researching, preparing, and organizing your speech. Why take the chance of reducing the impact of your speech by writing your notes at the last minute?

Following is an example of a set of speaker's notes. The transformation from planning outline to key-word outline is noticeable in terms of length and detail. Transitions, delivery hints, and the parts of the outline are emboldened.

Sample speakers' notes from the speech,

Young Women Take Control of the Marriage Pool

(Introduction)

I. Sociology and the male/female dating ratio.
   A. Berkeley study: 3 million women born in 1950 will never have a mate
   B. Yale study

II. New Census Bureau data
   A. Ratio five single women to six single men in their twenties
   B. Advantage: women

(Look around room. Make eye contact. Slow down.)

(Men are finding it hard to meet mates. We will examine the problem and its implications.)

(Body)

(Slow down)

I. Closer look at data
   A. 19.9 million men, 20.4 million women in their twenties
   B. However, 2.3 million more unmarried men
      1. Women marry older men
      2. How declining birth rate affects pool of marriageable singles

II. Result for men: No dates
   A. Loneliness
   B. Pressure to marry from corporate America
      1. Unmarried "oddballs"
      2. Climb the corporate ladder: marry by thirty
   C. Young and old fight for same women
      1. William Beer, Brooklyn College sociologist: "Older men are poaching."
      2. Men are following tradition

(Why are younger women drawn to older men?)

III. More sophisticated.
   A. Time to explore interests and the world.
   B. *"The older men that I have met have done so much after college that I haven't done."* (Martha Catherine Dagenhart, senior at U. of NC at Chapel Hill.)

IV. More money
   A. Working longer
   B. Money in the bank

V. More powerful.
   A. Relationships based on status of man
      1. E.g., administrative assistant marries boss
      2. Stereotype: May-September marriages
   B. Older men cultivate the image of power

(Conclusion)

(Make eye contact during list)

I. Date older women
   A. Plenty of women over thirty
   B. Women have always dated older men

II. Be less picky
   A. "I'm not willing to settle."
   B. Try to meet someone through the Internet

III. Accept and adjust

A Brief Analysis of Speaker's Notes

Including your specific purpose and thesis statement in your speaker's notes is unnecessary. Speaker's notes follow exactly the pattern of the planning outline so you maintain the organizational structure and flow of your speech. The introduction, body, and conclusion are labeled, although it is possible you might only need the initial letters "I," "B," and "C" to note these divisions. Nonessential words are eliminated, although some facts are included in the speaker's notes to avoid misstatement. Delivery instructions help emphasize that your speech has implications to your listeners and can help personalize the message.

The more experience you have as a speaker, the more you will come to rely on both your planning outline and speaker's notes, as both are indispensable to a successful presentation.

Summary

The first step in organizing your speech is to determine your main points. Organize your efforts around your specific purpose and thesis statement, then brainstorm to generate specific ideas, and finally, group similar ideas.

Your second step is to use supporting material to develop each main point. In step three, choose an organizational pattern. Arrange your ideas in chronological order, use a spatial organizational pattern, follow a pattern of cause and effect, look at a problem and its solutions, or choose a topical pattern. Your final step is to connect your main ideas through transitions, internal previews, and internal summaries.

As you develop your speech, your primary organizational tool is the planning outline, which includes most of the information you will present. The outline uses a traditional outline format, which establishes a hierarchy of ideas. The number of main points developed in your speech should be between two and five. The planning outline also uses complete sentences, labels transitions, and includes a reference list.

Speakers' notes, the notes you use during your presentation in an extemporaneous speech, are less detailed than the planning outline. They serve as brief reminders of what you want to say and the order in which you say it. They may include complete quotations and statistical data as well as important delivery suggestions. Speakers' notes are organized around phrases, not sentences, and they use the same format as the planning outline.

Name____ Date_______________

Exercise 8.1 Chapter 8 – Organizing and Outlining Your Ideas

General Purpose: Inform
Specific Purpose: To inform about my life past, present, + future
Attention-Getter: Quote
Pattern of Organization: Chronological

I. April 4, 1968. None of us were around to remember what happened this day, but our parents could probably tell us exactly what they were doing when they heard that one of the most influential men that has ever lived had been murdered.
   A. The death of Dr. King will always be a painful memory, but his life should be greatly celebrated for the inspiration he gave.
   B. Good morning. My name is Brittany Jackson and my purpose today is to tell you how the life of one man has inspired me to work hard, take action, and dream big.

II. The first thing Dr. King has inspired me to do is to work hard.
   A. Dr. King was a diligent student.
      1. He worked hard to graduate from high school and enter Morehouse College at 15 years old.
      2. He continued his schooling at Crozer Theological Seminary and Boston University and earned multiple degrees.
   B. It was not common that a young black man growing up in the Jim Crow South had the opportunity or the drive to go this far in education.
   C. Today, in an integrated society, I realize that I have more opportunities and an even greater chance to succeed.

III. The next thing that Dr. King has inspired me to do is to take action.
   A. During a time when civil injustice was at its peak, many people complained but were afraid to do anything about it.
   B. Dr. King saw the need for a social change.
      1. In December 1995, he organized a bus boycott, which led to the Supreme Court ruling bus segregation unconstitutional.
      2. Dr. King was arrested, his home was bombed, and he received personal abuse.
   C. Whatever you see that you feel needs to be changed, don't sit back and complain about it. TAKE ACTION!

IV. Lastly, Dr. King has inspired me to dream big.
   A. Mostly everyone is familiar with Dr. King's famous "I Have a Dream" speech.
      1. In that speech, he stated that one of his dreams was that his children would be judged by the content of their character and not the color of their skin.
      2. Dr. King never saw his dream come true, but he never gave up on believing in it.
   B. The most valuable lesson I have learned from Dr. King is to dream big, even thought it seems impossible.
   C. We all have dreams. They may not be dreams to change humanity, but they are still important to us.
      1. If you dream small, the outcome is likely to be small.
      2. If you dream big, then the possibilities are endless.

Name____ Date_______________

Exercise 8.1 Chapter 8 – Organizing and Outlining Your Ideas

Instructions: Transform the previous sentence outline into a key word(s) outline.

General Purpose:
Specific Purpose:
Attention-Getter:
Pattern of Organization:

I. April 4, 1968
  A. life, greatly celebrated
  B. work hard, take action, dream big
II. work hard
  A. diligent student
    1. Morehouse 15 years old
    2. Crozer and Boston College
  B. opportunity or drive for education
  C. Today more opportunities
III. take action
  A. afraid to do anything
  B. need social change
    1. bus segregation unconstitutional
    2. arrested.
  C.
IV.
  A.
    1.
    2.
  B.
  C.
    1.
    2.

9

After reading this chapter, you should be able to:

- ❐ Identify the four methods of the delivery of a speech
- ❐ Explain the aspects of vocal delivery when giving a speech
- ❐ Explain the aspects of physical delivery when given a speech

Key Terms

Articulation	Gestures	Pauses
Emphasize	Impromptu speaking	Pitch
Extemporaneous speaking	Manuscript delivery	Pronunciation
Eye contact	Memorization delivery	Rate
	Non-fluencies	Volume

9 Scenario

"Oh shoot!" Kevin muttered under his breath as he crouched down to pick up his note cards.

The class buzzed with chatter as Kevin collected his note cards, trying to place them back in order. Mr. Nahuel cleared his throat, "Class, you are being rude to Mr. Reynolds. Are you ok up there Mr. Reynolds?"

Kevin cleared his throat, "Of course. Now, where was I? Oh yea, now we all know that dress codes aren't the way to go. I mean, right?"

A few members of the crowd turned around, wondering if Kevin wanted them to answer. Damien looked at his best friend and shook his head as a group of kids in the back of the class giggled and laughed. Kevin could hear his breath coming short. He looked down at his feet and continued on with his speech and fiddled with the note cards in his hands.

"Mr. Reynolds, forgive my interruption but you are looking down at your feet." Mr. Nahuel commented, "We are up here." He motioned toward his face.

Kevin chuckled nervously, "Of course. Sorry about that. Like I was saying, dress codes limit our um…" Kevin trailed off as he tried to remember the word he was looking for. A girl in class caught his attention and pointed to his note cards. He nodded at her in appreciation before finding his sentence, "The dress code limits our creativity, and that's why it should be banned. Thank you."

People clapped out of pity as he staggered back to his seat. Kevin groaned and slid down in his seat, wishing he could disappear. He closed his eyes.

"Alright everyone, speeches will resume on Thursday. For those who went today, I have your grades," Mr. Nahuel announced before dismissing the class.

Members of the class trickled out as Kevin got up the nerve to approach Mr. Nahuel's desk.

"Mr. Reynolds, you gave an interesting speech today," Mr. Nahuel commented as he handed Kevin his evaluation card.

"Seems like I gave a horrible speech today, Mr. Nahuel," Kevin sighed. A 'C-' is a little harsh, don't you think?"

"Kevin, there some adjustments you have to make if you want a better grade," Mr. Nahuel said.

"Like what?" Kevin asked.

"Well for starters, you'll need to learn to be comfortable in front of a crowd," said Mr. Nahuel.

Kevin scoffed, "I am comfortable in front of the class. I always talk in class."

Mr. Nahuel laughed. "Yes, you do make the lessons interesting with your opinion, but it's different when you have a speech. It's as if you're an actor and you have lines. To convey the character well, you have to be comfortable delivering your lines in front of the audience. You have to get over your stage fright. Don't fidget or break eye contact, but stand tall and look everyone in the eyes. Confidence is key, Mr. Reynolds."

"I understand that now," Kevin moaned. "Just please tell what I have to do to make this up."

"Work harder on your next speech, Mr. Reynolds," Mr. Nahuel said. "Work harder on the next one and apply everything that was stated on your evaluation sheet."

Kevin nodded, "Ok, Mr. Nahuel. Thanks."

"Oh and Mr. Reynolds," Mr. Nahuel stopped Kevin before he could leave, "And don't be afraid to ask for help. The man that succeeds the most does this with the help of others. Remember that Mr. Reynolds."

Kevin smiled genuinely, "I got it. I got it, Mr. Nahuel."

What do you remember after a speaker is finished? Although you may walk away with the speaker's ideas buzzing through your mind, it is often the quality of the performance that remains with you long after you have forgotten the content of the message. That is to say, the *how* of public speaking—the speaker's style of delivery—often makes the most lasting impression.

Words alone are not enough to make audiences want to listen to a speech. Many brilliant people—scientists, lawyers, politicians, engineers, environmentalists—never connect with their listeners, not for lack of trying, but for problems with the delivery of their speech. Maybe they are too stiff or appear uninvolved. Worse, they may try to imitate other speakers and be something they are not.

Delivery affects your credibility as a speaker. Your ability to communicate information, persuade, and entertain is influenced by the manner in which you present yourself to your audience. An effective delivery works *for* you, an ineffective delivery against you—even when the content of your message is strong.

Methods of Delivery

The following section identifies four different methods of delivery. You may find comfort in one style more than the other, but hopefully, you will have an opportunity to explore different methods of delivery during your public speaking course. Each of the four methods is appropriate in certain situations. As a speaker, you need to be aware of your audience and the occasion when choosing the method of delivery that is most appropriate and effective. Performance guidelines accompany each method of delivery. These are aspects to consider as you plan to deliver the speech. Your four choices are to memorize your speech, speak from a manuscript, use carefully prepared notes and speak extemporaneously, or give an impromptu, spur-of-the-moment speech.

Memorization

It is every speaker's nightmare: You are in the middle of a ten-minute speech and you cannot remember the next word. Because you memorized the speech (or so you thought), you have no note cards to help you through the crisis. This nightmare becomes reality on a regular basis in public speaking classes. Nervous students who have memorized their speeches find themselves without a clue as to what to say next. Even those who spend hours preparing for the presentation may forget everything when facing an audience. This situation is made worse if you are part of a group presentation because other people depend on you.

While memorization is unnecessary in many situations, there are times when having your speech memorized is preferable. For example, when you know you will be receiving an award or recognition, memorization may be a useful delivery tool. Special occasions, such as toasting the bride and groom or delivering a *brief* commencement address, are also opportunities for delivering a memorized speech. Memorization enables you to write the exact words you will speak without being forced to read them. It also makes it easier to establish eye contact with your audience and to deliver your speech skillfully.

If you find yourself in a situation where memorization is necessary, consider the following four performance guidelines.

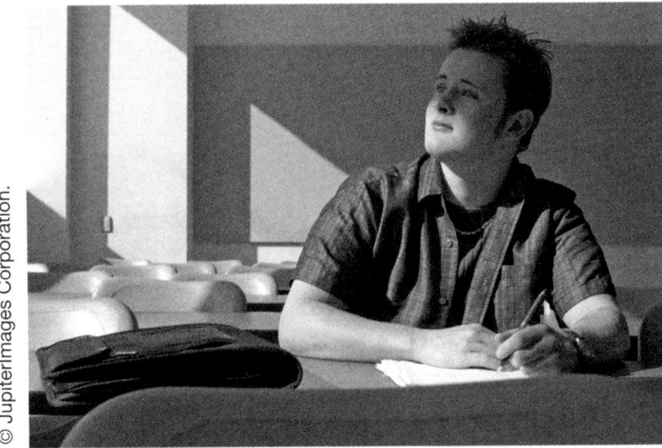
© JupiterImages Corporation.

Memorize small sections of your speech at a time.

Start memorizing the speech as soon as possible. You do not want to delay the process so that you are under a severe time constraint. (Such as the night before!) Make sure you have ample time to work on the memorization aspect of your delivery. Even experienced professional speakers have to work hard to remember their lines.

Memorize small sections of your speech at a time. Do not allow yourself to become overwhelmed with the task. Memorizing small sections of your speech at a time will help minimize the chance that you will forget your speech during the delivery. Remember that some people can memorize speeches more easily than others, so work at your own pace and do not compare yourself to the classmate who memorized her speech in a very short period of time.

Determine where you need pauses, emphasis, and vocal variety. You want to convey the appropriate tone for your speech—enthusiasm, excitement, anger, bewilderment. You can achieve this by emphasizing certain words, speaking faster or more slowly, and increasing or lowering your volume and/or pitch. More about vocal aspects of delivery will be discussed shortly.

Avoid looking like you are trying to remember the speech. As instructors, sometimes we feel as though we can *see* the speaker trying to remember the words, as though the speaker has a disk in his/her head, and he/she is trying to access the right file. The speaker might look up, look to the side, or simply look pensive as he/she tries to "retrieve" the information.

Overall, delivering a memorized speech can be very effective, but it is also a gamble. In addition to the actual task of memorization, students need to make sure they work on vocal variety, so they can connect with their audience. For the student in the basic public speaking class, a memorized speech is seldom what an instructor wants to hear.

Using a Manuscript

Manuscript reading involves writing your speech out word for word and then reading it. A manuscript speech may be considered in formal occasions when the speech is distributed beforehand or if it is archived. Many presidential speeches are manuscript speeches. The president is expected to follow a teleprompter, which is frequently used. On occasion, scholars give speeches that are then printed in the "proceedings" of a conference. On other occasions, the speaker may be addressing an international conference, and the manuscript is translated into one or more languages. Having a manuscript speech minimizes the temptation to add remarks during the speech.

If an issue or occasion is controversial or sensitive, a speaker may choose to rely on a manuscript. Having a carefully crafted statement may help avoid misstating a position. You may also choose to read from a manuscript when addressing a hostile audience because you know your listeners are ready—and waiting—to attack your statement. You want to be sure your communication is exact.

For those who are not professional speakers, a manuscript may be troublesome. If the font size is too small, it may be difficult to read. Each time you look up and then back down, it is possible to lose your place in the manuscript. Some people tend to sound as though they are reading rather than speaking when working from a manuscript. We encourage students to avoid writing out their speeches verbatim, but recognize that there are occasions when manuscript speaking is appropriate. If you find yourself involved in one of these occasions, we offer four performance guidelines.

Pay special attention to preparing the written text. If you cannot read what you have written, your delivery will falter. Avoid using a handwritten manuscript. Make sure you choose a large enough font to see without squinting, and have the lines spaced well enough that you do not lose your place.

Practice. The key to successful manuscript speaking is practice and more practice. One run through is not sufficient.

Express yourself naturally and communicate your personality. You do not want to look frozen in time. Think about what you want to emphasize and vary the pitch of your voice to avoid being monotone. Pronounce words as you would in normal speech and be conscious of speaking too quickly or too slowly.

Make eye contact with your audience. Glance back and forth between your manuscript and your audience. Take care not to bob your head in the process. When a speech is memorized, this is not an issue. However, when you are dependent on a manuscript, you need to make sure it does not *sound* like you are reading to the audience. Looking up from the manuscript and making eye contact with members of your audience are important aspects of manuscript delivery.

Expressing yourself naturally helps you connect with your audience.

A big mistake students make is typing the entire speech on the required number of note cards (even though they have been warned not to do this). A five- to eight-minute speech is typed on three to five note cards. The outcome is not pretty. Students find themselves unable to read the cards—font size is six, and twelve lines of type are on each note card. They cannot read, they lose their place, they stumble as they try to decipher the words, and even worse, because they are concentrating so hard on reading the notes, they forget about the vocal aspects of delivery! The lesson learned? Use a manuscript *only* when the occasion suggests it.

Extemporaneous Speaking

The most appropriate mode of delivery for students of public speaking is **extemporaneous speaking,** a method of delivery that involves using carefully prepared notes to guide the presentation.

Extemporaneous speaking has many advantages. In particular, speakers can maintain a personal connection with their listeners and can respond to their feedback. The most effective public speaking is often described as the speaker's response to the listener's reaction. This takes shape in the communication transaction. The extemporaneous mode of delivery allows this interaction to occur as you adjust your choice of words and decide what to include—or exclude—in your speech. You can shorten a speech (you may want to follow the advice of the Reverend William Sloane Coffin (1988) who said about the length of an effective sermon, "No souls are saved after twenty minutes") or go into greater detail than you originally planned. This mode of speaking provides flexibility.

Speaking extemporaneously means that your word choice is *fresh*. Although you know the intent of your message in advance, you choose your words as you are delivering your speech. The result is a spontaneous, conversational tone that puts you and your audience at ease. This is not to say that as you practice your speech, key words or phrases will not remain with you. On the contrary, the more you practice, the more likely you are to commit a particularly fitting word or phrase to memory. Extemporaneous speaking gives you the freedom to gesture as you would in conversational speech. With both hands free, (you can gesture with note cards in one hand) you can move about and emphasize key points with forceful gestures. Consider the following guidelines as you prepare for your extemporaneous speech.

Prepare carefully. In terms of preparation, use the same care you would use when preparing a written report. Choose your purpose, develop your core idea, research your topic, organize your ideas, and select the language and presentation style that is most appropriate for your audience.

Prepare both a full content and key-word speaker's outline. Recently, a student gave his own eulogy as a special occasion speech. He worked from a very brief outline. His speech was too short, and he seemed to have a lapse of memory. Had he used a more fully-developed outline, these problems would have been eliminated.

Develop an outline containing main points and subpoints, then create a key-word outline that can be transferred to index cards of the appropriate size. Cards should be large enough to accommodate information from your key-word outline, yet small enough to be unobtrusive. Cards may be held or placed on a lectern.

Extemporaneous speaking allows you to move freely and emphasize points with gestures.

Place detailed information on separate note cards. Facts, figures, and quotations may be written on separate note cards for easy reference. Always remember your ethical responsibility not to misrepresent facts or opinions that require careful and precise explanations. Rather than take the chance of misquoting people or facts, it may help to have the information written on separate cards.

Write legibly. Your notes are useless if you cannot read them, so print your words boldly and consider highlighting critical ideas. If typing, use an appropriate font size. Remember, too, that your visual aids can serve as notes to some extent.

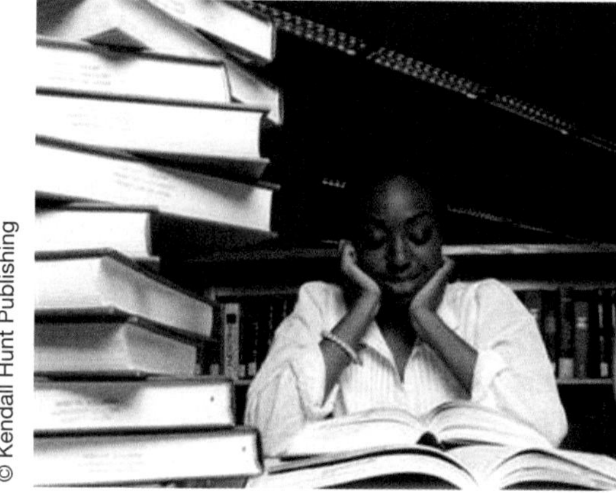

Be sure to develop an outline that contains main points and subpoints before moving on to key-words only.

Use your notes as a prompter. Notes enable you to keep your ideas in mind without committing every word to memory. Notes also make it possible to maintain eye contact with your listeners. You can glance around the room, looking occasionally at your cards, without giving anyone the impression that you are reading your speech.

Impromptu Speaking

Impromptu speaking term involves little to no preparation time. This means using no notes or just a few. In your lifetime, there may be many occasions when you are asked to speak briefly without any advanced notice. For example, you may be a principal of a high school attending a local school board meeting, and someone on the school board asks you to comment on the recent basketball victory. Or, at that same meeting, a school board member may decide it is the right moment to recognize the accomplishments of a retiring teacher. During other occasions, you may be asked to "say a few words" about a newlywed couple, the dearly-departed, or a scholarship you just received.

In a public speaking class, many instructors include impromptu speaking opportunities throughout the semester. In particular, it is helpful for students to give a brief impromptu speech at the beginning of the semester just to get on their feet and face the audience. Instructors generally feel that the more opportunities we give students to present, the more comfortable students will feel in the speaking environment. You may have an activity in class where you introduce yourself or someone in the class. You may be called upon to give an impromptu speech on "my proudest moment," or "my favorite vacation spot."

Not everyone has the ability of Marcus Garvey, African American nationalist leader, to speak on the spur of the moment. Dorothy L. Pennington, an expert in the rhetoric of African Americans, describes Garvey's oratorical style:

> He often spoke impromptu, gleaning his topic and remarks from something that had occurred during the earlier portion of the program. For example, in speaking before the conference of the Universal Negro

Improvement Association in August 1937, Garvey showed how his theme emerged: "I came as usual without a subject, to pick the same from the surroundings, the environment, and I got one from the singing of the hymn 'Faith of our Fathers.' I shall talk to you on that as a theme for my discourse." This type of adaptation allowed Garvey to tap into the main artery of what an audience was thinking and feeling (Duffy and Ryan 1987, 170).

Who knows when you'll be called upon to give a toast to someone celebrating a special occasion?

Impromptu speaking forces you to think on your feet. With no opportunity to prepare, you must rely on what you know. Here are several suggestions that will help you organize your ideas:

Focus your remarks on the audience and occasion. Remind your listeners of the occasion, or purpose of the meeting: ("We have assembled to protest the rise in parking fines from $10 to $25.") When unexpectedly called to speak, talk about the people who are present and the accomplishments of the group. You can praise the group leader ("She's done so much to solve the campus parking problem"), the preceding speaker, or the group as a whole. You may want to refer to something a previous speaker said, whether you agree or disagree: ("The suggestion to organize a petition protesting the fine increase is a good one.") The remarks give you a beginning point, and a brief moment to think and organize your comments.

Use examples. Be as concrete as possible. ("I decided to become active in this organization after I heard about a student who was threatened with expulsion from school after accumulating $500 in unpaid parking fines.") Keep in mind that as an impromptu speaker, you are not expected to make a polished, professional speech—everyone knows you have not prepared. But you are expected to deliver your remarks in a clear, cogent manner.

Do not try to say too much and do not apologize. Instead of jumping from point to point in a vague manner, focus on your specific purpose. When you complete the mission of your speech, turn the platform over to another speaker. Never apologize. Your audience is already aware it is an impromptu moment, apologizing for the informality of your address is unnecessary. You do not need to say anything that will lessen your audience's expectations of your speech.

Aspects of Vocal Delivery

The speaker should never forget about the needs of the audience, and this applies to vocal delivery, also. It is always beneficial to speak clearly. A German friend of ours once said, "Americans speak as though they have hot potatoes in their mouths." Indeed, many of us mumble, leave off the endings of our words, and fail to pronounce words correctly. When presenting in public, consider the following aspects of vocal delivery: articulation, pronunciation, volume, rate, pitch, pauses, and emphasis.

The informal, careless speech you use when talking with friends is not polished enough for a presentation.

Articulation

A person who articulates well is someone who speaks clearly and intelligibly. **Articulation** refers to the production of sound and how precisely we form our words. The more formal the situation, the more precise our articulation needs to be. The more casual the situation, the more likely we are to be relaxed in our speech. Thus, when you are giving a speech in front of an audience, the sloppy or careless pronunciation patterns you use with your friends and family should not find their way into your presentation.

Words should be crisp and clear. The listener should be able to distinguish between sounds and not be confused. The popular phrase, "Da Bears" shows how we mainstream some of our inarticulation. Leaving off the "g" in going, driving, shopping, etc. is common in American culture. Saying "I wanna," "I coulda," and "I hafta" are other examples of sloppy articulation which is perfectly acceptable in informal situations, but not so in a formal context.

Remember to adapt to your audience. In a formal setting, such as a commencement speech or an awards ceremony, you want to be as articulate as possible. In an informal setting, articulation is not as big of an issue, but it is *always* important to be understood.

Work to eliminate bad habits. Reflect a moment about how you articulate. Do you speak clearly? Do you mumble? Do you have certain words that you mispronounce? Do you leave the endings off of words? You should make a conscious effort to think about articulation. Following are several tongue twisters. You might want to see how well you do.

> Betty Botter had some butter,
> "But," she said, "this butter's bitter.
> If I bake this bitter butter,
> it would make my batter bitter.
> But a bit of better butter—
> *that* would make my batter better."
>
> So she bought a bit of butter,
> better than her bitter butter,

and she baked it in her batter,
and the batter was not bitter.
So 'twas better Betty Botter
bought a bit of better butter.

A big black bug bit a big black bear,
made the big black bear bleed blood.
Toy boat. Toy boat. Toy boat.

Pronunciation

In contrast to articulation problems, mispronunciation is not knowing how to say a word and, as a result, saying it incorrectly. Sometimes speakers simply do not know the word and mispronounce it; other times, a word is mispronounced because of dialect differences among speakers. For example, you may have heard President George W. Bush leave off the "g" in "recognize," so the words sounds like "reconize." Politicians or their detractors sometimes talk about "physical" responsibility, instead of the two-syllable word, "fiscal" responsibility. People also present "satistics" instead of "statistics," and talk about the "I-talians" and the people from "I-raq."

One of your authors lives in Illinois, near a town called Mattoon. Residents of the area can tell when someone is not from the area, because at first, they say, "Ma-toon" instead of "Mat-toon." Are you someone whose name is always mispronounced? If so, you know it can be annoying.

Check pronunciation of unfamiliar words. Part of the ethical responsibility of a speaker is to check his or her pronunciation. The speaker should know how to pronounce all words in his or her speech, including the names of people and places and foreign terms.

Do not comment on your pronunciation. Do not say, "or however you pronounce that" or "I cannot pronounce that." While we are likely to forgive regional differences, our credibility will be reduced if our listeners see we have made little or no effort to determine the correct pronunciation.

Practice the pronunciation of difficult words. You do not want to stumble or draw attention away from the point you are making.

Volume

If your audience cannot hear you, your speech serves little purpose. The loudness of your voice is controlled by how forcefully air is expelled through the trachea onto the vocal folds. This exhalation is controlled by the contraction of the abdominal muscles. The more forcefully you use these muscles to exhale, the greater the force of the air, and the louder your voice.

Do not mistake shouting for projection. Shouting involves forcing the voice from the vocal folds, which is irritating to the folds, instead of projecting the sound from the abdominal area. Straining your voice will only make you hoarse. Instead, work on your posture and breathing from the diaphragm.

Use volume to add interest and variety to your speech. Maybe you want to add a bit of humor to your introduction of a speaker. Using a "stage whisper," you could say something like, "And if we all clap very loudly, we can coax him on to the stage...." On his television show, Dr. Phil uses volume effectively by getting loud when he thinks people should be annoyed by what is happening and speaking softly when he is showing amazement or shares a startling fact.

Do not talk to the podium. If you have your notes on the podium and your head is bent, the audience will not be able to hear.

Rate

During the first week of teaching at the University of Arkansas at Little Rock, a student said to Dr. Mason, "You are not from around here, are you?" When asked what gave it away, the student replied that it was the rate of speech. In the United States, Southerners generally speak more slowly than Northerners. Overall, the average rate of speech for Americans is between 120 and 160 words per minute.

Nervousness may affect your normal pattern.When practicing alone, you may be relieved when you find that in timing your speech you are just over the minimum time required. However, under the pressure of giving a speech, you may find yourself speeding up ("The faster I talk, the faster I'll finish") or slowing down. Rate is also affected by mode of delivery. If you read a manuscript rather than speak extemporaneously, you may find yourself running a verbal road race.

Choose an appropriate rate. Your rate of speech should be consistent with the ideas being expressed and for the context. For example, it makes sense that a sportscaster announcing a basketball game speaks faster than a sportscaster at a golf match.

Vary your rate of speech. By changing your rate, you can express different thoughts and feelings. You may want to speak slowly to emphasize an important point or to communicate a serious or somber mood. A faster pace is appropriate when you are telling your audience something it already knows (many speeches include background information that sets the scene) or to express surprise, happiness, or fear.

Pitch

Pitch refers to your vocal range or key, the highness or lowness of your voice produced by the tightening and loosening of your vocal folds. The range of most people's voices is less than two octaves. Pitch is a problem when your voice is too high-pitched; in men a high-pitched voice may sound immature, and in women it may sound screechy.

Vary your pitch. Variety adds interest to your presentation. Avoid a monotone. When you do not vary the pitch of your voice, you risk putting your listeners to sleep.

Use your voice potential. Take advantage of the fact that our voices have incredible range. To add color, lower the pitch of a word or phrase you want to emphasize. Resist the temptation to raise your voice too much at key points.

Pauses

Pausing during a presentation can help listeners process the information you're conveying.

Some speakers talk nonstop until, literally, they run out of breath. Others pause every three or four words in a kind of nervous verbal chop. Still others, particularly those who read their speeches, pause at the wrong times—perhaps in the middle of an important idea—making it difficult for their listeners to follow.

Pauses add color, expression, and feeling to a speech. They should be used deliberately to achieve a desired effect. If used effectively, pauses also can add power and control to your speech. They may get you into trouble when it seems like you have lost your place or forgotten what you were going to say. This may suggest you are unprepared and have not practiced sufficiently.

Pauses serve multiple purposes. First, they communicate self-confidence. Pauses deliver the nonverbal message that you are relaxed enough to stop talking for a moment. Second, they help listeners digest what you are saying and anticipate what you will say next. Third, a significant pause also helps you move from one topic to the next without actually telling your listeners what you are doing. Fourth, a pause signals *pay attention*. (This is especially true for long pauses lasting two or three seconds.) According to Don Hewitt, producer of *60 Minutes*, "It's the intonation, the pauses, that tell the story. They are as important to us as commas and periods are to the *New York Times*"(in Fletcher 1990, 15).

In October 2009, President Barack Obama delivered remarks on Small Businessess and Health Insurance Reform at the Eisenhower Executive Office Building. The following is an excerpt of his address:

> "I asked you here today to talk about health insurance reform and why it's so critical to the success of small businesses across our country. But before I do, let me talk a minute just briefly about the new economic numbers that were released this morning.
>
> I am gratified that our economy grew in the third quarter of this year. We've come a long way since the first three months of 2009, when our economy shrunk by an alarming 6.4 percent. In fact, the 3.5 percent growth in the third quarter is the largest three-month gain we have seen in two years. This is obviously welcome news and an affirmation that this recession is abating and the steps we've taken have made a difference.
>
> But I also know that we got a long way to go to fully restore our economy and recover from what's been the longest and deepest downturn since the Great Depression. And while this report today represents

real progress, the benchmark I use to measure the strength of our economy is not just whether our GDP is growing, but whether we're creating jobs, whether families are having an easier time paying their bills, whether our businesses are hiring and doing well. And that's what I'm here to talk with you about today.

I know many of you have come from different corners of our country to be here, and looking out at all of you I'm reminded of the extraordinary diversity of America's small businesses. You're owners of coffee shops, and diners, and hotels. You're florists, exterminators, builders. Each of your shops and firms reflects different passions, and different ideas, and different skills.

But what you share is a willingness to pursue those passions, take a chance on those ideas, and make the most of those skills. What you share is an entrepreneurial spirit, a tireless work ethic, and a simple hope for something better that lies at the heart of the American ideal. Businesses like yours are the engines of job growth in America. Over the past decade and a half, America's small businesses have created 65 percent of all new jobs in this country. And more than half of all Americans working in the private sector are either employed by a small business or own one."

Try reading the excerpt aloud, using pauses where you find commas. Try using pauses of different lengths. While his words are powerful, they gain greater impact as he pauses before or after key words or phrases.

Pause when you introduce a new idea or term. This gives your listeners time to absorb what you are saying. It helps listeners keep up with you.

Tie your pauses to verbal phrasing. To a speaker, a phrase has a different meaning than it does to a writer. It is a unit you speak in one breath in order to express a single idea. Each pause tells your listeners you are moving from one thought to the next.

Use pauses to change the pace and add verbal variety. Pauses can be an effective tool speakers use to keep attention or to draw attention to a particular thought or emotion. Pause just before you speed up or pause just before you slow down. In both cases, the pause indicates to the audience that something is going to happen.

Extend pauses when displaying a visual. This tactic enables your audience to read the information on the visual without missing your next thought. It is important to pause after the display, not before it. Try pausing for two or three seconds.

Pause for two or three seconds when displaying a visual to let your audience read it without missing your next comment.

Emphasis

A speaker uses emphasis to draw attention to a specific word or phrase. It involves stressing certain words or phrases. It can add weight to what you say, and make a particular word or phrase more noticeable or prominent. An emotion can be highlighted through the use of emphasis. Emphasis is a nonverbal way of saying, "Listen to this!"

Think about how many ways you can say "Come in." Depending on how they are said and how they are accented by nonverbal behavior, these words can be:

A friendly invitation	(from one friend to another)
A command	(from a supervisor to an employee)
An angry growl	(from a mother with a headache to her teenage son who has already interrupted her five times)
A nondescript response	(to a knock at your office door)

These changes give meaning to a word or phrase. By singling out a few words for special attention, you add color to your speech and avoid monotony. Emphasis can be achieved by using different techniques.

Change your volume and pitch. Whether you choose to speak more loudly or more quietly, you draw attention to your speech through contrast. A quieter approach is often a more effective attention-grabber. When you speak in a monotone, you tell your listeners you have nothing to emphasize. When you vary the pitch of your voice, you let them know that what you are saying is important.

Pause when changing your speaking rate. A change of pace—speeding up or slowing down—draws attention to what will come next: Pausing can do the same.

Use emotion. Emphasis comes naturally when you speak from the heart. When you have deep feelings about a subject—drug abuse, for example, or the need to protect the environment from pollution—you will express your feelings emphatically. Anything other than an impassioned delivery may seem inadequate.

Work with the previous excerpt from Barack Obama's speech. Read it aloud. The first time, do not emphasize anything. Read it in a monotone, just as you would a telephone book. It is hard to get involved, is it not? Now, underscore the words or phrases that, if emphasized, would add meaning to the speech. Then read it a second time, adding the emphasis and emotion you think appropriate. You may find that the words seem to take a life of their own as they demand attention.

Eliminating Non-fluencies

Non-fluencies are meaningless words that interrupt the flow of our speech. We may use them unintentionally, but we need to work consciously to avoid them. Non-fluencies are also known as filled pauses or vocal fillers. While pauses can work *for* you, non-fluencies distract your listeners. These include: "you know," "uh," "um," "so," and "okay." If your economics professor says "okay" after every concept presented, or your history professor adds "uh" or "um" after every thought, it can cause you to lose focus. A sociology professor told us his students once kept track of his non-fluencies, and reported to him after class that that he said "you know" thirty-two times during the fifty- minute period. Non-fluencies are verbal debris; they add nothing to the content of your speech, and they also annoy an audience. Avoid them.

Throw out other types of speaking debris as well: giggling, throat clearing, lip smacking, and sighing. These interrupt the flow of speech and can also be annoying to the audience. As you give speeches during this term, think about any habits you have that may distract your audience. We do not expect you to be perfect, but striving to improve your speaking ability is a realistic goal.

Be aware of your speech patterns. Many people do not realize they use fillers. If you have been videotaped, listen for them as you watch your speech. Or, you can record your own phone conversation on a tape recorder. You can also ask friends to identify them when they hear you use fillers, or ask your teacher or classmates to keep track of non-fluencies.

Train yourself to be silent. Work actively to rid your speech of non-fluencies. Pause for a second or so after completing a phrase or other unit of thought. Because fillers indicate, in part, a discomfort with silence, this approach will help you realize that pauses are an acceptable part of communication.

What are the two central themes throughout this discussion of vocal delivery? *To practice and use vocal variety.* It is important to practice your speech so it flows smoothly. Practice pronouncing unfamiliar words so they come easily to you when you give your speech. Try varying pitch, rate, and volume to keep the audience's attention. Create interest in your speech, and stress key words, phrases, and thoughts. You have something relevant to share with your audience. You want to make it easy for them to understand you, and you want to keep them interested in what you have to say.

Aspects of Physical Delivery

Your physical delivery may convey professionalism or lack thereof. It can convey self-confidence or nervousness. Your delivery communicates enthusiasm or lack of interest. The ways you gesture, move, look at people, and dress say a great deal about you. More importantly, these elements leave a lasting impression that affects the speaker-audience connection. Although mastering the art of nonverbal communication will not guarantee your speaking success, it will help you convince your audience to pay attention.

Gestures

Gestures involve using your arms and hands to illustrate, emphasize, or provide a visual experience that accompanies your thoughts. Before we discuss the importance of gestures, body movement, and eye contact, we have a story about Katie, a non-traditional student who returned to school after five years of working for the loan department of a bank. She gave a speech adapted specifically to her audience. Her specific purpose was to explain how recent college graduates abuse credit cards and wind up owing thousands of dollars. She began:

> When you receive your first credit card, think of it as a loaded gun. If you don't use it properly you may wind up killing your credit for up to ten years.
>
> That means that no one will loan you money to buy a car, a plasma TV, or a house. You may not get the job you want because your credit is bad (prospective employers check applicants' credit ratings). And you'll go through a lot of torment while this is going on.
>
> Take my word for it. I've seen it happen dozens of times to people just like you.

Making a connection between a credit card and a loaded gun is a great attention-getter. Also, college students are usually fairly new to using credit cards, so the message is an important one to the audience. Although Katie's message was effective, her delivery was stiff and uncomfortable. She grasped the lectern for dear life, as if she were afraid to move from her spot. She was a talking statue, and her listeners responded by becoming restless and uncomfortable themselves. During the post-speech criticism, one audience member explained what he was feeling: "You looked so wooden that I had trouble listening to what you were saying, which is amazing since I'm already in credit card trouble."

Katie's problem was a lack of gestures and body movement, which her audience could not ignore despite the inherent interest of her speech. Gestures tell an audience that you are comfortable and self-confident. As an outlet for nervous energy, they actually help you feel more at ease. Gestures encourage an enthusiastic presentation. If you put your body into your speech through movement and gestures, it is difficult to present a stilted speech. Gestures also have a positive effect on breathing, helping you relax the muscles that affect the quality of the voice.

Gestures are especially important when you are speaking to a large audience. People in the back rows may not be able to see the changes in your facial expressions, and gestures may be their only way of seeing your involvement with your speech.

You can tell if your gestures are effective by checking where your listeners are looking. If they are focusing on the movement of your arms and hands instead of your face, your gestures are a distraction rather than a help. If this situation occurs, reduce the amount of gestures duringthe rest of your speech. Think about the following three guidelines as your practice using gestures.

When speaking to a large audience, gestures play a key part in reinforcing the ideas in your message.

Use natural gestures. Your gestures should reinforce both the ideas in the message and your own personality. Stand straight, with your arms bent at the waist and your hands relaxed, so you are ready to gesture. Pay attention to the position of your elbows. If they hang stiffly at your sides, your gestures will look shortened and artificial. To move your hands and forearms freely, make sure there is plenty of room between your elbows and your body.

Gesture purposefully. Gestures should be meaningful and enhance your message. They should not appear random. For example, if you were trying to persuade people to donate blood, you might want to give your audience three reasons for doing so. When you say, "three reasons," you can hold up three fingers. When you say, "First," hold up one finger, and then when you say, "Second," hold up two fingers. You get the picture. These gestures are meaningful because they serve as an organizational guide. They tell your audience where you are in your speech. The same thing is true if you were giving an after-dinner speech in which you were trying to convince your audience to stop complaining. You could put up one or both hands in the "stop" position when you say, "Stop complaining" to your audience. This is meaningful because it emphasizes your assertion.

Gesture appropriately. Gestures should be timely. You do not want to hold three fingers up before or after you say "three reasons," but *as* you are saying it. You do not want arms flailing around as you speak; they should match what you are saying. Appropriate gestures are timely, and they should make sense within the context of your message. If you are speaking before a large audience, gestures are bigger and, generally, more dramatic. Those same gestures may look awkward and exaggerated in a smaller environment.

Actions That Inhibit Gesturing

The preceding three guidelines are designed to help you gesture effectively. As you deliver your speech, try to avoid the following:

For your next speech, work to make your gestures appear more natural. Ask a friend or colleague to comment on your movement and gestures. Gestures should *not* draw attention to themselves and away from the ideas.

Using Note Cards

Many instructors restrict the number and size of the note cards you may use during your speech. Follow their instructions, and consider the following:

- View your note cards as an extension of your arm, gesturing as you would without the note cards.

If you hold your hands behind your back, you won't be able to gesture.

Clasping your hands together.	It makes gesturing impossible except if you are willing to raise both hands at once.
Hugging your body.	It makes you look as though you are trying to protect yourself from assault.
Clasping your hands in the "fig leaf" stance.	Holding your hands together at your crotch is another protective position, and it may be distracting.
Locking your hands behind your back.	That position may encourage you to rock back and forth. This "at ease" military stance is not appropriate for the classroom.
Putting your hands in your pocket.	This restricts movement and may encourage you to play with change in your pocket or something else that will make sound and distract your audience.
Grasping and leaning into the lectern.	Some students do this for support when they are nervous. You can touch the lectern; just do not hold it in a death grip. Free your hands so you can gesture. Release your energy through your movement.

- Cards should fit into your hand comfortably.
- Generally, 4" x 6" cards are going to be easier to read than 3" x 5" cards.
- Number your note cards so you are able to keep them in order as you write them, transport them, and use them when you deliver your speech.
- Check to see that they are in sequence before speaking.
- Never staple your note cards.

Common Problems Using Note Cards

Using note cards effectively is not as easy as it seems. Sometimes, students wait until the last moment to create their note cards. Just like every other aspect of speaking, students should practice their speech using note cards, and consider the following pitfalls.

Holding note cards with both hands. Holding on to note cards with both hands may be distracting to the audience because cards are relatively small pieces of paper that do not need the support of both hands. Holding on with both hands restricts your movement, also.

Putting too much on the note cards. You only need enough information on your note cards to trigger your thoughts. If you have practiced enough, you do not need many notes. Also, if you have most of your speech on your note cards, you may end up sounding like you are reading to the audience.

Having too many note cards. Teachers sometimes swap stories about how many note cards a particular student used. The assignment may call for three note cards, and a student has a quarter-inch pile of note cards—sometimes as many as twenty for a four- to six-minute speech. This is not necessary if you have practiced your speech!

Writing on both sides of the card. Sometimes students misinterpret the "three cards rule" and use three note cards, but write on both sides. It is easy to lose your place when you have written on both sides, and it can be distracting to the audience ("Hey! She used bright pink ink for her notes!"), and it usually means that you are relying too heavily on your notes. Practice!

Using a Legal Pad

Traditionally, public speaking instructors wince at the notion of allowing students to use something other than note cards. Our professors taught us to use note cards, and we teach our students the same. In reality, not every occasion calls for small note cards. It is certainly not uncommon to see speakers using note pads or legal pads of some kind in the corporate world. Long and detailed presentations may be better served by using a note pad instead.

Your instructor may allow the use of a note pad in your class, or you may be in a situation where having a pad of paper makes sense. Once you have your notes on something larger than your hand, it may be more distracting when you gesture. You do not want a pad of paper waving around in the air. It should *not* be used as an extension of your arm. Hold the pad in one hand, at a distance from your eyes that allows you to see your notes but not covering your face. Gesture with your free hand.

Physical Movement

Remember the second problem related to Katie's delivery? She appeared glued to the lectern. After a while, her listeners got tired of watching her. Katie's mistake is typical. Like many speakers, she failed to realize that an active speaker can encourage an active response from an audience, but an immobile speaker can leave listeners listless. When you move from one place to another while you speak, your listeners are more likely to keep their eyes on you. Movement has an additional advantage of helping to reduce your nervous energy. It can work against you, however, if you look like a moving target or if your movement has no purpose. Think about the following three guidelines as you prepare your speech.

Move naturally. Relax and use movement reasonably. Do not pace back and forth like a caged lion or make small darting movements that return you to the safety of the lectern.

Tie your movements to your use of visual aids. Walk over to the visual as you are presenting it and point to its relevant parts. Walk back to the lectern when you are through. Make sure the movement is fluid.

Be prepared. Your instructor and the speaking environment will influence the opportunities for physical movement. Your instructor may allow or prohibit you from speaking behind a lectern or podium. In informal situations, it may be appropriate to walk through the aisles as you talk. In a small room, you can walk around without a microphone and still be heard. In a large room, you may need the help of a wireless microphone. Be prepared to adapt to your instructor's rules and the speaking environment. Remember that movement is a way to connect with the audience, get them involved, and keep their attention.

When you don't make eye contact with your audience, it may be interpreted as a lack of interest in your subject.

Eye Contact

No other aspect of nonverbal behavior is as important as eye contact, which is the connection you form with listeners through your gaze. You engage your audience by drawing them in through eye contact. Sustained eye contact can communicate confidence, openness, and honesty. It suggests you are a person of conviction, you care what your listeners are thinking, and you are eager for their feedback. Making eye contact with your audience is a way for you to express nonverbally, "I want you to understand me."

When your eye contact is poor, you may be sending unintentional messages that the audience interprets as nervousness, hostility, being uncomfortable, or lack of interest. The audience may think you have something to hide or that you are not prepared.

In the process of writing this text, one of the authors attended a recognition ceremony where several honorees gave brief speeches. One speaker began by looking at her notes, then made eye contact with the audience, looked back at her notes, and then appeared to look at something on the wall to her right. She repeated these behaviors throughout her speech. Audience members were observed looking up at the same spot. The speaker admitted to being nervous before her speech. Clearly, this nervous tic distracted her audience.

Sometimes students only look at the instructor during their speech. Do not do this! It makes teachers uncomfortable and you are excluding the rest of the audience. Also, some student speakers ignore half the class by looking at the right side or the left side of the class only.

When you turn on the nightly news, you see the anchor looking straight at you. As a result of television, eye-to-eye contact is what you expect from every speaker; it is the norm. When a speaker looks away, we sense that something is wrong. We offer the following four performance guidelines for reflection.

Distribute your gaze evenly. Work on sustained eye contact with different members in the audience. Avoid darting your eyes around or sweeping the room with your eyes. Instead, try maintaining eye contact with a single person for a single thought. This may be measured in a phrase or a sentence. It may help to think of your audience as divided into several physical sectors. Focus on a different person in each sector, rotating your gaze among the people and the sectors as you speak.

Glance only briefly and occasionally at your notes. Do not keep your eyes glued to your notes. You may know your speech well, but when you are nervous, it may feel safer to keep looking at your notes. However, this is counterproductive.

Do not look just above the heads of your listeners. Although this advice is often given to speakers who are nervous, it will be obvious to everyone that you are gazing into the air.

Appearance

Standards for appearance are influenced by culture and context. Americans visiting the Vatican will find that shoulders and knees should be covered in order to gain entry. It is okay for students to wear baseball caps outside, but some in some contexts, it may be offensive to keep one on inside. In high school, you may have violated the student conduct code by wearing something that was deemed inappropriate. Most school districts have clearly-stated standards related to appearance. However, these standards differ from one district to another.

An effective speaker is aware of the norms and expectations for appearance as he or she moves from one culture to another. In a 1989 summit between Soviet President Mikhail Gorbachev and Chinese leader Deng Xiaoping, Gorbachev made a nearly fatal blunder: He wore a pair of beige loafers with his formal suit, a choice that offended the Chinese who believed that "holiday shoes" should not be worn on such a special occasion. Gorbachev's advisors failed to provide him with such relevant information.

We do not have to move from one country to another to experience differences in perspectives on appearance. Some businesses allow more casual attire; others expect trendy, tailored clothing. As rhetorical theorist Kenneth Burke (1969, 119) reminds us, your clothes make a rhetorical statement of their own by contributing to your spoken message.

Your choice of shoes, suits, dresses, jewelry, tattoos, hair style, and body piercings should not isolate you from your listeners. If that occurs, the intent of your speech is lost. We offer the following guidelines for appearance, but the bottom line is, *do nothing to distract from the message.*

Your appearance should be in harmony with your message. Communication professor Leon Fletcher (1990) describes a city council meeting addressed by college students pleading for a clean-up of the local beaches. Although the speeches were clearly organized, well-supported, and effectively presented, the unkempt physical appearance of the speakers conflicted with their message. They wore torn jeans, T-shirts and sloppy sandals. Their hair looked ungroomed. The city council decided to take no action. Several months later, the same issue was brought before the council by a second group of students, all of whom wore ties and sport jackets—symbols of the neatness they wanted for the beaches. This time the proposal was accepted (14).

Although no one would tell you that wearing a certain suit or dress will make your listeners agree with your point of view, the image you create is undoubtedly important. Research on employment interviews suggests that "physical appearance and grooming habits are factors in the hiring process" (Shannon and Stark 2003, 613).

Be clean and appropriately dressed and groomed. In your public speaking class, your shoe choice is not likely to create a stir. However, your audience expects that you will be clean and appropriately groomed. Your instructor may provide you with specific guidelines regarding your appearance on the day you speak. A general guideline is to be modest and slightly more formal than your audience.

Avoid clothing that detracts from your message. If the audience focuses on your appearance, your speech loses effectiveness. Wearing a cap is usually frowned upon. The audience wants to see your eyes, and you should not ignore the possibility that your instructor views caps as outdoor, not indoor, wear.

Avoid shirts that have writing on them. It is probably not wise to give a persuasive speech on the day you wear a t-shirt with "I make stuff up" on it. One of our female students held her poster in front of her, with the word "Hooters" showing on her t-shirt, just above the visual aid. Whether what is written on your t-shirt is witty or offensive, it takes focus off the message.

Some students may need the following gentle reminder: Your instructors, and probably many of your classmates are not interested in seeing your belly or *any* type of cleavage. And a note to the females—if you wear a tight shirt or a short skirt, and you tug or pull on it, you draw attention to yourself, not what you are trying to say.

Summary

The four methods of speech delivery are memorization, manuscript speaking, extemporaneous speaking, and impromtu speaking. Each method is appropriate in varying circumstances. Following the guidelines for the method you choose will enhance the effectiveness of your speech. In this chapter we focus on extemporaneous speaking, a method in which you prepare the content of your speech in advance, but speak from a key-word outline. Impromptu speaking involves speaking without preparation.

Nonverbal communication is an important part of delivery. Your vocal and physical delivery affect your presentation. Aspects of vocal delivery include articulation, pronunciation, volume, rate, pitch, pauses, and emphasis. Guidelines for effective vocal delivery are provided. In addition, an effective speaker has relatively few non-fluencies. Aspects of physical delivery include gestures, physical movement, eye contact, and appearance. A good speaker will use nonverbal delivery to capture and maintain the attention of the listeners.

Name____ Date_______________

Exercise 9.1 Chapter 9 – Delivery

Review the guidelines of each of your required speeches by addressing the criteria included on the speech evaluation form. Ask your instructor to explain any terms that are unfamiliar to you.

Speech Evaluation Form

Name__________________________________ Time________ Grade__________ Date________

Thesis Statement____

Type (purpose) of Speech ____

1= Excellent 2= Good 3= Average 4= Fair 5=Poor

Adaptation	*Language*	*Content*
___ Awareness of listeners	___ Appropriateness	__ Accuracy of material
___ Adaptation to conditions	___ Economy	__ Familiarity of material
___ Appropriate topic	___ Vividness __ Clarity	__ Sources cited & qualified
___ Friendliness	___ Sentence Structure	__ Specific evidence
Physical Delivery	*Organization*	*Vocal Delivery*
___ Posture and movement	___ Introduction	___ Pitch ___ Quality
___ Facial expression	___ Thesis___ Body	___ Rate___ Loudness
___ Gestures	___ Transitions	___ Sound Production
___ Eye contact	___ Conclusions	___ Conversational quality

Overall Rating of Speech with General Comments:

____

____

____

____ Examiner:____________________

10

Speaking to Inform

After reading this chapter, you should be able to:

- ❑ Distinguish between informative and persuasive intent
- ❑ Describe the different types of informative speeches
- ❑ Indentify the goals and strategies for informative speaking

Key Terms

Definition through example
Operational definitions
Speeches of demonstration
Speeches of description
Speeches of explanation
Repetition

Courtesy of Hampton University. Photo by Reuben Burrell.

HAMPTON UNIVERSITY

10 Scenario

Cassandra banged on the keyboard in frustration. She leaned back and sighed. As she glanced over at the calendar, the date of her speech jumped at her. She had less than a week to finish this informative speech.

"Come on Cassie you can do this," She told herself as she turned her gaze back to the wordless blank document on her computer.

When Cassandra was asked to deliver a speech informing her fellow students on the impact of AIDS in the world she thought it would be fairly easy. It was a topic she was passionate about and knew firsthand due to the fact that her mother served as an administrator for the World Aids Foundation. However, there was so much to discuss and different routes Cassandra could take. She could discuss the AIDS impact in Africa or even the epidemic among young people her age. Cassandra thought, "Oh man how can I be certain that my speech measures up to everyone's expectations. I know I want my speech to be accurate. I want it to be objective and clear. I certainly want it to have meaning, and of course, be memorable."

Cassandra sat up and looked at all the books and pamphlets that were scattered across her desk. She rolled her neck and went back to work, determined to develop a speech that would fulfill all of these goals.

"A terrific speech," she signed. "Yes!"

Informative Speaking

When you deliver an **informative speech,** your goal is *to communicate information and ideas in a way that your audience will understand and remember.* Whether you are a nurse conducting CPR training for new parents at the local community center, a museum curator delivering a speech on impressionist art, or an auto repair shop manager lecturing to workers about the implications of a recent manufacturer's recall notice, you want your audience to gain understanding of your topic. An important caveat for students of public speaking to remember is that the audience should hear *new* knowledge, not facts they already know. For example, the nurse conducting CPR training for new parents would approach the topic differently than if the audience was comprised of individuals from various fields working on their yearly recertification. New parents may have never had CPR training, whereas the others receive training at least once a year.

In this chapter, we first distinguish an informative speech from a persuasive one. The different types of informative speeches are identified, and goals and strategies for informative speaking are presented.

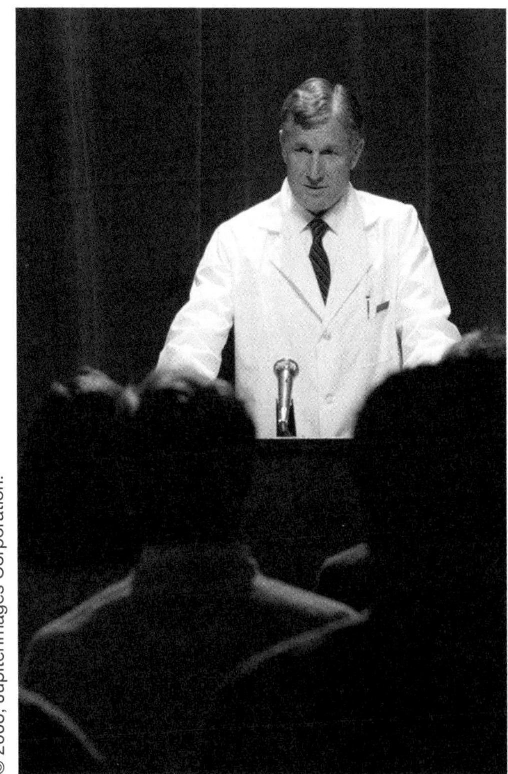

Is your goal to expand the audience's understanding of a topic? If this doctor is outlining the latest advances in neurosurgery, he is giving an informational speech.

Informative Versus Persuasive Intent

When you deliver an informative speech, your intent is to enlighten your audience—to increase understanding or awareness and, perhaps, to create a new perspective. In contrast, when you deliver a persuasive speech, your intent is to influence your audience to agree with your point of view—to change attitudes or beliefs or to bring about a specific, desired action. In theory, these two forms are distinctly different. In practice, as we noted earlier, this may not be the case.

For example, if during an informative speech on the ramifications of calling off a marriage you suggest to the engaged couples in your audience that safeguards may have to be taken to prevent emotional or financial damage, you are being persuasive implicitly. If you suggest to the men in your audience that they obtain a written statement from their fiancées pledging the return of the engagement ring if the relationship ends, you are asking for explicit action, and you have blurred the line between information and persuasion.

The key to informative speaking is intent. If your goal is to expand understanding, your speech is informational. If, in the process, you also want your audience to share or agree with your point of view, you may also be persuasive. In describing the different kinds of assault rifles available to criminals, you may persuade your audience to support measures for stricter gun control. Some of your listeners may write to Congress while others may send contributions to lobbying organizations that promote the passage of stricter gun control legislation. Although your speech brought about these actions, it is still informational because your intent was educational.

To make sure your speech is informational rather than persuasive, start with a clear specific purpose signifying your intent. Compare the following two specific purpose statements:

> **Specific purpose statement #1 (SPS#1)** To inform my listeners about the significance of the bankruptcy of the leading American energy company, Enron Corporation

> **Specific purpose statement #2 (SPS#2)** To inform my listeners why the investment firm Drexel Burnham Lambert was a symbol of Wall Street greed, power, and the corruption that marked the decade of the 1980s

While the intent of the first statement is informational, the intent of the second is persuasive. The speaker in SPS#1 is likely to discuss the fallout of Enron's bankruptcy, such as decrease in consumer confidence, changes in federal securities laws, and how employees were affected. The speaker in SPS#2 uses subjective words such as "greed, power, and corruption." Most likely this speech would focus more on the unethical practices that resulted in employees and investors losing their life savings, children's college funds, and pensions when Enron collapsed.

Types of Informative Speaking

Although all informative speeches seek to help audiences understand, there are three distinct types of informative speeches. A speech of **description** helps an audience understand *what* something is. When the speaker wants to help us understand *why* something is so, they are offering a speech of **explanation.** Finally, when the focus is on *how* something is done, it is a speech of **demonstration.** Each of these will be discussed in more detail.

Speeches of Description

Describing the circus to a group of youngsters, describing the effects of an earthquake, and describing the buying habits of teenagers are all examples of informative speeches of description. These speeches paint a clear picture of an event, person, object, place, situation, or concept. The goal is to create images in the minds of listeners about your topic or to describe a concept in concrete detail.

Here, for example, is a section of a speech describing a reenactment of the 1965 civil rights march in Selma, Alabama. We begin with the specific purpose and thesis statement:

> **Specific purpose.** To have my audience learn of the important connections between the civil rights marches in Selma, Alabama in 1965 and 2005.
>
> **Thesis statement.** Civil rights marchers returned to Selma, Alabama, in 2005 to commemorate the violence-marred march forty years earlier.
>
> Thousands of civil rights marchers came together in Selma, Alabama, to walk slowly across the Edmund Pettus Bridge. The year was 2005 and the reason for the march was to commemorate the brutal and violent march that took place in Selma forty years earlier. The first march awakened the country to the need to protect the civil liberties of African Americans, but this one was a time of celebration and rededication to the cause of civil rights.
>
> The 2005 march was peaceful. Only sound effects reminded participants of the billy club-wielding state troopers, of the screams and clomping horse hoofs, of the beatings and the inhumanity (Smothers, 1990).

In this excerpt, the speaker is making a contrast between two similar events that occurred forty years apart. Audience members are provided with images of what was named "Bloody Sunday," in 1965, and they can picture the peaceful, even celebratory, mood of the similar event forty years later. Specific, concrete language conveys the information through vivid word pictures.

Speeches of Explanation

Speeches of explanation deal with more **abstract** topics (ideas, theories, principles, and beliefs) than speeches of description or demonstration. They also involve attempts to simplify complex topics. The goal of these speeches is audience understanding. A psychologist addressing parents about the moral development of children or a cabinet official explaining U.S. farm policy are examples of speeches of explanation.

To be effective, speeches of explanation must be designed specifically to achieve audience understanding of the theory or principle. Avoid abstractions, too much jargon, or technical terms by using verbal pictures that define and explain. Here, for example, a speaker explains the concept of depression by telling listeners how patients describe it.

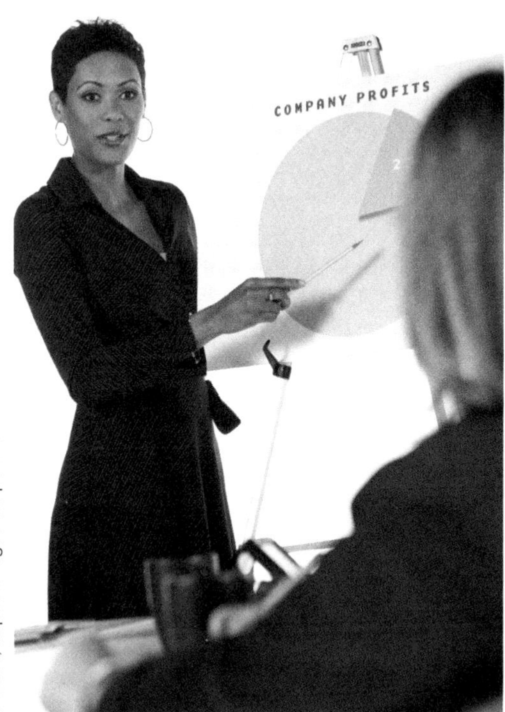

Speeches of explanation may come from a corporate officer outlining business policy to people in the company.

> Serious depression, a patient once said, is "like being in quicksand surrounded by a sense of doom, of sadness." Author William Styron described his own depression as "a veritable howling tempest in the brain" that took him down a hole so deep that he nearly committed suicide.
>
> Veteran and senior CBS correspondent Mike Wallace reached a point in his life where he found himself unable to sleep, losing weight, and experiencing phantom pains in his arms and legs. "Depression is palpable," explained Wallace. "You begin to feel like a fake and a fraud. You second guess yourself about everything" (1990, 48–55).

Compare this vivid description with the following, more abstract version:

> Severe depression involves dramatic psychological changes that can be triggered by heredity or environmental stress. Depression is intense and long lasting and may result in hospitalization. The disease may manifest itself in agitation or lethargy.

If the second is presented alone, listeners are limited in their ability to anchor the concept to something they understand. The second explanation is much more effective when combined with the first.

Speeches of explanation may involve policies: statements of intent or purpose that guide or drive future decisions. The president may announce a new arms control policy. A school superintendent may implement a new inclusion policy. The director of human resources of a major corporation may discuss the firm's new flextime policy.

A speech that explains a policy should focus on the questions that are likely to arise from an audience. For example, prior to a speech to teachers and parents before school starts, the superintendent of a school district implementing a new inclusion policy needs to anticipate what the listeners will probably want to know—when the policy change will be implemented, to what extent it will be implemented, when it will be evaluated, and how problems will be monitored, among other issues. When organized logically, these and other questions form the basis of the presentation. As in all informative speeches, your purpose is not to persuade your listeners to support the policy, but to inform them about the policy.

Speeches of Demonstration

Speeches of demonstration focus on a process by describing the gradual changes that lead to a particular result. These speeches often involve two different approaches, one is "how," and the other is a "how to" approach. Here are four examples of specific purposes for speeches of demonstration:

- To inform my audience *how* college admissions committees choose the most qualified applicants
- To inform my audience *how* diabetes threatens health
- To inform my audience *how to* sell an item on Ebay
- To inform my audience *how to* play the Internet game Bespelled

Speeches that take a "how" approach have audience understanding as their goal. They create understanding by explaining how a process functions without teaching the specific skills needed to complete a task. After listening to a speech on college admissions, for example, you may understand the process but may not be prepared to take a seat on an admissions committee.

Let us look more closely at a small section of a "how" speech.

> How are shows selected by the networks to be placed in prime time for an upcoming television season? The answer to this question describes a complex process involving a host of people ranging from developers with an idea to advertising executives responsible for deciding whether or not to sponsor a program. When the proposed television programs are presented to advertisers, the process engaged is one which can allow advertisers to have some influence over the content of programs they choose to sponsor. Before this sort of influence takes effect, the network officials and advertising executives go through what is called "speculation season." In early spring those involved in the decision-making process may consider about 100 hours' worth of programs. Usually no more than 23 to 25 hours of airtime eventually make it. The networks may develop 30 to 40 projects, while many more do not get past a one-page plot outline (Carter 1992).

Although this sample begins to explain how television programs are selected for the fall season, its primary goal is understanding, not application.

In contrast, *"how to"* speeches try to communicate specific skills, such as selling an item on Ebay, changing a tire, or making a lemon shake-up. Compare the previous "how" example discussing network television show selection with the following "how to" presentation on "how to" make a lemon shake-up.

> In front of me are all the ingredients for a lemon shake-up: lemons, water, sugar, a knife, and two cups. First, cut the lemons into quarters. If you love the tart taste of lemons . . .

> The main object of Bespelled is to win points by connecting letters or "tiles" on a board to spell words that are at least three letters long. After downloading the game from msn.com and pressing "play," look at the board. Seven rows of seven letters are arranged randomly, and to the left of the board, you'll see a wizard and a score box. Look for words arranged in any fashion. One letter of a word must be connected to the next letter. You use the mouse to highlight each letter, and then click when you have finished the word.

> Points are based on two things: the length of the word, and value of the letters. A second object is to keep letters or "tiles" that catch on fire from reaching the bottom of the board. The game is over when a burning tile ignites the whole board. So, you need to put out the fire by creating a word that incorporates the burning letter. If you avoid one burning tile, more will appear. Each burns the tile beneath them, and at some point, the board goes up in flames . . .

At the end of this speech of demonstration, the listener should know the ingredients and how to make a lemon shake-up.

One clear difference between the speech of demonstration and the speeches of presentation and explanation is that the *speech of demonstration benefits from presentational aids.* When your goal is to demonstrate a process, you may choose to complete the entire process—or a part of it—in front of your audience. The nature of your demonstration and the constraints of time determine your choice. If you are giving CPR training, a partial demonstration will not give your listeners the information they need to save a life. If you are demonstrating how to cook a stew, however, your audience does not need to watch you chop onions; prepare in advance to maintain audience interest and save time.

After a speech of demonstration about how to plan an Internet game, you should know the object of the game and be able to play it.

Goals and Strategies of Informative Speaking

Although the overarching goal of an informative speech is to communicate information and ideas in a way that the audience will understand, there are other goals that will help you create the most effective informative speech. Whether you are giving a speech to explain, describe, or demonstrate, the following five goals are relevant: be accurate, objective, clear, meaningful, and memorable. After each goal, two specific strategies for achieving that goal are presented.

Research is crucial to attain correct information to present in your speech.

1. Be Accurate

Facts must be correct and current. Research is crucial to attaining this goal. Do not rely solely on your own opinion; find support from other sources. Information that is not current may be inaccurate or misleading. Informative speakers strive to present the truth. They understand the importance of careful research for verifying information they present. Offering an incorrect fact or taking a faulty position may hurt speaker credibility and cause people to stop listening. The following two strategies will help speakers present accurate information.

Question the source of information. Is the source a nationally recognized magazine or reputable newspaper, or is it from someone's post on a random blog? Source verification is important. Virtually anyone can post to the Internet. Check to see if your source has appropriate credentials, which may include education, work experience, or verifiable personal experience.

Consider the timeliness of the information. Information can become dated. There is no hard and fast rule about when something violates timeliness, but you can apply some common sense to avoid problems. Your instructor may take this decision-making out of your hands by requiring sources from the last several years or so. If not, the issue of timeliness relates directly to the topic. If you wanted to inform the class about the heart transplant process, relying on sources more than a few years old would be misleading because scientific developments occur continuously.

2. Be Objective

Present information that is fair and is unbiased. Purposely leaving out critical information or "stacking the facts" to create a misleading picture violates the rule of objectivity. The following two strategies should help you maintain objectivity.

Take into account all perspectives. Combining perspectives creates a more complete picture. Avoiding other perspectives creates bias, and may turn an informative speech into a persuasive one. The chief negotiator for a union may have a completely different perspective than the administration's chief negotiator on how current contract negotiations are proceeding. They may be using the same facts and statistics, but interpreting them differently. An impartial third party trying to determine how the process is progressing needs to listen to both sides and attempt to remove obvious bias.

Show trends. Trends put individual facts in perspective as they clarify ideas within a larger context. The whole—the connection among ideas—gives each detail greater meaning. If a speaker tries to explain how the stock market works, it makes sense to talk about the stock market in relation to what it was a year ago, five years ago, ten years ago, or even longer, rather than focus on today or last week. Trends also suggest what the future will look like.

3. Be Clear

To be successful, your informative speech must communicate your ideas without confusion. When a message is not organized clearly, audiences can become frustrated and confused and, ultimately, they will miss your ideas. Conducting careful audience analysis helps you understand what your audience already knows about your topic and allows you to offer a clear, targeted message at their level of understanding. The following five strategies are designed to increase the clarity of your speech.

Carefully organize your message. Find an organizational pattern that makes the most sense for your specific purpose. Descriptive speeches, speeches of demonstration, and speeches of explanation have different goals. Therefore, you must consider the most effective way to organize your message. *Descriptive speeches* are often arranged in spatial, topical, and chronological patterns. *Speeches of demonstration* often use spatial, chronological, and cause-and-effect or problem-solution patterns. *Speeches of explanation* are frequently arranged chronologically, or topically, or according to cause-and-effect or problem-solution.

Define unfamiliar words and concepts. Unfamiliar words, especially technical jargon, can defeat your purpose of informing your audience. When introducing a new word, define it in a way your listeners can understand. Because you are so close to your material, knowing what to define can be your hardest task. The best advice is to put yourself in the position of a listener who knows less about your topic than you do or ask a friend or colleague's opinion. In addition to explaining the dictionary definition of a concept or term, a speaker may rely on two common forms of definitions: operational and through example.

Operational definitions specify procedures for observing and measuring concepts. We use operational definitions to tell us who is "smart," based on a person's score on IQ test. The government tells us who is "poor" based on a specified income level, and communication researchers can determine if a person has high communication apprehension based on his or her score on McCroskey's Personal Report of Communication Apprehension.

Definition through example helps the audience understand a complex concept by giving the audience a "for instance." In an effort to explain what is meant by the term, "white-collar criminal," a speaker could provide several examples, such as Jeff Skilling, (former Enron executive convicted on federal felony charges relating to the company's financial collapse), George Ryan (former Illinois governor indicted on federal racketeering, fraud, and conspiracy charges), and Duke Cunningham (former congressional representative from California, convicted of various bribery and fraud charges).

4. Be Meaningful

A meaningful, informative message focuses on what matters to the audience as well as to the speaker. Relate your material to the interests, needs, and concerns of your audience. A speech explaining the differences between public and private schools delivered to the parents of students in elementary and secondary school would not be as meaningful in a small town where no choice exists as it would be in a large city where numerous options are available. Here are two strategies to help you develop a meaningful speech:

The setting makes a difference as to what information is important to people, and you should plan your focus accordingly.

Consider the setting. The setting may tell you about audience goals. Informative speeches are given in many places, including classrooms, community seminars, and business forums. Audiences may attend these speeches because of an interest in the topic or because attendance is required. Settings tell you the specific reasons your audience has gathered. A group of middle-aged women attending a lifesaving lecture at a local YMCA may be concerned about saving their husbands' lives in the event of a heart attack, while a group of nursing students listening to the same lecture in a college classroom may be doing so to fulfill a graduation requirement.

Avoid information overload. When you are excited about your subject and you want your audience to know about it, you can find yourself trying to say too much in too short a time. You throw fact after fact at your listeners until you literally force them to stop listening. Saying too much is like touring London in a day—it cannot be done if you expect to remember anything.

Speakers who are enthusiastic, genuine, and creative make a long-lasting and favorable impression upon their audience.

Information overload can be frustrating and annoying because the listener experiences difficulty in processing so much information. Your job as an informative speaker is to know how much to say and, just as importantly, what to say. Long lists of statistics are mind-numbing. Be conscious of the relationship among time, purpose, and your audience's ability to absorb information. Tie key points to anecdotes and humor. Your goal is not to "get it all in" but to communicate your message as effectively as possible.

5. Be Memorable

Speakers who are enthusiastic, genuine, and creative and who can communicate their excitement to their listeners deliver memorable speeches. Engaging examples, dramatic stories, and tasteful humor applied to your key ideas in a genuine manner will make a long-lasting impact.

Use examples and humor. Nothing elicits interest more than a good example, and humorous stories are effective in helping the audience remember the material. When Sarah Weddington (1990), winning attorney in the Roe v. Wade Supreme Court case, talks about the history of discriminatory practices in this country, she provides a personal example of how a bank required her husband's signature on a loan even though she was working and he was in school. She also mentions playing "girls" basketball in school and being limited to three dribbles (boys could dribble the ball as many times as they wanted).

While these stories stimulate interest and make the audience laugh, they also communicate the message that sex discrimination was pervasive when Weddington was younger.

Physically involve your audience. Ask for audience response to a question: "Raise your hand if you have . . . " Seek help with your demonstration. Ask some audience members to take part in an experiment that you conduct to prove a point. For example, hand out several headsets to volunteers and ask them to set the volume level where they usually listen to music. Then show how volume can affect hearing.

Guidelines for Effective Informative Speeches

Regardless of the type of informative speech you plan to give, there are characteristics of effective informative speeches that cross all categories. As you research, develop, and present your speech, keep the following nine characteristics in mind.

Consider Your Audience's Needs and Goals

Considering your audience is the theme of the book, but it is always worth repeating. The best informative speakers know what their listeners want to learn from their speech. A group of Weight Watchers members may be motivated to attend a lecture on dieting to learn how to lose weight, while nutritionists drawn to the same speech may need the information to help clients. Audience goals are also linked to knowledge. Those who lack knowledge about a topic may be more motivated to listen and learn than those who feel they already know the topic. However, it is possible that technology has changed, new information has surfaced, or new ways to think about or do something have emerged. The speaker needs to find a way to engage those who are less motivated.

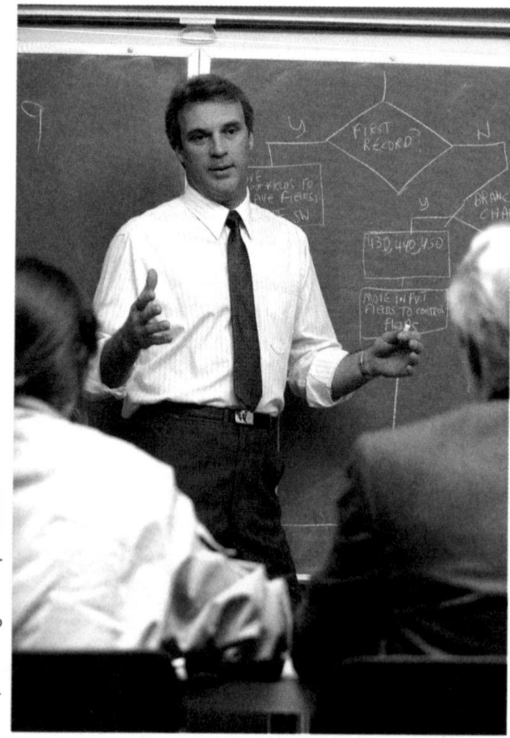

The best informative speakers know what their audiences want to learn from their message.

Make connections between your subject and your audience's daily needs, desires, and interests. For example, some audience members might have no interest in a speech on the effectiveness of half-way houses until you tell them how much money is being spent on prisons locally, or better yet, how much each listener is spending per year. Now the topic is more relevant. People care about money, safety, prestige, family and friends, community, and their own growth and progress, among other things. Show how your topic influences one or more of these and you will have an audience motivated to listen.

Consider Your Audience's Knowledge Level

If you wanted to describe how to use eSnipe when participating in Ebay auctions, you may be speaking to students who have never heard of it. To be safe, however, you might develop a brief pre-speech questionnaire to pass out to your class. Or you can select several individuals at random and ask what they know. You do not want to bore the class with mundane minutia, but you do not want to confuse them with information that is too advanced for their knowledge level. Consider this example:

> As the golf champion of your district, you decide to give your informative speech on the game. You begin by holding up a golf club and saying, "This is a golf club. They come in many sizes and styles." Then you hold up a golf ball. "This is a golf ball. Golf balls are all the same size, but they come in many colors. Most golf balls are white. When you first start playing golf, you need a lot of golf balls. So, you need a golf club and a golf ball to play golf."

Expect your listeners to yawn in this situation. They do not want to hear what they already know. Although your presentation may be effective for an audience of children who have never seen a golf club or ball, your presentation has started out too simplistic even for people who have some knowledge of the game.

Capture Attention and Interest Immediately

As an informative speaker, your goal is to communicate information about a specific topic in a way that is understandable to your listeners. In your introduction, you must first convince your audience that your topic is interesting and relevant. For example, if you are delivering a speech on white-collar crime, you might begin like this:

> Imagine taking part of your paycheck and handing it to a criminal. In an indirect way, that's what we all do to pay for white-collar crime. Part of the tax dollars you give the federal government goes into the hands of unscrupulous business executives who pad their expenses and over-charge the government by millions of dollars. For example, General Dynamics, the third-largest military supplier, tacked on at least $75 million to the government's bill for such "overhead" expenses as country-club fees and personal travel for corporate executives . . .

This approach is more likely to capture audience attention than a list of white-collar crimes or criminals.

Sustain Audience Attention and Interest by Being Creative, Vivid, and Enthusiastic

Try something different. Change your pace to bring attention or emphasis to a point. Say the following phrase at a regular rate, and then slow down and emphasize each word: "We must work together!" Slowing down to emphasize each word gives the sentence much greater impact. Varying rate of speech can be an effective way to sustain audience attention.

Show some excitement regardless of your topic!

Also, show some excitement! Talking about accounting principles, water filters, or changes in planet designations with spirit and energy will keep people listening. Delivery can make a difference. Enthusiasm is infectious, even to those who have no particular interest in your subject. It is no accident that advertising campaigns are built around slogans, jingles, and other memorable language that people are likely to remember after a commercial is over. We are more likely to remember vivid language than dull language.

Cite Your Oral Sources Accurately

Anytime you offer facts, statistics, opinions, and ideas that you found in research, you should provide your audience with the source. In doing this, you enhance your own credibility. Your audience appreciates your depth of research on the topic, and you avoid accusations of plagiarism. However, your audience needs enough information in order to judge the credibility of your sources. If you are describing how the HBO show *Deadwood* became an acclaimed yet controversial drama, it is not sufficient to say, "Ashley Smith states . . ." because Ashley Smith's qualification to comment on this show may be based on the fact that she watches television regularly. If the speaker said, "Ashley Smith, television critic for the Chicago Tribune, states . . ." then we know she has some expertise in the area.

Signpost Main Ideas

Your audience may need help keeping track of the information in your speech. Separating one idea from another may be difficult for listeners when trying to learn all the information at once. You can help your audience understand the structure of your speech by creating oral lists. Simple "First, second, third, fourth . . ." or "one, two, three, four . . ." help the audience focus on your sequence of points. Here is an example of signposting:

Having a motorized scooter in college instead of a car is preferred for two reasons. The first reason is a financial one. A scooter gets at least 80 miles per gallon. Over a period of four years, significant savings could occur. The second reason a scooter is preferred in college is convenience. Parking problems are virtually eliminated. No longer do you have to worry about being late to class, because you can park in the motorcycle parking area. They're all around us . . .

Signposting at the beginning of a speech tells the audience how many points you have or how many ideas you intend to support. Signposting during the speech keeps the audience informed as to where you are in the speech.

Relate the New with the Familiar

Informative speeches should introduce new information in terms of what the audience already knows. Analogies can be useful. Here is an example:

A cooling-off period in labor management negotiations is like a parentally-imposed time-out. When we were children, our parents would send us to our rooms to think over what we had done. We were forbidden to come out for at least an hour in the hope that by the time we were released our tempers had cooled. Similarly, by law, the President can impose an 80-day cooling-off period if a strike threatens to imperil the nation's health or safety.

Most of us can relate to the "time out" concept referred to in this example, so providing the analogy helps us understand the cooling-off period if a strike is possible. References to the familiar help listeners assimilate new information.

Use Repetition

Repetition is important when presenting new facts and ideas. You help your listeners by reinforcing your main points through summaries and paraphrasing. For example, if you were trying to persuade your classmates to purchase a scooter instead of a car, you might have three points: (1) A scooter is cheaper than a car; (2) A scooter gets better gas mileage than a car; and (3) You can always find a nearby parking spot for your scooter. For your first point, you mention purchase price, insurance, and maintenance cost. As you finish your first point, you could say, "So a scooter is cheaper than a car in at least three ways, purchase price, insurance, and maintenance." You have already mentioned these three sub-points, but noting them as an internal summary before your second main point will help reinforce the idea that scooters are cheaper than cars.

© Corbis.

Use effective presentational aids in your informative speech to hold your audience's attention.

Offer Interesting Visuals

Using pictures, charts, models, PowerPoint slides, and other presentational aids helps maintain audience interest. Jo Sprague and Douglas Stuart, (1988) explain:

> "Your message will be clearer if you send it through several channels. As you describe a process with words, also use your hands, a visual aid, a chart, a recording. Appeal to as many senses as possible to reinforce the message . . . If a point is very important or very difficult, always use one other channel besides the spoken word to get it across" (299).

Use humorous visuals to display statistics, if appropriate. Demonstrate the physics of air travel by throwing paper airplanes across the room. With ever-increasing computer accessibility and WiFi in the classroom, using computer-generated graphics to enhance and underscore your main points and illustrations is a convenient and valuable way to help you inform your audience effectively.

Ethics of Informative Speaking

Think about the advertising you see on television and the warning labels on certain products you purchase. Listening to a commercial about a new weight-loss tablet, you think you have just found a solution to get rid of those extra twenty pounds you carry with you. Several happy people testify about how wonderful the drug is, and how it worked miracles for them. At the end of the commercial, you hear a speaker say, "This drug is not for children under 16. It may cause diarrhea, restlessness, sleeplessness, nausea, and stomach cramps. It can lead to heat strokes and heart attacks. Those with high blood pressure, epilepsy, diabetes, or heart disease should not take this medicine . . . " After listening to the warnings, the drug may not sound so miraculous. We have government regulations to make sure consumers make informed choices.

As an individual speaker, *you need to regulate yourself*. A speaker has ethical responsibilities, no matter what type of speech he or she prepares and delivers. The informative speeches you deliver in class and those you listen to on campus are not nearly as likely to affect the course of history as those delivered by high-ranking public officials in a time of war or national political campaigns. *Even so, the principles of ethical responsibility are similar for every speaker.*

The President of the United States, the president of your school, and the president of any organization to which you belong all have an obligation to inform their constituencies (audiences) in non-manipulative ways and to provide them with information they need and have a right to know. Professors, doctors, police officers, and others engaged in informative speaking ought to tell the truth as they know it, and not withhold information to serve personal gain. You, like others, should always rely on credible sources and avoid what political scientists label as "calculated ambiguity." **Calculated ambiguity** is a speaker's planned effort to be vague, sketchy, and considerably abstract.

You have many choices to make as you prepare for an informative speech. Applying reasonable ethical standards will help with your decision-making. An informative speech requires you to assemble accurate, sound, and pertinent information that will enable you to tell your audience what you believe to be the truth. Relying on outdated information, not giving the audience enough information about your sources, omitting relevant information, being vague intentionally, and taking information out of context are all violations of ethical principles.

Summary

Informative speeches fall into three categories. Speeches of description paint a picture of an event, person, object, place, situation, or concept; speeches of explanation deal with such abstractions as ideas, theories, principles, and beliefs; and speeches of demonstration focus on a process, describing the gradual changes that lead to a particular result.

A somewhat blurry line exists between informative and persuasive speaking. Remember that in an informative speech your goal is to communicate information and ideas in a way that your audience will understand and remember. The key determinant in whether a speech is informative is speaker intent.

As an informative speaker, you should strive to be accurate, objective, clear, meaningful, and memorable. Preparing and delivering an effective informative speech involves applying the strategies identified in this chapter. In order to increase accuracy, make sure you question the source of information, consider the timeliness, and accurately cite your sources orally. Being objective includes taking into account all perspectives and showing trends. Crucial to any speech is clarity. To aid your audience, carefully organize your message, define unfamiliar words and concepts, signpost main ideas, relate the new with the familiar, and use repetition.

Audience members have gathered for different reasons. No matter what the reason, you want your speech to be meaningful to all listeners. In doing so, consider the setting, your audience's needs and goals and knowledge level, and try to avoid information overload. An informative speaker also wants people to remember his or her speech. In order to meet that goal, try to capture attention and interest immediately, sustain audience attention and interest by being creative, vivid, and enthusiastic, use examples and humor, offer interesting visuals, and physically involve your audience.

As you prepare your informative speech, make sure the choices you make are based on a reasonable ethical standard. You have an obligation to be truthful, and we presented many ways to accomplish this as you prepare your speech as well as when you deliver it.

TTYL (Talk to Your Listener)

In an informative speech, you are likely to encounter questions, comments, and interruptions while you speak. Here are some tips to cope with these unpredictable events.

Decide whether you want questions during your presentation or at the end. If you prefer they wait, tell your audience early in your speech or at the first hand raised something like, "I ask that you hold all questions to the end of this presentation, where I have built in some time for them."

When fielding questions, develop the habit of doing four things in this order: thank the questioner, paraphrase the question in your own words (for the people who may not have heard the question), answer the question briefly, and then ask the questioner if you answered their question.

Note that the second step in answering questions is to paraphrase the question in your own words. This provides you with the opportunity to point questions in desirable directions or away from areas you are not willing to go. Paraphrasing allows the speaker to stay in control of the situation.

For any question, you have five options: (1) answer it, and remember "I do not know" is an answer; (2) bounce it back to the questioner, "Well, that is very interesting. How might you answer that question?"; (3) Bounce it to the audience, "I see, does anyone have any helpful thoughts about this?"; (4) Defer the question until later, "Now you and I would find this interesting, but it is outside the scope of my message today. I'd love to chat with you individually about this in a moment"; (5) Promise more answer later, "I would really like to look further into that. May I get back to you later?" Effective speakers know and use all five as strategies to keep their question-and-answer period productive and on track.

When random interruptions occur, do not ignore them. Call attention to the distraction. This allows your audience to get it out and then return their attention to you. One speaker was interrupted when a window washer suspended outside the building dropped into view, ropes and all. The speaker paused, looked at the dangling distraction and announced, "Spiderman!" Everyone laughed, and he then returned to his speech. At a banquet, a speaker was interrupted by the crash of shattering dishes from the direction of the kitchen. She quipped, "Sounds like someone lost a contact lens." Whether humorous or not, calling attention to distractions is key to maintaining control.

The heckler is a special kind of distraction that requires prompt attention. If you notice a man in the audience making comments for others to hear that undercut your message, first, assume he is trying to be helpful. Ask him to share his comments for all to hear. This will usually stop the heckler. If it does not, ask him his name, and use it as often as you can in your message. This usually works because oftentimes the heckler simply wants more attention. When all else fails, enlist the assistance of your audience. Ask if anyone wants to hear what you have to say more than what the heckler is saying. (Your audience will indicate they do.) Then ask if there is a volunteer, preferably a big one, who can help us all out. The combination of humiliation and the implied threat should do the trick.

Name____ Date_______________

Exercise 10.1 Chapter 10 – Speaking to Inform

Part I

Oral Communication for Today's Student states that there are three types of informative speaking: Speeches of Description, Speeches of Explanation and Speeches of Demonstration. Select an informative speech topic. Write a key word outline for your topic first as a *speech of description*, then as a *speech of explanation* and lastly as a *speech of demonstration.*

After making your topic selection, consider how the three types of speeches differ and how are they similar.

Part II

Regardless of whether you are giving a speech to *explain*, *describe* or *demonstrate*, your speech should meet the five goals of informative speaking. Does it?

☐ Be accurate

☐ Be objective

☐ Be clear

☐ Be meaningful

☐ Be memorable

11

Speaking to Persuade

After reading this chapter, you should be able to:

- ❒ Describe the elements of persuasion
- ❒ Describe the dimensions of speaker credibility
- ❒ Discuss pathos and the power of emotion
- ❒ Discuss logos and the power of logical appeals and arguments
- ❒ Explain the three types of inductive reasoning
- ❒ Demonstrate an understanding of deductive reasoning
- ❒ Discuss the goals of persuasion
- ❒ Identify persuasive aims
- ❒ Explain the types of persuasive claims
- ❒ Discuss the use of Monroe's Motivation Sequence as a method of organizing persuasive argument
- ❒ Demonstrate an understanding of the role that ethics play in persuasive speaking

Key Terms

Adoption
Analogies
Belonginess and love needs
Causal reasoning
Continuance
Deductive reasoning
Deterrence
Discontinuance
Dynamism
Ethics
Esteem needs
Ethos
Inductive reasoning
Inference
Logos
Monroe's Motivation Sequence
Pathos
Physiological needs
Proposition of fact
Proposition of policy
Proposition of value
Reasoning
Reasoning from sign
Safety needs
Self actualization

HAMPTON UNIVERSITY
SEAL OF THE PRESIDENT OF THE UNITED STATES

11 Scenario

Kevin laughed as his best friend, Damien, stuck his hand in the fishbowl. Mr. Nahuel's class watched in anticipation as Damien opened his sheet of paper. He groaned loudly, which caused Kevin and the rest of the class to howl with laughter.

"What is it man?" Kevin asked.

"Mr. Nahuel can I pick again?" Damien begged.

Mr. Nahuel shook his head, "You know the rules Mr. Damien. Now what topic did you choose?"

"I have to write an informative speech on the "Woman's Suffrage Movement." Damien huffed.

"Very interesting moment in U.S.history," Mr. Nahuel smiled, "Can't wait to hear it. You next Kevin."

Kevin smiled as he stuck his hand in and quickly pulled out a piece of paper. He unfolded it and read it silently. He looked up at the class and smirked. He stood to his feet and looked around the room, "Ladies and Gentlemen, I by far have the best topic ever. Feel free to hate on me now."

"Kevin enough with the drama, what did you pick?" Mr. Nahuel asked.

"I have to write a persuasion speech on the "Elimination of The Student Dress Code." Kevin smirked, "A piece of cake."

"How do you figure?" Damien asked.

"My dad makes speeches like this all the time. I've watched him do it and it's easy. He says all you have to do to persuade someone is to focus on whether you're trying to change someone's attitude or to get people to take some kinda action."

Damien looking uncertain, "for real? Is that right, Mr. Naheul?"

Well, Damien persuasion is little more involved than that but I have to admit that's where we start."

Kevin smiled. "See, I told you! No problem."

Individuals engage in persuasive speaking at all levels of communication. Interpersonally, we try to convince people to share our opinions or attitudes about very small things ("Burger King fries are better than McDonald's fries") and very significant things ("We shouldn't have children until we've been married for ten years"). We also engage in persuasive discourse at a societal level ("Homosexuals should be allowed to marry"). The ability to express one's self is a cornerstone of our democracy. The power of free speech is most clearly realized in speeches to persuade. Here is one example.

Sharing your opinion on something even as simple as where you will go to eat lunch involves persuasion skills.

After the defeat of the "Clinton health care program" in the fall of 1994, Hillary Clinton stepped up the efforts to bring a more universalized system of healthcare to the American public. Her steadfast belief in this cause resulted in extensive worldwide campaigning, which led to her giving a speech before the World Health Organization (WHO) on September 5, 1995.

> At long last, people and their governments everywhere are beginning to understand that investing in the health of women and girls is as important to the prosperity of nations as investing in the development of open markets and trade . . . (Remarks to the World Health Organization Forum on Women and Health Security. Delivered in Beijing, China.)

Clinton's speech stressed the need to come together as a worldwide community with the goal of bettering the health and well-being of all women and families so the new century would open with marked improvement in the lives of women.

Clinton continued by outlining the basic needs that women have not had access to in the past. Women have lived without the necessities that help anyone look forward to a full life of health and productivity. These necessities include medical care, education, legal protection, the chance to better their economic position, and human rights. There are many places in the world where womens' health is in jeopardy because health care is not available or does not do enough to adequately meet needs. Often health care is simply too expensive for those who need it. Even the most basic needs, such as good, clean drinking water and good nutrition are not readily available. Moreover, many women are the victims of sexual abuse and ignorance of health concerns.

Too many women have been suffering for too long, Clinton proclaimed. She said the state of their health is one of continuous pain. The women who are suffering could be any woman in the world or any girl in the world. You could be looking in the mirror at that woman. Or it could be another person very close to you . . . your friend, your sister, your child, your neighbor.

In her speech, Clinton quoted compelling statistics about how many women in the world die or nearly die because of serious difficulties during childbirth. She expanded the information about reproductive issues, citing statistics about women who do not use any family planning methods due to a lack of education, no access to such services, or just because of their poverty. Because of this, Clinton stated that millions of women end up having abortions that are unsafe and ultimately result in lifelong medical problems or even death. More women are facing unplanned, unwanted pregnancies when they themselves can scarcely be called women, as young as they are. Good opportunities available for those babies born to very young mothers are few and far between. Mother and child both suffer in so many ways.

Another topic Clinton spoke out against was violence, saying that women not only suffer because of violence, but they also die. Violence takes many forms against women, whether it takes place within the home or outside the home. She said that violence, too, is an issue of health.

Breast cancer statistics also served as startling reminders to show the numbers of women throughout the world who suffer from this disease and who ultimately die because of it. Clinton even mentioned how many women would have died in the amount of time it took for her to deliver her speech that day.

Clinton remarked that using tobacco products kills as well and it is a killer that can be prevented. Even though it is not one of those things that people immediately think of as being deadly, it is one that causes horrible suffering to those who are affected by it. Along with such diseases as AIDS, there needs to be a focus on this killer as well. There is much that can be done to prevent those deaths that are caused by tobacco use.

Clinton closed her speech with a plea for all the nations who had representatives present that day to make every effort to ensure that the childbearing years of womens' lives should be a healthy and safe time. She implored every nation to do everything possible to make health care accessible and affordable for all women. She made a call for action on the issue.

Although retrospectives of Clinton's stay as First Lady often point to the failure of the "Clinton health care plan," her remarks before the WHO led to a substantial change in the healthcare of both women and their children.

Elements of Persuasion

Hillary Clinton's speech embodies the critical elements of persuasion that have been defined by generations of rhetorical scholars, starting with Aristotle. Persuasion is intended to influence choice through appeals to the audience's sense of ethics, reasoning, and emotion. Aristotle's views on the use of what he termed ethos, pathos, and logos provide the underpinnings of our modern study of persuasion.

Ethos and the Power of the Speaker's Credibility

Aristotle believed that **ethos,** which refers to speaker credibility, makes speakers worthy of belief. Audiences trust speakers they perceive as honest, especially "on points outside the realm of exact knowledge, where opinion is divided." In this regard, he believed, "we trust [credible speakers] absolutely. . . ."(Cooper 1960, 8). Hillary Clinton appealed to her audience through her own credibility as First Lady of the United States and as Chairwoman of the Task Force on National Health Care Reform. Due to her experiences with health and healthcare, Clinton was viewed as a credible source on several dimensions.

Dimensions of Speaker Credibility

What your audience knows about you before you speak and what they learn about your position during your speech may influence your ability to persuade them. Credibility can be measured according to four dimensions: perceived competence, concern for the audience, dynamism, and ethics.

© JupiterImages Corporation.

Persuasive speakers have the ability to convey to listeners that you are on their side.

Perceived competence. In many cases, your audience will decide your message's value based on perceived speaker competence. Your listeners will first ask themselves whether you have the background to speak. If the topic is crime, an audience is more likely to be persuaded by the Atlanta chief of police than by a postal worker delivering his personal opinions. Second, your audience will consider whether the content of your speech has firm support. When it is clear that speakers have not researched their topic, their ability to persuade diminishes. Finally, audiences will determine whether you communicate confidence and control of your subject matter through your delivery.

Concern for audience. Persuasion is also influenced by concern for your audience. Communication Professor Richard L. Johannesen (1974) differentiates between speakers who engage in "dialogue" and those who engage in "monologue." A **dialogue** takes into account the welfare of the audience; a **monologue** focuses only on the speaker's self-interest (95). Audiences sense a speaker's concern by first analyzing the actions a speaker has taken before the speech. If the group has formed to protest the location of a highway through a residential community, the audience will consider what the speaker has already done to convince highway officials to change their minds. Second, audiences listen carefully to the strength and conviction of the speaker's message. For instance, does the speaker promise to fly to Washington, D.C., if necessary, to convince federal officials to withhold funds until a new site is chosen? Persuasive speakers are able to convince their audiences that they are on their side.

Dynamism. Your credibility and, therefore, your ability to persuade are also influenced by the audience's perception of you as a dynamic spokesperson. A person who is dynamic is lively, active, vigorous, and vibrant. Your listeners will ask themselves whether you have the reputation for being someone who gets the job done. They will listen for an energetic style that communicates commitment to your point of view, and for ideas that build upon one another in a convincing, logical way.

Ethics. Finally, your ability to persuade is influenced by the audience's perception of your ethical standards. If you come to the lectern with a reputation for dishonesty, few people will be persuaded to trust what you say. If your message is biased and you make little attempt to be fair or to concede the strength of your opponent's point of view, your listeners may question your integrity. They may have the same questions if you appear manipulative (Sprague and Stuart 1988, 208–10).

If you analyze Hillary Clinton's speech to the WHO, all four dimensions of speaker credibility can be seen. *Perceived competence* is illustrated by her official positions (First Lady and Chair of the Task Force on National Health Care Reform) and her research. She cites several statistics related to childbirth complications, violence against women, breast cancer, and tobacco usage. *Concern for audience* is found in her topic selection and approach. Her target audience is members of the World Heath Organization, so the variety of health-related topics addressed by Hillary Clinton is appropriate. Also, she shares information rather than lectures, and approaches the topics as issues "we" need to address rather than what "you" need to be concerned about. *Dynamism* is shown through her articulate and energetic presentation, and the straight-forward approach. Known concern for women's health issues and use of statistics suggest a solid set of *ethics*.

Does credibility make a difference in your ability to persuade? Researchers have found that, in many cases, the most credible speakers are also the most persuasive (Aronson, Turner, and Carlsmith 1963). One powerful way speakers enhance their credibility is by creating a strong sense of identification in their audiences.

The Strategy of Identification: Seeking Common Ground

Your credibility and your ability to persuade may increase if you convince your audience that you share "common ground." In his classic work, *Public Speaking*, published in 1915, James A. Winans introduced the concept of "common ground." "To convince or persuade a man," he writes, "is largely a matter of identifying the opinion or course of action which you wish him to adopt with one or more of his fixed opinions or customary courses of action. When his mind is satisfied of the identity, then doubts vanish" (Day 1959).

Labor leader Cesar Chavez forged a common bond with his audience after a twenty-day fast in 1968 to call attention to the plight of California farm workers by proclaiming that the end of his fast was not the true reason for the gathering. Rather, people had come to observe that, "we are a family bound together in a common struggle for justice. We are a Union family celebrating our unity and the nonviolent nature of our movement." Chavez explained why he had fasted: "My heart was filled with grief and pain for the suffering of farm workers. The Fast was first for me and then for all of us in this Union. It was a Fast for nonviolence and a call to sacrifice." Chavez concluded with, "We have something the rich do not own. We have our own bodies and spirits and the justice of our cause as our weapons. It is how we use our lives that determines what kind of men we are. . . . I am convinced that the truest act of courage, the strongest act of manliness is to sacrifice ourselves for others in a totally non-violent struggle for justice. To be a man is to suffer for others. God help us to be men" (Hammerback and Jensen 1987, 57).

Cesar Chavez established a common ground with his audience and effectively used emotional arguments.

In this instance, Chavez establishes a common ground through identifying with his audience and provoking them to identify with him. Moreover, Chavez also makes effective use of emotional arguments, which Aristotle referred to as *pathos*.

Pathos and the Power of Emotion

Aristotle believed in the power of speakers to persuade through emotional appeals. He explained, "Persuasion is effected through the audience, when they are brought by the speech into a state of emotion; for we give very different decisions under the sway of pain or joy, and liking or hatred. . . ."(Cooper 1960, 9). Hillary Clinton appealed to the emotions of her listeners with the words, "In too many places, the status of women's health is a picture of human suffering and pain. The faces in that picture are of girls and women who, but for the grace of God or the accident of birth, could be us or one of our sisters, mothers, or daughters." This call to visualize harm to one's own family members served as a powerful example of utilizing emotion to appeal to the sensibilities of her audience members.

Appeal to Audience Emotion

Emotional appeals have the power to elicit happiness, joy, pride, patriotism, fear, hate, anger, guilt, despair, hope, hopelessness, bitterness, and other feelings. George Kennedy (1991), a scholar of classical rhetoric, tells us, "Emotions in Aristotle's sense are moods, temporary states of mind (123–4). But according to persuasion theorists Martha Cooper and William Nothstine (1992), "modern research into motivation and the passions moved beyond Aristotle's emphasis on the emotions themselves and moved extensively into broader theories of human psychology" (74). The persuader, they advise us, can influence his or her audience by using appeals to create an emotional, as well as a cognitive, state of imbalance in listeners, which arouses feelings that something is wrong and something must be done. By taking the essential needs of an audience into consideration, the persuader can develop lines of reasoning that respond to pertinent needs. Yes, human needs can be described in terms of logic or what makes sense to a listener, but needs are immersed in emotions of the individual as well.

Psychologist Abraham Maslow classified human needs according to the hierarchy pictured in figure 10.1. An analysis of these needs will help you understand audience motivation as you attempt to persuade. Maslow believed that our most basic needs—those at the bottom of the hierarchy—must be satisfied before we can consider those on the next levels. In effect, these higher level needs are put on "hold" and have little effect on our actions until the lower level needs are met.

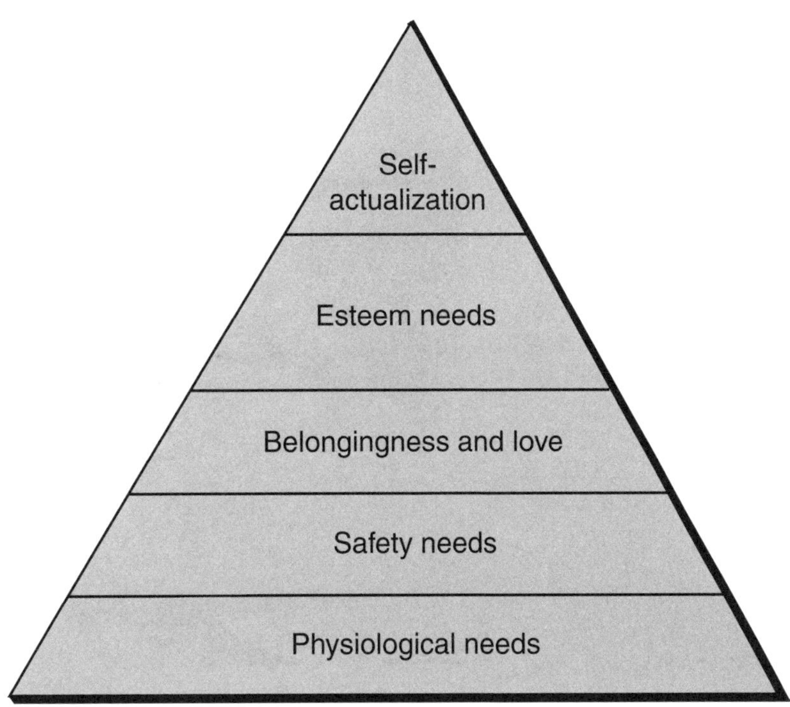

FIGURE 10.1 Maslow's Hierarchy of Needs

Physiological needs. At the bottom of the hierarchy are our biological needs for food, water, oxygen, rest, and release from stress. If you were delivering a speech in favor of a proposed new reservoir to a community experiencing problems with its water supply, it would be appropriate to appeal to the need for safe and abundant water.

Safety needs. Safety needs in-clude the need for security, freedom from fear and attack, a home that offers tranquility and comfort, and a means of earning a living. If you are delivering the same speech to a group of unemployed construction workers, you might link the reservoir project to jobs and a steady family income.

Belongingness and love needs. These needs refer to our needs for affiliation, friendship, and love. When appealing to the need for social belonging, you may choose to emphasize the camaraderie that will emerge from the community effort to bring the reservoir from the planning stage to completion.

Esteem needs. Esteem needs include the need to be seen as worthy and competent and to have the respect of others. In this case, an effective approach would be to praise community members for their initiative in helping to make the reservoir project a reality.

Self-actualization needs. People who reach the top of the hierarchy seek to fulfill their highest potential through personal growth, creativity, self-awareness and knowledge, social responsibility, and responsiveness to challenge. Addressing this audience, you might emphasize the long-range environmental and ecological implications of the reservoir. Your appeal may include the need to safeguard the water supply for future generations.

Maslow's Hierarchy of Needs can guide you in preparing a persuasive speech when you think about the feelings of your audience and how you can reach them in combination with the factors of credibility and sound argument. Understanding the basis for Maslow's hierarchy is critical to your success as a persuasive speaker, for if you approach your listeners at an inappropriate level of need, you will find them unable or unwilling to respond.

Our emotions are powerful ingredients in our human composition. You accept an ethical responsibility when you use emotional appeals. *The ethically responsible speaker does not distort, delete, or exaggerate information for the sole purpose of emotionally charging an audience in order to manipulate their feelings for self-centered ends.*

Everyone has attachment needs and can identify with appeals for friendship and camaraderie.

Yet, emotional appeals are often the most persuasive type of appeal because they provide the motivation listeners need to change their minds or take action. Instead of simply listing the reasons high fat foods are unhealthy, a more effective approach is to tie these foods to frightening consequences:

> Jim thought nothing could ever happen to him. He was healthy as an ox—or so he thought. His world fell apart one sunny May morning when he suffered a massive heart attack. He survived, but his doctors told him that his coronary arteries were blocked and that he needed bypass surgery. "Why me?" he asked. "I'm only 42 years old." The answer, he was told, had a lot to do with the high fat diet he had eaten since childhood.

Some subjects are more emotionally powerful than others and lend themselves to emotional appeals. Stories such as personal health crises, children in need, or experiences with crime and deprivation engage the emotions of listeners. Delivery also has an impact. Your audience can tell if you are speaking from the heart or just mouthing words. They respond to the loudness of your voice, the pace and rhythm of your speech, and to your verbal cues. Finally, the placement of the appeal is important. Corporate speech consultant James Humes suggests using an emotional ending to motivate an audience to action. In his view, the same emotions that stir people in their private lives motivate audiences. He explains, "CEOs tell me, 'Listen, Jim, I'm not trying to save England, I'm just trying to get a message across to the company.' Well, you still want to ask the employees to join you in something. End on an emotional pitch. Work that audience up" (Kleinfeld 1990).

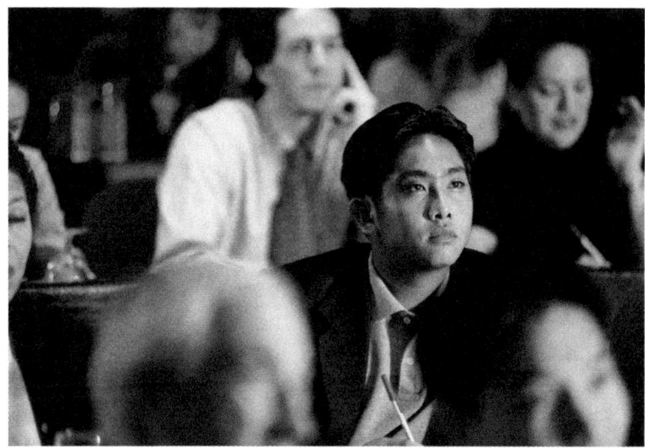

Your audience can tell if your expressions, tone, and gestures are genuine.

Because of their power, emotional appeals can be tools of manipulation in the hands of unscrupulous speakers who attempt to arouse audiences through emotion rather than logic. These speakers realize that fear and other negative emotions can be more powerful persuaders than reason when the audience is receptive to their emotional message.

Logos and the Power of Logical Appeals and Arguments

In addition to ethical (ethos) and emotional (pathos) appeals and arguments, logos or logical appeals and arguments are critical to the persuasive process. A logical appeal is rational and reasonable based on evidence provided. For example, if a friend tried to convince you *not* to buy a new car by pointing out that you are in college, have no savings account, and are currently unemployed, that friend would be making a logical argument. Aristotle saw the power of persuasion relying on logical arguments and sound reasoning. Clinton appealed to her audience's reasoning by constructing an inequality of healthcare as evidenced by the positions of doctors, scientists, and nurses.

Reasoning refers to the sequence of interlinking claims and arguments that, together, establish the content and force of your position. Although we believe the treatment of public speaking throughout this book promotes being reasonable, *no aspect of our book is more instrumental in guiding you to improve your critical thinking than reasoning as logical appeal.* Logical thought as critical thinking is intended to increase your ability to *assess, analyze*, and *advocate* ideas. As a persuasive speaker you will reason logically either through induction or deduction. Your responsibility is to reason by offering your audience factual or judgmental statements based on sound inferences drawn from unambiguous statements of knowledge or belief (Freeley 1993, 2).

To construct a sound, reasonable statement as a logical appeal for your audience you need to distill the essential parts of an argument:

1. The evidence in support of an idea you advocate;
2. A statement or contention the audience is urged to accept; and,
3. The inference linking the evidence with the statement.

Of the three parts to an argument, the most difficult part to understand is often the inference. It may be an assumption that justifies using evidence as a basis for making a claim or drawing a conclusion. For example, suppose you take a big bite out of food you have taken for dinner in your cafeteria or apartment and claim, "This is the worst piece of meat I have ever put in my mouth." With this claim you are making a statement that you *infer* from tasting the meat.

What is the evidence? The meat before you. The statement or contention is, "The meat is awful." The relation of the evidence to the claim is made by an inference, which may be an *unstated belief* that spoiled, old, or poorly prepared meat will taste bad. Stephen Toulmin, the British philosopher acknowledged as an expert on argument, speaks of the inferential link between evidence and claim as the *warrant.* Toulmin points out that a warrant is the part of the argument that states or *implies* an inference (Vancil 1993, 120–24).

When you reason with your audience by trying to persuade the listeners with an argument you want them to accept and act upon, you must use evidence, inferences, and statements as contentions the audience can understand and accept. Sound reasoning is especially important when your audience is skeptical. Faced with the task of trying to convince people to change their minds or do something they might not otherwise be inclined to do, your arguments must be impressive.

Supporters in an audience may require arguments in the form of reinforcement. You may have to remind a sympathetic crowd of the reasons your shared point of view is correct. This reminder is especially important if your goal is audience action. If you want a group of sympathetic parents to attend a board of trustees meeting to protest tuition increases, you must persuade them that a large turnout is necessary. It is up to you, through the presentation of an effective argument, to make action the most attractive course.

In persuasion, ethical and emotional appeals may be powerful factors, but reasoning or logical appeal can be your most effective tool. Well-developed reasons stated without exaggeration tell your listeners that you trust them to evaluate the facts on their merit rather than emotional appeal. Through the framework of a logical appeal, we piece together important elements to persuade listeners to accept our position and respond to a call to action. The framework for logical appeal is based on inductive and deductive modes of reasoning, in particular reasoning by analogy, reasoning from cause, and reasoning from sign.

To persuade your audience that a claim or conclusion is highly probable, you must have strong evidence and show that you have carefully reasoned the support of your points. Only when strong probability is established can you ask your listeners to make the inductive leap from specific cases to a general conclusion, or to take the deductive move from statements as premises to a conclusion you want them to accept. We will look more closely now at inductive and deductive reasoning.

You must have strong evidence and show that you've carefully supported your points to convince your audience that your claim has merit.

Inductive Reasoning

Aristotle spoke of inductive reasoning in his *Rhetoric* (Cooper 1960, 10). Through inductive reasoning, we generalize from specific examples and draw conclusions from what we observe. Inductive reasoning moves us from the specific to the general in an orderly, logical fashion.

When you argue on the basis of example, the inference step in the argument holds that what is true of specific cases can be generalized to other cases of the same class, or of the class as a whole. Suppose you are trying to persuade your audience that the disappearance of downtown merchants in your town is a problem that can be solved with an effective plan you are about to present. You may infer that what has worked to solve a similar problem in a number of highly similar towns is likely to work in the town that is the subject of your speech.

One problem associated with inductive reasoning is that individual cases do not *always* add up to a correct conclusion. Sometimes a speaker's list of examples is too small, leading his/her audience to an incorrect conclusion based on limited information. Here, as in all other cases of inductive reasoning, you can never be sure that your conclusions are absolutely accurate. Because you are only looking at a sample, you must persuade your audience to accept a conclusion that is probable, or maybe even just possible.

Reasoning by Analogy

Analogies establish common links between similar and not-so-similar concepts. They are effective tools of persuasion when you can convince your audience that the characteristics of one case are similar enough to the characteristics of the second case that your argument about the first also applies to the second.

A **figurative analogy** draws a comparison between things that are distinctly different, such as "Eating fresh marshmallows is like floating on a cloud." Figurative analogies can be used to persuade, but they must be supported with relevant facts, statistics, and testimony that link the dissimilar concepts you are comparing.

Although figurative analogies can provide valuable illustrations, they will not prove your point. For example, before the United States entered World War II, President Franklin D. Roosevelt used the analogy of a "garden hose" to support his position that the United States should help England, France, and other European countries already involved in the war. In urging the passage of the Lend-Lease Bill, he compared U.S. aid to the act of lending a garden hose to a neighbor whose house was on fire. Although this analogy supplied ethical and emotional proof, it did not prove the point on logical grounds. It is vastly different to lend a garden hose to a neighbor than it is to lend billions of dollars in foreign aid to nations at war (Freeley 1993, 119).

Whereas a figurative analogy compares things that are distinctly different and supply useful illustrations, a literal analogy compares things with similar characteristics and, therefore, requires less explanatory support. One speaker in our class compared the addictive power of tobacco products, especially cigarettes, with the power of alcoholic beverages consumed on a regular basis. His line of reasoning was that both are consumed for pleasure, relaxation, and often as relief for stress. While his use of logical argument was obvious, the listener ultimately assesses whether or not these two things—alcohol and tobacco are sufficiently similar. It may be that their differences diminish the strength of the speaker's argument. The distinction between literal and figurative analogies is important because only literal analogies are sufficient to establish a logical proof. The degree to which an analogy works depends on the answers to the following questions:

1. Are the cases being compared similar?
   Only if you convince your listeners of significant points of similarity will the analogy be persuasive.
2. Are the similarities critical to the success of the comparison?
   The fact that similarities exist may not be enough to prove your point. Persuasion occurs when the similarities are tied to critical points of the comparison.
3. Are the differences relatively small?
   In an analogy, you compare similar, not identical, cases. Differences can always be found between the items you are comparing. It is up to you as an advocate for your position to decide how critical the differences are.

4. Can you point to other similar cases?
   You have a better chance of convincing people if you can point to other successful cases. If you can show that the similarities between your position and these additional cases are legitimate, you will help sway audience opinion (Freely 1993, 119–20).

Reasoning from Cause

When you are reasoning from cause the inference step is that an event of one kind contributes to or brings about an event of another kind. The presence of a cat in a room when you are allergic to cats is likely to bring about a series of sneezes until the cat is removed. As the preceding example demonstrated, causal reasoning focuses on the cause-and-effect relationship between ideas.

Cause: inaccurate count of the homeless for the 2000 census

Effect: less money will be spent aiding the homeless

An advocate for the homeless delivered the following message to a group of supporters:

> We all know that money is allocated by the federal government, in part, according to the numbers of people in need. The census, conducted every ten years, is supposed to tell us how many farmers we have, how many blacks and Hispanics, how many homeless.
>
> Unfortunately, in the 2000 census, many of the homeless were not counted. The government told us census takers would go into the streets, into bus and train station waiting rooms, and into the shelters to count every homeless person. As advocates for the homeless, people in my organization know this was not done. Shelters were never visited. Hundreds and maybe thousands of homeless were ignored in this city alone. A serious undercount is inevitable. This undercount will cause fewer federal dollars to be spent aiding those who need our help the most.

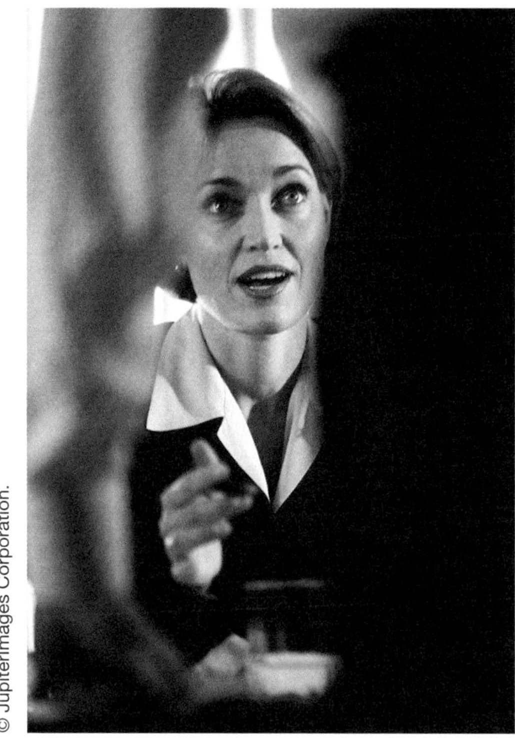

Causal reasoning is effective if your argument can withstand scrutiny.

When used correctly, causal reasoning can be an effective persuasive tool. You must be sure that the cause-and-effect relationship is sound enough to stand up to scrutiny and criticism. To test the validity of your reasoning, ask yourself the following questions:

1. Do the cause and effect you describe have anything to do with one another?
   Some statements establish a cause-and-effect relationship between ideas when the relationship is, at best, questionable. Ask yourself whether other factors contributed to the change. You may be attributing cause and effect where there is only coincidence.

2. Is the cause acting alone or is it one of many producing the effect?
   Even if the connection you draw is valid, it may be only one of several contributing factors that bring about an effect. To isolate it as solely responsible for an effect is to leave listeners with the wrong impression.
3. Is the effect really the effect of another cause?
   To use a medical example, although fatigue and depression often occur simultaneously, it may be a mistake to conclude that depression causes fatigue when other factors may also be involved. Both conditions may be symptoms of other illnesses such as mononucleosis, or the result of stress.
4. Are you describing a continuum of causes and effects?
   When you are dealing with an interrelated chain of causes and effects, it is wise to point out that you are looking at only one part of a broader picture.
5. Are the cause and effect related but inconsequential?
   Ask yourself whether the cause you are presenting is sufficient to bring about the effect you claim.
6. Is your claim and evidence accurate?
   To be an effective persuasive tool, causal reasoning must convince listeners that the link you claim is accurate. Your listeners should be able to judge probability based on your supporting evidence. They will ask themselves if your examples prove the point and if you explain or minimize conflicting claims (Sprague and Stuart 1988, 165–66).

To be effective, causal reasoning should never overstate. By using phrases like, "This is one of several causes," or "The evidence suggests there is a cause-and-effect link," you are giving your audience a reasonable picture of a complex situation. Public speakers could learn from medical researchers who are reluctant to say flatly that one thing causes another. More often than not, researchers indicate that cause-and-effect relationships are not always clear and that links may not be as simple as they seem.

Reasoning from Sign

In the argument from sign, the inference step is that the presence of an attribute can be taken as the presence of some larger condition or situation of which the attribute is a part. As you step outside in the early morning to begin jogging, the gray clouds and moist air can be interpreted as signs that the weather conditions are likely to result in a rainy day. Argumentation Professor David Vancil (1993) tells us that, "arguments from sign are based on our understanding of the way things are associated or related to each other in the world with them, [so] we conclude that the thing is present if its signs are present. The claim of a sign argument is invariably a statement that something is or is not the case" (149).

The public speaker who reasons from sign must do so with caution. Certainly, there are signs all around us to interpret in making sense of the world, but signs are easy to misinterpret. Therefore, the responsible speaker must carefully test any argument before using it to persuade an audience.

Deductive Reasoning

Aristotle also spoke of deduction as a form of reasoning in persuasive argument. Through deductive reasoning, we draw conclusions based on the connections between statements that serve as premises. Rather than introducing new facts, deductions enable us to rearrange the facts we already know, putting them in a form that will make our point. Deductive reasoning is the basis of police work and scientific research, enabling investigators to draw relationships between seemingly unrelated pieces of information.

At the heart of deductive reasoning is the syllogism, a pattern of reasoning involving a major and a minor premise and a conclusion. Syllogisms take this form:

a = b

b = c

c = a

Here is an example:

1. All basketball players can dribble the ball.
2. Anthony is a basketball player.
3. Anthony can dribble the ball.

Using this pattern of logic, the conclusion that Anthony can dribble the ball is inescapable. If your listeners accept your premise, they are likely to accept your conclusion. The major premise in this case is statement (1) "All basketball players can dribble the ball," while the minor premise is statement (2) "Anthony is a basketball player." Whether the deductive reasoning is stated in part or not, it leads us down an inescapable logical path. By knowing how two concepts relate to a third concept, we can say how they relate to each other.

Recognizing that people do not usually state every aspect of a syllogism as they reason deductively, Aristotle identified the **enthymeme** as the deductive reasoning used in persuasion. Because speakers and listeners often share similar assumptions, the entire argument may not be explicitly stated, even when the elements of a syllogism are all present. This truncated, or shortened, form of deductive reasoning is the enthymeme. The inference step in reasoning with an enthymeme is that the audience, out of its judgment and values, must supply and accept the missing premises or conclusions. If a classmate in a persuasive speech makes the claim that a newly elected congressional representative will probably take unnecessary trips costly to the taxpayers, your classmate's claim is drawn from the major premise (unspoken) that most, if not all, congressional representatives engage in unnecessary and costly travel.

The interrelationships in a syllogism can be established in a series of deductive steps:

1. **Step One:** Define the relationship between two terms.
   Major premise: Plagiarism is a form of ethical abuse.

2. **Step Two:** Define a condition or special characteristic of one of the terms.
   Minor premise: Plagiarism involves using the words of another author without quotations or footnotes as well as improper footnoting.
3. **Step Three:** Show how a conclusion about the other term necessarily follows (Sprague and Stuart 1988, 160).
   Conclusion: Students who use the words of another, but fail to use quotations or footnotes to indicate this, or who intentionally use incorrect footnotes, are guilty of an ethical abuse.

Your ability to convince your listeners depends on their acceptance of your original premise and the conclusion you draw from it. The burden of proof rests with your evidence. Your goal is to convince your listeners through the strength of your supporting material to grant your premises and, by extension, your conclusion. Considering persuasion from the vantage point of such outcomes will be considered next.

Outcomes and the Power of Goals, Aims, and Claims

Since Aristotle, scholars have focused on the elements of ethos, pathos, and logos as the primary aspects of persuasion. Some researchers have added to these principles an emphasis on outcomes. Gary Woodward and Robert Denton, Jr. (1992), explain: "Persuasion is the process of preparing and delivering messages through verbal and nonverbal symbols to individuals or groups in order to alter, strengthen, or maintain attitudes, beliefs, values, or behaviors" (18–19). Careful consideration of the goals of persuasion, the aims of your speech, and the type of claim you are making will help your message achieve the influence that will allow you to advance your agenda.

Goals of Persuasion

Critical to the success of any persuasive effort is a clear sense of what you are trying to accomplish. As a speaker, you must define for yourself your overall persuasive goals and the narrower persuasive aims. The two overall goals of persuasion are **to address attitudes** and **to move an audience to action.**

Speeches that focus on attitudes. In this type of speech, your goal is to convince an audience to share your views on a topic (e.g., "The tuition at this college is too high" or "too few Americans bother to vote"). The way you approach your goal depends on the nature of your audience.

When dealing with a negative audience, you face the challenge of trying to change your listeners' opinions. The more change you hope to achieve the harder your persuasive task. In other words, asking listeners to agree that U.S. automakers need the support of U.S. consumers to survive in the world market is easier than asking the same audience to agree that every American who buys a foreign car should be penalized through a special tax.

By contrast, when you address an audience that shares your point of view, your job is to reinforce existing attitudes (e.g., "U.S. automakers deserve our support"). When your audience has not yet formed an opinion, your message must be geared to presenting persuasive evidence. You may want to explain to your audience, for example, the economic necessity of buying U.S. products.

Speeches that require action. Here your goal is to bring about actual change. You ask your listeners to make a purchase, sign a petition, attend a rally, write to Congress, attend a lecture, and so on. The effectiveness of your message is defined by the actions your audience takes.

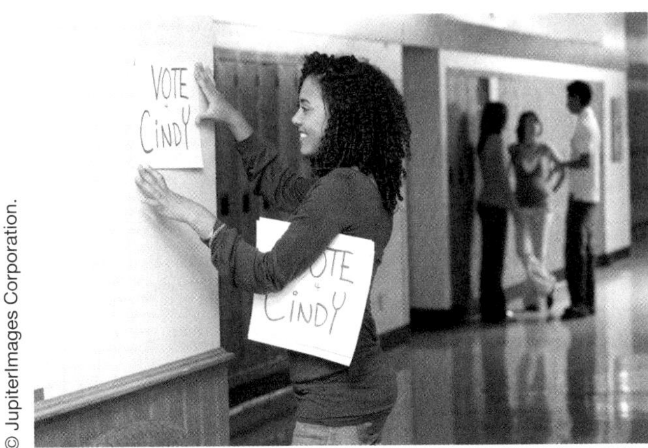

Even if you convince a group that you are the best candidate, they may not bother to vote in the election.

Motivating your listeners to act is perhaps the hardest goal you face as a speaker, since it requires attention to the connection between attitudes and behavior. Studies have shown that what people feel is not necessarily what they do. That is, little consistency exists between attitudes and actions (Wicker 1969, 41–70). Even if you convince your audience that you are the best candidate for student body president, they may not bother to vote. Similarly, even if you persuade them of the dangers of smoking, confirmed smokers will probably continue to smoke. Researchers have found several explanations for this behavior.

First, people say one thing and do another because of situational forces. If support for your position is strong immediately after your speech, it may dissipate or even disappear in the context in which the behavior takes place. For example, even if you convince listeners to work for your political campaign, if their friends ridicule that choice, they are unlikely to show up at campaign headquarters.

Researchers have found that an attitude is likely to predict behavior when the attitude involves a specific intention to change behavior, when specific attitudes and behaviors are involved, and when the listener's attitude is influenced by firsthand experience (Zimbardo 1988, 618–19). Firsthand experience is a powerful motivator. If you know a sun worshipper dying from melanoma, you are more likely to heed the speaker's advice to wear sun block than if you have no such acquaintance. An experiment by D. T. Regan and R. Fazio (1977) proves the point:

> A field study on the Cornell University campus was conducted after a housing shortage had forced some of the incoming freshmen to sleep on cots in the dorm lounges. All freshmen were asked about their

attitudes toward the housing crisis and were then given an opportunity to take some related actions (such as signing a petition or joining a committee of dorm residents). While all of the respondents expressed the same attitude about the crisis, those who had had more direct experience with it (were actually sleeping in a lounge) showed a greater consistency between their expressed attitudes and their subsequent behavioral attempts to alleviate the problem (28–45).

Therefore, if you were a leader on this campus trying to persuade freshmen to sign a petition or join a protest march, you would have had greater persuasive success with listeners who had been forced to sleep in the dorm lounges. Once you establish your overall persuasive goals, you must then decide on your persuasive aims.

Persuasive Aims

The aims of persuasion, or the type and direction of the change you seek, is the important next consideration. You must define the narrower aims of your speech. Four persuasive aims define the nature of your overall persuasive goal.

Adoption. When you want your audience to start doing something, your persuasive goal is to urge the audience to adopt a particular idea or plan. As a spokesperson for the American Cancer Society, you may deliver the following message: "I urge every woman over the age of forty to get a regular mammogram."

Continuance. Sometimes your listeners are already doing the thing you want them to do. In this case, your goal is to urge continuance. For example, the same spokesperson might say:

> I am delighted to be speaking to this organization because of the commitment of every member to stop smoking. I urge all of you to maintain your commitment to be smoke free for the rest of your life.

Speeches which urge continuance are necessary when the group is under pressure to change. In this case, the spokesperson realized that many reformed smokers constantly fight the urge to begin smoking again.

Discontinuance. You attempt to persuade your listeners to stop doing something:

> I can tell by looking around that many people in this room spend hours sitting in the sun. I want to share with you a grim fact. The evidence is unmistakable that there is a direct connection between exposure to the sun and the deadliest of all skin cancers—malignant melanoma.

Deterrence. In this case, your goal is avoidance. You want to convince your listeners not to start something, as in the following example:

> We have found that exposure to asbestos can cause cancer twenty or thirty years later. If you have flaking asbestos insulation in your home, don't remove it yourself. Call in experts who have the knowledge and equipment to remove the insulation, protecting themselves as well as you and your family. Be sure you are not going to deal with an unscrupulous contractor who is likely to send in unqualified and unprotected workers likely to do a shoddy job.

Speeches that focus on deterrence are responses to problems that can be avoided. These messages are delivered when a persuasive speaker determines that an audience possesses something which the speaker sees as highly threatening or likely to result in disaster. The speaker may try to bring about some sort of effective block or barrier to minimize, if not eliminate, the threat or danger. New homeowners, for example, may find themselves listening to persuasive presentations about the purchase of a home security system. The thrust of such a persuasive speech is the need to prevent burglary through use of an effective and economical security system.

Types of Persuasive Claims

Within the context of these persuasive goals and aims, you must decide the type of persuasive message you want to deliver. Are you dealing with a question of fact, value, or policy? To decide, look at your thesis statement which expresses your judgment or point of view. In persuasive speeches, the thesis statement is phrased as a proposition that must be proved.

For example, if your thesis statement was, "All college students should be required to take a one-credit Physical Education course each year," you would be working with a proposition of policy. If instead, your thesis statement was, "Taking a Physical Education course each year will benefit all college students," this would be a proposition of value.

Propositions are necessary because persuasion always involves more than one point of view. If yours were the only way of thinking, persuasion would be unnecessary. Because your audience is faced with differing opinions, your goal is to present your opinion in the most effective way. The three major types of propositions are those of *fact*, *value*, and *policy*.

Proposition of fact. Because facts, like beauty, are often in the eye of the beholder, you may have to persuade your listeners that your interpretation of a situation, event, or concept is accurate. Like a lawyer in a courtroom, you have to convince people to accept your version of the truth. Here are two examples of facts which would require proof:

1. Water fluoridation can lead to health problems.
2. American corporations are losing their hold on many world markets.

When dealing with propositions of fact, you must convince your audience that your evaluation is based on widely accepted standards. For example, if you are trying to prove that water fluoridation can lead to health problems, you might point to a research article that cites the Environmental Protection Agency (EPA) warning that long-term exposure to excessive fluoridation can lead to joint stiffness and pain and weak bones. You may also support your proposition by citing another research study that reports that children who are exposed to too much fluoridation may end up having teeth that are pitted and/or permanently stained.

Informative speakers become persuasive speakers when they cross the line from presenting facts to presenting facts within the context of a point of view. The informative speaker lets listeners decide on a position based on their own analysis of the facts. By contrast, the persuasive speaker draws the conclusion for them.

Proposition of value. Values are deep-seated beliefs that determine what we consider good or bad, moral or immoral, satisfying or unsatisfying, proper or improper, wise or foolish, valuable or invaluable, and so on. Persuasive speeches that deal with propositions of value are assertions based on these beliefs. The speaker's goal is to prove the worth of an evaluative statement, as in the following examples:

1. It is *wrong* for men to leave all the housework and childcare to their working wives.
2. Plagiarism is terribly *dishonest* for anyone who engages in it to complete an assignment.

    When you use words that can be considered judgments or evaluations, such as those italicized above, you are making a proposition of value.

Proposition of policy. Propositions of policy are easily recognizable by their use of the word "should":

1. Campus safety should be the number one priority of the college.
2. Student-athletes should adhere to the same academic standards as other students.

    In a policy speech, speakers convince listeners of both the need for change and what that change should be. They also give people reasons to continue listening and, in the end, to agree with their position and to take action.

A speaker's persuasive appeal, in summary, derives from the audience's sense of the speaker's credibility as well as from appeals to an audience's emotion and logic. At times, one persuasive element may be more important than others may. Many speakers try to convince audiences based primarily on logical appeal, some use mainly emotional appeals, and others rely on their image and credibility as a speaker. The most effective speakers consider their intended outcomes and appropriately combine all persuasive elements to meet a variety of audience needs and achieve their ultimate persuasive ends. Now we will turn our attention to a powerfully influential sequence of steps often used to organize persuasive messages.

Monroe's Motivated Sequence

As emphasized throughout this text, communication is a process connecting both speaker and audience. This awareness is particularly important in speeches to persuade, for without taking into account the mental stages your audience passes through, your persuasion may not succeed. The *motivated sequence*, a widely used method for organizing persuasive speeches developed by the late communication professor Alan H. Monroe (1965), is rooted in traditional rhetoric and shaped by modern psychology.

The method focuses on five steps to motivate your audience to act, and as Monroe would tell his students, they follow the normal pattern of human thought from attention to action. The motivated sequence clearly serves the goal of action if all five steps are followed. When the goal is to move your audience to act, each of the following five steps would be needed.

If someone wants only to persuade the audience there is a problem, then only the first two steps are necessary. If the audience is keenly aware of a problem, then a speaker may focus only on a solution.

Attention. Persuasion is impossible without attention. Your first step is to capture your listeners' attention in your introduction and convince them that you have something to say that is of genuine importance to them. You have several possibilities, including making a startling statement, using an anecdote, and asking a rhetorical question.

Need. In the *need step*, you describe the problem you will address in your speech. You hint or suggest at a need in your introduction, then state it in a way that accurately reflects your specific purpose. Your aim in the need step is to motivate your listeners to care about the problem by making it clear the problem affects them. You can illustrate the need by using examples, intensifying it through the use of carefully selected additional supporting material, and *linking* it directly to the audience. Too often the inexperienced speaker who uses the motivated sequence will pass through the need step too quickly in haste to get to the third step, the satisfaction step.

How can you capture an audience's attention in your introduction to keep them listening?

Satisfaction. The *satisfaction step* presents a solution to the problem you have just described. You offer a proposal in the form of an attitude, belief, or action you want your audience to adopt and act upon. Explanations in the form of statistics, testimony, examples, and other types of support ensure that your audience understands exactly what you mean. You clearly state what you want your audience to adopt and then explain your proposal. You have to show your audience how your proposal meets the need you presented. To be sure everyone understands what you mean, you may wish to use several different forms of support accompanied by visuals or audiovisual aids. An audience is usually impressed if you can show where and how a similar proposal has worked elsewhere. Before you move to the fourth step, you need to meet objections that you predict some listeners may hold. We are all familiar with the persuader who attempts to sell us a product or service and wants us to believe it is well worth the price and within our budget. In fact, a considerable amount of sales appeal today aims at selling us a payment we can afford as a means to purchasing the product, whether it is an automobile, a vacation, or some other attractive item. If we can afford the monthly payment, a major objection has been met.

Visualization. The *visualization step* encourages listeners to picture themselves benefiting from the adoption of your proposal. It focuses on a vision of the future if your proposal is adopted and, just as important, if it is rejected. It may also contrast these two visions, strengthening the attractiveness of your proposal by showing what will happen if no action is taken.

Positive visualization is specific and concrete. Your goal is to help listeners see themselves under the conditions you describe. You want them to experience enjoyment and satisfaction. In contrast, negative visualization focuses on what will happen without your plan. Here you encourage discomfort with conditions that would exist. Whichever method you choose, make your listeners feel part of the future.

Action. The *action step* acts as the conclusion of your speech. Here you tell your listeners what you want them to do or, if action is not necessary, the point of view you want them to share. You may have to explain the specific actions you want and the timing for these actions. This step is most effective when immediate action is sought.

How far would any politician get if he/she failed to directly ask people to vote for him?

Many students find the call to action a difficult part of the persuasive speech. They are reluctant to make an explicit request for action. Can you imagine a politician failing to ask people for their vote? Such a candidate would surely lose an election. When sales representatives have difficulty in closing a deal because they are unable to ask consumers to buy their products, they do not last long in sales. Persuasion is more likely to result when direction is clear and action is the goal.

In review, remember the five-step pattern if you want to lead your audience from attention to action. The motivated sequence is effective, and like all tools of persuasion, can be misused. The line between use and abuse of persuasive tools warrants further examination.

Ethics and Persuasive Speaking

Do you want to be lied to—by anyone? Even when the truth hurts, we prefer it to deception. Telling the truth is the paramount ethical standard for the persuasive speaker. The importance of ethics in public speaking is stressed both implicitly and explicitly throughout this book. Ethics provide standards for conduct that guides us. Persuasive speaking requires asking others to accept and act on ideas we believe to be accurate and true. The ethics of persuasion merit particular consideration in our plans for persuasion.

Think for a few moments about rhetoric as persuasive speaking. Rhetoric is framed and expressed in language and presents ideas within a range of choice. As a speaker, when you make choices, some degree of value is involved in your choosing, whether you speak about the quality of the environment or television programs to select. When choice is involved, ethics are involved. Rhetoric and ethics are bound together.

As a speaker, you must decide not only what to tell your audience, but also what you should avoid saying. In a persuasive speech, you are asking listeners to think or act in ways needed to achieve your specific purpose, a desired response. Emotional appeals entail ethical responsibility, and this responsibility extends to other appeals as well. Consider the four habits as applied to ethical persuasion:

1. **The habit of search**, in which we look for information to confirm or contradict a point of view, demands that we express genuine knowledge of our subject and an awareness of its issues and implications. As a persuasive speaker, you know that controversy exists in matters requiring persuasion. Your task, within the time constraints you face and resources you utilize, is to develop sound and good reasons for the response you desire from an audience. This task is centered in a careful search for the truth.
2. **The habit of justice** asks that you be fair in your search, selection, and presentation of facts for the audience to consider and accept. You should not distort ideas or hide information that an audience needs to properly evaluate your speech, neither should you use loaded language or guilt-by-association tactics.
3. **The habit of preferring public to private motivation** stems from the fact that when you are involved in public speaking, you act as public persons. As such, you have a responsibility to disclose any special bias, prejudice, and private motivations in your sources and in your own motives. There are times in our society when political, religious, or economic spokespersons will articulate a public position that clearly indicates motives in the public interest when, in fact, their persuasive message is actually rooted in a private agenda that is self-serving.
4. **The habit of respect for dissent** requires that, as a persuasive speaker, you must recognize the legitimate diversity of positions that differ from yours. As a persuader, you are not compelled to sacrifice principle but, as Karl Wallace (1955) puts it, you should "prefer facing conflict to accepting appeasement" (9). Leaders who serve as spokespersons, from local community centers to the centers of power in Washington, DC, are constantly being challenged about their opinions, policies, and actions. As a persuasive speaker, you can ask with respect for dissent: "Can I freely admit the force of opposing evidence and argument and still advocate a position that represents my convictions?"

The ethics of persuasion call for honesty, care, thoroughness, openness, and a concern for the audience without manipulative intent. The end does *not* justify the means at all costs. In a society as complex as ours, one marked in part by unethical as well as ethical persuaders, the moral imperative is to speak ethically.

Summary

Your credibility as a speaker is determined by the way the audience perceives you. Credibility is measured in terms of perceived competence, concern for the audience, dynamism, and ethics. According to rhetorical theorist Kenneth Burke, you can increase your credibility and ability to persuade if you convince your audience that you share "common ground" by identifying with your listeners.

Emotional appeals (pathos) can be powerful because they provide the motivation for action and attitude change. Through emotional appeals you can elicit the full range of human feelings in your listeners. To strengthen your appeal, use concrete detail and emotional language, and concentrate on delivering your speech effectively. Persuasive speaking also invites ethical responsibility (ethos). As a persuasive speaker, you should be conscious of ethical standards and what the implications are of the choice you are asking your audience to make. The audience needs to be treated to the truth, without manipulative intent.

Understanding Abraham Maslow's hierarchy of human needs is helpful to persuasive speakers. The five levels of Maslow's hierarchy form a pyramid, with the basic levels forming the base. From bottom to top, these needs are physiological, safety, belongingness and love, esteem, and self-actualization. If you approach your listeners at an appropriate level of need, you will find them more able or willing to respond.

When making logical arguments (logos), one can take an inductive or deductive approach. Inductive reasoning enables you to generalize from specific instances and draw a conclusion from your observations. Deductive reasoning draws a conclusion based on the connections between statements. Depending on your purpose for persuasion, you may choose to reason from examples, analogies, causal relations, or with enthymemes. Choosing the right amount of support, the most persuasive kind of evidence, and then reasoning carefully are essential for successful persuasion.

The two overall persuasive goals are to address audience attitudes and to move an audience to action. Four specific persuasive aims define the focus of your speech. These aims include adoption, continuance, discontinuance, and deterrence. Your point of view, or thesis statement, is expressed in the form of a proposition that must be proved. Propositions take three basic forms: fact, value, and policy.

An effective method for organizing a persuasive speech is Monroe's Motivated Sequence that includes five steps designed to motivate the audience to action: attention, need, satisfaction, visualization, and action. The motivated sequence is a widely used method for organizing persuasive speeches which follows the normal pattern of human thought from attention to action.

Name____ Date________________

Exercise 11.1 Chapter 11 – Speaking to Persuade

Today's student is bombarded by thousands of persuasive messages each day. *Communication for Today's Student* traces persuasion from Aristotle's elements of ethos, pathos and logos to persuasive claims to Monroe Motivated Sequence, etc. The list of the methods of persuasion is lengthy. First, list and give a brief definition of each of the methods of persuasion.

Next, you will locate Emancipation Oak or a site on campus designated by your instructor. Pick a *single* blade of grass from under the tree. Place the single blade of grass in an envelope and write in red ink on the outside of the envelope your name and date. Along with the blade of grass, prepare a one page statement using the methods of persuasion to convince your instructor that the blade of grass did indeed come from beneath The Emancipation Oak or designated site. Each time you use a method of persuasion label it in parenthesis ( ). Use as many methods as you can!!!!

Remember, place the blade of grass and the explanation in the envelope and seal it. Please be prepared because your instructor may decide to share your work with the class.

12

What are the Roles of Leadership and Power in Group Dynamics?

After reading this chapter, you should be able to:

- ❐ Define and distinguish between leadership and power
- ❐ Discuss the different types of leadership syles
- ❐ Discuss the six basic bases of power in small groups
- ❐ Describe the types of conflict that can occur in small groups
- ❐ Discuss the role of culture and conflict management strategies in small groups

Key Terms

Autocratic leader
Certainty
Coercive power
Collectivistic cultures
Democratic leader
Empathy
Expert power
Extrinsic conflict
High context culture
Individualistic cultures
Influence
Interpersonal linkage
Intrinsic conflict
Laissez-Faire leader
Leadership
Legitimate power
Low context culture
Maintenance leaders
Neutrality
Power
Power distance
Problem orientation
Provisionalism
Reciprocal
Referent power
Reward power
Situational leadership
Spontaneity
Strategy
Substantive conflict
Superiority quality
Task leaders
Task Roles
Theory X
Theory Y
Transformational
Transformational leader
Uncertainty avoidness

12 Scenario

BJ looked around as the auditorium filled with students. He smiled and waved at a few people he knew before settling in a seat by himself. He usually sat alone when he went to meetings like this so he could concentrate and focus on the speaker.

After a few minutes, Ms. Linwood, the Vice President of Student Activities, stood behind the podium. "Good evening everyone. I'm so pleased that you could be with us today. As some of you may know, I am the Vice President of Student Activities and one of my duties is to select the new student leaders of our school, also known as the Student Ambassadors.

BJ knew the moment he stepped on the college campus, he wanted to be a student leader. He wanted to help lead his classmates and provide a positive example for the members of the lower classes. As Ms. Linwood went on to discuss the different types of leaders, this allowed BJ to think about what type of leader he would be. Ms. Linwood described three types of leaders. She discussed the autocratic leader, the leader that leads with a strong hand and doesn't listen to the input of others within the group. Autocratic leaders reminded BJ of a dictatorship, which he thought could never work on a college campus. The next type of leader Ms. Linwood talked about was the laissez-faire leader. This person takes a hands-off approach to leadership. From the way Mrs. Linwood described the Student Ambassador organization, laissez- faire leaders are too passive and not motivated enough to evoke change.

"None of these leaders sound like me," BJ thought to himself.

"Those examples of leaders are okay, but they are not the type of leaders we need for this program. We need transformational leaders. Does anyone know what makes a transformational leader?" Ms Linwood asked the audience.

BJ looked around, wondering if anyone knew. He certainly didn't. As Ms. Linwood described a transformational leader, it seemed as though someone was describing BJ perfectly. The transformational leader is charismatic, generates awareness of vision, stimulates interest among colleagues, and helps their followers see past their interests for the benefit of the group.

BJ smiled and nodded as Ms. Linwood continued to discuss the role of the Student Ambassadors on campus. He truly believed at that moment he had found the organization perfect for him.

Introduction

How can my group manage itself to be productive and make quality decisions? That's a very hard question! One way to get some insight is to learn the chapter objectives. Even if you have the best group staffed with very bright and highly motivated members, most groups still need some help. You will have to find ways to help the group coordinate all its efforts, as well as help the members remain civil with each other. After all, the groups we are talking about are challenged with complex problems requiring information gathering, analysis, debate, and commitment. All that activity needs to be coordinated to keep the group on track. The members will require occasional motivation and, perhaps, even some discipline. In addition, because this process is rarely completed overnight, the potential for conflict is very high. It's natural for people to become irritated with each other and argue, especially when they spend a lot of time together. We're people; it's what we do! We have to find ways to keep that conflict under control and to use it to help our groups make the best decisions.

Groups are challenged with complex problems requiring a coordinated work approach.

To help answer all these questions, this chapter addresses three separate but related topics: leadership, power, and conflict.

Are Power and Leadership the Same Thing?

Leadership is the ability to influence the behavior of others. A leader is someone who can use interpersonal *influence* to move people to action. A person exercising leadership uses persuasion to motivate people to action. **Power,** by contrast, is the ability to *control* the behavior of others. Power can be based on legitimate authority or position, access to information, or access and control of desired resources.

The use of power and the use of influence are not the same thing. It is possible to use one without using the other. For example, a group member in a leadership role could be very successful at motivating other members to complete tasks in the effort to accomplish the group goal, but that leader could have no source of power. Conversely, a group member with some form of power (control over desired resources, for example), might be able to control the behavior of other group members, but he or she might not be personally persuasive or motivating.

In reality, many leaders likely use a combination of influence and power to accomplish tasks with groups of people. Good leaders try not to rely on power to motivate people, because a reliance on power damages the motivation and creativity of group members, and it results in flawed decisions and inferior products.

Leadership and power will be treated separately because they are different, but the discussion will emphasize the relationship between the two concepts.

How does a leader motivate others in the group?

What is the Role of Leadership?

Forsyth says that leadership is a specialized form of social interaction. It is a "reciprocal, transactional, and sometimes transformational process in which cooperative individuals are permitted to influence and motivate others to promote the attainment of group and individual goals." Let's look at the parts.

Reciprocal suggests that leadership is an ongoing process and is defined by the leader, the group members, and the particular situation that the group happens to be experiencing. There is a give-and-take relationship between the leader and the members in which the followers allow themselves to be influenced by the leader. There is no leadership without followers.

Leaders and group members work together in a *transactional* process "exchanging their time, energies, and skills to increase their joint rewards." The leader specifies what follower behaviors are needed to solve the problem and how the group's or followers' needs would be satisfied as a result.

In a give-and-take relationship, followers allow themselves to be influenced by the leader.

Transformational means that leaders can communicate a group vision that members find appealing. This vision motivates and empowers followers to become leaders themselves and influence the outcomes of group tasks. The leader's task is to make the vision clear to the followers. It asks them to make the group goals perhaps more important than their own individual goals.

As we mentioned earlier, leadership is really a *cooperative* process that uses persuasion instead of power and control. Members with the most influence usually emerge as leaders over time, and they are followed by the other members of the group. Remember that we are talking about the member with the most influence, and not *necessarily* the person who was appointed or elected leader of the group. Finally, leadership should function to help the group to adapt to changing circumstances and remain focused on *accomplishing goals.* Leadership helps to provide the direction that moves the group toward its objectives.

Influence of a Leader

Leadership is not "built in" to particular people who possess certain personality characteristics. That is, people are not born or destined to be leaders or followers. Instead of leadership being determined by a set of personality traits, we suggest that it depends more on experience and skills that can be learned and developed. Leadership is given or attributed to a person by others in the group. Even though we have suggested that personality characteristics or traits do not determine who has the ability to lead others, personal qualities do seem to affect *perceptions* of leadership.

How can you emerge as a leader within your group?

Take a Closer Look

A study by Geier reports that a process of elimination of contenders for leadership takes place in the initial meetings of any group. If you want to contribute to the goals of the group and become a leader, take these steps:8

1. *Be informed:* Being uninformed is seen as a negative characteristic that eliminates most contenders.
2. *Participate:* Groups typically judge quiet members as nonparticipative and unsuitable for leadership.
3. *Be flexible:* Try to remain open to new ideas or methods, especially when your ideas or methods are in conflict with group norms or goals, and be willing to compromise.
4. *Encourage:* Encourage other members to participate; don't try to make all the decisions yourself or dominate the discussion.

If your group does have an appointed leader, it doesn't necessarily mean that he or she will be the most influential person in the group. Leadership is not the sole possession of *the* leader. Many members of the group could provide leadership in different areas or at different times as the group progresses through a task. For example, if your group is working on a project related to the responsible use of energy resources, and even though you might not be *the* leader, you could be influential in decision making because you know a lot about the issue, because you are interested in energy policies, or because you belong to an active energy conservation organization. Whenever you influence the course the group takes, or when you help move the group toward the accomplishment of its goals, you have provided *leadership*.

Task and Maintenance Leadership

Task roles are oriented toward helping the group accomplish it's goals, while maintenance roles are focused on the social and relational issues that arise whenever people work together.

What role does a task leader play in a group?

Consistent with this model, **task leaders** are those group members who help the group with organization and advancement toward making a decision of completing a job. They are sometimes perceived as the leader of the group, but they can also be group members who are influential in a particular situation. Task leaders often *emerge* from the interaction of the group over time, but they could also be appointed or elected by the members. The presence of effective task leadership results in the group spending more time on task and staying focused on specific topics. Groups with leaders have longer attention spans than groups without leaders.

Maintenance leaders focus on relational issues, the development of an open and supportive climate, motivation of members, and conflict management. This type of leader also emerges from the interaction of the group. This function is far more than a cruise director sort of position. Maintenance leaders are critical to quality decision making because they mediate differences of opinion and interpersonal conflicts, maintain a high set of standards for group behavior and contributions, and encourage the participation of all the group members.

Both task and maintenance functions are essential to groups interested in making important decisions or completing complex tasks. Keep in mind these important functions of leaders as you consider the three perspectives on leadership presented in the next section.

Leadership Styles

© Andresr, 2008, Shutterstock.

Theory Y assumes that people are creative and imaginative in problem solving.

The **styles approach** to leadership is focused on the behaviors of the leader. McGregor tells us that the behavior of a leader is based on assumptions that he or she makes about the members of the group. These assumptions are divided into two groups, Theory X and Theory Y, which were designed to show leaders two ends of a continuum of leadership possibilities.

Theory X Assumptions

- People don't like to work and require the control of a leader.
- People do not like responsibility and they will resist it.
- People are not creative problem solvers.
- People are motivated by lower level needs such as security, food, and money.

Theory Y Assumptions

- People like to work; it comes as naturally as play to them.
- People are capable of self-direction.
- People are attracted to self-control and responsibility.
- People are creative and imaginative in problem solving and like to make decisions.
- People are motivated by higher-level needs such as recognition and self-actualization.

The practical application of these assumptions can be seen in the leadership styles: autocratic, laissez-faire, and democratic. Autocratic and democratic leadership capture the ends of the continuum, and those will be the primary focus of our illustration.

© Dmitriy Shironosov, 2008, Shutterstock.

What does the autocratic style of leadership accomplish?

The autocratic leader. The **autocratic leader** follows the Theory X assumptions most closely and creates an authoritative atmosphere that is based on direction and control. This type of leader does not solicit follower feedback. Instead, he or she makes the decisions and supervises followers to make sure the task is being accomplished. Members do not communicate much with each other. Instead, they communicate mostly with the leader, and communication is mostly task-related questions. There is very little discussion. An example of autocratic leadership can often be found in military organizations and on the shop floor in factories geared for high-volume production.

The autocratic style normally results in high efficiency and a high quantity of work, but it is low on cohesiveness, creativity, and member satisfaction. Lewin found that groups with autocratic leaders had the highest incidents of aggressive activity and exhibited the most productivity, but only when closely supervised. Additionally, employees who had low needs for independence and were authoritarian performed best under autocratic supervision.

The laissez-faire leader. **The laissez-faire leader** is one who takes a hands-off approach to leadership and provides very little direction to those being led. This leader seems to be a nonleader, because he or she does so little to guide the group. He or she abdicates responsibility, delays decisions, gives no feedback, and makes little effort to help followers satisfy their needs. There is no exchange with followers or any attempt to help them grow. This is rarely an effective style.

The democratic leader. The **democratic leader** adopts the Theory Y assumptions and creates an atmosphere of member integration, self-control, and participatory decision making; the input of subordinates is encouraged and is used to make decisions. This type of leadership is most effective with groups who have some knowledge about how to complete the task at hand and are fairly motivated to do so. Followers tend to be motivated by higher-level needs such as self-esteem and job satisfaction. In this case, a leader who is too authoritative will only serve to inhibit the group's creative processes.

Why are democratic conditions better when searching for a creative solution?

The democratic leader facilitates group discussion and participation in the decision-making process. In Lewin's study, groups with democratic leaders had the highest levels of individual satisfaction and functioned in the most positive and orderly fashion. Likewise, employees with a high need for independence and who are not authoritarian performed best under a democratic supervisor.

The strength of the styles approach is its focus on leader behaviors and assumptions made by leaders about followers. Some styles would only be effective in particular situations. For example, the autocratic style should bc useful in a factory type setting where work is repetitive and high quantity is expected. By contrast, a group trying to find a creative solution to a complex problem would probably perform better in a democratic condition. The situation, the task, and the composition of the group members will determine what style will produce the best outcomes.

Situational Leadership

Situational leadership assumes that a leader's effectiveness is contingent, or dependent, upon how well the leader's style fits the context. The situational leadership model by Hersey, Blanchard and Johnson argues that leadership effectiveness is built on a combination of task-based and relationship-based behaviors of the leader. The composition of the group will determine what leadership approach will work best. People in leadership positions should first analyze the group, and then implement one of a variety of leadership styles designed to address the situation.

How does a leader effectively analyze the group?

The primary factors that leaders look for are the ability of members to complete a particular task and their motivation to do so. As we discussed earlier, groups function on two levels: a task level (which is focused on goal achievement) and a relationship level (which is focused on maintaining the group as a unit and motivating members). As such, after situational leaders examine the abilities and motivation levels of followers, they must determine what combination of task and relationship leadership behaviors will work for the group in this situation. Hersey, Blanchard, and Johnson have outlined four leadership styles that consider these issues: telling, selling, participating, and delegating.

1. *Telling*. A high-task and low-relationship approach is used when group members have low levels of ability and low motivation. Groups that are not motivated to perform a task need and expect the leader to be direct in telling them what they should do. Communication is one-way and the leader decides what should be done and how. This leader typically uses a clear, confident, and directive communication style.
2. *Selling*. A high-task and high-relationship approach is used when the members have low levels of ability but high motivation to complete the task. The leader is comparable to a salesperson and works to gain acceptance of a particular course of action by explaining why it is the right or best one to take. The communication used by this leader offers emotional support, and it is motivational, encouraging, and, at times, stern.
3. *Participating*. A low-task and high-relationship approach is used when the members have high levels of ability but low motivation to complete the task. The leader and the group work together to determine what should be done, how, and when. It is similar to the democratic style mentioned earlier. It requires the leader to be less directive, more supportive, and to include the members in decision making. The leader utilizes an open communication style conducive to facilitating discussion, sharing ideas, and encouraging input.
4. *Delegating*. A low-task and low-relationship approach is used when the members have high levels of ability, as well as high levels of motivation to complete the task. This group needs very little guidance

or motivation. The leader outlines what needs to be accomplished and the group gets the job done its own way and at its own pace. This requires the leader to use feedback as well as clear communication that fosters a supportive climate, while still maintaining a sense of his or her role as a facilitator. The leader demonstrates confidence in the group by delegating more responsibilities.

The strength of the situational approach to leadership is its focus on member assessment and thinking through what and why a particular leadership approach should be used. For example, we may be more authoritative when a quick response is due and more facilitative when we are working with a mature group and have the time for facilitation. In addition, individuals from high context and collectivistic cultures may not ever use an authoritative (i.e., telling) style, as this approach would cause both leaders and followers to lose face. Please see the cultural discussion later in this chapter.

Transformational Leadership

A **transformational leader** is someone who possesses the charisma necessary to motivate followers and evoke change. Transformational leaders have charisma and vision, provide intellectual stimulation, and inspire their followers:

- They stimulate interest among colleagues and followers to view their work from new perspectives.
- They generate an awareness or a vision of the mission for the group.
- They develop colleagues and followers to higher levels of ability and potential.
- They motivate colleagues and followers to look beyond their own interests toward those that will benefit the group.

Transformational leaders are visionary and inspire followers to achieve higher goals. Lee Iacocca, a transformational leader, joined the Chrysler Corporation in 1978 when the company was on the verge of bankruptcy. From 1979 to 1986, Iacocca was able to turn the company around and make it profitable. Stephen Sharf, who was the head of manufacturing for Chrysler when Lee Iacocca took over, attributed the Chrysler transformation to Iacocca's leadership style. Iacocca is described as someone who knew what he was doing, someone who was well liked, and a person who took charge. Sharf states: "His tremendous self-confidence radiated to whomever he talked to—workers, suppliers, banks, and the government. He was articulate and a motivator. There was no doubt in his mind that he could turn Chrysler around and people began to believe he really could." Iacocca was a transformational leader and a visionary who was able to share that vision with others and transform Chrysler's way of doing business. Lee Iacocca is still regarded as a folk hero because of his leadership and achievements at Chrysler.

Other examples of transformational leaders include John Kennedy, Sam Walton, Steve Jobs, Abraham Lincoln, and Franklin D. Roosevelt.

As with the other leadership approaches mentioned in this chapter, there are some weaknesses of transformational leadership. One is the possibility that passion and confidence may be mistaken for truth and reality. Additionally, the energy these leaders exert can become unrelenting and exhausting because the followers and leaders of this type tend to see the big picture at the expense of the details. However, this approach helps us to understand why some leaders are more successful than other leaders.

How to Destroy a Group: Understanding What Not to Do

In order to improve our communication skills, understanding what not to do is important. Communication scholar D. M. Hall jokingly suggests eight ways in which a group member should not behave in groups:

1. Never prepare in advance; speak spontaneously. It keeps things on a superficial level.
2. Always take your responsibility lightly. This reduces your anxiety level and increases the frustration levels of others.
3. Never try to understand the group's purposes. This guarantees you'll accomplish nothing.
4. Always do the lion's share of the talking. None of the others have good ideas anyway.
5. Never give credit; hog it all for yourself. The rest love a braggart.
6. Always speak of your many years of experience. This compensates for your lack of ability.
7. Never tell anyone how to do it, else you may lose your prestige and position.
8. Always encourage the formation of cliques. The group can't last long when they begin to fight among themselves.

Have you engaged in any one of these communication behaviors?

If so, what can you do to avoid doing so in the future?

Source: Written by D. M. Hall, summarized by Murk (1994).

They can empower individual members to perform beyond their own expectations. This kind of motivation can create strong group identity and often changes the culture of entire organizations.

You don't need to be born with certain personality traits to be a good leader. You can rise to leadership if you take the time to develop the skills and gain experience. Hackman and Johnson tell us that skill development is a continuous, life-long process. The moment you think you have "arrived" as a leader, the progress stops.

From the discussion of leadership styles and types in this chapter, you should learn that a single leadership type will not always be successful. There is no absolute or formula that will be perfect in every situation. To be a successful leader, you should be able to analyze the task, the context of the task, and the group of people who will be making the decision or working on the task. When you have completed that analysis, you should gain some insight into what kind of leadership approach will be most useful in that situation. However, you should not get comfortable! Groups mature, motivation levels change, and the nature of the task could vary as you move toward completion.

Good leaders always adapt their approach as the group changes.

You should always pay attention to these changes and be ready to adapt and to alter your leadership approach as needed to best achieve your group's goals.

What is the Role of Power?

At the beginning of this chapter, we defined power as the ability to control the behavior of others. As you read before, power can be based on legitimate authority or a person's position in an organization, access to information, and access to or control of desired resources. It is possible to use power without being influential (i.e., exhibiting leadership), and it is possible to be influential without using power. The best situation exists when leadership and power are combined: the influential leader who uses power at the appropriate times and in moderation can be very successful at helping groups accomplish goals.

French and Raven identified five foundations of power that are typically used in small groups:

1. Legitimate power
2. Coercive power
3. Reward power
4. Expert power
5. Referent power

This section looks more closely at these five power sources, plus one more—interpersonal linkage.

Legitimate Power

Legitimate power exists as a function of someone's position in an organization. Followers defer to the *authority* carried by the position regardless of who occupies the position. Respect for the individual in the position of legitimate power is not required for control. The higher the position in the organization, the more legitimate power a person typically has. An example of the amount of influence and psychological effects legitimate power can have over an individual can be found in the studies of Stanley Milgram. This series of studies found that people would obey legitimate power even when it conflicted with what they believed to be the right thing to do. The best condition exists when the person holding the legitimate power in the organization is also respected by the subordinates. In this condition, the power can be used to direct activities rather than to control group members.

Is using coercive power an effective way to lead?

Coercive Power

Coercive power could also be called power to punish. Members follow leaders with coercive power because they want to avoid reprimand or punishment. Followers allow themselves to be controlled in order to avoid the punishments or sanction that could be associated with the failure to comply. Such punishments could include criticism, social ostracism, poor performance appraisals, reprimands, undesirable work assignments, or dismissal.

Coercive power ends when the power holder is no longer able to inflict punishment. Unless it is necessary, it is a good idea to avoid the use of this type of power because it is uncomfortable for most people and it can have a negative effect on the motivation and creativity of group members.

Reward Power

Reward power is just the opposite of coercive power. Where coercive power threatens to punish (or remove access to some desired resource) for noncompliance, reward power offers access to some desired resource as payment for compliance. The primary motivation of the follower is to comply with the leader to get the reward. Your teacher could reward you with bonus points for coming to class on a very cold day, or your boss could give you a bonus for completing a project on time or under the budget. Other rewards at your workplace could include pay increases, recognition, interesting job assignments, or promotions.

Like coercive power, this individual's power ends when he or she is no longer able to provide rewards. Individuals with only reward and not coercive power promise fewer rewards than someone who has both coercive and reward power. Likewise, those who possessed coercive power without reward power were more likely to invoke coercive power more frequently.

These first three power bases can be considered as what Porter and his colleagues termed *position power,* which includes power that is granted as a result of a person's position in an organization rather than by the unique characteristics of the individual. Position-based power is an impersonal source of power. It is also granted to those who have supervisory positions.

The last two bases of power identified by French and Raven and one identified by Hocker and Wilmot are forms of personal power. Unlike position power, these are granted based on individual knowledge, skills, or personality. These power bases often transfer from role to role and are used by either supervisors or subordinates.

Expert Power

A person with **expert power** is able to assist the group in reaching its goals because of his or her expertise on a given topic. Group members comply because they don't have the knowledge to complete the task without help. Followers perceive that the expert has the knowledge to achieve the group's goals. This person can easily lose power if his or her knowledge base is needed for just one subject and if the knowledge is no longer needed or desired.

Referent Power

Referent power is based on the personal liking or respect that one person has for another. The person with referent power is influential because others respect or admire the way he or she does a job or if the power holder possesses personal qualities that others would like to emulate. When people admire you and want to be liked or admired by you, they are often willing to be influenced. You could say that people who have referent power have charisma. As long as followers feel connected with this leader, he or she will exert referent power. If, for some reason, followers' perceptions are altered, then this leader's power is diminished.

A person with referent power is influential because others respect or admire the way he/she works.

Interpersonal Linkages

In addition to the five bases of power identified by French and Raven, Hocker and Wilmot identified a power base that comes from the power holder's access to people who control desired resources. The **interpersonal linkage** is power based on who you know and what resources those people control. If your group needs information from a government agency, for example, and you happen to know somebody at that government agency who can get the information for you, then that can be a source of influence. You don't have access to the information, but you know somebody who does!

Power bases give us insight into the reasons that some leaders are effective. Power can be based on one's position in a company, as we see with legitimate, coercive, and reward power. Power such as expert, personal linkage, and referent can be based on one's individual qualities. Any group member can have this kind of power, and it is dependent on the context and task facing the group. When you possess this kind of power, it is essential that you are ethical with its use. You should be aware of the unethical use of power and question it when it comes in direct conflict with your moral and ethical standards.

Does My Group have to have Conflict?

Just as you can count on the sun coming up in the morning, you can count on the presence of conflict in small groups. Whenever you get two or more people together who are trying to do something, there will be conflict! Even though many of us are quite similar, we still have individual differences that make us unique. We see the world around us in our own unique ways. When we come together as a small group, those individual differences are going to clash to create misunderstandings and disagreements. Conflict!

How is group conflict a good thing?

Conflict involves disagreement over task and procedural issues, over personality and affective issues, and over competitive tensions among group members. It can arise from differences of opinion, incompatible personalities, and even from geographical and cultural differences.

Conflict is inevitable in small groups. It is not something that you can avoid. But don't walk away from this discussion with the idea that conflict is always a bad thing. Conflict is a central and essential element for groups trying to solve complex problems. One of the primary reasons that groups make better decisions than individuals working alone is the multiple perspectives that group members bring to the table. It is when these perspectives conflict that new ideas, points of view, and solutions are created. This is group synergy in action!

Conflict related to the problem challenging a small group is central to the group's success, but it has a darker side. Conflicts based on personality clashes or competitive group members can be a distraction to groups, prevent the group from thoroughly completing the decision-making plan, and even threaten the existence of the group. However, personality-related conflicts can serve a maintenance function. Members of even friendly and cohesive groups get upset with each other now and then. Conflict provides those members with an outlet for hostile feelings, and it can facilitate a close examination of relationships. The bottom line is that if conflict is properly managed, it can be productive on both the task and relationship levels.

As you might have guessed by now, we will be discussing two kinds of conflict: conflict *intrinsic* to the task and conflict *extrinsic* to the task.

Intrinsic Conflict

Intrinsic conflict usually centers on disagreements related to the task facing the group. Intrinsic conflict can take two forms. It can be *substantive conflict,* which involves issues directly related to the content of the decision being made. It is unrelated to personal tensions that might exist between group members. Substantive conflict helps groups achieve their goals. Intrinsic conflict can also be *procedural,* which involves group policies and methods of solving problems. Members could disagree, for example, on what is the best way for reaching agreement. Some members might favor voting, for example, while other members believe that all decisions made by the group should have the complete agreement of all members. To prevent procedural issues from taking too much time, some groups adopt explicit policies that specify member responsibilities and decision making processes. Some groups even adopt standard policies such as *Robert's Rules of Order*.

Young, et al. provide us with a comparison of three standard procedures for reaching decisions: voting, compromise, and consensus. If your group gets stuck deciding how to decide, consider adopting of these procedures as your standard policy. Before you choose one, however, carefully look at the strengths and weaknesses of each procedure. We have ranked them good, better, and best, but all decision making experts might not agree with our assessment.

If your group gets stuck on substantive or procedural differences, then you should consider adopting a policy that will help you resolve or manage them. If intrinsic conflict is not managed well, it distracts from the group working on the task. In addition, it could get out of control and lead to extrinsic conflict. The decision-making plan (DMP) is a comprehensive procedure designed to help you understand and solve complex decisions. The three strategies just described will be very useful as your group navigates its way through the DMP procedure.

Standard Procedures for Reaching Decisions

- *Good: Voting.* Voting is quick and it solves the problem efficiently, but it creates a majority and a minority. The majority gets everything it wants, so its members are satisfied and committed to carrying out the decision. The minority gets nothing that it wants, so the commitment level of its members is often low, which results in a lack of motivation to follow through with implementation.
- *Better: Compromise.* In this situation, the members made trade-offs to make the decision. All of the members get some of what they want, and all of the members have to give up something to gain the agreement of the group. The resulting level of commitment is only moderate from all members, so follow through on decision implementation could be weakened. Compromise is not as quickly accomplished as voting.
- *Best: Consensus.* Consensus implies unanimous agreement of all members. Because all the members are satisfied and take ownership of the outcome, commitment to the decision is high and all are motivated to follow through on implementation. Consensus could take a very long time with complex issues. You should also beware that a consensus decision, because it has to please all the members to gain agreement, might not always be the most creative or best decision.

Extrinsic Conflict

When most people think of conflict, they are probably thinking of **extrinsic conflict.** This kind of conflict is related to the personalities and relationships between members. It can arise when you *just don't like* another group member, or when some basic incompatibility exists between members that cause tension.

There are multiple causes of extrinsic conflict:

- Recall that group communication implies interdependence among the people. When the communication becomes less interdependent and more competitive, the potential for conflict is high. Group members who are committed to the group's goals (creative solution to the problem facing the group) are at odds with members who are more committed to their own individual goals (promotion, money, job recognition).
- The use of power such as threats and punishments and the poor application of legitimate power by leaders or other members can lead to extrinsic conflict.
- Extrinsic conflict can arise when individuals do not understand the reasons for the behaviors of others. If the reasons are not understood, then the behaviors can easily be misinterpreted and lead to resentment. For example, geographic diversity and cultural differences are often a source of conflict. These will be described in the next section.
- Extrinsic conflict often arises from the ways the members communicate with each other. Sometimes it is not *what* you say but *how* you say it that creates the problem. If communication makes another member defensive, then extrinsic conflict becomes more likely. The final section of this chapter looks at communication that can create defensive climates and strategies that can help you avoid conflict.
- Extrinsic conflict can arise because you just don't like another group member. Maybe he or she reminds you of the kid who broke your pencil in kindergarten or the bully who beat you up. If it's all inside your head, then here's some friendly advice: *It's time to be an adult and let go of it!* If, however, the other person feels the same way about you, you should handle the problem in private. If you and the other member can't resolve these differences, try to agree on a strategy for at least managing your relationship while you are working with the group. If you can both commit to the goals of the group, petty differences can be put aside and maybe you can share a friendly, professional relationship.

As stated before, extrinsic conflict can serve a useful maintenance function. However, unmanaged extrinsic conflict often causes harm to a group. If unmanaged, even minor extrinsic conflicts can turn into major problems. Conflicts that go unresolved or unmanaged generally do not go away. They can "explode," and the group cannot go about the business of making decisions because it is caught up in destructive conflict.

Whatever the kind of conflict that arises in your group, the key to making it work for you is **conflict management.** Some strategies you can use for managing extrinsic conflict include the following.

1. *Do everything you can to encourage cooperation among group members.* Look for opportunities to agree whenever possible. Small agreements can eventually lead to larger agreements and cooperation.
2. *Try to encourage participation of all members.* Approach reticent or shy members in a nonthreatening way and ask for their opinions. Listen to their answers. When they realize that other members listen to them, participation will increase.

Example: Countering Extrinsic Conflict

A group member complains, "Steve is always late for our meetings. He says we meet too far from his house. That really burns me up. Let's throw him out of the group!"

Problem: Extrinsic conflict leads to low member satisfaction, a lack of agreement, the loss of the cooperative climate, low productivity, and even the disintegration of the group. What do you do when you see escalating extrinsic conflict?

Strategy: Individual group members can successfully counteract extrinsic conflict by turning disruptive acts (that would normally escalate the conflict) into constructive contributions. This helps defuse the situation and refocus the attention of each member to the task at hand. You could turn that expression of anger into a constructive suggestion by saying, "Let's meet at Steve's house. That way, he can't be late! Besides, we can watch the game on his HDTV and his refrigerator is always full of food!"

3. *Be honest about your intentions.* Don't play games or try to manipulate other members.
4. *Maintain a supportive climate.* Look at the final section of this chapter and be able to recognize the difference between defensive and supportive climates. If the climate in your groups becomes defensive, use some of the strategies suggested to move toward a more supportive, cooperative atmosphere.
5. *Keep the group goals as a priority.* They should take precedence over the individual goals of members.

How can Cultral differences Lead to Extrinsic Conflict?

Cultural influences have a profound effect on decision quality and the overall decision-making process. Chances are, you have already worked in a group made up of people from a variety of cultural and ethnic backgrounds. If not, get ready! The world is becoming increasingly *flat*. This means that collaboration and competition for jobs is open to people from all over the world, not just those who live near you or even in your country! Instantaneous communication technology in the "digital age" is shaping the way we manage our lives and do business, and that business is increasingly conducted with others around the globe. Because diverse groups are more likely to experience extrinsic conflict than homogeneous groups, we will briefly examine some of the cultural dimensions that affect groups.

How has the "digital age" changed the way we do business?

If you are aware of the cultural influences on others, and if you are aware of your own cultural influences and biases, you will be better able to adapt to new situations when they present themselves. Instead of moving directly to an extrinsic conflict situation, you should be willing to understand (and possibly explain to others in the group) that the source of your differences is culture related and perhaps not a fundamental interpersonal disagreement.

Geert Hofstede used the term *cultural dimensions* to refer to the common elements or the key issues of a culture that can be studied and analyzed in meaningful ways. Hofstede's value orientations are used to test and understand culture's influence in today's digital world. Some of these dimensions can be directly applied to the small-group context.

Individualism/Collectivism

In **individualistic cultures**, people are taught personal autonomy, privacy, self-realization, individual initiative, independence, individual decision making, and an understanding of personal identity as the sum of an individual's personal and unique attributes. People from individualistic cultures are taught that their needs and interests are just as important, if not more important, than the needs and interests of others. Some examples of individualistic societies are Australia, Great Britain, Canada, and the United States.

Group members from individualistic cultures are most comfortable working on projects alone and have a tendency to do all the work or none at all. This is not because they are uncooperative or difficult. Rather, it is because they are not socialized to collaborate like those from collectivistic cultures. For individualists, the group experience can be exceedingly frustrating. When an individualist approaches group projects and collaboration with a collectivistic mindset, he or she may find that to put group goals before personal goals is not necessarily a losing position.

Collectivism characterizes a culture in which people, from birth, are integrated into strong, cohesive in-groups. Collectivistic cultures emphasize emotional dependence on groups and organizations, less personal privacy, and the belief that group decisions are superior to individual decisions. They believe in interdependence, an understanding of personal identity as knowing one's place within the group, and concern about the needs and interests of others.

Group members from individualistic cultures are most comfortable working on projects alone.

Collectivistic cultures include China, Hong Kong, India, Japan, Pakistan, and Taiwan. Group members from collectivistic cultures experience less frustration when working with group members who also have collectivistic tendencies. This is largely due to the practice they have had collaborating with their own families, friends, and colleagues. Their frustration with groups is more likely experienced when they are collaborating with people who approach group work as individualists.

High Power Distance/Low Power Distance

Power distance is the extent to which the less powerful members of organizations and institutions accept and expect that power is distributed unequally. Individuals from low power-distance cultures believe that inequality in society should be minimized, that all individuals should have equal rights, that power should be used legitimately, and that powerful people should try to look less powerful than they are. Individuals from high power-distance cultures stress coercive and referent power and believe that power holders are entitled to privileges, and that powerful people should try to look as powerful as possible.

Participating effectively in small groups may be more challenging for group members from high power-distance cultures. Likewise, decision-making processes and approaches to conflict resolution are likely to be influenced by the group's power distance level. For instance, conflict management in teams with a low power-distance factor is based on principles of negotiation and cooperation, while in high power-distance teams, conflict is resolved primarily by the power holder. On the one hand, those who come from low power-distance cultures think that group decisions should be made by consensus, should have shared leadership, and that role responsibilities should be based on expertise. On the other hand, people from high power-distance cultures use voting, expect leaders to lead, and are uncomfortable in teams where they are asked to take on more autonomy and responsibility.

Uncertainty Avoidance

Uncertainty avoidance refers to the extent to which risk and ambiguity are acceptable conditions. Hofstede suggests that it is the extent to which the members of a culture feel threatened by uncertain or unknown situations. This is one of the cultural dimensions most problematic for groups. Group members from high uncertainty avoidance cultures interact based on a need for rules, suppression of deviant ideas and behavior, and resistance to innovation. They are motivated by security, esteem, and belongingness. Some countries with high uncertainty-avoidance cultures are Greece, Portugal, Guatemala, Uruguay, and Japan. Low uncertainty-avoidance cultures include the United States, Sweden, Jamaica, Singapore, and Hong Kong.

Group members from low uncertainty-avoidance cultures are more tolerant of different opinions, prefer as few rules as possible, are more calm and contemplative, and they are not expected to express emotions. They are better able to function within a group that is less structured. Such groups are characterized by loose deadlines, undefined roles, few rules, and a high tolerance for innovation and "outside-of-the-box" thinking. Understanding the uncertainty avoidance tendencies of members can help groups structure a productive decision-making environment. Such an environment would provide a balance of structure for those high in uncertainty avoidance. They would still maintain a spirit of innovation and encourage unique approaches to decision making for those who are low in uncertainty avoidance.

High Context/Low Context

Hall divided cultures into high and low context according to their ways of communicating. A **high-context culture** uses communication in which most of the information is either in the physical context or internalized in the person. To understand high-context communication, one should consider the content of the messages and the context together. Context is the situation, background, or environment connected to an event, a location, or an individual. Very little is explicitly stated. High-context communication is typically indirect, ambiguous, harmonious, reserved, and understated. A **low-context culture** is just the opposite. The majority of information is stated explicitly. Low-context communication is direct, precise, dramatic, open, and based on feelings or true intentions.

High Context Cultures

↑

Japan
Arab Countries
Greece
Spain
Italy
England
France
North America
Scandinavian Countries
German-speaking Countries

↓

Low Context Cultures

Source: Hall & Hall (1990) Understanding Cultural Differences

When interacting with people who are from a high-context culture, using communication that is too direct can result in embarrassment or even anger. Likewise, when interacting with someone from a low-context culture, using communication that is indirect or implied can result in confusion and frustration because it is perceived that the communicator does not say what he or she means. For instance, if a North American supervisor is unsatisfied with a subordinate's sales proposal, the response will probably be explicit and direct: "I can't accept this proposal as submitted, so come up with some better ideas." A Korean supervisor, in the same situation, might say, "While I have the highest regard for your abilities, I regret to inform you that I am not completely satisfied with this proposal. I must ask that you reflect further and submit additional ideas on how to develop this sales program." The message is essentially the same, but as you can see, the approach is different.

In addition to personal and ideational differences that normally exist between people, multicultural groups have a high potential for intrinsic conflict based on their different points of view. The potential for extrinsic conflict is even higher, considering the number of potential misunderstandings and interpersonal transgressions resulting from the clash of cultural expectations. An awareness of different cultural expectations will help keep nonproductive conflict to a minimum and promote the level of communication, understanding, and cooperation necessary for making creative decisions.

How is Communication a Source of Extrinsic Conflict?

A frequent source of extrinsic conflict is communication itself. Sometimes it's not what people say that creates the problem but the way they say it.

Defensive versus Supportive Behaviors

Defensive and supportive climates can be created and maintained with communication behaviors

Defensive Behaviors

1. Control strategies
2. Superiority
3. Evaluation
4. Neutrality
5. Strategy
6. Certainty

Supportive Behaviors

1. Problem orientation
2. Equality
3. Description
4. Empathy
5. Spontaneity
6. Provisionalism

Control/Problem Orientation

Most of us need to feel we have some control over our lives. So we respond to control with *psychological reactance*. In response to feeling controlled, we do the opposite of what we are told to do. Communication typical of **control strategies** includes statements such as, "You need to be more considerate," "You must stop procrastinating," and "You have to listen to me." Statements like these create psychological reactance and lead to defensiveness, which leads to extrinsic conflict. Gibb says that hidden in attempts to control is the assumption by the controlling person that the other is somehow inadequate. Wouldn't that make you feel defensive?

Using a **problem orientation** allows others an equal contribution to the discussion and decision making. It sends the relational message that the other's position, opinions, and concerns are important. When you take a problem orientation approach to interacting with others, they are likely to be more committed to the resolution of

Take a Closer Look

Sometimes when your group has a competitive environment or spirit, it means that there is a lack of compatibility between group goals and the goals of individual members. What should you do?

Try this: Create a cooperative climate!

Instead of allowing the competitive attitudes of group members to become more intense and inhibit cooperation in the group, try to find something on which all members can agree. Even if the members don't go along with you, discovering these opportunities to agree should push the group climate toward the more cooperative end of the continuum. Agreement tends to be reinforcing in that, before too long, others in the group will begin to "pay back" your agreement with their cooperation. Over time, the environment of your group should become more cooperative.

the problem. Just as individuals may respond with psychological reactance when feeling controlled, individuals who feel they have a voice in decision making are more likely to commit to the decision's implementation. Statements that illustrate a problem orientation include, "We are in this together," "What can we do to solve this problem?" and "What do you think?"

Superiority/Equality

Communicating **superiority** creates defensiveness by demonstrating that we perceive ourselves to be better than others, and that quickly leads to extrinsic conflict. Superiority is characterized by comments such as, "You do not know what you are doing," and, "I have had more experience with this type of situation; I will handle it." This sends the relational message that the other's opinion is not worthy, his expertise is not valued, or that he is not important.

Equality, by contrast, involves treating others with respect and valuing their thoughts and opinions, regardless of their knowledge about the topic, their status, age, or position. People who *appear* to be of lower status or position are capable of having profound insights. Communication illustrating equality would be, "What do you think?" and, "I never thought of it that way; let's explore this idea together further."

Evaluation/Description

If a communicator appears to be evaluating you, either through tone of voice, expression, or message content, you will likely go into a protection mode. This kind of communication is often perceived as an attack on a person's self-esteem. The person feeling attacked then focuses energy on defense, which draws his or her focus from the problem to be solved. When communicating with others, you should first *describe* before forming evaluations. This is not to say that you cannot evaluate behavior, but before jumping to conclusions, you should demonstrate that you are attempting to understand. Through description, you may create a more supportive climate. To be descriptive is to be factual without offering an opinion.

If you look at the descriptions provided in the box, can you say with certainty that the behaviors indicate rudeness, pushiness, or unfairness? Based on the behaviors described, there *may* be other possible interpretations. Could Kate have not realized she bumped into someone? Or did she softly say she was sorry but was not heard? Could Tom have had an urgent message? Could Stacey have valid reasons for her decision that were, indeed, fair? The answers to these questions are, *maybe*. We cannot be entirely sure without more information. The point is we need to be descriptive if we want to avoid extrinsic conflict by creating a defensive climate.

Neutrality/Empathy

One of the best ways to devalue someone is to respond in a way that communicates a lack of caring. **Neutrality** communicates that you simply do not care about the person or what he or she is saying. Using the supportive strategy of **empathy** means approaching a discussion with the intent to understand the other person's position from his or her point of view. This is not to be confused with sympathy, or responding with how we would feel in a particular situation. To be empathic is

Take a Closer Look

Kate is rude.	Tom is pushy.	Stacey is unfair.

Each of these statements is an evaluation. Now, if we were to take the time to describe the behavior that made us conclude that Kate is rude, Tom is pushy, and Stacey is unfair, we might come up with the following descriptive statements:

- Kate bumped into me without acknowledging it. She didn't say she was sorry or excuse herself.
- Tom kept phoning me after I told him I was too busy to talk.
- Stacey didn't give me the opportunity to work on the marketing project.

to express genuine interest in hearing what others have to say; it is one of the most confirming communication forms. Some examples of empathic responses are, "Kate, you must feel very upset by your layoff," and, "Stacey, I can only imagine how you must feel right now." To respond with neutrality, you might use responses like, "It doesn't matter to me," and, "Whatever you want."

If you want to create and maintain a supportive climate in your group, practice responding in ways that demonstrate that you care and understand.

Strategy Versus Spontaneity

To use **strategy** is to communicate that you have a hidden agenda. There is something motivating your communication that is not initially revealed to others. You try to manipulate others in the effort to gain some advantage. Have you ever had someone ask you, "What are your plans Friday night?" And you respond with, "I am free. Do you want to do something?" only to hear, "Oh good, can you babysit?" Somehow, this approach asking us to babysit feels like a trick. Another stereotypical example is the feeling when you walk into a sales presentation. You suspect that everything from the first handshake to the free dinner is carefully scripted to get you to buy something. Your defenses are activated and you begin to interpret everything that is said to you as part of a sneaky plot to buy that time-share in an exotic resort area. Strategic communication is revealed when you feel that people are flattering you for their own personal gain, or using self-disclosure to get you to reciprocate.

Spontaneity is characterized by honesty, directness, and good faith. It is saying: "I really need a babysitter Friday night; if you are free I would greatly appreciate your help." In a spontaneity condition, you probably won't be as suspicious of others and you will take things they say at face value. If they attempt to shake your hand, you can be sure it's an invitation to friendship and nothing else. When you get into the defensive mode, it is easy to misinterpret and start looking for hidden meanings in things that people say.

Certainty Versus Provisionalism

People who communicate **certainty** seem to know all the answers. There is nothing they don't know, and they are quite sure about it. We tend to see this dogmatic individual as needing to be right and "wanting to win an argument rather than solve a problem." This behavior communicates to others a lack of interest in their position on an issue. The defensiveness that is created by certainty can be countered by provisionalism. **Provisionalism** means trying to explore issues, look for solutions, and consider the points of view of other group members.

Research tells us that supportive climates not only produce happier and more satisfied group members, but that groups with predominately supportive climates are more productive. When the climate becomes defensive, group members become distracted by the suspicion that they are being manipulated or attacked, the potential for destructive extrinsic conflict is high, messages are consistently misinterpreted, and the group loses sight of the problem to be solved. All the assumptions that we make about groups making better decisions are based on the broad assumption that the members are fully engaged in the solution of the problem. When the attention of the group is distracted from that problem-solving goal, defective decisions will be the result.

Summary

There was a lot of territory covered in this chapter, so we'll try to boil down the answer to the question, "What should I take from this chapter?" First, you should understand that every group member has the potential for leadership. You don't have to be *the* leader to exhibit leadership; you just have to use influence to help the group somehow mover closer to its goals. You should also understand that every group is unique, and that there is no single leadership style or approach that is going to be successful in every group. You will have to understand the functions of leadership, and then you will have to adapt what you know to each particular situation. There are many suggestions in this chapter to help you accomplish this. Look at the leadership styles approach, the situational leadership approach, and the information on transformational leadership to get some insight about how to adapt to your group.

You should also try to understand the bases of interpersonal power and how they can be used as a tool of leadership. Remember that those power bases can be easily abused, especially legitimate and coercive power, and that abuse can prevent your group from accomplishing its goals.

Finally, you should take with you an appreciation for conflict. If you are a member of a small decision making group, conflict can be your best friend and your worst enemy. Conflict related to the task, intrinsic conflict, unleashes the real power of small groups by allowing the clash of divergent points of view. This clash leads to a synthesis of ideas which the group members could not have created if they were working alone. This clash exploits the synergy of the group and makes the solution of complex problems possible.

However, conflict can also be your worst enemy. Extrinsic conflict, related to personalities, can distract your group from its task and even destroy the group itself. Although there are a lot of sources of extrinsic conflict, this chapter explored two common causes: differences in culture (very important in the age of the global economy), and the defensive climates that are created when interpersonal sensitivity is overlooked in conversations. Being aware of the roots of conflict and understanding management strategies can help your group stay together, make complex decisions, and provide all the members with a satisfying experience!

Name____ Date______________

Exercise 12.1 Chapter 12 – What are the Roles of Leadership and Power in Group Dynamics?

Answer the survey below to determine your strengths and weaknesses as a transformational leader. Would you make an excellent, fair, or poor candidate for the Student Ambassador Program?

5 Strongly Agree.....4 Agree....3 Somewhat Agree .....2 Disagree.....1 Strongly Disagree

______________ I handle difficult people well in difficult situations.

______________ I listen to conflicting opinions without criticism.

______________ When I critique others, I focus on their actions and not their personality.

______________ I encourage others to give input when working in a group.

______________ I contribute valuable information when working in a group.

______________ I encourage suggestions that are divergent from groupthink.

______________ I am adaptable in stressful situations.

______________ I do not participate in sidebar conversations.

______________ I am punctual and encourage others to be.

______________ I use humor when dealing with stressful tasks.

Total: _________

Now, that you have completed the survey and computed your score, let's talk about your ability to be a transformational leader?

13

Small Group Presentations

After reading this chapter, you should be able to:

- ❐ Discuss the aspects of participating in a small group
- ❐ Describe the characteristics of small groups
- ❐ Explain the role responsibilities of small group members
- ❐ Identify ways to create effective small group experiences
- ❐ Explain the application of the reflective thinking process in small group problem solving
- ❐ Describe the small group presentation formats

Key Terms

Brainstorming
Forum
Group-oriented goals
Panel discussion
Primary audience
Process
Reflective thinking process
Secondary audience
Self-oriented goals
Small group
Symposium

13 Scenario

Nathalie's head went back and forth like she was watching Serena and Venus Williams in a tennis match. She was sitting in her dorm's study room with her group from her psychology class. The class had been interesting, but challenging. Her teacher opened up a new door for Nathalie, opened up her interest in psychological disorders.

However, this group project was proving to be the worst part of the course. At first glance, Nathalie thought she had really lucked up with the group in which she was placed. She was placed with some of the brightest in the class. They all participated in class discussions and performed very well on tests and quizzes. But after one group meeting, Nathalie realized that this group may not have been the best. Everyone in the group wanted to do things in his or her own way, but didn't want to take on any responsibility. Nothing was ever accomplished and there was always an argument.

"Brandon we can't show this to Dr. Millian," Mya said as she threw Brandon's poster board across the room.

"Hey watch it!" Brandon spat as he walked over to the corner where his poster landed. "I paid good money for that poster board. Oh and by the way you, all owe me five dollars."

"Five dollars!" Everyone exclaimed.

Brandon simply nodded, "Yes, five dollars."

"You must have lost your mind." Kevin waved him off.

"Oh trust me, he has!" Mya said.

"I actually have an idea about our visual presentation..." Ryan murmured as he adjusted his glasses. His voice was drowned out by their loud ones.

Nathalie closed her eyes as their voices grew louder and louder. Finally, in one swift motion, she stood to her feet and bellowed, "Everyone quiet!" Everything came to a startling halt as her voice bounced off the walls. "This is getting ridiculous. We all want to continue to do well in this class. We have to organize and use our strengths. Mya and Brandon you both are five-year MBA majors, correct?"

Mya and Brandon nodded as Nathalie continued. "You two should come up with our presentation outline. Come up with a script of what we should say during our presentation. Kevin and I are English majors; we'll collaborate on the paper. Since Carl is a graphic design major, he can come up with the visual aspects of our presentation. Is that fine with everyone?"

Everyone nodded. Nathalie looked over at Kevin and winked. Kevin smiled as he packed up his bags.

Small Groups in Life

Small groups are a part of life. If you are on the editorial board of your school newspaper or are an organizer of the community blood drive, you are a member of a small group. If you are a member of a church, a musical, athletic, or academic group, you are a member of a small group. Think about how many groups you have participated in, and realize your membership in small groups may increase after you leave college. In business, academic life, government, and civic affairs, tasks are defined and completed through small-group communication. Many of the major decisions affecting your life are made by small groups. College admissions departments, school boards, and zoning boards are a few groups whose policies directly influence behavior.

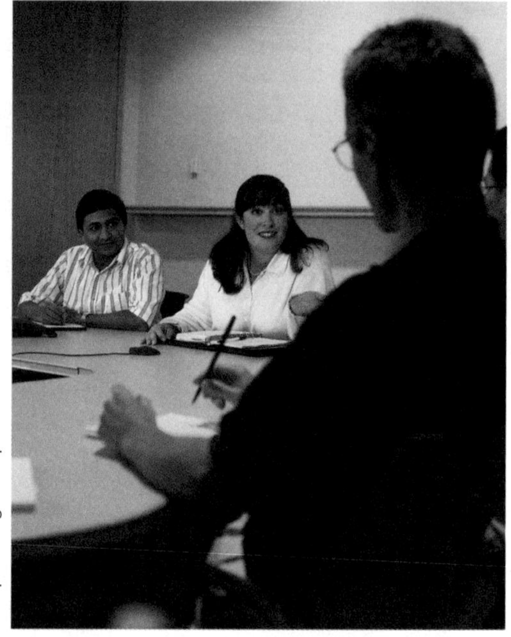

Small groups are a part of life and you may have opportunities to speak before your city council, school board, or other community groups.

As a homeowner, you may have an opportunity to present before a governing board. Perhaps you are a budding environmentalist who has noticed that the city has been pruning trees excessively or is making plans to eliminate landmark trees in order to widen streets. You take an opportunity to encourage the city council to approach city growth in a more "green" fashion. As a parent, you speak before the school board to convince them to eliminate vending machine drinks that contain sugar and/or caffeine. You argue that these are not healthy choices for young school children. In these situations, you have asked to speak before some group. As a professional, however, you receive requests to speak before a group because of your expertise. A state senator might talk to the local League of Women Voters about proposed state legislation. An insurance agent presents a bid before the city council or school board. As the chair of a university-funded organization, you present a budget request before the school's Apportionment Board, the group that allocates funds to college organizations.

Participating in a Small Group

The most common way to be involved in groups is to participate in a small group. Groups meet for a variety of purposes. Sometimes the purpose of a small group meeting is to discuss a current problem. For example, if your organization is low on funds. You must find a way to raise money. A group of individuals wanting to become a recognized group on campus, needs to think of a strategy for presenting your case to the appropriate governing body. Everyone contributes to the discussion, and usually a designated leader facilitates the discussion. In college, study groups, sororities and fraternities, residence halls, honorary societies, academic groups, athletic groups, and church groups are just some of the possible ways you connect with others through small group communication.

Chances are you've been involved in various small groups, such as a study group, during college.

Speaking as an Individual Before a Group

A second way to be involved with a small group is by speaking before one. This is considered public speaking and is the focus of this text book. Unlike regular public speaking, however, you may have two audiences, not one. The *primary audience* is the small group, such as a seven-member school board, a five-member city council, or a ten-member Apportionment Board. Your purpose is to provide information, to express a concern, or attempt to persuade. Also in attendance, however, may be a *secondary audience*. This is a collection of individuals who attend the open meeting for any number of reasons, including simply observing its proceedings. It's possible these individuals may have no knowledge or interest in your specific topic, and did not know you were planning to speak.

In a situation involving both primary and secondary audiences, do you construct a message for the primary audience, accepting the fact that the secondary audience may not understand the context, concern or content? Or do you construct a message that takes into account both audiences, knowing that for members of the primary audience, some of the information will be unnecessary or redundant? Complexity of the issue, size of the secondary audience, and time constraint are a few of the factors to consider before developing your message.

Speaking as a Member of a Group Before a Group

Alternatively, you may find yourself in a third speaking situation where you are a member of a small group presenting before another group. This may occur in your business class when you are part of a group presenting a case study, in a psychology class when your group presents results of its research project, or in a public relations class when you are asked, as a group, to present your public relations campaign. There are many instances in college when you work as a group to accomplish a task and report the results to your classmates. In your community, as a health care professional, you may be asked to join a panel with several other health care professionals to discuss the health care crisis before a group of senior citizens. The focus is not just on you, but on your group.

Many contexts are possible with the small group presentation, including being the only person who speaks before a small group or being one of many individuals who speak before a group. In some instances you will find yourself on a panel with individuals you have never met and in others you will participate in significant small group interaction before your group presents. Given our interest in helping you become the most effective speaker possible regardless of context, this chapter will focus on (1) working in small groups, and (2) presenting in small groups. In order to work in a small group, it is helpful to know the characteristics of small groups, including purpose, goals, and size. When presenting in small groups, each person should understand his or her role responsibilities, and the members should consider which group format is most appropriate for the purpose and audience. Included in this chapter are suggestions for working in a small group and small group performance guidelines.

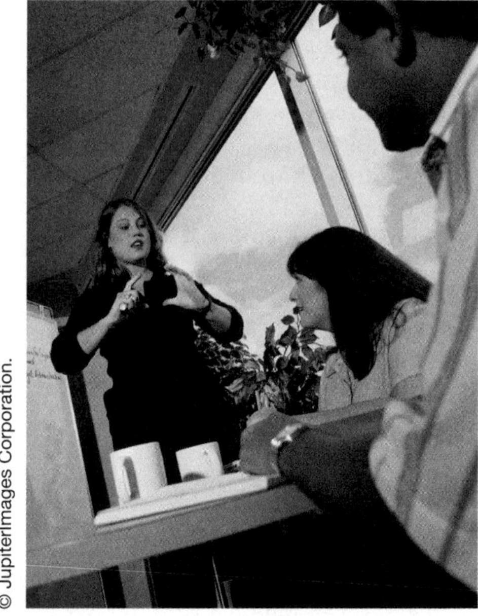

When presenting in small groups, members need to consider which format is most appropriate for the occasion.

Working in a Small Group

In a college classroom, whether or not you were able to choose your "groupmates," the members of your group, these are the individuals with whom you must interact and cooperate. Each person brings to the group his or her own predispositions, attitudes, work ethic, personality, knowledge, and ability. You may find your groupmates friendly, fascinating, frustrating, or infuriating. Likewise, they will have their own perceptions of you and of each other. Regardless, in all but the most dire circumstances, you will traverse the hills and valleys of group work with these people.

Characteristics of Small Groups

We should acknowledge that many academic institutions have semester-long courses devoted to the topic of small group communication, and we could discuss small group characteristics indefinitely. However, for our purposes, three characteristics seem to be most relevant to the public speaking classroom.

Shared purpose. One characteristic of a small group is that group members share a purpose for communication, unlike a collection of individuals who share the same physical space. Seven people waiting in line for tickets to see the Los Angeles Lakers are not considered members of a small group.

Neither are five people sharing a taxi from the Dallas-Fort Worth airport or eight people sitting in a dentist's waiting room. They lack a communication purpose. But if the individuals waiting in line for tickets interact with each other to form a cooperative so that only one of the seven individuals will wait in line for tickets at subsequent games, they would then have a shared purpose that would guide communication in all future meetings.

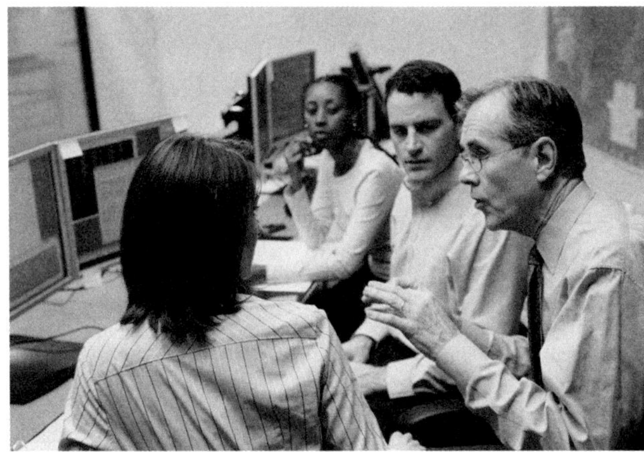
© Corbis.

A group with an even number needs to determine what to do in the event of a tie vote on an issue.

Group-oriented and self-oriented goals. A second characteristic of small groups is that members usually have both group-oriented and self-oriented goals. **Group-oriented goals** center around specific tasks to be performed, whereas **self-oriented goals** relate to the individual's personal needs and ambitions. Say you are a member of a small group charged with the responsibility of determining policies of a new campus radio station. Some of the tasks you face are developing station operating policies, purchasing equipment, and attracting advertisers. As an individual, however, a self-oriented goal may be to emerge as leader of the group in order to demonstrate leadership potential. Self-oriented goals may complement group-oriented goals, or they may provide distracting roadblocks.

Size. A third characteristic of small groups is group size. Scholars agree that a group must have a minimum of three members to be considered a small group. Communication professor Vincent DiSalvo notes that the ideal group size is from five to seven members (DiSalvo 1973, 111–112). According to Philip E. Slater, "These groups are large enough for individuals to express their feelings freely and small enough for members to care about the feelings and needs of other group members" (Slater 1958). However, a three-person group may lose effectiveness if one member is left out or if one member withdraws or chooses not to contribute. Also, groups with even numbers need to have some mechanism in place for solving the problem of a potential tie. As groups grow in numbers, the need for coordination and structure increases.

Role Responsibilities

When you become a group member, how you communicate is shaped, in large part, by your role in the group. If you have been appointed leader or have a special expertise that sets you apart from the other members, you may be given more responsibility than the other members.

Roles quickly emerge in small groups. While one group member emerges as the leader, taking the initiative in setting the group's agenda, another is uncommunicative and plays a minor role in group discussions. Still other members of the group may try to dominate the discussion, oppose almost every point raised, and close their minds before the discussion begins (Bales 1953, 111–61).

The role you assume determines how you will communicate in the group and how effective the group will be. Although there are many types of roles, we focus on two broad categories: your role as a group leader and your role as a group member.

Group roles evolve quickly and if you are the appointed leader, you will likely have more responsibility than other members.

Leader Responsibilities

You may be elected or appointed as leader of a group, or you may emerge as leader over time. As leader, you need to be aware of the group's *process and the relationships* among group members. Behaviors that relate to *process* are designed to help the group complete the task. These include *providing direction and purpose, keeping the group on track, and providing clarifying summaries.*

Provide direction and purpose. As part of your responsibility to provide direction and purpose, you may choose to open the meeting with action-directed comments ("We are here to establish whether or not it is feasible to add another organization to our college") or to examine items on an agenda. Once the discussion begins, others will contribute, but it is the leader's role to focus the meeting at the start.

Keeping the group on track. Keeping the group on track simply means making sure the group does not drift too far from the task at hand. If you are talking about offering healthy alternatives in the cafeteria line, it is easy to start talking about favorite foods or incidents that occurred in the cafeteria or people who work or who eat in the cafeteria. While *some* extraneous conversation help build relationships among group members, the leader is responsible for making sure time is not wasted and the group does not get side-tracked on irrelevant issues.

Provide a clarifying summary. Groups, like the individuals who comprise them, can be confused by the information they hear. Warning signs include questions for clarification, puzzled looks, and drifting attention. When you sense confusion, one of the best ways to move forward is to provide a clarifying summary, which recaps what has just occurred. For example, after hearing evidence and testimony at a student disciplinary hearing, the board voted that a student (Martin) was guilty of vandalism. After some time, the group was getting nowhere in terms of determining a punishment. As a leader, you say,

> We've agreed that Martin is guilty of vandalism, and that his actions are worthy of punishment, but we seem to be stuck on the concept of expulsion. We agree that suspension is too lenient, and expulsion is more warranted. The confusion seems to rest on how we are interpreting `expulsion,' with some thinking the student may never return to our school and others thinking the student may return after a specified period of time, provided certain conditions are met.

With this type of clarifying summary, you have eliminated suspension from further discussion and identified the source of confusion. Clarifying summaries help bring focus back to the meeting.

In addition to facilitating the group's *process*, an effective group leader is concerned with *relationship* aspects, which facilitate communication. An effective leader will draw information from participants, keep group communication from being one-sided, and try to maintain the cohesiveness of the group. Ultimately, the relationship aspects allow the group to accomplish its task.

Draw information from participants. Each person has something to contribute to the group, whether it is in the form of offering specific information, analyzing the issue, or being creative. However, some people are hesitant to speak even when they have something valuable to contribute. Their reasons may range from communication anxiety to uncertainty about their role in the group. As a leader, draw information from participants by directing questions to those who remain silent, asking each group member to speak, and being supportive when a normally quiet member makes a comment in the hope of encouraging additional responses at a later time. Getting everyone to contribute is particularly important when one or more members of the group seem to dominate the discussion. It is up to the group leader to make sure the group benefits from the combined wisdom of all its members.

Try to keep group communication from being one-sided. A leader should try to keep group communication from being one-sided. We often have preconceived ideas of how something should be done. While dissent is healthy, these ideas may be obstacles to group communication if the leader allows the discussion to become one-sided. The leader needs to recognize when one point of view is dominating the discussion. Inviting others into the discussion or providing a varying opinion yourself may open up the discussion for multiple perspectives.

How can a group leader encourage everyone to contribute to the discussion?

Try to maintain the cohesiveness of the group. As a leader, you should try to maintain the cohesiveness of the group. You want the group to see themselves as a group and function as a group, not as a collection of individuals. Everyone needs to work toward the group goal, while not ignoring his or her personal goals. Nothing is inherently wrong with a heated discussion, especially when the issue is controversial. But when the discussion turns into a shouting match, it is no longer productive. In a conflict situation, the leader should acknowledge the person's point of view but suggest that the problem be analyzed from other perspectives as well. Conflict is healthy, but unproductive conflict is a major obstacle to task completion. Keeping communication flowing effectively and making sure members feel their contributions are valued are important to the overall cohesiveness of the group.

Member Responsibilities

Being an active participant is the most important responsibility of each group member. An active participant contributes to the discussion, shares responsibility for task completion, and works effectively with other group members. Some group members believe that their participation is unnecessary because others will pick up their slack. Others view the experience as less important than other college work or activities. Complaining about group members is nothing new. Here are common complaints about other group members:

- Doesn't work or prepare enough
- Others have to nag group members to get work done
- Procrastinates
- Doesn't keep group members informed of content of presentation
- Information in presentation overlaps too much
- Information is excessive or too brief
- Too controlling
- Too apathetic
- Doesn't return calls or email
- Difficult to contact
- Doesn't stay after class to check with group
- Doesn't come to class on group work days
- Doesn't proofread PowerPoint

The previous is only a partial list of complaints we hear about group members. We understand that students take several academic courses. They have a social and/or work life, and priorities differ among students. But once you are part of a group, your actions have an impact on the other people in that group. In a classroom setting, you may not be thrilled with the topic, the assignment, or the other group members. But you do need to work with your group in order to complete the required assignment. Actively working to complete your individual tasks and being available and cooperative will make the situation better for all involved. Fulfill a commitment to the group.

Suggestions for Group Members

The following seven suggestions are designed to create the most effective small group experience within the context of your classroom. Many of these translate easily to experiences outside the college classroom. The suggestions are derived partially from *Speak from Success* by Eugene Ehrlich and Gene R. Hawes (1984, 133).

Know the constraints of the assignment. Read the syllabus or any other material given to you related to the assignment. Make sure everyone agrees as to the constraints of the assignment. The following are some questions that may guide your group:

- When does the group present?
- How much time does the group have to present?

- Does each speaker have the same amount of time?
- What information needs to be included in the presentation?
- Are presentational aids required?
- Does each speaker use a set of note cards? Is there a restriction?
- Is there audience involvement at some point during the group presentation?
- Can group members interrupt each other to comment or add insight?
- Is there a paper required? Or an outline?
- How many and what type of sources are required, and should they be cited during the presentation?
- Does the group choose its format, or is there a particular format that is required?
- Are students being graded individually, as a group, or both?
- Will there be any peer evaluations?

When you feel strongly about your position, you can try to convince others that you're correct. Ultimately, though, you need to put the group's goals above your own.

Work to achieve group goals. Instructors understand that each individual is concerned about his or her own grade. However, the purpose of a group assignment is to work collectively and collaboratively. Make group goals your top priority. Making a commitment to the group means making a commitment to achieve group goals at each meeting. When you feel strongly about your position, it is legitimate to try to convince the group you are correct. But if others disagree, it is important that you listen to their objections and try to find merit in them. You need an objective detachment from your own proposals to enable you to place the group's goals above your own. A group needs a shared image of the group, in which individual aspirations are subsumed under the group umbrella that strives for the common good.

Be responsible for completing your part of the assignment. Group membership brings with it a set of roles and responsibilities. It may not have been your choice to work in a group or to work with that specific group of individuals. The fact is, the assignment is mandatory. Everyone has a life. Everyone has distractions in their lives. You may be very busy, or you may be uninterested, but your group needs your help. If a group member volunteers to make the PowerPoint presentation consistent from speaker to speaker, you need to make sure that person has your slides when they are requested. If you are supposed to make contact with city officials or individuals who may help with a fundraising idea, you need to come to the group with that information. Do not be responsible for the group's progress being delayed, or the task not completed. If you cannot attend a meeting, make sure someone knows. Send your work with someone else. If you do get behind, make sure group members know so they have an opportunity to respond in some way.

Research sufficiently. Most group work involves research of some type. When you are finished researching, you should feel confident that you have ample support or that the topic or issue has been covered in enough depth. Depending on the group's purpose or goal, research may involve surfing the Internet, conducting a library search, looking through the local Yellow Pages, calling different social service agencies in town, or interviewing members of the local city council. If your group sought to determine what Americans consider the most important political issues for the 2008 presidential campaign, locating *one* website or *one* magazine article is not sufficient. If your group wanted to determine which pizza place in town served the best pizza, selecting two from the Yellow Pages is not sufficient, particularly in a city that has ten or more places that sell pizza. If you have been assigned to interview city council members, talking to one person for five minutes is not sufficient.

Most group work involves some research so you feel confident that the topic has been covered in enough depth.

Communicate effectively and efficiently. Different people bring to a group a wide range of knowledge and views that help complete the task. Group discussion often produces creative approaches that no one would have thought of alone. Group involvement through communication increases the likelihood that the group's decision will be accepted and supported by all group members and by the broader community. Do not waste time and do not monopolize the group discussions or the presentation.

Avoid personal attacks. Comments like, "You have to be an idiot to believe that will work," or "My six-year-old cousin has better ideas than that," accomplish nothing. On the contrary, these comments are so antagonistic that they make it virtually impossible for people to work together. If you do not like an idea, say so directly by focusing on the idea, not the person, such as "It may be difficult to get funds for that project," or "I don't think parents will want to volunteer their time for that." Try not to make your disagreement too negative. Find areas of agreement, where possible.

Leave personal problems at home. Group conflicts are often the result of personal problems brought to the group meeting. A fight with a family member, a poor test grade, an alarm clock that failed to ring, a near-accident on the highway, or school or work pressure can put you in a bad mood for the meeting and lessen your tolerance for other group members.

Antagonistic comments can be permanently damaging and make it impossible for the group to function.

Although an outburst of anger may make you feel better for the moment, it can destroy the relationships you have with other members of the group.

Reflective Thinking Process

You may be called upon in a college course or in an organization to work with others on a problem-solving task. On campus for example, the Student Senate needs to find ways to get more students involved in campus events, while off campus the local Chamber of Commerce is trying to find ways to entice new businesses to join their organization. Groups are faced with small and large problems on a regular basis. Almost 100 years ago, John Dewey developed a theory of reflective thinking that is now applied to group communication (1910). If you are working on a problem-solving task, consider following the following seven steps:

1. Identify and Define the Problem

The first step of this process is to make sure group members understand and agree on what the problem is. Otherwise, the discussion may scatter into many different directions and time will be misused, for example, a newly elected Student Senate member wants to work with a group to deal with student complaints about residence hall assignments. One problem is that students are not given enough options about where they may live or with whom. A second problem is that the administration does not process complaints effectively. Third, students are unhappy about meal plan options and residence hall rules and contracts. Does the group want to take on all of these problems, or to focus on the complaint process? The first thing the group needs to do is identify the problem.

2. Analyze the Problem

In the process of analyzing the problem, group members need to identify what they know about the problem, what they do not know, and what resources are available to help them acquire more information. In this step, group members should find out what caused the problem, how long the problem has been an issue, and the extent of the problem. If only one student has complained about her residence hall assignment, there is not much of a problem. But if significant staff time is devoted to addressing students' complaints, then the problem is significant. Perhaps the problem started when a new administrator took office. Perhaps the problem is ongoing. This is the information-gathering, sorting, and evaluation stage of the reflective thinking process.

3. Determine Criteria for an Acceptable Solution

Many groups skip this step, whether they are newly formed groups in a college classroom or well-established policy groups in a community. However, it is a mistake to come into the problem-solving process with a firm idea of what you think is the best solution. Whatever solution your group suggests must meet agreed-upon criteria or standards. Criteria will differ vastly from situation to situation. For example, if four students turned in a group paper that was clearly plagiarized, before determining the punishment, an instructor might consider the following criteria:

- Is (the punishment) it fair (to the four students and the rest of the class)?
- Is it appropriate (given the nature of the misconduct)?
- Will it deter future misconduct (on the part of the students who cheated as well as other students who might be contemplating misconduct)?

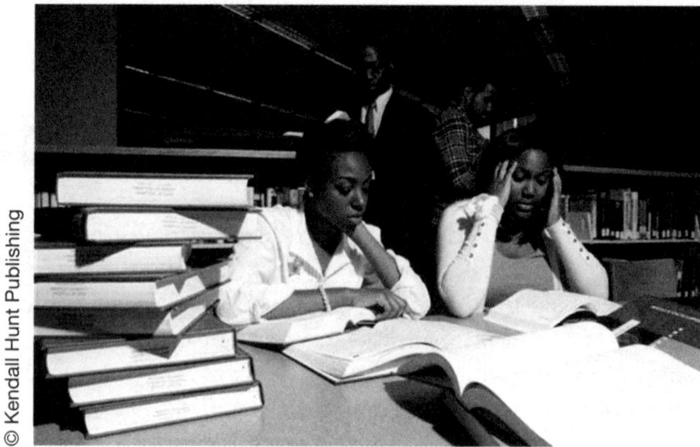

In order to present a solution, there needs to be sufficient information-gathering, sorting, and evaluation of the problem.

Criteria related to the residence hall complaints issue might include the following:

- Does the solution consider both the needs of students and college administrators?
- Does the solution apply to all students living in residence halls, not just incoming freshmen?
- Does the solution allow students to change residence halls?
- Does the solution recognize that freshmen do not have cars?

Establishing criteria keeps group members from simply proposing their solution. Any solution presented needs to meet the criteria established by group members.

4. Generate Possible Solutions

According to Dewey, suspended judgment is critical at this point in the decision-making process (Ross and Ross 1989, 77). Group members need to identify available options without stifling the process by providing immediate evaluation. **Brainstorming,** which involves generating as many solutions as possible without critical evaluation, may be useful during this step of the reflective thinking process. Be creative. Encourage group members to think "outside the box." Avoid the temptation to say, "that won't work," "that's not possible," or worse, "that's a dumb idea." Instead, generate ideas until you agree you have exhausted the possibilities. If possible, give yourselves time to think about these solutions before evaluating or moving on to the next step. For the teacher who caught the group of students plagiarizing, some of the punishment options include ignoring it, talking to the students, requiring them to give a group presentation on the evils of plagiarism, requiring them to write another paper, lowering their grade on the paper, failing them for the assignment, failing them for the semester, and reporting the students to the Office of Judicial Affairs.

Regarding the problem of residence hall complaints, the group may develop several options, including changing the forms students fill out, suggesting a policy change, providing clearer, more specific information to students, and establishing a committee to hear complaints not resolved between students and administration. The important thing is to *have* alternatives, and not be single-minded in your approach.

5. Choose the Solution That Best Fits the Criteria

Each solution identified in Step Four needs to be evaluated based on the criteria established in Step Three. Ideally, the best solution is one that meets all the established criteria. If that does not happen, the group may need to revisit the possible solutions, and determine if amending one of the solutions might result in it meeting all of the established criteria. The instructor who caught students plagiarizing needs to evaluate her possible options by the criteria she has set. For example, if she ignores the misconduct, is that fair to those in the class who did not plagiarize? Is failing the students for the course an appropriate punishment for the students' misconduct?

In terms of the residence hall complaints, does changing the form students fill out meet both the needs of students and administrators? Will the form address the issue of changing residence hall assignments? Will a committee be formed to hear complaints from all students in residence halls? An option might not meet each of the criteria perfectly, but the point of this step is to choose the solution that best meets the criteria. If multiple options are acceptable, the group needs to determine how it will decide on which solution to implement.

6. Implement the Solution

Implementing the solution means putting it into effect. It is one thing to decide that a car wash will raise the most money; it is another thing to advertise, staff, supply, and conduct the fundraiser. The work involved in implementing the solution will vary according to the problem. For example, an instructor dealing with plagiarism can determine the best solution and then communicate that decision to the students and/or administration. If the group dealing with residence hall complaints decides to form a committee to hear complaints, then implementing the solution entails setting up committee structure, policies and procedures, soliciting membership, and informing students about the committee.

In a public speaking class, your group may be involved in determining a solution and suggesting how it could be implemented, but it is possible the group will not be involved with the actual implementation. For example, your group may be given the task of determining how to get students more involved in their department's activities. Your group could work through Step Five and decide that the best solution is to advertise activities earlier so that students can work them into their schedules. As a group, you may present Steps One through Five to a faculty committee, but Step Six might ultimately be the committee's responsibility.

7. Reassess

Reassessing at some point prevents the group from saying "we're done" after implementing the solution. It is an important part of the process because you evaluate your group's success or lack thereof.

Fundraisers are carefully planned and executed, but still may fail. New policies are developed with the best intentions, but may still be ineffective. Do you try the same fundraiser again? Do you keep the new policy? Before you answer "yes" or "no" to these questions, the group needs to answer some other questions. Did the fundraiser fail because it was held at a bad time? Was it advertised sufficiently? Did it ask too much of the people working it or attending the fundraiser? In other words, the group needs to decide what contributed to the lack of success. Similarly, with the ineffective policy, did administration evaluate its effectiveness too soon? Were students inadequately informed? Was administration insufficiently trained? Those engaged in reassessment need to discuss what factors influenced the lack of success. In a sense, this final step can be the beginning step of a new process, if the solution has not been effective.

The seven-step reflective thinking process is one way to help groups move through the problem-solving process. It is certainly not the only way. However, regardless of the approach groups take, it is important that a clear process be established that allows for rational, deliberative discussion of all relevant aspects of the problem. A leader should help the group through this process, and group members should contribute productively throughout the process.

Presenting in Small Groups

Just because you are part of a small group discussion does not mean that you will report your results through some type of oral presentation. Some groups prepare written reports that some administrator, council, or committee will evaluate. Sometimes the results of your deliberation are presented before a group, and in many instances a group presents before another group for other reasons. For example, a group of teachers who attended a workshop on working with gifted students present their observations of the workshop to the group of teachers who were unable to attend. Members of the League of Women Voters who attended the national convention present a summary of their experiences to the rest of the membership. Also, many careers have national conferences where people with similar interests have the opportunity to attend or present seminars and panel presentations.

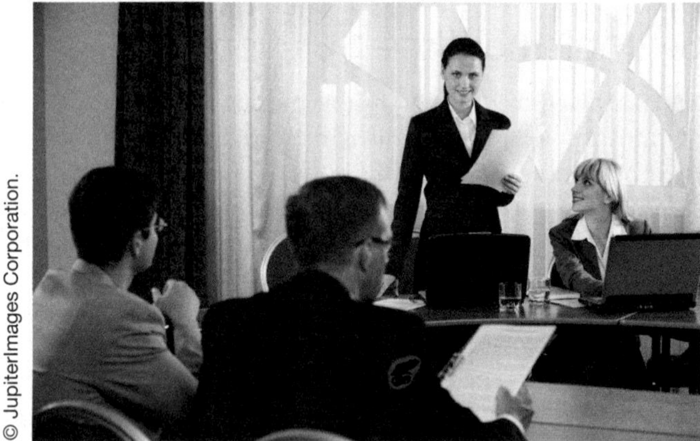

When speaking in a small group format, you need to be aware of how your message fits in with those of the other group members.

Whether presenting as a group or as an individual to a group successful public speaking strategies are necessary. So all information presented in this textbook is relevant to this context. Audience analysis is essential. Any presentation you prepare should have a clear introduction, body, and conclusion. Your presentation should be well-research, sufficiently supported, and organized effectively. Your delivery should be engaging and extemporaneous. Be sure you are not too dependent on notes.

Speaking as a member of a group, however, involves additional reflection. First, it is important to find a small group format that best suits your purpose. Second, it is important that the speeches all group members give flow as though they were one coherent speech. The last section of this chapter describes a variety of small group formats concerns that need to be addressed before the group speaks, and makes suggestions for the presentation.

Small Group Formats

Most of your group work in class occurs before the day you present. You spend time defining your purpose, setting goals, distributing the work load, researching your topic/issues, and organizing your research into something meaningful. If in business or civic life, you are already an expert on the topic, your task is to determine what you need to bring to this particular presentation. It is possible that you never meet the other group members until moments before the presentation.

Most of your group work occurs before you present, as you spend time defining your purpose, researching, and organizing your message.

In a public speaking class, your instructor may suggest a particular small group format. In business or civic life, a moderator or facilitator decides how the group should present. It is also possible that you determine your format. Regardless, there are three main small group formats: panel discussion, symposium, and forum.

Panel Discussion

In a panel discussion, group members have an informal interchange on the issues in front of an audience. The positive and negative features of issues are debated, just as they were in the closed group meeting, but this time in front of an audience. When you are part of a panel discussion, it is important to keep in mind that you are talking for the benefit of the audience rather than for other group members. Although your responses are spontaneous, they should be thought out in advance, just as in any other public speaking presentation.

Panel discussions are directed by a moderator who attempts to elicit a balanced view of the issues and to involve all group members. The role of the moderator is to encourage the discussion—he or she does not take part in the debate. Moderators coordinate and organize the discussion, ask pertinent questions, summarize conclusions, and keep the discussion moving. Once the discussion is over, the moderator often opens the discussion to audience questions.

As you can tell from the previous description, the critical elements of a panel discussion are: (1) it is an informal discussion moderated or facilitated by someone who is not an active participant, (2) interaction should be distributed equitably among group members with no pre-determined time limit for each group member, and (3) generally, there are no prepared remarks.

Symposium

A symposium is more formal and predictable than a panel discussion. Instead of focusing on the interaction among group members, it centers on prepared speeches on a specified subject given by group members who have expertise on the subject. The topic and speakers are introduced by a moderator. A symposium is structured, and speakers are generally given a time frame for their comments. After the formal presentation, a panel discussion or forum may follow. This allows for interaction among group members, and for the audience to ask questions of individual speakers.

Forum

In a forum, group members respond to audience questions. Someone may provide a prepared statement, but it is also possible to introduce group members and their credentials, and then ask for audience questions. Unlike a panel discussion or the second half of a symposium, a forum does not include interactions among group members. The forum is very audience-centered.

The success of the forum depends on how carefully the audience has thought about the topic (the topic is announced in advance) and the nature of their questions. For example, school boards hold public hearings about their annual budget. In addition to the school board, the superintendent and district financial officer will be present. Generally, there is a presentation by the financial officer, and then anyone present at the meeting may ask questions. Questions could be asked about transportation, food service, athletics, computer equipment, and so on. If several concerned citizens show up with questions in mind, the meeting could last for hours. If no one in the community attends the meeting, then it will be very short.

A forum also needs a moderator. When the League of Women Voters holds a candidates' forum, selected League members collect questions from the audience and give them to the moderator who then addresses questions to the appropriate panelists. A forum is not just a collection of individuals, but a group of people who have been chosen for their interest in the topic/issue or because of their expertise.

Preparing to Present as a Group

When you prepare a speech for class, you are responsible for all aspects of the speech. As an individual, you need to prepare, practice, and present. Once you join a group, however, you need to be prepared, but you also need to be aware of how your speech fits into the other speeches, and the group needs to make sure everyone is viewing the presentation from a similar perspective. With this interest in mind, we present the following aspects of the presentation to consider *before* the group speaks. All group members should know and be in agreement with the following:

1. Speaker order
2. Formality of the presentation
   Can group members interrupt each other?
   Can group members wander from their prepared remarks?
3. Determine where will the group sit/stand?
   Group members need to realize that if they are all in front of the class, whether standing or speaking, audience members will be aware of them, even when they are not speaking.
   Will all sit and then stand up to speak or will all stand throughout the entire presentation?
   Should the group sit to the side and have the speaker stand in the middle of the front of the class?
4. Delivery
   Use note cards? Legal pad? PowerPoint slides?
   Prepare individually—think about eye contact (speak to the group, not the instructor), gestures, and vocal aspects
5. Time constraints for each speech
6. Determine how to signal if someone is speaking too long or if the group is going too long
7. Introduction, body, conclusion
   Who will deliver the group's introduction and conclusion?
   How will each person's introduction and conclusion relate to the group?
   How do you make transitions between speeches so all presentations are connected?
8. Presentational aids
   What is available in the classroom?
   Will they benefit the presentation?
   Who will be responsible for making them and setting them up?

If group members wait until they approach the front of the room to address these concerns, they will appear unprepared. Deciding where to stand, how to signal each other, and what the speaking order is will reduce awkwardness and uncertainty, and should give a more professional, polished look to the presentation.

General Suggestions for Presenting in a Small Group

The following guidelines will help you be a successful participant in a panel discussion, symposium, or forum. Many of the guidelines apply to all three group formats, but others apply just to one.

Limit the number of points you make. Since you will be given some time constraints, limit the number of points you make. Remember that each person has information to present. Your audience cannot process an overload of material. Be brief. Make your point as briefly and clearly as possible and do not confuse your listeners with too many details.

Avoid repetition. Avoid repetition by learning in advance what the other panelists will cover in their speeches. The job of assigning topics should be the responsibility of the presentation organizer. If the organizer is negligent, you may want to get in touch with the other panelists yourself. Keep communication channels open with your group members so you do not find yourself giving the same presentation as the person who spoke before you.

Try to meet in advance. Try to meet your fellow panelists in advance. When group members meet for the first time on stage, there is often an awkwardness in their interchange that comes from not knowing one another. This discomfort may be communicated to the audience.

Restrict your speech to the allotted time. If speakers exceed the time limit, the audience will find it difficult to sit through the entire program, and little opportunity will remain for a panel interchange or a question-and-answer period. In addition, by violating the time constraints, you may cause another speaker to modify his or her speech significantly. Staying within the allotted time frame is a necessary courtesy to the other group members.

Prepare for audience questions. Because the question-and-answer period is often the most important part of the program, spend as much time preparing for the questions as you did for your formal remarks. Anticipate the questions you are likely to be asked and frame your answers. During the question-and-answer period, be willing to speak up and add to someone else's response if none of the questions are being directed to you. When a fellow panel member finishes a response, simply say, "I'd like to make one more point that ..." If, on the other hand, a question is directed to you that you think would be better handled by another panel member, say, "I think that considering her background, Therese is better able to answer that question."

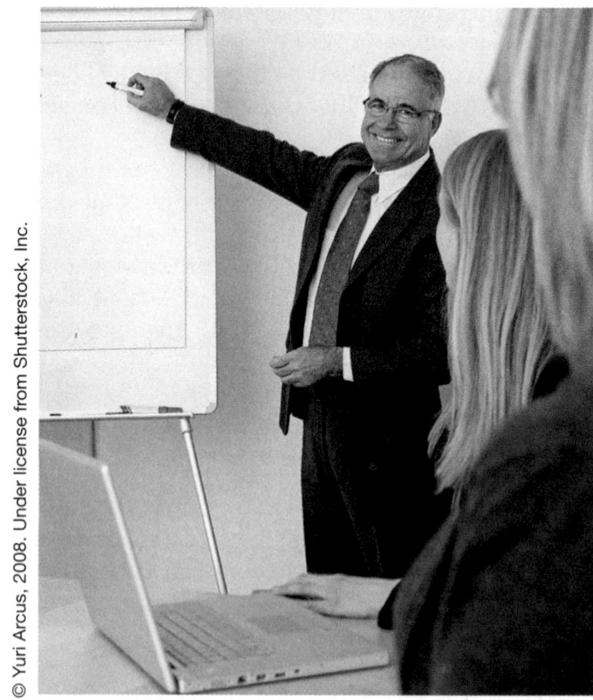

Simple visual aids are appropriate for group presentations, as long as you coordinate with other members.

Consider enhancing your presentation with visual aids. Simple visual aids are as appropriate in group presentations as they are in single-person public speaking. Coordinate the use of visual aids so information is not repeated by multiple speakers. Be consistent and professional. It is inconsistent to allow one group member to use the blackboard when the rest of the group has PowerPoint slides.

Summary

We are all involved in small group activities whether they occur within or outside of the classroom. Opportunities exist for interacting within a group or speaking before a group. As a speaker, consider both primary and secondary audiences. As group members, we share a purpose for communication. Also, group members usually have both group-oriented and self-oriented goals, and group size influences the need for structure and how we communicate.

Each individual has responsibilities within the group setting regardless of the person's role. As leader, you can contribute to the group's process by providing direction and purpose, especially at the beginning of the meeting, keeping the group on track throughout the meeting, and providing a clarifying summary when appropriate. In terms of helping the group communicate effectively, the leader should draw information from participants, try to keep group communication from being one-sided, and try to maintain the cohesiveness of the group.

As a group member, you have several responsibilities, including knowing the constraints of the assignment, working to achieve group goals, being responsible for completing your part of the assignment, researching sufficiently, communicating effectively and efficiently, avoiding personal attacks, and leaving your personal problems at home. Following the seven-step reflective process helps to keep the group organized and focused and helps to make sure that members do not jump to quick solutions without sufficient analysis and deliberation.

When the occasion arises for you to present as a group member before an audience, it is important to determine whether a panel discussion, symposium, or forum best suits your needs and the needs of your audience. Your knowledge of public speaking and your individual skills come into play as you present before the group. However, it is important to meet as a group beforehand to determine such things as speaker order, amount of speaking time allotted for each individual, whether or not presentational aids will be useful, and who will be responsible for preparing such aids. Each person's presentation should cover only a few points. The presentations should not overlap, and group members should be prepared for audience questions. An effective presentation involves preparation on the part of all group members as well as attention to detail regarding content connection, transitions from speaker to speaker, and overall professional performance.

Name____ Date_______________

Exercise 13.1 Chapters 13 – Small Group Presentations

Groups are organized for a wide variety of reasons. Most often groups meet to discuss and solve a current problem. In this exercise, after agreeing on a leader and a set of operating rules, your group will follow the Reflective Thinking Process to solve a problem.

After completing the process, the group leader should prepare the group survey to submit to the instructor. The group reporter should be prepared to share the group experience with the class.

Part One:

Group membership:

____

____

____

____

____

____

Group Rules:

1.

2.

3.

4.

5.

6.

7.

8.

9.

10.

*Leader ____

Topic: ___________________________________

Step One: Identify and Define the Problem
Application:

Step Two:
Application:

Step Three:
Application:

Step Four:
Application:

Step Five:
Application:

Step Six:
Application:

Step Seven: Reassess
Application:

Part Two:

Group Membership:

____

____

____

____

____

____

Submit a copy of the survey below. All group numbers must have input in the final responses of the survey.

A. Identify the type of group in which you have just participated.

B. Who is the leader of the group?

C. What type of leader is he/she? Why?

D. Did you use the *seven* suggestions to create the most effective small group experience? Give us an example of how some of the suggestions were used.

E. What conflict did the group experience? What was the reason?

F. How was the conflict solved?

G. If your group were to be convened to address another problem, what recommendations would you make to ensure the group operates effectively?

*Leader____

Glossary

A

Acceptance: Refers to our awareness of the feelings and emotions involved in diverse approaches to relationships and communication.

Acronym: a word abbreviated in such a way that it creates a new word or phrase so that something (a concept or process) is easy to remember

Action-oriented listener: Listeners that prefer error-free and concise messages and they get easily frustrated with speakers who do not clearly articulate their message in a straightforward manner.

Active strategies: Require us to engage in interactions with others to learn additional information about others.

Adaptors: behaviors that can indicate our internal conditions or feelings to other people

Adoption: When you want your audience to start doing something.

Affect display: a form of nonverbal behavior that expresses emotions

Aggressive talk: Talk that attacks a person's self concept with the intent of inflicting psychological pain.

Ambushing: Type of listener who will listen for information that they can use to attack the speaker.

Appreciative listening: This type of listening is for the pure enjoyment of listening to the stimuli.

Articulation: The verbalization of distinct sounds and how precisely words are formed.

Assertiveness: Taking the responsibility of expressing needs, thoughts, and feelings in a direct, clear manner.

Attitudes: Deeply felt beliefs that govern how one behaves. Also, a group of beliefs that cause us to respond in some way to a particular object or situation.

Attitudes: Learned predispositions to respond in favorable or unfavorable ways toward people or objects.

Attribution theory: The dominant theory that explains how people explain their own and others' behavior.

Autocratic leader: leadership method based on direction and control of the leader. There is little discussion among followers

Avoidance: A refusal to deal with conflict or painful issues.

B

Beliefs: One's own convictions; what one thinks is right and wrong, true and false. Also, they are classified as statements of knowledge, opinion and faith.

Beliefs: Our personal convictions regarding the truth or existence of things.

Biased information search: Our propensity to seek out certain types of information and avoid others.

Bid: A question. Gesture, look, touch, or other single expression that says, "I want to feel connected to you."

Blind pane: That area in the Johari Window as an accidental disclosure area.

C

Certainty: behavior that communicates to others a lack of interest in their position on an issue; the person seems to know all the answers

Channel: The route traveled by a message; the means it uses to reach the sender-receivers.

Coercive power: power to punish; members follow coercive leaders to avoid reprimand or punishment

Collectivistic cultures: cultures in which people practice collaboration with family, friends, and colleagues

Commitment: A strong desire by both parties for the relationship to continue. In groups, is it the willingness of members to work together complete the group's task.

Communication: Any process in which people share information, ideas, and feelings.

Compatibility: Similar attitudes, personality, and a liking for the same activities.

Complaint: Expression of dissatisfaction with the behavior, attitude, belief, or characteristics of a partner of or someone else.

Comprehensive listening: This type of listening involves mindfully receiving and remembering new information.

Computer-mediated communication (CMC): A wide range of technologies that facilitate both human communication and the interactive sharing of information through computer networks, including e-mail, discussion groups, newsgroups, chat rooms, instant messages, and web pages.

Concrete: Refers to messages that are well-defined.

Conflict resolution: Negotiation to find a solution to the conflict.

Connotative meanings: reflect your personal, subjective definitions

Consensus: Considers whether the behavior is unique to the individual or if they are behaving in the way that would be typically expected of others.

Consistency: Refers to whether an individual behaves the same way across contexts and at various times.

Constitutive rules: tell us how to "count" different kinds of communication, revealing what we feel is appropriate

Constructivism: Refers to the process we use to organize and interpret experiences by applying cognitive structures labeled schemata.

Content-oriented listener: Listeners that focus on the details of the message, and they pick up on the facts of the story and analyze it from a critical perspective.

Context: The place that the communication occurs.

Costs: The problems associated with relationships.

Covariation theory: The idea that we decide whether peoples' behavior is based on either internal or external factors by using three different and important types of information: distinctiveness, consensus, and consistency.

Criticism: A negative evaluation of a person for something he or she has done or the way he or she is.

Cultural information: Information used in making predictions based on person's most generally shared cultural attributes such a language, shared values, beliefs, and ideologies.

Culture: Shared perceptions which shape the communication patterns and expectations of a group of people.

Culture: The ever-changing values, traditions, social and political relationships, and worldview created and shared by a group of people bound together by a combination of factors (which can include a common history, geographic location, language, social class, and/or religion.

D

Decoding: Once the message is perceived and understood by the receiver, the decoding process occurs and that process is reversed.

Deductive reasoning: Drawing conclusions based on the connections between statements that serve as premises.

Defensive Communication: When one partner tries to defend himself or herself against the remarks or behavior of the other.

Defensive listening: This type of listener perceives a threatening environment.

Definition through example: Helps the audience understand a complex concept by giving the audience a "for instance."

Democratic leader: adopts the Theory Y assumptions and creates an atmosphere of member integration, self-control, and participatory decision making; the input of subordinates is encouraged and is used to make decisions

Denotative meanings: literal, dictionary definitions that are precise and objective

Derogatory language: consists of words that are degrading or tasteless

Deterrence: Your goal is to convince your listeners not to start something.

Disconfirming: Listeners that deny the feelings of the speaker.

Discontinuance: An attempt to persuade your listeners to stop doing something.

Discriminate listening: This type of listening helps us understand the meaning of the message.

Distinctiveness: Refers to whether or not a person typically behaves the same way with the target, or receiver, of the behavior.

Diversity: Refers to the unique qualities or characteristics that distinguish individuals and groups from one another.

Dual perspective: recognize another person's point of view and take that into account as you communicate

Dynamism: A lively, active, vigorous, and vibrant quality.

E

Emblem: a nonverbal behavior that has a distinct verbal referent or even a denotative definition, and it is often used to send a specific message to others

Emotional intelligence: The ability to understand and get along with others.

Empathetic listening: This type of listening is used to help others.

Empathy: approaching a discussion with the intent to understand the other person's position from his or her point of view

Empathy: The process of mentally indentifying with the character and experiences of another person. The ability to recognize and identify with someone's feelings.

Empty words: overworked exaggerations

Encoding: The process of transforming mental images into words and placing these words into logical messages with meaning.

Equivocal words: have more than one correct denotative meaning

Ethical Communication: Communication that is honest, fair, and considerate of others' rights.

Ethnicity: Refers to the common heritage, or background, shared by a group of people.

Ethnocentrism: Refers to the tendency to perceive our own ways of behaving and thinking as being correct, or acceptable, and judging other behaviors as being "strange," incorrect, or inferior.

Ethos: Ethical appeal, makes speakers worthy of belief.

Evaluative listening: This type of listening involves critically assessing messages.

Evaluative statements: Expressions that involve a judgment.

Examples: Support that helps illustrate a point or claim.

Expectancy violations theory: suggests that we hold expectations about the nonverbal behavior of others, and when communicative norms are violated, the violation may be perceived either favorably or unfavorably, depending on the perception that the receiver has of the violator

Expert power: a person who is able to assist the group in reaching its goals because of his or her expertise on a given topic

Explicit learning: Learning that involves actual instructions regarding the preferred way of behaving.

Extemporaneous speaking: A method of delivery that involves using carefully prepared notes to guide the presentation.

External attribution: Situational factors.

External Noise: Includes any factors outside of the communicators that make it difficult or prevent the message from being understood.

Extrinsic conflict: conflict related to the personalities and relationships between members

Extrinsic Costs: The sacrifices, loses, or suffering as a result of things that occur outside the relationship (could not include having as much time for your friends or sharing your friends with your partner)

Extrinsic Rewards: The gifts, prizes, and recompenses that occur outside the relationship (could include liking the people your partner has introduced you to or the friends he or she hangs out with)

Eye contact: direct visual contact made with another person; helps us to communicate in at least four ways: it can open a channel of communication, demonstrate concern, gather feedback, and moderate anxiety

Eye contact: The connection you form with listeners through your gaze.

F

Forum: Group members respond to audience questions.

Fundamental attribution error: When attempting to explain others' negative behaviors, we tend to overestimate the internal factors or causes and underestimate the external factors or causes.

G

Gestures: Using your arms and hands to illustrate, emphasize, or provide a visual experience that accompanies your thoughts.

Grammar: syntax, a patterned set of rules that aid in meaning

H

Hearing: Involves the physical process of sound waves traveling into the ear canal, vibrating the ear drum, and eventually sending signals to the brain.

Hidden pane: That area of the Johari Window where self-knowledge is hidden from others- a deliberate non-disclosure area in which there are certain things you know about yourself that you do not want known and deliberately conceal them from others.

Homophily: The idea that we choose to be with people who are similar to us.

I

Illustrator: a gesture that is used with language to emphasize, stress, or repeat what is being said

Implicit learning: Learning that occurs via observation.

Impromptu speaking: Involves little or no preparation time; using no notes or just a few.

Indirect aggression: (also called passive aggression) People who use this form of communication often feel powerless and respond by doing something to thwart the person in power.

Individualistic cultures: cultures in which people are taught personal autonomy, privacy, self-realization, individual initiative, independence, individual decision making, and an understanding that their needs and interests are just as important, if not more important, than the needs and interests of others

Inductive reasoning: Generalizing from specific examples and drawing conclusions from what we observe.

Instrumental costs: The problems associated with relationships.

Instrumental rewards: The pleasures that come as result of being in a relationship.

Intentionality: Described as being stable or persistent and often refers to behaviors that are likely to be exhibited repeatedly across a variety of contexts.

Interactive strategies: Typically involve a face-to-face encounter between two individuals to reduce uncertainty.

Intercultural Communication: When a message is created by a member of one culture, and this message needs to be processed by a member of another culture.

Intercultural communication: When a message is created by a member of one culture, and this message needs to be processed by a member of another culture.

Internal attribution: Dispositional factors.

Internal Noise: Interference with the message that occurs in the minds of the sender-receivers when their thoughts or feelings are focused on something other than the communication at hand.

Interpersonal Communication: One person interacting with another on a one-to-one basis, often in an informal, unstructured setting.

Interpersonal linkage: power based on who you know and what resources these people control

Interpretation: The subjective process of making sense of our perceptions.

Intersubjective: meaning can exist only when people share common interpretations of the symbols they exchange

Intrapersonal Communication: Communication that occurs within you; it involves thoughts, feelings, and the way you look at yourself.

Intrinsic conflict: conflict that centers on disagreements related to the task facing the group

Intrinsic costs: The obligation to return the attention, warmth, and affection you receive, and the time you will spend listening, communicating, and self-disclosing.

Intrusion of territory: violation, invasion, or contamination of your space

J

Jargon: specialized professional language

Johari Window: A model of the process of disclosure in interpersonal relationships, developed by Joseph Luft and Harry Ingham.

K

Kinesics: the study of our use of the body to communicate

Knowledge: Refers to the theoretical principles and concepts that explain behaviors occurring within a specific communication context. Also refers to understanding what reaction or action is best suited for a particular situation.

L

Laissez-faire leader: one who takes a hands-off approach to leadership and provides very little direction to those being led

Language: a shared system of symbols structured in organized patterns to express thoughts and feelings

Leadership: the ability to influence the behavior of others to move people to action

Legitimate power: exists as a function of someone's position in an organization

Limited capacity processors: We are described as this because we have innate limitations in our ability to process information.

Linear Communication: One-way communication that has no feedback.

Listening styles: A set of attitudes, beliefs, and predispositions about the how, where, when, who, and what of the information reception and encoding process.

Listening: Involves the physical process of hearing, but it also involves the psychological process of attending to the stimuli, creating meaning, and responding.

Loaded words: sound like they're describing, but they're actually revealing your attitude

Logos: An appeal that is rational and reasonable based on evidence provided.

M

Maintenance leaders: focus on relational issues, the development of an open and supportive climate, motivation of members, and conflict management

Meaning: symbols must be shared in order to be understood

Message credibility: The extent to which the speech is considered to be factual and well-supported through documentation.

Message: The ideas and feelings that a sender-receiver wants to share.

Monopolizing: Involves taking the focus off the speaker and redirecting the conversation and attention to themselves.

N

Needs: Strong feelings of discomfort or desire which motivate to achieve satisfaction or comfort.

Negative feedback: Refers to verbal and nonverbal behaviors that are often discouraging to a source to continue communicating.

Neutrality: communicates that you simply do not care about the person or what he or she is saying

Noise: Interference that keeps a message from being understood or accurately interpreted.

Noise: Refers to anything that interferes with the reception of a message.

Non-fluencies: Meaningless words that interrupt the flow of our speech; also known as filled pauses or vocal fillers.

Nonverbal Communication: Information we communicate without using words.

Novelty: Refers to the tendency to pay attention to stimuli that new or different.

O

Open pane: The area of the Johari Window that involves information about yourself that you are willing to communicate, as well as information you are unable to hide.

Operational definitions: Specify procedures for observing and measuring concepts

Opinions: Points of view that may or may not be supported in fact.

Organization of ideas: The placement of lines of reasoning and supporting materials in a pattern that helps to achieve your specific purpose.

Organization: Refers to the process of placing stimuli or information into categories in order to make sense of it.

Owned message: (also known as an I-message): An acknowledgement of subjectivity by a message-sender through the use of first-person singular terms.

P

Panel discussion: Group members have an informal interchange on the issues in front of an audience.

Paraphrasing: Involves restating a message in your own words to see if the meaning you assigned was similar to that which was intended.

Passive strategies: Typically involve observation and social comparison to learn information about others.

Pathos: Persuading through emotional appeals.

People-oriented listener: Listeners that seek common interests with the speaker and are highly responsive; interested in the speaker's feelings and emotions.

Perception: How we interpret and assign meaning to others' behaviors and messages based on our background and past experiences. The process of selecting, organizing, and interpreting stimuli into something that makes sense or is meaningful.

Personal constructs: Bipolar dimensions of meaning used to predict and evaluate how people behave.

Personal orientation system: Predispositions that are comprised of one's needs, beliefs, values, and attitudes.

Personal space: a small amount of portable space that you carry with you all the time; you control who is and who is not permitted inside that space

Phonological rules: regulate how words sound when you pronounce them

Pitch: Vocal range or key, the highness or lowness of your voice produced by the tightening and loosening of your vocal folds.

Positive feedback: Refers to verbal and nonverbal behaviors that encourage the speaker to continue communicating.

Power distance: the extent to which the less powerful members of organizations and institutions accept and expect that power is distributed unequally

Primacy and recency: Refers to arguments delivered first and last.

Primary sources: Firsthand accounts such as diaries, journals, and letters, as well as statistics, speeches, and interviews. They are records of events as they are first described.

Primary territory: space on those items you personally control

Problem orientation: allows others an equal contribution to discussion and decision making

Proposition of fact: Persuading your listeners that your interpretation of a situation, event, or concept is accurate.

Proposition of policy: Easily recognizable by their use of the word "should."

Proposition of value: Persuading your listeners based on deep-seated beliefs.

Prototypes: Refers to knowledge structures which represent the most common attributes of a phenomenon.

Provisionalism: behavior that tries to explore issues, look for solutions, and consider the points of view of other group members

Proximity: Refers to the physical distance between two people.

Proximity: The close contact that occurs when people share an experience such as work, play, or school.

Pseudo-listening: This type of listening is used when we are pretending to listen.

Psychological information: The kind of information that is the most specific and intimate because it allows you to know individual traits, feelings, attitudes, and important personal data.

Psychological Noise: Idiosyncrasies that occur within the speaker that interfere with the speaker's ability to express or understand the intended message.

Public Communication: The sender-receiver (speaker) sends a message (the speech) to an audience.

Public territory: available to anyone; so any space you try to claim is only temporary

R

Race: The term used to refer to genetically inherited biological characteristics such as hair texture and color, eye shape, skin color, and facial structure.

Rapport talk: Analogous to small talk or phatic communication.

Rate: The pace at which you speak.

Reasoning from sign: The inference step is that the presence of an attribute can be taken as the presence of some larger condition or situation of which the attribute is a part.

Reasoning: The process of using known and believed information to explain or prove other statements less well understood or accepted. Refers to the sequence of interlinking claims and arguments that, together, establish the content and force of your position.

Reference(s): consist of thoughts, experiences, and feelings about the referent

Referent power: based on the personal liking or respect that one person has for another

Referent: the thing that we want to communicate about that exists in reality

Regional differences: Speech patterns, attitudes, and values may differ significantly depending on the geographic location.

Regionalisms: words or phrases that are specific to one part of the country

Regrettable Talk: Saying something embarrassing, hurtful, or private to another person.

Regulative rules: tell us when, how, where, and with whom we can talk about certain things

Regulator: a turn-taking signal that helps control the flow, the pace, and turn-taking in conversations

Reinforce: Refers to messages that are consistent with our views.

Report talk: Involves discussions about facts, events, and solutions. Refers to talking to accomplish goals.

Research: The raw material that forms the foundation of your speech.

Response to a bid: A positive or negative answer to somebody's request for emotional connection.

Reward power: offers access to some desired resource as payment for compliance

Rewards: The pleasures that come as a result of being in a relationship.

S

Schemata: Refers to mental filing cabinets with several drawers or organized clusters of knowledge and information about particular topics.

Script theory: The idea that we often interact with others in a way that could be described as "automatic" or even "mindless."

Scripts: Knowledge structures that guide and influence how we process information.

Secondary sources: Generally provide an analysis, an explanation, or a restatement of a primary source.

Secondary territory: not your private property; not owned by you, but typically associated with you

Selection: We are continually making choices about the amount and type of information that we choose to notice.

Selective attention: Refers to the decision to pay attention to certain stimuli while simultaneously ignoring others.

Selective exposure: Refers to the choice to subject oneself to certain stimuli.

Selective listening: Type of listening that occurs when a listener focuses only on parts of the message.

Selective retention: Refers to the choice to save or delete information from one's long-term memory.

Self-disclosure: Involves divulging personal information to another individual and is often delivered through face-to-face or computer mediated channels.

Self-disclosure: Process by which one person tells another something he or she would not tell just anyone.

Self-serving bias: States that we tend to manufacture, or construct, attributions which best serve our own self-interests.

Semantic rules: govern the meaning of specific symbols

Semantic triangle: a model that demonstrates how words come to have meaning

Sender-receivers: In communication situations, those who simultaneously send and receive messages.

Setting: Where the communication occurs.

Situational leadership: assumes that a leader's effectiveness is contingent, or dependent, upon how well the leader's style fits the context

Size: Refers to the magnitude of the stimuli.

Skills: Specific communication behaviors which contribute to competent and effective interpersonal communication.

Slang: consists of words that are short-lived, arbitrarily changed, and often vulgar ideas

Small Groups: gatherings of 3 to 13 who meet to do a job, solve a problem, or maintain relationships.

Small talk: Social conversation about unimportant topics that allows a person to maintain contact with a lot of people without making a deep commitment.

Small-group Communication: It occurs when a small number of people meet to save a problem. The group must be small enough so that each member has a chance to interact with all the other members.

Social class: Stratification based on educational, occupational, or financial backgrounds, resulting in classifications and status differentials.

Social identity theory: An explanation for our tendency to evaluate in-groups more positively than out-groups.

Social penetration: The process of increasing both disclosure and intimacy in a relationship.

Socialization: Refers to the process of learning about one's cultural norms and expectations.

Sociological information: Information that tells you something about others' social groups and roles.

Speaker credibility: The extent to which a speaker is perceived as a competent spokesperson.

Specific purpose: The precise response you want from your audience.

Spontaneity: communication characterized by honesty, directness, and good faith

Statistics: The collection, analysis, interpretation, and presentation of information in numerical form.

Stereotypes: Impressions and expectations based on one's knowledge or beliefs about a specific group of people which are then applied to all individuals who are members of that group.

Strategy: 1. a plan; 2. a form of communication often making others defensive because they suspect a hidden agenda

Symbol: Something that sends for something else.

Symbols: arbitrary labels that we give to some idea or phenomenon

Symposium: Centers on prepared speeches on a specified subject given by group members who have expertise on the subject.

Syntactical rules: present the arrangement of a language; how the symbols are organized

T

Task leaders: group members who help the group with organization and advancement toward making a decision or completing a job

Task roles: contribute to the group's productivity and are concerned with moving the group toward achieving its goals

Testimony: Citing the experience or opinion of others; either directly or through paraphrasing.

Thesis statement: The core idea; identifies the main ideas of your speech.

Topophobia: The fear of speaking in public.

Transactional Communication: Communication that involves three principles: (1) people sending messages continuously and simultaneously; (2) communication events that have a past, present, and future; and (3) participants playing certain roles.

Transformational leader: someone who possesses the charisma necessary to motivate followers and evoke change

Transitions: Verbal bridges between ideas; words; phrases, or sentences that tell your audience how ideas relate.

Trite words: words that have been overused and lose power or impact

U

Understanding: Applying knowledge to specific situations in an attempt to explain the behaviors that are occurring.

Unknown pane: Area of the Johari Window that is known as a nondisclosure area and provides no possibility of disclosure because it is unknown to self or to others.

Utility: The perception that particular messages are immediately useful.

V

Verbal Symbol: A word that stands for a particular thing or idea.

Volume: The loudness of your voice, controlled by how forcefully air is expelled through the trachea onto the vocal folds.